ESSAYS ON
CONTEMPORARY
BRITISH
DRAMA

edited by

HEDWIG BOCK

AND

ALBERT WERTHEIM

Max Hueber Verlag

1. Auflage
3. 2. 1.
1984   83   82   81

© 1981 Max Hueber Verlag München

Book Design: Stephanie Wicks
Printed in U.S.A.

ISBN 3-19-00.2214-3

PR
737
E8
1981

CONTENTS

INTRODUCTION

The tradition of British Drama is a long and rich one. It boasts such playwriting talents as William Shakespeare, Christopher Marlowe, Ben Jonson, John Webster, John Dryden, William Congreve, Richard Brinsley Sheridan, George Bernard Shaw, and Noel Coward. Like the fraternity of playwrights that formed during the reign of Queen Elizabeth I, there is today, during the contemporary reign of Queen Elizabeth II, a new group of playwrights whose dazzling, trend-setting works have created a new renaissance in English drama. Harold Pinter, Edward Bond and Tom Stoppard—perhaps the Shakespeare, Marlowe and Jonson of our day—are at the center of a theatre movement that has won praise both in England and abroad.

This volume draws together critical essays on specific contemporary British playwrights. The authors of the articles are primarily German, American and British scholars, whose diverse backgrounds and approaches are a testimony to the richness of the playwrights they discuss. The purpose of this volume, moreover, is to introduce readers to the work of scholars from several countries in the hope that American and British readers will become more aware of the work of German scholars and vice-versa.

The editors would like especially to thank the Deutscher Akademischer Austauschdienst, the Deutsche Forschungsgemeinschaft and the British Council whose generous aid made this volume possible. The ongoing scholarly and faculty exchange between the Universität Hamburg and Indiana University likewise facilitated the creation of this volume. The editors wish to thank as well Dr. Roland Irmer of Max Hueber Verlag.

Hedwig Bock, Universität Hamburg
Albert Wertheim, Indiana University

John Osborne:
Look Forward in Fear

STEVEN H. GALE

In 1956 John Osborne's *Look Back in Anger* exploded across the English stage with intense anger in a bitter indictment of modern British life. A mixture of despair and black humor were contained in the attacks on humanity, social classes, politics, economics, and the educational system leveled by Jimmy Porter, the drama's main character. Jimmy's expressions of wrath were frequently indiscriminate and overwhelming. While he attempted to expose his wife to the realities and meanings of life so that she would be moved out of her complacency, the underlying hurt which motivated Jimmy's actions was so massive that it controlled him as often as he controlled it.

For a quarter of a century critics have classified *Look Back in Anger* as one of the turning points in the history of twentieth-century English theatre. They have pointed to Osborne's choice of topics, his working-class characters, the realistic language, setting and situations which characterize the play, and which have influenced a generation of playwrights. *Look Back in Anger* is both a good play and an important one. In spite of all the acclaim, however, it is not great, nor is it as thoroughly innovative as has been claimed. What does raise it above its predecessors is its emotional power, an emotional power that is so strong that it almost serves as a sub-structure. And it is clear that this emotion surges forth out of Osborne's own experiences and being.

Between 1956 and 1965, when *A Patriot for Me* was produced, Osborne wrote seven dramas, a teleplay, and three filmscripts. Many of the topics found in *Look Back in Anger* are dealt with in these works, but the quality, power, and vigor of the anger steadily declines. The studied seriousness of the themes in *A Patriot for Me* and their treatment suggest a cool detachment in Osborne's approach to his material by this time.

A PATRIOT FOR ME

A Patriot for Me was first produced at the Royal Court Theatre in London on June 30, 1965. For five years the Lord Chamberlain had refused to license the play for public performance unless certain cuts and alterations were made and Osborne refused, so the play was staged by the English Stage Society "by arrangement" with the English Stage Company as a club production which placed it outside the Lord Chamberlain's jurisdiction.[1] The question of censorship is important, for once again Osborne explores territory heretofore avoided in the British theatre: homosexuality. Whether this topic is really what the play is about, or whether it is used as a means of expressing a more significant theme is another question.

The plot is simple, though Osborne's revelation of his main theme is so distended that the audience feels that they are caught in the midst of a film co-directed by Antonioni and Fellini in which no one is quite sure what is going on (and they are not involved enough to care to find out). In Act I Alfred Redl's homosexuality is gradually exposed. In Act II he is faced with the consequences of his sexual preference and he is seen trying to function in several social situations. In Act III society forces him to commit suicide.

Despite this simple plot, critics have not come to a consensus of opinion, other than the common complaint that the play is vaguely "unsatisfactory."[2] But when looking at the play in retrospect and in the context of Osborne's later works, certain meanings do become clear. For example, the lengthy exposition of the homosexuality theme allows the dramatist to demonstrate who is involved in such activities, and how they are involved, and it permits him to point out how difficult it is to tell who is homosexual. At the same time that all levels of society are presented, the importance of the establishment is emphasized throughout Act I so that when the Baron's drag ball is presented in Act II, Osborne is striking at the very heart of society.

The first clue of Redl's homosexuality appears when he serves as Siczynski's second at the duel with von Kupper, who has called Siczynski "Fräulein Rothschild."[3] The theme of the death of characters who do not fit into society in Osborne's later works is established early in this play when von Kupper kills his homosexual opponent easily and mercilessly. Similarly, there is a forewarning of Redl's end implied in Siczynski's observation "you're not what they call sociable" (p. 18) by the juxtaposition of these elements. Later, Redl will admit to the Countess Delyanoff that he has never confided in anyone, that the only ones he might have trusted "were killed" (p. 58). Since von Kupper has accused Siczinski of homosexuality, and since the implication is that Siczinski, having died in

Redl's arms, is one with whom Redl could have discussed his problem, it may be assumed that homosexuality is the secret which Redl is trying to hide. Ironically, Redl's inclinations are so obvious that even a stranger in a café recognizes them: "I know what *you're* looking for" (p. 67). It has been suggested that Redl's "failure is one of self-awareness," and that he does not know of his homosexual nature until the climax of Act I,[4] but this seems unlikely. The point of the play does not revolve around Redl's "self-discovery" so much as it does around his attempts to avoid exposure. After all, half of the drama takes place after the revelation occurs. Moreover, there is very little feeling of inner conflict over his sexuality. Instead, what dominates is his fear of being found out as a homosexual, a spy, or both, as he acknowledges to Oblensky (p. 114). Redl's *"stricken"* look in the café confrontation is a result of his realization that he can no longer hide, and the audience becomes privy to what has been bothering him in the very next scene.

In *A Patriot for Me* Osborne's concern is more with society than, as in his earlier plays, with an individual's plight. Redl is an individual, certainly, but his problem is symptomatic of a larger set of circumstances that have a broad, impersonal application. This determines and simultaneously grows out of the dramatist's techniques. Osborne states in a program note for the play's premiere that "The story ... is true." The drama's historical basis limits the author. As with his literary adaptations, the result is not as forceful as when he works with his own premises. The locale and time of the play (Austria and Hungary between 1890 and 1913) create a distancing effect which produces less emotional content than in his preceding plays. This is reinforced by the sense of a detached observer, perhaps a carry-over of the technique employed in *Inadmissable Evidence* (performed the previous year). The audience is not presented with the protagonist's point of view, as was the case with Jimmy; Redl is characterized through other people's eyes. And it is not the prototypical Osborne hero who emerges. In some ways *A Patriot for Me* is a one-man play, but Redl is not another Jimmy. Dashing, attractive, sometimes warm, he is described by Colonel von Möhl as overpowering and forceful because of his disciplined character (pp. 51–52), though members of the Baron's party and Oblensky (p. 97) have different opinions. Like Jimmy, Redl comes from the working class: he is the eighth of eleven children, and his father was a second grade railway clerk. Unlike Jimmy, he tries to escape his heritage and/or his sexuality through hard work. He is extremely successful at the War College, and the Baron and Kunz comment that he throws himself into his work in order to change his circumstances (p. 82), which may apply to both situations. His sister's death does not move him (he thought about it for ten minutes). He is naturally reticent, and instead of imposing his personality on those around him, à la Jimmy, he tries to hide his true self. Still, his willingness to commit suicide with the pistol given him by his superiors is not to avoid the issue of being a traitor in the service of the Russians, but as the ultimate expression of his individualism.

Redl finally does make Jimmy-like statements, but they do not come until his Act III monologs when he berates his ex-lover's wife, his current lover, and Spanish society. The monolog technique is not utilized in the first two acts because Osborne is too involved in establishing the character of the society to explore his protagonist's character. A combination of other techniques and the play's meaning prevent a clearer picture of Redl from developing. The *coup de théâtre* ball scene, the humor ("Queen Victoria was quite clearly a man" —p. 83), the parallel between the scientific gobbledygook of the pseudo-Freudian, anti-homosexual Dr. Schoepfer (Act II, scene 2) and the crazy Mischa's ramblings (Act III, scene 3) contribute little to an understanding of Redl, for instance. The abundant sensory images (the smell of peppermints, the foul tasting mouths, the sounds of different characters walking, of music, of crowd noises, and of love-making) keep the audience physically aware, yet except for Redl's moans and his reactions to light during sexual activity, they provide scant information that will lead to insights into his character. Further complicating the issue are the inordinate number of parts (92), and the swift movement through twenty-three scenes. Osborne may have improved his techniques for dealing with peripheral characters and creating realistic social milieux, but the delineation of Redl suffers. Shakespeare was able to impart an immense amount of information about his characters by quickly shifting from scene to scene (as with Hal and Hotspur); Osborne's episodic treatment seems to be an experimental attempt to recreate the effect of cinematic structure through rapid jump cuts between public and private scenes. Unfortunately, his talent for strong portrayals of his protagonists is diluted in the process.

In spite of the critics' consternation over this turn of events, it is obvious that Osborne has chosen this path purposefully, and that he has accomplished what he set out to do. Because his concern is for society in *A Patriot for Me* (by definition "patriot" refers to society), his attention to the individual must perforce be diminished. In fact, too fully-developed a protagonist would destroy the drama's effectiveness because homosexuality is not the subject of this play; it merely serves as a metaphor. The protagonist's personal troubles are symbolically interlocked with a diseased society. Actually, homosexuality becomes equated with more than just a corrupt society; it is also related to power and to the decay of civilization. Osborne's presentation leads to the conclusion that Redl's world picture is not of a "deviant subculture"—it *is* the world.[5] Two characters in the play make observations that support this thesis. First, Kunz replies to the Countess' ironic "I can't think of anything more admirable than not having to play a part" by saying, "We all play parts" (p. 49). Second, the Baron interprets the gay life at his ball (and presumably of the world) with the prophetic announcement "We are none of us safe" (p. 77), an early sounding of the themes of uncertainty and frustration that dominate the later plays.

Oblensky's role is a key to understanding the play, for it is through him that the audience becomes aware of certain things. For instance, he reads aloud the love letter to the Countess in which Redl complains, "This is a difficult time" (p. 62). A commentary on the faltering love affair, this also reflects the general *Angst* suffered by a goal-less, decadent society. In the third act meeting during which Redl is reprimanded for initiating the arrest of one of Oblensky's best agents, the espionage officer states, "It isn't any fun having no clear idea of the future is it? And you can't re-make your past" (p. 114).

Many critics have been unsure how the title and the drama are related, even though Osborne explains the title in the program note mentioned above. His explanation is straightforward and enlightening: "It was the Emperor Francis II who first used the term 'A Patriot For Me'. One day, when a distinguished servant of the Empire was recommended to him for special notice, his sponsor remarked that he was a staunch and loyal patriot. The old Emperor looked up sharply: 'Ah! But is he a patriot for me?' The Hapsburgs ... were not interested in German patriotism ... they were interested only in Imperial patriotism." As with many of Osborne's allusions, there seems to be no direct application of this story to the play. But the words, with the emphasis on "me," suit Redl perfectly. His loyalty is not to a society into which he does not fit, his friends, his fellow officers, his religion, or his country—his loyalty is to himself. He is his own patriot and object of patriotism. The social element in Redl's death is underscored by the fact that representatives of society supply him with the instrument of death, and the final scene, in which Oblensky examines Dr. Schoepfer's dossier in the same way that he did Redl's in Act I, indicates that everything will continue as before. Society is willing to exploit both sides to gain its own ends.

There is a paradox in the need to use an individual to show the workings of society. When an individual places loyalty to self above loyalty to society, society destroys the individual in an automatic self-protective response. That Redl dies because he does not fit looks forward to *West of Suez* and *Watch It Come Down*.

Between the premiere of *A Patriot for Me* and today, Osborne has continued his prolific output. Eleven new stage dramas, including adaptations of Lope de Vega's *La Fianza Satisfecha* (as *A Bond Honoured*), Henrik Ibsen's *Hedda Gabler,* and Oscar Wilde's novel *The Picture of Dorian Gray,* a "reworking" of Shakespeare's *Coriolanus* (as *A Place Calling Itself Rome*), six teleplays, two filmscripts, and numerous newspaper and journal articles have appeared.

The two most notable features of this list are the increased number of plays written for television, and Osborne's interest in literary subjects. As might be expected, this interest is reflected in the themes of the plays he wrote during the same period. Moreover, his characters typically are involved in filmmaking, television, or writing, and literary allusions are abundant. Interestingly, as these elements become more important in Osborne's writing, there is a corresponding diminishment in emotional impact and in his characters' vitality. It is as though he has adopted the nonchalance and emotional sterility of *Look Back in Anger*'s Helena. Gratification has replaced antagonism as the operative motivation.

In two of Osborne's more recent major plays, though—*West of Suez* and *Watch It Come Down*—a new ingredient is apparent, and it is clear that there has been another shift in the perspective out of which Osborne writes, as fear for the future evolves as his main concern. This shift is especially significant when the emotion that underlies *Look Back in Anger* is compared with these two dramas, for the emotions are opposites. Two minor dramas which signal this transition both opened at the Royal Court Theatre in 1968. *Time Present* (first performed on May 23) and *The Hotel in Amsterdam* (first performed on July 3) stand between *A Patriot for Me* and *West of Suez* in terms of both content and technique.

TIME PRESENT and THE HOTEL IN AMSTERDAM

Time Present is really not much more than an extended character sketch. Pamela is in some ways just another Jimmy. She can be cruel, telling Constance that "perhaps" she meant to upset her,[6] and announcing that she has turned down "better" people, but she is not as vital as Jimmy is. Possibly this is because her posturing precedes her father's death.

Pamela, whose long-lasting love affair ended the previous year, has moved into Constance's apartment. The differences between the two roommates' furnishings provide the first clues to Pamela's character. Constance, a Member of Parliament, has decorated the apartment with modern, straight-lined Scandinavian furniture. In contrast with Constance's neatness, the untidy Pamela has cluttered the room with relics from her actor father's past: a wall poster features him in the role of Macbeth and a faded production photograph of him in Shakespearean costume stands on the table.

In an awkward exposition, the kind that a Harold Pinter avoids at all costs, Osborne provides more information about Pamela through dialogs between her mother, Edith, and her younger sister, Pauline, before his protagonist appears on stage. Physically, while Pamela is attractive, she is not pretty; like her father, she is a talented performer; her relationship with her mother is not close (they are not even "friends"), but she and her father are quite close. Further details evolve out of the contrasts between Pamela and Constance or Pauline.

The theme of the play is simple, too simple perhaps. Pamela needs, but is unable to respond to others. "I believe in love," she says, "Just because I don't know how to doesn't mean I don't" (p. 28). Constance, too, observes that "You need love more than anyone I've ever known" (p. 72). But Pamela rejects her closest friends. "Look after Murray," she tells Constance, and Murray, Constance's lover and the father of Pamela's unborn child, is dismissed in favor of an abortionist's services.

Pamela is unable to accept her friends' love because she is living in time present. Osborne includes an excerpt from *Ecclesiastes* as an epigraph in the printed version of the play: "A time to embrace and a time to refrain from embracing. A time to get and a time to lose: a time to keep and a time to cast away." Unfortunately, Pamela is not capable of moving from time to time. More appropriate for her are the opening lines of T. S. Eliot's "Burnt Norton": "Time present and time past/ Are both perhaps present in time future,/ And time future contained in time past." Clearly, Pamela is not an existential heroine. In some ways a familiar Osborne character, isolated and antagonistic, she chooses not to adjust to a changing world. Pauline, who is involved in the drug culture, hippie mentality of the mid-1960's, states, "Your scene is really out" (p. 25). Pamela, noting that she and her sister are not close and know very little about one another (which she sees as "no loss" — p. 22), replies, "Just like my father." And this is the key to the play, of course. Pamela is not trapped so much in her own past as she is influenced by her father's past. Her relationship with her father is symbolized in his chosen name. Born Tristram Prosser, Pamela's father, unlike Pamela, tried to escape his past and his Welsh heritage by adopting the name Giddeon Orme.[7] For Pamela the significance of the surname may lie in the components *or/me* — which complete her identification with her father. In Pamela's vision, Sir Giddeon's prime was during an era of class and taste, and she finds herself unfit to compromise with the vulgar, modern world that surrounds her. As a rejoinder to her sister's criticism she says, "It's impossible to argue with someone wearing such cheap clothes" (p. 25).

Time is important in this play. Constance asserts, "Time is in short supply in the present" (p. 33). Pamela suggests that "we should keep it in its place. Whenever we can. Just because we can't win." But in fact she is paralyzed by time. It is significant that while she is thirty-four, she contradictorily admits to being both twenty-six and twenty-nine. The great irony is that the present in which she is trying to live is actually already past.

Time Present is the first of Osborne's plays which look back not in anger but nostalgically. In an interview Osborne has said "the theatre as I know it ... has probably got a limited life ... the literate theatre of words and rounded psychological characterization is a decadent art form." He goes on to say, however, that he intends to continue writing for the stage, and it may be that herein lie the seeds of his lack of success with this drama. Pamela's world is much narrowed from Redl's; hers is a stage, and she speaks of it in terms of "timing." Her concern is with a style of life. She is not motivated by a workingclass consciousness, economics, or politics, and her resultant calm detachment is the reverse of Jimmy's. This is true of the supporting characters in the play, too. Pamela speaks bitingly and bitterly about a competing actress, Abigail, but when Abigail appears, the confrontation is anything but dramatic. Pamela's foils are not fully realized as characters; they are straw men, and consequently Pamela herself never quite comes to life as a character. The play lacks the energy and enthusiasm of *Look Back in Anger*. It is too cerebral. Redl is less abrasive and less funny than Jimmy, and the characters in *Time Present* are still further removed from life. Indeed, one of the most important presences in the play never appears on stage. In Act I Sir Giddeon is already in the hospital dying; in Act III he has been dead for several weeks.

Even the generation gap is not seriously considered. Pauline is a caricature. Her philosophy of life is not meant to be taken as an alternative to Pamela's lifestyle. She is too foolish, and the slang which fills her speech and delineates her as a representative of time future was going out of date when the play was mounted in 1968.[8] Of course, this may be part of Osborne's point: even the future is becoming the past. Ultimately, the audience does not feel for Pamela, though the problem of how to avoid her fate has been raised.

Osborne's style interferes with the effectiveness of the drama, too. His writing has become more ostentatious and obvious, and the repetitive pattern in his phrasing seems artificial. For example, "He is, he is dying" (p. 19) and "my own, my own walls" (p. 59) probably do not carry the intensity of emotion intended. So, also, is it with the use of literary and political allusions. Although there is some reflection of the characters in their names and their references to Addison (p. 43) and Vietnam (p. 27), the allusions lend as much to building a cultural milieu as they do to an understanding of the immediate situation. Actually, at times it appears that the inclusion of a reference for its own sake is at least as important as the associations connected with it.

As Osborne proceeds from this point, death, the arts, homosexuality, and related topics become more and more central in his writing. In relation to these subjects the past becomes increasingly important. The plays are set in the past, or the characters are linked to a past in such a way that they are somehow out of joint with the present. And this lack of connection with the present is reenforced by the foreign element: the characters were born abroad (Pamela in India) or the play takes place in a foreign setting as though to reiterate that Osborne's protagonists are not at home in to-day's England.

In *The Hotel in Amsterdam* the characters are again greatly influenced by an off-stage presence, and while they are a part of the art world of modern London, they have tried to escape both, in this case by fleeing to a foreign locale. This play is a little more thematically complex than *Time Present,* though, and it is also more entertaining. In large part this is due to Osborne's better handling of his characters.

The situation is minimal. A group of three married couples takes a long weekend vacation together in Amsterdam as a means of escaping their boss, the movie producer referred to only by his initials, K. L. These characters are different from Osborne's earlier ones. Stylish, well-to-do, fortyish intelligentsia, they come together for a chance to reaffirm what is valuable in their lives—the need for and the enjoyment of the others in their small group. As Laurie, the most articulate, witty, and vocal member of the gathering notes, "it's not natural. It's bloody unnatural. How often do you get people so different as we all are still all together all friends and who all love each other" (p. 98). This sentiment is immediately undercut by Annie's parody of a Barbra Streisand song ("people who need people are the ghastliest people in the world"), but this is done in a Noel Cowardish manner which looks forward to *West of Suez.* In fact, these characters are relatively well-adjusted, and while Laurie, Osborne's new hero, contains some of Jimmy's self-pity, he is also affectionate and able to express his feelings for his friends. The invective is missing.

Almost no dramatic action takes place on stage; this is because the group is a collection of talkers, and their topics do not lend themselves to action. As Annie comments, "I can tell you what everyone will do—just talk. About what to do, where to go, what we should wear" (p. 114). Even if the social commentary and class consciousness of *Look Back in Anger* were present, these people would not do anything about them. Their targets are comparatively insignificant: the Welsh, Japanese, and Americans, travel, mothers, homosexuality, sex (with a Freudian linking of mothers and rape), sleep, the generation gap, the pill. When class differences are mentioned, it is only in passing (p. 90). The characters are too concerned with having escaped their "monster" of a boss for several days and with congratulating themselves for having done so.

The combination of escape and congratulatory motifs is an interesting one. Very early in Act I it is made clear that the characters are, indeed, escaping (p. 89), and this theme is repeated throughout the drama. They are sure that K. L. will be amazed at their "naughtiness" (p. 93). Yet Margaret's contention that "Here we are congratulating ourselves on escaping from him and we've hardly stopped talking about him" (p. 94) is so obvious that it really does not need to be stated. And in Act II, after having been in Amsterdam for two days, Gus's "we really have had quite a time" (p. 121) has a hollow ring. The continual restatement sounds too much as though everyone is trying to confirm or to convince everyone else that this is true. There is an amusing and revealing parallel in Laurie's joke that only an annual notice of one's birthday in the London *Times* is confirmation of one's existence (p. 102).

The Hotel in Amsterdam is a slice of life. A very special kind of life, to be sure, but a slice of life nonetheless, and it is the differences between the characters and their interactions that make this so. In general each has a personality (perhaps the mixture represents civilized society: e. g., Dan is from a working-class background, Gus is slow but solid). At the same time, the group dynamics, the give and take, the supportiveness are elements which flesh out the play and simultaneously demonstrate Osborne's advance in characterization. The reality of their situation and their exchanges are more vital than the posturing in *Time Present*. These people do not play roles when they are together in the way that they do for K. L., according to Gus (p. 93), and thus they come closer to self-knowledge and to knowing each other than do any characters in Osborne's work since *Inadmissable Evidence*. This extends so far as the perceptive Gus' recognizing that K. L. may be an indispensable linkage in their relationships (p. 117). The irony is that the group is defined by its exclusion of K. L. The double irony is that K. L. apparently needed them. "Where would K. L. be" without his writer and editor, Laurie asks facetiously (p. 100). Apparently the answer is that without his friends he is dead. When K. L. commits suicide, it is with the knowledge that the group is gone and cannot save him, unlike the sham suicide staged by Margaret's younger sister, Gillian.

The ending is melodramatic; the climax does not fit. There have been vague comments about K. L.'s vulnerability and reliance on the group, but they have been countered by the group's words and actions. The tragedy at the end of the drama seems tacked on, separate from the rest of the play. One critic suggests that the conclusion serves as a warning rather than a prophecy of disintegration, now that there is an open recognition of need,[9] yet this has been admitted throughout. Another critic discusses the unconsummated love avowed by Annie and Laurie as a potential for renewal which is undercut by the ending.[10] But what if Osborne's point is that K. L. died because he was not supported? In the final analysis, however, K. L.'s death may be nothing more than exposing the audience to the senseless violence that marks *West of Suez* and *Watch It Come Down*. It may also be an indication that Osborne did not know how to end this play effectively.

Stylistically *The Hotel in Amsterdam* does incorporate some interesting developments. The monologs are shorter, wittier, and less vindictive than previously. More important, though, is Osborne's use of language. Words themselves are important, as evidenced by the characters' concern with Dutch and Laurie's "Italian." Osborne's attempts to reproduce banal, everyday conversation, with some wit thrown in for characterization (in spite of Laurie's sophomoric humor—El Fag Airlines and the Golden Sanitary Towel Presentation), emphasizes the slice of life surface of the play. A limited optimism may be found in the presence of Constance, a successful representative of modern society, on stage as *Time Present* closes, and Laurie's curtain line that the group probably will not return to Amsterdam, "But I expect we might go somewhere else" (p. 143), offers the possibility of a similar gathering. But there is a touch of sinister irony in the fact that these extremely verbal characters frequently resort to vulgarities. This use of vulgar language in the mouths of cultured and sophisticated people is more than an example of the liberating effect of the ending of the Licensing Act; it is an early psychological signal of the evolving fear which will permeate *West of Suez*.

A SENSE OF DETACHMENT

A Sense of Detachment, first staged at the Royal Court Theatre on December 4, 1972, has largely been ignored by the critics, and rightly so. Osborne's use of language for its shock value as an attention-getter, like Henry Miller's, has overwhelmed his content. An anomaly in Osborne's canon, and possibly an attempted parody of 1960's happenings, psychodrama, and plays like *Hair*, the drama comes across as nasty and dirty, the sort of thing that might be expected of an undergraduate Beyond the Fringe or Goodies revue.

Osborne focuses on a diversity of subjects normally touched only in passing in his other dramas (sex, the generation gap, politics, religion, the battle of the sexes), and in part this may account for the work's failure. It affects a purposeful formlessness, and the stage directions call for improvisation, but within the limits of insult and bad taste.[11] The sense of unstructured happening produces moments of low-brow fun, yet the overall result is something like a Godard film, a lack of connection mixed with stridency, because of the author's aggressive attack on his audience.

The employment of theatrical devices—music, records, film projection, characters seated in the audience, references directed at the audience, literary and theatrically based jokes—are simultaneously used to deride these same devices and to involve the audience as though, in Grandfather's words, "all life is a theatre" (p. 13). This curious mixture is emphasized by the apparent detachment of the actors, and the playwright for that matter. There may be general agreement with the criticism of the two actors placed in the audience, however. Osborne's low opinion of his audience parallels that stated in his non-dramatic writing and interviews, and the playwright may well intend to drive the play-goers away. Given the coarse, vulgar language and the raunchy topics expounded upon in Act I, there is little wonder that the post-intermission stage directions begin *"As the audience returns, if it does"* (p. 27). For those who do return, the second act is more of the same, reenforced by the juxtaposition of pornography and quotations from a variety of poems and songs on miscellaneous subjects, though commonly revolving around love. Does this mean that pornography and love are equatable? The play ends on its most positive note as the Chap and the Girl embrace in preparation for sexual activity.

The social satire incorporated in this non-play is hardly redeeming. It seems that Osborne has momentarily slipped a cog; but *A Sense of Detachment* surely exemplifies the psychological set that drives the dramatist to express his frustrations and fears more seriously in other plays during this period.

WEST OF SUEZ, THE END OF ME OLD CIGAR, and WATCH IT COME DOWN

Osborne's next two major plays have dark endings. While they are separated in time by a very minor work, *West of Suez* and *Watch It Come Down* represent the dramatist's new view of life. There is an extension of certain themes that began to be developed in *Time Present* and *The Hotel in Amsterdam*, and their tone reflects Osborne's concern with the implications of the new world that he sees.

West of Suez was first performed at the Royal Court Theatre on August 17, 1971. Like *The Hotel in Amsterdam*, the drama is about a small group of sophisticated English men and women who are in a foreign locale, but the earlier play's seeds of anxiety become portents of fear for the future as they blend with nostalgia for the past and the combination is overpoweringly significant in Osborne's development. The movement from anger to fear is now complete.

The action takes place at the villa "Mesopotamia" on a sub-tropical island which is *"neither Africa nor Europe, but some of both, also less than both."* [12] Like the settings in Graham Greene's novels, it is a place conducive to deterioration. As Frederica notes, "Nothing heals, everything goes rotten or mildewed. Slimy" (p. 39). That the Tigris and Euphrates valley was the cradle of western civilization, that there are no longer British military posts in Mesopotamia, and that the island setting is between two worlds, literally and figuratively, has more than coincidental bearing on the play's meaning.

The characters also reflect a way of life that is on the wane. When Frederica says "Ah—home to England" (p. 61), she is speaking ironically, for all of the major characters are foreign born. Wyatt, his four daughters, the Brigadier, and Lamb were born in exotic former Empire outposts in the East: Srinigar, Ceylon, Singapore, Mesopotamia, Rangoon, Kuala Lumpur. As the play unfolds, it will be seen that many of their professions are passive. Wyatt and Lamb are writers (with writer's names); Patrick, Robin's husband, is a retired brigadier who is "happy pottering around" (p. 18) and serving as a leftover representative of Colonel Redfern's Edwardian world; Edward, Frederica's husband, is in pathology, a field of medicine "Somewhat inhuman and requiring a detachment that's almost unscientific" (p. 15); Robert, Mary's husband, is a teacher; Wyatt's secretary lives on what his employer does; and Alastair is a homosexual hairdresser. There are also several Americans on the scene: Harry seems to be a beachcomber, the cruise ship tourists are "Helpless and hopeless" (p. 31), and Jed is a special case, a professional student. More about Jed later.

The opening dialog between Frederica and Edward seems to be setting up a Noel Cowardish atmosphere as the couple wittily discusses servants, sleep, relatives, and similar shallow subjects. Their talk is at cross-purposes, for they are not truly listening to each other. Ironically, Edward tells his wife to "Listen to those birds" (p. 12). Later Wyatt will observe pompously, "Birds chatter and *that* is their mortal flaw. Chatter sins against language, and when we sin against the word, we sin against God"

(p. 57). Despite Wyatt's pronouncement, like the characters in *The Hotel in Amsterdam*, these people are talkers, and anyone who talks so much does not have time to listen, which will cost them dearly when their civilized battle of the sexes is pushed aside by more critical events.

Actually, language assumes the importance of a character in this drama. Frederica and Edward consciously play with words in their extended opening dialog. They talk about Miss Nomers (p. 13), joke about bird lovers ("If one can still use [the term] in the feathered sense" — p. 14), refer to Edward's medical specialty as "Blood and shit" (p. 15), and comment on the "syntactical swing" of their sentences (p. 16). When Wyatt speaks, it is in a consciously abbreviated style filled with counterbalancing italics (e.g., pp. 38–41). In contrast, long-haired Jed is almost speechless until his diatribe at the end of the play. Asked where he is going, his answer is simply "Wherever" (p. 50). Apparently a rootless student, his subsequent comment that "Anyplace is home for me" (p. 69) seems to be an extension of his "Wherever," but, as his later outburst reveals, the fact that he feels at home everywhere is especially chilling in its implications.

Language is important to Wyatt and his sophisticated companions because it is a badge of their culture. The dark-skinned servant Leroi's sole words are an announcement that Mrs. James has arrived (p. 69), and Frederica complains that none of the servants listen to orders. One of the characteristics of the ex-patriot British is their propensity for working around native cultures by transporting English social elements wherever they go, and this often includes listening to the BBC. The pseudo-economic, pseudo-sociological jargon of the program descriptions which Robert reads in Act II are not from the real world. In fact, in tone they are suspiciously similar to the pornographic descriptions recited in *A Sense of Detachment*.

The literary allusions that self-consciously lard the dialog are further cultural indicators. There are references to St. Paul (p. 18), King Lear (p. 34), George Moore (p. 38), Yeats (p. 38), Rupert Brooke (p. 41), Cranmer's *Book of Common Prayer* (p. 44), "Papa" Hemingway (p. 68), Samuel Johnson (p. 72), St. Augustine (p. 72), and the King James Bible (p. 73). Wyatt even has a hat that belonged to George Moore, a self-revelatory Irish novelist. This is fitting, given Wyatt's self-centered nature.

The most amusing allusion is to Osborne's own *Look Back in Anger* when Robin repeats Jimmy's words ("as someone said"): "if you've no world of your own, it's rather pleasant to regret the passing of someone else's" (p. 35). Jimmy is speaking almost sentimentally about Colonel Redfern's world, a world that no longer exists, but which was solid and secure and comfortable. By referring to his own earlier work Osborne recognizes his personal alienation from the contemporary world, recognizes that the source of his alienation has changed (his literary, artificial insertion suggests that he has lost the intensity and the ability to create strong emotional impacts based on sincere feelings which characterized that play—instead of creating anew, now he must rely on quoting from his past). He is also clearly stating the theme of cultural decline.

Having established the above in an almost Shavian fashion, Osborne introduces an interview format to express Wyatt's apolitical nature. This apolitical stance is obviously related to the cultural element, and ultimately it is the cause of what happens, for it is nothing more than a form of blindfolding. Mrs. James begins by asking Wyatt, "What do you think of as being Utopia?" to which he answers, "A place without pain, passion or nobility. Where there is no hatred, boredom or imperfection" (p. 71). She then asks, "What do you think of man?" and he replies, "As a defect, striving for excellence." This is the context within which all of Wyatt's answers must be considered. He desires a comfortable world and he is living as though such a world is real. For example, in a world that has a servant class he can answer the query, "In these changing times, do you still believe that words in themselves have any meaning, value or validity?" by saying "I still cling pathetically to the old bardic belief that 'words alone are certain good'" (p. 74).

Wyatt cannot see because of his love of words, or he loves words because he cannot see—the result is the same. "What are your feelings about the island and the people," Mrs. James asks. "All the good things I've seen of the island seem to be legacies of the British, the Spanish and the Dutch. ... As for the people, they seem to me to be a very unappealing mixture of hysteria and lethargy, brutality and sentimentality" (p. 75), Wyatt replies.

The colonial mind set is appealing because it is easy to live at the expense of others—if there is no sensitivity to the plight of those others. Mrs. James wants to know "What do you think about the class situation in England?" Wyatt answers, "Like many of the upper class, I've liked the sound of broken glass" (pp. 75–76). Throwing champagne glasses into the fireplace following a toast is fine, so long as there is no worry about the expense of replacing the glasses and there is someone to clean up the mess.

The two most important questions come near the end of the interview. Mrs. James asks "How would you describe yourself politically?" and Wyatt states "I wouldn't attempt to." In spite of this, the play's ending is foreshadowed when Mrs. James asks, "What do you dread most at this stage of your life?" Wyatt's answer is ironic in its foreshadowing and in its perceptiveness: "Not death. But ludicrous death. And I also feel it is in the air" (p. 78). It is too bad that he is not as perceptive anywhere else in the play.

A final language/culture connection is seen in the way that the natives are described. Frederica's contention that they are an odd ethnic mixture of "Lethargy and hysteria" and "Brutality and sentimentality" (p. 12) is obviously contradictory (and probably a repetition of her father's stereotyping). In Act II she demonstrates her lack of sensitivity when she comments on the islander's music: "I suppose they think it has a simple, brooding native charm and intensity. Which is about the last thing any of them have got. Anyway, they never stop playing it" (p. 81). This is the kind of insensitivity that Jimmy railed against, and it may be founded in the same class basis. Edward is more insightful. He finds the natives "Perched between one civilization and the next."

When armed islanders step out of the bush and shoot down Wyatt, everything comes together. The ending is shocking, not because the native uprising is barely expected, but because the senseless violence has not been prepared for. That it is Wyatt who dies, though, is fitting, for he represents the attitudes and values against which the natives are rebelling. He claims that "Protest is easy. But grief must be lived" (p. 73), yet he mouths the words without understanding them. Edward and Frederica's combined "We can't be—/ Responsible for others" (p. 19) is ironic as applied to doctors, but actions in the play demonstrate the results of generalized applicability in political and social terms.

Colonial types in an imperialistic setting create a cultural metaphor in *West of Suez*. Osborne demonstrates that both colonialism and culture are things of the past. They are not viable in the modern world. This is not his main point, however. For one thing, he does not appear to be especially fond of his characters. Wyatt, the most engaging, does not come on stage until a third of the way into the drama, and in spite of his wit, he is pompous and shallow. Collectively his family are non-productive aesthetes whose main delight is in the sound of their own idle verbosity and bickering. With the exception of Jed, the killers are not developed. There hardly can be sympathy for a group which is invisible and unknown until it steps out of the darkness for a few moments of butchery. And Jed's tirade destroys his credibility because it is filled with meaningless revolutionary rhetoric and clichés: "Fuck all your *shit*. ... You're pigs, babies" (pp. 82–84). Critics point out that this most forceful dialog in the play strikingly resembles Osborne's "Damn you England" letter to the *Tribune,* and one wonders if the dramatist "created the chatter only to destroy it."[13] Perhaps this should be taken a step farther. Wyatt spoke about chatter previously, and it may be that Jed is chattering just as the sophisticated characters do, but in a different idiom.

Again, language provides the key to the play. American revolutionaries may help shoot down seventy-year-old men, and American tourists may overcome civilization with litter, cartons, beer cans, cokes, and more hotels (pp. 23, 32), but these are merely symptoms of the disease before which Osborne cringes. The use of four-letter words by cultured characters is too facile to be part of their stereotyping, or to be a means of devaluing the language with which they play, so the words represent more than Osborne's rejection of the characters or their words; they represent insecurities and fears that psychologically can be manifested only in this way. Jed's alternative forms of expression are dismissable. So what is left? Frustration and despair.

The play's title reenforces Osborne's theme. It is a perverted allusion to Somerset Maugham's fifty-year-old drama, *East of Suez*. Maugham's play has little relevance to this work other than that it is about problems Englishmen face when they do not understand a native population. Possibly more important is the simple reference to an earlier, grander, more civilized time. The focus on Suez is interesting, of course, since the Suez Crisis in 1956 was devastating evidence of the Empire's decline. By placing his drama west of Suez, Osborne moves beyond the Edwardian period into contemporary times, and he draws attention to the symbolic setting sun of the Empire.

The final lines sum up the play's meaning. Standing over the murdered Wyatt, Edward recalls an old English saying: "My God—they've shot the fox" (p. 85). Fox hunting is the prototypical English upper-class sporting activity (expensive, complex, rigid, meaningless activity). Shooting a fox, therefore, is the grossest conduct imaginable. It is contrary to the social code and is done only by outcasts and enemies of society.[14] It is proper that this interpretation is uttered by a pathologist who has diagnosed the situation to someone whose background is lacking the elements which would give the saying any meaning. And this explicitly expresses the theme of *West of Suez*. culture and the members of cultured society can be destroyed without reason and without warning by those who neither know nor care what they are destroying. There have been numerous examples of this throughout history, from the Thugees to the Boxers to the Mau Maus, but Osborne must have felt horribly like a prophet when barely a year after the play opened eight people were massacred by natives with submachine guns on a golf course on the island of St. Croix.

The End of Me Old Cigar, first performed at the Greenwich Theatre on January 16, 1975, is the slightest piece that Osborne has written for the stage. It is on a par with some of his lesser television scripts, like *Jill and Jack* (fittingly published in the same volume), and like *A Sense of Detachment*, it seems something of an anomaly.

In Act I of this social satire Lady Regina Frimley and her female friends are established as fighters for women's liberation who are trying to gain control of Great Britain by having "enticed almost every man in England"[15] to a large country house where the men have been filmed, without their knowledge, while being seduced. The film is to be used to embarrass the men into giving up their role of running the world's affairs. The characters are pure stereotype. Aggressive, plain, unwashed man-haters mingle with shy, downtrodden housewives in working for this common cause, and they speak in clichés befitting their stereotypes.

The upshot is that the women's plans break down under the pressure of good old romantic love and masculine superiority (the housewife finds her appointed conquest more attractive than her assignment, and Lady Regina's male consort tells the victims everything and provides them with a key to the film vault). The battlers for women's rights degenerate into ineffectual recriminations and name calling, and the play ends with the quotation, "A WOMAN IS A WOMAN BUT A GOOD CIGAR IS A *SMOKE!*" (p. 56).

Patently anti-feminist, the play is a male chauvinist's view of women at their worst. While funny at times in its obvious play on spoken and conceptual clichés, it has none of the power of Osborne's previous works, and he seems to be trying to get by on vulgarities and superficial stylishness. Osborne may realize what has happened to his style and technique and be trying to move from the depressive negatism that has characterized his latest dramas. Perhaps *The End of Me Old Cigar* is self-parody. It may be amusing, but it is not good drama.

Watch It Come Down, first performed at the Old Vic on February 24, 1975, may be the culmination of thematic lines that began appearing in *Time Present*. The overriding fear and frustration that underlie Osborne's latest dramas and break through so violently in *West of Suez* are present, perhaps even in greater intensity, yet Osborne's statements are clearer and his style is more controlled than previously.

The movement from *A Patriot for Me*'s European past to the present in *West of Suez*'s former colonial setting terminates in today's rural England in this play. Having established his concern for a kind of character in *West of Suez*, Osborne brings his fears home to his British audience by placing *Watch It Come Down* in a familiar locale. As a metaphor, the converted country railway station presents the image of a faded past, but more significantly, it says that what happened on an anonymous, foreign, sub-tropical island can just as easily happen to native-born Britons in merry old England. The parallels between the two plays are devastatingly significant; *Watch It Come Down* corroborates the theme of a culture under attack.

The characters are typical of those in Osborne's plays during this period. Some of them are admirable; all of them are cultured, bright, and artistically sophisticated. As a film director, Ben Prosser represents the new "plastic" arts. He is successful, with Oscars and awards at Cannes, but he does not like "people," and he is weak.[16] Friends, however, are important, and his sexual desire for his ex-wife, his wife's painter sister, and Jo seems to be stimulated more by his liking them as human beings than by attacks of satyriasis (e.g., pp. 38–39); there is a sense of the comradeship that is present between Laurie and Annie in *The Hotel in Amsterdam*. He also loves his daughter and his dog.

Ben's wife Sally, a writer, is cruel. She is ready to inflict pain at a moment's notice, as when she derides Marion and Ben's daughter (p. 18), yet her cruelty is a defensive reaction to situations that might expose her vulnerability. As Ben says, she "can't face the future" (p. 28), a conclusion that she repeats in despair later.

Ray, a homosexual in the "rag trade," is a sophisticated version of *Look Back in Anger*'s Cliff. He is pleasant; he is sensitive; he likes those around him; and he is either helpful or used by them, or both. This latter aspect of his personality is important thematically. Ben and Sally are game players. They are as witty and bitter as Edward Albee's George and Martha:

> SALLY: . . . The only joke you don't see is yourself.
> BEN: You should have been a writer. (p. 29)

Like George and Martha, they go too far occasionally. When Sally assails Ben's relationship with Marion and his daughter, his response is indicative of his pain: "Will you . . . for one minute, just stop that fucking pile of shit spewing out of your fucking mouth!" (p. 19). When they go too far, they are sorry (pp. 19, 31), but they are incapable of forcing themselves to comfort one another, even though they want to, so Ray's role is to provide sympathy and understanding. He also serves as their tool; he is used to inform Glen, Jo, and Shirley that Ben and Sally are separating. Although the couple does not intend to separate and is only pretending in order to evoke their friends' reactions, ironically they admit that a separation is possible, and Ray explains to Glen that it is almost as though they want their friends to make a decision for them (p. 49).

The game playing is symptomatic; Ray's analysis is that they "Didn't know what they were doing" (p. 50). Ben "had heavy moral scruples" about testing his friends (p. 13), but play with them he does. He also states that the "one thing" that he has not been able to do is tell Sally the truth (p. 33). Her response is "I'm tired of this." The game gets on their nerves, yet they cannot separate games from reality, as is evident when she interrupts Ben's call to Marion and when Ben retaliates by tearing the new outfit that he has brought Sally (p. 34). This is apropos of Osborne's theme of degeneration of the artistic/aristocratic class, involved with game playing because they are no longer vital, certainly not in a Shavian sense. The world from which they sprang, the world of Sally's dead father, who was in "The Colonial Service" (p. 15), is no longer in effect and it has been replaced by play. When Sally recognizes this ("All the days are long the way we live"), Ben cannot help her escape the trap in which they are both caught: "Oh, knock it off for five minutes. Do your cabaret somewhere else" (p. 14). There is a lack of communication. Ben says, "I don't think you really. . . . Have feelings for anyone. Except dogs. . . . How *little* you know." Sally answers, "How little *you* know" (p. 55). Yet there is feeling. When Ben is shot, Sally cries, "Oh Ben, don't go. Don't leave me" (p. 57). Her personal grief becomes a class lament, though, when she continues, "We all, *the few of us,* need one another."

Glen and Jo contrast with Ben and Sally. Throughout the play Ben and Sally's outbursts of bitterness and violence are followed immediately by tender moments between the second couple, as when the opening confrontation over Ben's family is juxtaposed with Jo's affirmation that Glen "really [is] so very gentle" (p. 20), and Ben's ripping of Sally's present is followed by a quietly affectionate scene. Ben and Sally are emotional, irrational, and noisy, and the action of the play centers on them. Glen and Jo are the intellectual center of the drama, and they articulate the thematic meaning for which Ben and Sally supply the practical examples. Glen is dying. Admirable in a washed-out way, a remnant of an earlier era, he is a homosexual novelist who has come to the last page of his latest book (p. 20). His spectacles are broken (p. 40), but he is the most perceptive character. Glen delivers the play's intellectual commentary throughout. His first statement focusing on Osborne's theme details contemporary England: "Suspicion, cupidity, complacency, hostility, profiteering, small, greedy passions, tweedy romance. . . . Beef barons, pig and veal concentration camps. . . . The Country. It's the last of England for them, the one last, surviving colony. This is England. . . . The fuzzy wuzzies from Durham and the Rhondda are at the last gate" (p. 21). The country is explicitly representational for all of England, and the appellation "fuzzy wuzzies," traditionally applied derogatorily to pagans in foreign countries, is ironically used to label residents of rural and lower working class Britain. Furthermore, Ben and Sally become symbolic representatives of their class when Glen continues in words that appear to be an extension of the above thoughts, but that refer to his friends: "How *did* it happen? They needed one another. But no more. Who's going? . . . Is this really *it* this time?"

The theme of transition, of people caught between dying and emerging cultures, is called up by Glen's allusion to Yeats' "The Second Coming."

"So," he says, "it *does* all fall apart" (p. 22). His perceptiveness is further demonstrated when he continues, "We've seen the future *and it doesn't work.*" And he offers a reason for what he sees happening. Books, his culture symbol, are declared "an outmoded form of communication" (p. 23). Later he expands on this when he explains that he became a writer to "show us what we are yesterday and today. They're starting to wonder. But too late. My book's no good. It's too late. The century pulled the carpet out from me" (p. 40). One of Ben's moments of insight corroborates Glen's view: "How can you be a romantic in a world that despises imagination and only gives instruction in orgasms?" Ben also sums up Glen's role as a representative of bygone times: "I loved him because ... he made his own life out of the twentieth century and what a bad one *it* was. The century, I mean" (p. 52). As Sally notes, "What isn't broken? Dead? Disappearing?" (p. 43).

Jo lends credibility to Glen's perceptions because of her own character and her linking with him. Jo loves Glen, and she needs love. Her nature is so immersed in love, in fact, that she sees herself as love (p. 37), and interpersonal relationships, the love that she simultaneously requires and symbolizes, may be a source of salvation — "It's like religion without pain" (p. 39). Her mode of escape is couched in similar terms: "Release us from ourselves and give us each our other." Thus, when she says that "Glen is the life. If he goes. It all. Goes" (p. 43), she reenforces the impression that Glen is the key, and his pronouncements thereby gain additional substance. Her suicide underscores her contention that "it all goes" if Glen dies, and ironically conceals her sense of love as a source of salvation.

Jo unifies several other threads of plot and theme, too. In various guises the characters seek escape. Ben, for instance, looks to hide in women's arms. Actually, they all share a need for physical contact, for touching, from Jo's tender stroking of Glen's hand (p. 20) to Ben's wanting to hold her (p. 47). But there is no escape, for time has run out. Jo sees the end approaching: "The time is short and all our heads are sore and our hearts sick, oh, into this world, this century we've been born into and made and been made by" (p. 39). Even before events prove her right, Jo's words are confirmed by Sally ("...it *is* the time. Because it's running out, and we should be running away" —p. 45), and by Marion ("There's been a lot of time. A wasteland of it" —p. 53).[17]

The group gathered at the railway station hearkens back to those who stayed at the hotel in Amsterdam. In the earlier play the problems stemmed from the personalities involved. But in this play the problems are proof that the world is "all so bad, so brutish, so devilish, so sneering" (p. 51). This is the England described by Glen, and by Sally, who catalogs the "nasty, brutish issue of English Country Life" with armies of Japs and Texans who "slaughter" a "Wildlife Vietnam": "No, there's not much in the land. Fish and animals, yes; and the pigs who *own* it and *run* it" (p. 17).

With the violence and corruption implied in these descriptions, Osborne has come back to the islanders of *West of Suez*. Although the natives are not seen in *Watch It Come Down*, the confrontation between alien cultures is as destructive as it was in the previous drama (though the "muddied, grasping, well-off peasants from public schools and merchant banks" (p. 17) are more cruel and uncivilized in their actions than were the untutored natives). The conflict is epitomized by two events: the murder of Ben's dog and the assault on the railway station. The appalling incident of the dog's death and the characters' reaction to it are foreshadowed when Ben reports that "Major Bluenose" has offered £5 to any of his men who shoot Ben's dogs. The Major has also complained about Ben's cats worrying his sheep (!), and the "layabouts lolling about" (p. 16). Unable to accept those who do not belong, the local residents attack them in a senseless, lawless, violent way. As Sally describes it, "We saw them from the top of the hill, helpless. They tied [Ben's dog] to a tree and set all the male dogs on her. And then they shot her ... In front of us" (pp. 41–42). In a frenzy of uncontrolled fury and frustration over their loss and their impotence, Ben and Sally fly at one another, smashing, kicking, and tearing as the curtain falls on Act I. Striking out at each other in their grief is a reflection of the inner turmoil inherent in Osborne's world view.

The assault which brings down the final curtain in a flurry of anti-intellectual destruction is prepared for in the scene that foreshadows the dog's death when Ray accuses the Major of arranging the "smashing up the windows here last month." With Glen's death, Jo's suicide, and Ben's murder, the most talented, likeable, civilized, and social characters are removed. They may be homosexuals or effete literati who were never at the "center" and whose passion and primary success was in insignificant word play, but they would never shoot at the body of a dead woman. Dr. Ashton, the one outsider who appears, is an educated man, a professional who should heal and relieve suffering, yet his response is to blame the victims for not being "popular" with the "yobbos" (p. 56).[18] His lack of emotion may be stereotypically British stiff upper lip; his complete lack of sympathy and continuing condemnation of the sufferers is something else. "You've brought this on yourselves," he says reprovingly to a group who has done nothing more than move into a neighborhood, an action so sinister for the locals that they must destroy what they do not like or understand. The doctor's statement, "you do lead odd sorts of lives, don't you," again blames the victims and sums up the attitude of the yobbos (an attitude graphically portrayed in Sam Peckinpah's 1971 film *Straw Dogs).* He is not understated; he is coldly alien. Sally's reply has the ring of Osborne's truth to it: "Yes. . . . We do. Most of us. You must be glad."

The title of the play combines concepts from Eliot's "Journey of the Magi" and Yeats' "The Second Coming" in a modern idiom. A revolution is taking place in the twentieth century. This is a barbaric age; the old order is falling. The significance of the title also is revealed in Glen's anecdote: "I saw two signs. . . . One was a little triangle of green with a hedge and a bench. And a sign read: 'This is a temporary open space' . . . the other was a site of rubble near the Crystal Palace . . . where bank managers and cashiers fled at the beginning of our . . . century. It said 'Blenkinsop— Demolitionists. We *do* it. You *watch* it. *Come down'"* (p. 50). The linking of open spaces and demolition (near a cultural center) is obviously another reference to Osborne's primary theme.

Once more his theme is reflected in his stylistic elements. There is still pretentiousness in some of his constructions ("They're: splitting up"— p. 21), as though he is flaunting self-conscious, artificial literary techniques in the faces of those he despises and fears. More important, however, are his use of language and literary allusions to augment his themes. In general he is hardly more subtle in expressing his themes through dialog than he was in previous plays—indeed, Glen openly states them. Sex is an important metaphor, and the language reflects a preoccupation with sex. On the one hand, the outburst by Ben ("stop that fucking pile of shit") is neither civilized nor sophisticated. On the other hand, there are times when language and meaning combine perfectly. When Sally talks to Ben about his visit with Marion, she asks "Did you fuck her?" (p. 19). Not did you sleep with her, or make love, but the harsh, shocking, even brutal "Did you fuck her?" Sally is striking at Ben, trying to hurt him by degrading his relationship through these terms, but there is simultaneously a masochistic, self-inflicted punishment aimed at herself. By using these words she is exacerbating the pain which she feels that she deserves because of the nature of her own relationship with Ben.

Similarly, the playwright's allusions are better integrated, too. While there are relatively few literary references, they tend to be associated with death (Leo Tolstoy, p. 10; *Hamlet,* pp. 15, 19; Armageddon, p. 22; Christ's cross, p. 41) or cultures in upheaval (Yeats, p. 22; the Theatre of the Absurd, p. 41). Appropriately, the allusion to *The Death of Iván Ilyich* goes beyond the novel's theme, for Tolstoy died at a remote railway junction.

Overall, the combined effect of Osborne's tightly packed style, witty, real characters, and integration of language, allusions, and themes is to make good drama. *Watch It Come Down* is the best written of his latest plays—in spite of the disturbing, unsettling events depicted. His control makes his statement all the more powerful.

With the performance of *West of Suez*, Osborne's new concern for the future emerges fullblown; *Watch It Come Down* confirms and reenforces this theme. When he wrote *Look Back in Anger*, Osborne was indeed looking back in anger at an insensitive world and time. He was filled with rage. Now he is looking at another insensitive world and time, but he is looking forward and with fear. Where once he was aggressive and sought to goad his contemporaries into a life of feeling, he is now desperate in his fear of a world which is attacking him, and which will crush him and his way of life.

NOTES

1. The cuts demanded are published at the end of the Faber edition. Interestingly, the Lord Chamberlain's office was abolished in 1968, a fact which may be significant in Osborne's later work.

2. Mary McCarthy and Kenneth Tynan engaged in a celebrated literary feud over its meaning in *The Observer* (London), July 4 and 18, 1965, and Ronald Hayman concedes to being mystified (*John Osborne*. New York: Ungar, 1972).

3. *A Patriot for Me* (London: Faber and Faber, 1965), p. 17. All subsequent page references to this play refer to this edition.

4. Simon Trussler, *The Plays of John Osborne: An Assessment* (London: Gollancz, 1969), pp. 139–40.

5. This is pointed out by Harold Ferrar in *John Osborne* (New York: Columbia University Press, Columbia Essays on Modern Writers series, 1973), p. 36.

6. *Time Present and The Hotel in Amsterdam* (London: Faber and Faber, 1968), p. 36. All subsequent page references to these plays refer to this edition.

7. This leads to several levels of irony, since the name Orme is of Celtic derivation, too. Interestingly, the name Prosser recurs in *Watch It Come Down*.

8. For example, "turned on and dropping out" (p. 21) and "trip" (p. 23).

9. Trussler, p. 195.

10. Ferrar, p. 41.

11. *A Sense of Detachment* (London: Faber and Faber, 1973), see pp. 14–15. All subsequent page references to this play will refer to this edition.

12. *West of Suez* (London: Faber and Faber, 1971), p. 11. All subsequent page references to this play refer to this edition.

13. Hayman, pp. 135–36.

14. There are also some interesting reverberations with the character of Volpone here.

15. *The End of Me Old Cigar and Jill and Jack* (London: Faber and Faber, 1975), p. 20. All subsequent page references to this play refer to this edition.

16. *Watch It Come Down* (London: Faber and Faber, 1975), p. 10. All subsequent page references to this play refer to this edition.

17. Marion's agonized reference to Eliot is filled with irony, for they have had time and yet they have accomplished nothing, and will accomplish nothing with more time. At the same time, her wasteland allusion resounds with double irony because of its statement about what that time holds in store.

18. Yobbos is derived from the children's game which reverses the spelling of words. It has come to mean oaffish, violent, Teddy-boy types.

Arnold Wesker:
The Celebratory Instinct

MARGERY M. MORGAN

Arnold Wesker dramatised one of his own stories as a television play, and this, *Love Letters on Blue Paper,* was later adapted for the stage. It is concerned with the final illness and death of Victor, a retired trade union leader who has also been a lover of the arts. Victor reads out to his younger friend, Maurice, a passage on an imaginary artist taken from an essay he has been writing:

> His is a playful rather than profound art; ... he reproduces the *patterns* of man's architecture rather than reflects the passion and personality that made it ... He seems unmoved by what moves man to contort his body or arrange the bones in his face ..., Only the sterile, geometric shapes of life seem to obsess him, not life itself.

By this reference to an art like Harold Pinter's, or even Beckett's, Wesker implies his own very different, essentially humanist intention. He came, like Pinter, from a Jewish family in London's economically and culturally deprived East End. But Pinter's grammar school and London drama school training gave him an educationally privileged background in comparison with Wesker's, and the lower-class material in Pinter's plays has been distanced, fictionalised and aesthetically transformed. Wesker's defence against similar neutralisation has been a dramatic style that critics have called prosaic and unimaginative, and, in his earlier plays, dramatic forms they have called naive.[1] 'Naturalism' is the term he himself has chosen to describe his mode of writing, defining his preference with the statement that 'there is no such thing as realistic art.'[2] It is an apt enough term for work that often lies close in technique to much film and television material, though without adopting the false stereotypes that Manfred, in *The Friends,* speaks of as the means whereby television persistently erodes and destroys working class reality.

The theatre in Britain—with rare exceptions on the extreme fringe—has resisted all this century's efforts to open it up to the mass of the people, though the long fight for a state-subsidised theatre to break the commercial stranglehold has resulted in a wide distribution of theatrical activity over the whole of Britain since the mid 1950s. Wesker has been particularly concerned to break the class barrier, and there is a close interrelationship between his plays and his project, known as Centre 42, for an organisation, based on and financed by the Trade Union Congress, to take the arts to industrial areas. He has been much criticised by fellow socialists on grounds articulated by John McGrath:

> Wesker's Crusade for Centre 42 to bring "culture" as he understood it ... "to" the working class rests on a completely false analysis. The idea ... that culture is a product to be sold ... is based on the bourgeois concept of culture.[3]

It may be argued in his defence that Wesker's great error was to misunderstand the British trade union movement itself as less 'bourgeois' than it actually is. Persistent campaigning won little beyond token support from the T.U.C., and in 1968 Wesker withdrew from Centre 42, after eight years' work and a record of one festival in 1961 and six festivals in 1962 in working class towns.

This experience of the failure of a grand design permeates his later plays, and the cultural project figures, in a transparent disguise, in *Their Very Own and Golden City* and, more astonishingly, under the guise of a chain of six trendy shops selling beautiful and high quality merchandise, in *The Friends*. Wesker evidently recognized some truth in McGrath's critique, and with more irony than he has been given credit for. In his 1966 Stockholm lecture,[4] he admitted:

> inside me is a little voice nagging and ... warning that ... all the Centre Fortytwos we may build ... can only be a patchwork if that society remains at heart a capitalist society.

Yet from the beginning there are signs in his work of an ambivalent attitude to the working class. In *Chicken Soup with Barley,* Ada refers to her husband's experience in the Army: 'Oh yes! the service killed any illusions Dave may once have had about the splendid and heroic working class.' Libby Dobson, Dave's old friend in *I'm Talking about Jerusalem,* explains his cynicism in one of the moral anecdotes Wesker likes to include in his plays:

> I went back to old Robert Owen. Five thousand pound my old man left me ... I found four other young men ... and I said 'Here's a thousand pounds for each of you ... no strings, no

> loans, it's yours! Now let's open our own garage and exploit no
> one but ourselves ... Can you guess the hell of a time they had
> planning to buy me out?

The dramatist's awareness of a potential danger in detaching himself from
his own class even to pass judgment on its corruption is revealed in his
choice of an aristocrat to be the main character in *Chips with Everything*.
Here Pip's condescension towards the low-class conscripts he has chosen
to be with ('You breed babies and you eat chips with everything') is in
conflict with his troubled sense of their humanity that prompts an attempt
to direct them, for their own good, against the established authority of the
Air Force officers. It is comparable to the attempt Ronnie Kahn has made
to educate the ignorant country girl, Beatie Bryant, in *Roots*; this is set in
critical perspective by the device of keeping Ronnie off stage, while his
words are relayed and his manner imitated by Beatie; and she then proceeds, like Shaw's Eliza Doolittle, to become a more fully alive and
independent being than the Pygmalion who moulded her may have intended. Among the later plays, *The Friends* surveys a number of attitudes
to the lower classes which were prevalent in the 1960s. Manfred speaks for
all whom the '50s gave social mobility, detaching them from their roots.
Only his self-knowledge and openness are abnormal: 'The working class,
my class, offend me. Their cowardly acquiescence, their rotten ordinari-
ness.' The apostles of popular culture are derided (by Macey) for applaud-
ing the 'stunted growths' they call 'working class values ' (Wesker's own
use of folk songs as a touchstone of authentic values, in *The Four Seasons*
as well as in *Roots* and *Chips with Everything,* falls under this indictment.)
Simone, the only upper-middle-class member of the group, impugns the
'alternative' politics of the '60s for 'the most "counter-revolutionary" act
of all,' attempting to mobilize support by acceptance of 'the most bigoted,
the most loud-mouthed, the most reactionary instincts of the people.' The
dying Esther's view of the ultimate cause of revolutionary violence, and the
deformation of humanity to enjoy that violence, corresponds to the summing up, in another play: 'Capitalism has created an enemy in its own
image, monstrous as itself.' With these words Victor, in *Love Letters on
Blue Paper,* is able to reconcile the faith he has had in his work with the
contempt he has come to feel for the men he represented. The bitter farce of
The Wedding Feast, based on a story by Dostoievsky, contributes an
oblique comment on attempts to bridge class divisions: Louis was a man of
the people, one who 'in 1936, during the fascist riots in the East End of
London ... was a young communist messenger'; but he has become an
employer of labour, and the whip of satire falls equally on him and on the
workers who reject his attempt to join in their celebration.

The East End in 1936 provides the image of the golden age when life and dream seem one, in *Chicken Soup with Barley,* the first full-length play of Wesker's to be produced. This play traces the course of British history from 1936 to 1956 through the lives of the Kahn family, acknowledged to be a version of Wesker's own. The apparently straggling action, with the lapse of years between acts and even scenes, can be accepted as a feature of documentary drama. The avoidance of a conventional invented plot allows the material to find its own form, and the play as a whole has a sure dramatic rhythm, a falling rhythm checked only at the end. The public occasion with which the play begins is the famous Cable Street counter-demonstration to the march of Mosley's Blackshirts, and the international context is dominated by the Spanish Civil War. Wesker's management of this act shows the influence of O'Casey's presentation of the 1916 rebellion in Dublin through the lives of the inhabitants of one tenement building, in *The Plough and the Stars.*[5] By introducing the young child, five-year-old Ronnie, to stand and gaze on the scene, Wesker puts the frame of an idealistic vision around his stage image of the day. It is youth's day, and the enthusiasm of 14-year-old Ada and 18-year-old Monty flows over all. The general mood of excited activity, confidence and comradeship is sharpened with a further urgency at the information that Dave Simmonds, beloved of Ada, is leaving next morning to fight in Spain: it is the day of heroes, which Ronnie will never forget.

Yet what has aroused him from sleep is a quarrel between his father and mother, Harry and Sarah. From this note of private distress there begins the train of sadness and disillusionment that gathers force as the play proceeds. Including the sly evasions of a weak man and the nagging of his strong, slightly older wife allows Wesker to blend the ideal vision into a more complex realistic pattern. Harry is the obvious weak spot in the community, though presented with a touch of humour that reveals the character's kinship to the more exaggerated 'Captain' Boyle in O'Casey's *Juno and the Paycock*: work-shy, comfort-loving, essentially timid — frightened above all of his wife —, but intelligent enough and still capable of putting up a show to conceal the weakness of his will. After this, decline sets in: Harry is chronically unable to keep a job, until successive paralytic strokes excuse him from the pretence of taking part in the struggle. The children leave the house through which the abundant life of the East End flowed in Act I, and first Ada, then finally Ronnie lose hope and the energy it gives. None of this is simply domestic in its interest. It epitomises the history of the British Communist Party, as its membership dwindled under the impact of international events: the splintering and treacheries of the Left in Spain; the Cold War and the revelations of persecution in Stalinist Russia, especially the persecution of the Jews; and finally the Russian tanks entering Hungary to suppress the 1956 rising. This is the news with which Ronnie, back from Paris, confronts his mother, the last bulwark of faith. His father represents to Ronnie what he most fears to discover in himself: apathy and the drift towards failure and purposelessness. Yet Harry's decline is not only, if at all, a moral delinquency; it is a natural process of decay through the seeds of constitutional weakness that develop into incapacitating illness and incontinence and carry him towards death. Sarah starts by fighting the process as aggressively as she would fight Fascism, but becomes gradually more accepting. Ronnie's panic contains within it the young adult's realisation that time and change carry all, himself included, towards death, and that the golden days of innocence belong ineluctably to the past.

The theme of dying unites Wesker's earlier and later plays. The minor characters of *Roots* remember their mortality in recurring and fearful awareness of vague discomforts or unidentified illness. Beatie Bryant, the heroine, shrinks from their broken-down, alcoholic neighbour, Stan Mann: 'I can't bear sick men. They smell.' Encountering him she admits: 'Ole age terrify me.' Yet his death is a key incident for her development, as, in the last play of the Trilogy, the second stroke and the death of Harry Kahn mark critical stages in Dave's and Ada's losing struggle to stay free of the industrial system and live out a life of rural craftsmanship. In these plays, death has no full symbolic significance; it is included as part of the fabric of reality. By contrast, no individual dies in *The Old Ones,* but anticipation of death moves to the centre of the play. Here it is Rosa, a female version of Ronnie, who most openly expresses the dread she feels:

> One day, Sarah, we will die ... It's the most terrible fact I know.
> ... You can't imagine how much I dread it. Says Boswell: 'But is
> not the fear of death natural to man?' Says Johnson, 'So much
> so, Sir, that the whole of life is but keeping away the thoughts
> of it.'

She belongs to the younger generation in the play, and her particular struggle is to rouse the children of the poor to a sense of their cultural deprivation and oppression and so provoke them into helping themselves. She learns how to do this only as the 'old ones' master their own fears and the temptation to isolate themselves in eccentricity and come together to help each other and to celebrate life. Old Jack's eccentricity is to carry a bell and cry his warning, which becomes a choric refrain to the play:

> Jack is a-dying, the young folk is living, Jack is a-going, the
> young folk is coming. Don't come you near me, the plague is
> upon me, the devil is in me, the young folk is living.

The character steps out of his apocalyptic role easily enough into a caring, shrewd and humorous response to the vague and gentle Millie, who keeps losing her grip on the present.

As a naturalistic playwright, Wesker is remarkable for the attention he gives to the experience of age and the richness of life he portrays in his nearly senile characters. (His television play, *Menace,* is most closely related to *The Old Ones* in its concern with communication across barriers of age and class.) His readiness to extend the privilege of eccentricity to the aged brings in its train a freedom of dramatic expression: norms of human behaviour have been abandoned, and a more intricate and sophisticated dramatic structure replaces the simply life-like presentation of incidents in a chronological narrative. The beginning of *The Old Ones* is a startling departure from Wesker's 'prosaic' method: the stage is in darkness through which the light of first dawn gradually filters, and out of the darkness come Manny's anguished cries and then the alarm sounds that he improvises by knocking stones together or shaking a piece of wood in an old kettle. There is an eerie contrast between this primitive, nocturnal creature—his night-mares drive him into the garden—and the resilient Manny of daylight who turns from his breakfast, on the verandah where he sleeps, to shaping a suit on his tailor's dummy, chatting with his wife, shouting at his brother who is shut in a neighbouring room. That he should work to tape recordings of himself singing is again surprising, but now the effect is amusingly odd and oddly cheerful. The suggestion it carries of the old stereotype of the little Jewish tailor, introduced here as a unit in a far from stereotypical mosaic, recalls Chekhov's techniques; as does the making of a play out of an *ensemble* of strongly defined, idiosyncratic characters, each with his or her own story. Wesker does not compress and miniaturise any of the elements to the scale of Chekhov's minor figures, and the separateness of episodes breaks up the flow of the action; consequently, though the emotional range and diversity of *The Old Ones* is as great as the Chekhovian masterpieces offer, the total effect is less like an impressionistic symphony, the realistic impact is undiminished.

One element of the *ensemble* is so extensive that it becomes estab-lished as a major counter-design in the whole composition. This is the battle of books carried on between the estranged brothers as their only mode of communication: Manny, optimistic and positive, and the pessimistic Boomy bombard each other with quotations from famous writers and thinkers, evidence for defence and prosecution in an informal trial of the universe, or its putative creator. Drawing upon Voltaire, or Carlyle, is an easy way of introducing eloquence and power into the dialogue without departing entirely from naturalism, while the humour of the quarrel mod-ifies the overingenious effect. The intellectual substance of the quotations adds weight to the emotion in the play; the simple dialectical device maintains a steady perspective. At the end Manny, like Beatie Bryant in *Roots,* starts to speak his own words in his own voice and offers his own definition of evil, which his brother has accused him of not understanding. Boomy himself has admitted: 'I've read too much! I've seen too much,' only to have his son, Martin, protest: 'Well that's you, not me. Stop drowning me with your experience of men.' The theme of the genuine search, stumbling beyond the accumulated wisdom men store in books, is conveyed in a different form through the deliberately tentative symbol of the 'Succah,' the ark decorated with branches that stands wobbling on the balcony of Sarah's flat. As Rosa reads from the book, the tenuously united 'family' group of unbelievers move with hesitation and embarrassment through what they can reconstruct of an old ritual to express new meanings, before they sit down to their meal together. The irony of such a ceremony for atheists underlies their need to gather together 'a habit of joy' to pit against their sense of doom, to praise life in the face of death.

The Old Ones is certainly one of Wesker's finest and potentially most moving plays. The life of his best work is in the emotion, controlled, conflicting, with too much sternness and strength within it to come near sentimentality. It flows more simply, with less elaboration, through *Love Letters on Blue Paper.* The dying Victor, prompted by his need to think about this reality he is going through, asks Maurice, his close friend and regular visitor, to speak of his own knowledge of death. Under this pressure, Maurice recalls his mother's dying:

> I sat close to her and cradled her in my arms instead, holding her hands. 'Ah, warmth, warmth!' she said. 'There's nothing like warmth.' 'Get into bed,' I said, 'that'll make you warm.' 'Not warm like this,' she said.

Such closeness makes a poignant contrast with the indirection Victor's wife, Sonia, has to practise to be able to express her love for him, and which gives Wesker the basis for a dramatic indirection that pays dividends. For the greater part of the play Sonia is outside Victor's room, sometimes attending to the washing in the garden, sometimes sitting at her desk writing the letters she sends to him. The actress's voice over speaks the text, when Victor gives Maurice the letters to read. On the rare occasions when she enters the sick room, she speaks hardly a word. In this instance, an 'alienation' device [6] serves to give the heart of the relationship with the eloquence of soliloquy, while leaving the objective view of the character, dour and almost graceless, a figure of reticence itself.

Love as an answer to death, and community as love, is part of the humanist faith of the plays. Neither love nor death is conceptualised and aesthetically transformed, as in the Romantic tradition, unless in the one play which directly equates disenchantment and death: *The Friends*. Here Wesker stresses the decadent luxury of the setting, which communicates the sick fascination through which death holds sway over the group and keeps them at Esther's bedside. They know themselves that this room is their Cherry Orchard (though Chekhov is not named):

> *TESSA:* ... We've built too much of ourselves into it ... and now we're trapped ...
> *SIMONE:* You should love it.... Memory, the past, signs of human activity—you should cherish them—I adore this room.
> *CRISPIN:* Millions starving and we've surrounded ourselves with thefts.

In revulsion, Tessa smashes the guitar she has been playing *'to pieces against the eighteenth-century chair.'* Esther dies, and the others are unable to leave the corpse. The imagery of necrophilia has already been introduced in Crispin's confession of his 'unnatural passions,' his love affairs with old women:

> it's like the glory of raising the dead to see red blood rise up in their faces and find their soft bones flutter with life ...

In the museum-like setting, the dead woman easily becomes an image of other deaths: of the enterprise they have been jointly involved in—the chain of six shops which correspond to the six cities of *Their Very Own and Golden City* and, ultimately, to the six festivals organised by Centre 42 in 1962, when, as Macey says of the decade: 'You never thought you'd grow old or die.'

There are many similarities to *The Cherry Orchard* in *The Friends*. The business that Wesker's characters have been engaged in has been neglected and is now bankrupt, like the Ranevsky estate. Macey, the older man who has managed the business, scolds and advises his 'boys' as Lopakhin does Madam Ranevska. Wesker employs music for the creation of mood as Chekhov does, and there is a specific parallel between Tessa's singing to the guitar and Yepihodov's playing of the mandolin in Act II of Chekhov's play. It is enhanced by a similar style of dialogue: the characters pursue their separate trains of thought aloud, so that the lines intersect, or brush past each other without fully engaging. But whereas nostalgia paralyses Chekhov's gentlefolk, until the sale of the estate brings release, the apathy and purposelessness of Wesker's people has more to do with loss of vision than any clinging to a rich tradition in decline. Through Simone, the dramatist reasserts the values of an 'aristocratic' culture, an inheritance available to all. (Wesker's rejection of popular culture as inadequate is as clear as was Sarah's rejection of East End cheating and stealing in *Chicken Soup,* though working-class morality may have a place for it, as for the factory worker's petty pilfering, in which Harry engages and which Dave carelessly continues, in *I'm Talking about Jerusalem.*) As if to demonstrate his attitude concretely, Wesker draws on a Shakespearean source for the audacious ritual with which the play ends: the silent ceremony of 'animating' and enthroning the corpse of Esther in a faintly comic, though more formal version of the moment when the still living woman was led to sit, in her robes, in the eighteenth-century chair. This is directly imitative of the setting up of the final tableau which shows the dead Cleopatra as a great queen in state, in the last Act of *Antony and Cleopatra.* The touches of comedy, which intermingle with the magnificence in the original context, seem to have inspired the jauntiness with which Wesker ultimately disposes of the corpse—of his own attempt to bring about a cultural revolution.

The Friends is an uneasy play. It is hard to believe in the North country working-class origins assigned to most of the characters, emotionally demonstrative as they are. They seem equally remote from the manners and spirit of the 'sixties' youth culture, which they are supposed to have survived. There could be no clearer evidence that Wesker has little histrionic talent for entering into the consciousness of strangers; he is no passionate observer of mankind. The intimate knowledge that belongs to love is the source of all that is most vivid and truthful in his plays and gives them power over the imaginations of others. Subjective experience in the face of illness, failure, aging, dying, the temptation to despair, informs his concern for the good society, as the attachment to family inspires his vision of true community and comradeship. 'There's something about people getting together and doing things,' says Andy, the central character in *Their Very Own and Golden City.* Though it runs the risk of dismissal as narrowly autobiographical, this latter play is stronger than *The Friends* in its very disdain for a disguise that falls short of complete imaginative distancing.

It is possibly more self-critical than *The Friends.* The form Wesker has devised for it presents innocence and experience as contraries held in tension, not comfortably resolved. The play opens with a scene in Durham Cathedral, where the young Andy has his vision of society transformed through art. (It is interesting to remember that a cathedral was the chosen symbol of the Bauhaus.) From this point, Wesker presents episodes in Andy's life from 1926 into the future (about 1990), but regularly alternating with returns to that first occasion and setting. Two distinct time schemes are combined, for what happens in the Cathedral provides one thread of continuous action intersected by the larger-scale, speeded-up review of a life-time's effort to turn the vision into a reality. Wesker's directions offer a choice of terms, 'flash-back' or 'flash-forward,' thus making it clear that neither of the continuities is more 'real' than the other; the two perspectives offered are equally valid. The final scene, Act II, scene 6, is very long, covering some forty years from 1948. Here, each episode dissolves into the next with an unbroken fluidity that recalls the technique of Strindberg's *Dream Play,* until the two perspectives are fused in Andy's consciousness at the very end: as it is the aged figure that is surrounded by the young companions of 1926 in Durham. Though Andy is an architect, ambitious to build six golden cities, his progress from a local Town Hall to the Trade Union Congress, seeking support for his plan, is evidently a version of the playwright's own experience. Yet the outer events and the substance of Andy's plan are subordinate, in the play, to the pattern of emotional experience: the contrast between the zest and exaltation of youth and the disheartening, embittering years of compromise, betrayal, guilt, fighting cynicism in others and in the self. Far from taking pride and pleasure in what he achieves against the odds, or feeling a sober satisfaction in what he learns of the art of the possible, Andy senses the futility of 'patchwork,' 'a little bit of order in the midst of chaos,' which will some day be overwhelmed again by chaos. He loses his faith in the ability of men to work without leaders (close, in this way, to Pip in *Chips with Everything*), and comes ultimately to doubt whether it was all worth doing. Outside his consciousness, hovering over the action, are the words first spoken by the trade unionist, Jake Latham: 'Defeat doesn't matter; in the long run all defeat is temporary. It doesn't matter about present generations but future ones always want to look back and know that someone was around acting on principle.' In the dramatic pattern, the Cathedral scenes continue to assert the principle, though the portrait of Andy raises troubling questions of motive and personality. Wesker has often been called a didactic writer, but the force of negative emotion can save his plays from abstract statement and argument, when simple affirmation is not possible.

Wesker's most objective play is *The Journalists*. He prepared himself to write it by spending the better part of three months in the offices of *The Sunday Times,* and—after delays caused by the objections of *Sunday Times* journalists—he has published a documentary account of the experience under the title of *Journey into Journalism*. Even a cursory comparison of the play with this reveals how closely the dramatic version keeps to the raw material. The composition itself is quite new, of course: incidents, themes, lines of dialogue have been freely organised into a sophisticated structure. In the journal he kept while working on the play,[7] he expresses doubts and dissatisfactions over the quality of what he was doing, but he makes no mention of the troubling intrusion of an invented plot into a context where factual veracity is strength. The dramatic intrigue involving Mary Mortimer's youngest son as member of an urban terrorist gang supporting the policies of the M.P. she is determined to destroy, has a cheapening effect on the whole. It is melodramatic, when in striking contrast the scene of Mary in her domestic setting, at the ritual monthly dinner with her family, is perhaps the strongest in the play, not least because it deepens with some sympathy the character Wesker has chosen to be villain of the piece. Mary's prime quarry, Morgan King, is described as a 'fiery socialist' and new political 'superstar.' He never appears on stage, but the reports of his speeches invite identification of him with Wesker himself: the phase which serves to link him with the urban guer-rillas, 'the patterns men can make for the pleasure of their living,' has been deliberately lifted from Andy, in *Their Very Own and Golden City,* and the account of King's attitude to the arts in society, given by Sebastian of the Arts Pages, confirms that here is a self-portrait of the dramatist. If there is a suggestion of embarrassing self-exposure in it, this is countered by the presentation of Mary as the opposite that idealism generates within itself In her daughter's words, 'It's as though you're fighting yourself, and it shows.' The visionary turned cynic, despising his fellow men, had put in an appearance as Libby Dobson, in *I'm Talking about Jerusalem;* and the life-affirming Manny of *The Old Ones* recognises an intimate *rapport* with his despairing brother: 'With his philosophy of doom he keeps me alive.' But only in *The Journalists* has Wesker attempted to focus centrally on the negative aspect of his own consciousness, corresponding as it does to an insidious and powerful element in the psychology of a fiercely competi-tive society.

Yet we may still be uneasy that the play's centre of gravity is held at the campaign against King, while the cracking sanity of Tamara, the foreign correspondent confronted by the horrors of large-scale starvation and disease, war and massacre, is used to give a squinting perspective on Mary Mortimer's destructive critical approach. A more radical question about newspapers and about the world to which they are a distorting mirror, is raised by the photographer who 'can't photograph peace' and whose brilliance depends on the substitution of curiosity for compassion, than by the woman journalist engaged in a personal vendetta. Staged according to the playwright's instructions, the newspaper would certainly establish itself as the total significant image, in which everything else is detail. To achieve this effect visually Hayden Griffin's designs, published with the text of the play, follow a medieval scenic principle: nine pre-set structures, representing different departments in the newspaper offices, are arranged about an unlocalised playing area to be used for scenes supposed to take place anywhere outside the building.[8] In addition, Wesker wanted to complete the view of the production processes by showing the presses at work and settled for projection of the machinery on a screen at the back of the set.

The last scenes of the play, including the revelation of the activities of Mary's son, are accompanied by the rolling of the presses, though their noise is subdued to let the dialogue be heard until the final crescendo. The image has been familiar in cinema since the days of D. W. Griffith, but neither cinema nor television can create such an effect of simultaneity as is possible in theatre, and as Wesker intends here: 'Activity must be continuous in all sections throughout the play,' he directs, qualifying the statement with a further indication that 'the rest of the action and the noise freezes' when the focus is on the centre space. In this respect, he is using the theatre as Erwin Piscator did, with a similar presentation of industrial processes. Yet Wesker significantly refers to the individual stages incorporated into the multiple set as 'frames,' and in his journal he likens his work on this play to the editing of lengths of film. Dialogue and action travel continually from one area of the set to another: now complete scenes, now snatches of dialogue, or even single speeches, are cut-in to each other as if they were camera shots. The technique has an obvious appropriateness to the particular subject of *The Journalists*. But its use here is also a reminder that Wesker had taken a short, part-time course in film production before his first play was accepted for stage performance.

How aware he was in writing his first stage piece, *The Kitchen*, that the work lent itself to the precisely drilled routines of Expressionist theatre remains uncertain in view of the debt he has acknowledged to the producer, John Dexter, for helping him to understand the theatrical aspect of his drama.[9] Irving Wardle has written lately of the policy of George Devine in encouraging close relationships between particular authors and play-directors working for the English Stage Company at the Royal Court Theatre.[10] To a varying extent it seems that the published texts of Royal Court plays have represented such a wedding of literature to stage practice as is necessary to all outstanding periods of dramatic history. Out of the style of actors' workshops at the Royal Court there evolved a number of plays which depended largely on the expressiveness of physical action, mime and virtually choreographed *ensemble* passages. Some of David Storey's plays, directed by Lindsay Anderson, were to show this quality to a supreme degree and thereby make a symbolic statement on the relation between the individual and society, or labour and art. The dialogue of *The Kitchen* is naturalistic; and the compression, in so short a play, of the separate stories of so many characters is simply a more extreme example of the basic design used by Gorky in *The Lower Depths*. Yet in performance it is the frenzied movement on a crowded stage, human bodies working together like the parts of a machine, that creates so vivid an image of industrial man's world. The parade-ground scenes and the silent action in which the conscripts make a living chain to steal the coal (demonstrating the order and discipline needed to oppose established order and discipline), in *Chips with Everything,* are the other most notable instances of similar technique from the first half of Wesker's playwriting career. The episodes based on workshops in which the Court Theatre dramatists participated stand out even more clearly from play after play. Indeed the critical question must concern the degree of integration that can be achieved between these passages and their dramatic context. There can be little doubt of the effectiveness of the deftly performed peeling of the orange by Sonia, in *Love Letters on Blue Paper*: it is the climax of a long train of physical actions, changing pillow-slips, preparing tea, spreading cream and jam on scones, hanging out washing on the line, taking it in again, setting out glasses on a tray, cutting roses and arranging them, polishing brass, all stage business which is her form of eloquence, giving as it does the outer substance of her life, the truth of her character, and the observance of her relationship to Victor. More than all the rest, her skill with the orange[11] conveys poignantly the careful, almost artistically loving control that she is maintaining over her intermingled grief and joy.

On the other hand, it is certainly debatable whether the making of the apfelstrudel, in *The Four Seasons,* may not distract attention from the experience of the lovers to itself; and Andy's acrobatics and mimicry are barely acceptable as idiosyncratic (like Gaev's imaginary billiards) and fit awkwardly as a sign that the author is moving away from naturalism in *Their Very Own and Golden City.* And the 'birth game' Ada plays with her unseen son, in *I'm Talking about Jerusalem,* may be an expressive set-piece in the hands of a clever actress, but it must stand out from the fabric of the rest of the play as the half-achieved, half-anti-climactic ceremony of the Succoth does not do, in *The Old Ones*: that is an essential part of the action, summing up the emotional hesitancy with which the characters half-celebrate a revived, yet still tenuous faith in life and in humanity.

Wesker's use of background music, as in film, and distinct from inset songs, began as early as *Chicken Soup* and *I'm Talking about Jerusalem,* where Ronnie 'conducts' classical music on radio or gramophone, and it persists in the playing of Janáček's Sinfonietta in *Love Letters.* The noise of the presses through the last part of *The Journalists* is a variation on this technique. *Love Letters on Blue Paper* makes the most extensive and moving use of contrast between the living voice and recorded speech, though the use of tapes in *The Old Ones* is also as meaningful as it is ingenious. There is some irony in the fact that no other contemporary British dramatist shows so consistent and developing a consciousness of his medium in terms of elements of space amd time, visual and aural possibilities, the vulnerable immediacy of the performer on stage and the technological aids that modern theatre can command — if one excepts Samuel Beckett.[12] Beckett's drama is, of course, much more claustrophobic than Wesker's, and there is an equally great contrast between Wesker's frankly advertised personal involvement in the matter of his plays and the cultivated detachment of the artist, god-like to the point of anonymity, which Beckett practices. Beckett's, and Pinter's, iron control and calculated manipulation of audience response are unmatched by Wesker; yet he is as resistant as they are to any form of audience participation. The instructions are unambiguous: 'He must *not* address the next speech to the audience' (*Their Very Own and Golden City,* Act II, scene 5); '*It is essential that* Rosa *does not appear to be addressing the audience*' (*The Old Ones,* Act I, scene 4). The stage is to contain the play, offering it as an object for contemplation. Though Wesker's stagecraft may seem to be part of the general liberation of British theatre through the influence of Brecht, he proves to be much less of a Brechtian dramatist than John Osborne. And ultimately the political content of his plays falls into perspective as one element in the complexity of consciousness where memory is part of the present and society is a function of the emotional life. He does not need to limit the world of his plays to the solitude *à deux* of two lovers, as in *The Four Seasons,* to create a drama that is in this sense lyrical. Even in *Chicken Soup with Barley,* Wesker's East End proves to be the earth that holds his emotional roots: 'The East End is a mother,' and Sarah is its human embodiment, first of the strong, loyal Jewesses, essentially Martha figures, women who serve and love and are contrasted with the professional women, the upper-class types, mistrustfully presented in the later plays. They do not have, finally, to be Jewish: Sonia, whose memories well up and find a voice, full-throated and soaring, is the most magnificent. 'The genuine creative instinct,' Victor had written, 'is and always has been a celebratory one.' The right to celebrate, like the right to despair, has to be earned by Wesker's *personae* — in a world that can be as bleak, or as rich, as Beckett's.

NOTES

1. An American critic who sums up most of the adverse judgments that have been passed on Arnold Wesker's drama is George Wellwarth, *Theater of Protest and Paradox* (New York University Press, rev. edition 1971), pp. 271–282. The specific charge of unimaginativeness is made by Bamber Gascoigne, *Twentieth Century Drama* (London: Hutchinson & Co., 1962) p. 200.

2. 'Theatre, Why?' *Fears of Fragmentation* (London: Cape, 1970), p. 98.

3. Quoted by Wesker in 'Casual Condemnations,' *Theatre Quarterly* I, no. 2 (April–June 1971), pp. 19–20. John McGrath's review of *The Friends* was published in *Black Dwarf,* 12 June 1970.

4. Published under the title, 'Tarnished Virtues and Confused Manners,' pp. 63–81, esp. p. 79.

5. See Bernard Leroy, 'Two Committed Playwrights: Wesker and O'Casey,' in *Aspects of the Irish Theatre,* ed. P. Rafroidi, R. Popot & W. Parker, (Lille: P.U.L., Paris, Editions universitaires, 1972), pp. 107–17.

6. Although Wesker's theatre shows superficial resemblances to Brecht's, especially in its preference for episodic structure and its free use of mechanical equipment for staging, he never attempts to diminish emotional impact. He may more properly be seen as heir to the techniques of Strindberg's later plays, as mediated especially through German theatre.

7. *Theatre Quarterly* VII, no. 26 (Summer 1977), pp. 3–17.

8. Fouquet's miniature, 'The Martyrdom of St. Apollonia,' is a well-known example of similar medieval staging.

9. Prefatory note to *The Friends.* See John Dexter, 'Working with Arnold,' *Plays and Players* (April 1962), p. 11, and 'Chips and Devotion,' *Plays and Players* (December 1962), p. 32.

10. *The Theatres of George Devine* (London: Cape, 1978), esp. pp. 199–201.

11. The present writer remembers being entertained, as a child, by a demonstration of this particular skill.

12. Wesker has expressed his great admiration for Beckett in 'Theatre, Why?' *loc. cit.*, pp. 97–8.

From Paradox to Propaganda: The Plays of John Arden

HENRY I. SCHVEY

In an interview published in 1965, John Arden claimed that

> Sheer propaganda in the theatre is a bore, and completely uncommitted play-writing is also a bore. I think what I'd like to do is to run somewhere between the two, so that one has a point of view, but one doesn't force it on the audience ... I don't regard it as the business of a dramatist to try and tell the audience to accept [my] views.[1]

Just over a decade later, in the essay "A Socialist Hero on the Stage," written by Arden and his wife and frequent collaborator Margaretta D'Arcy about their latest play, *The Non-Stop Connolly Show* (1975), the antithetical point of view is offered:

> ... [The play] is not so much 'propagandist' as exploratory and educational. But it *is* propagandist in that it finally brings the authors, and consequently the audience, to some 'partisan' conclusion. All conclusions about the state of contemporary affairs must inevitably be partisan—as we have stated, consensus is not possible in a divided society.[2]

What was it that brought Arden from his earlier dedication to the ideal of objectivity to the point where partisanship is not only felt to be justified but necessary? Even more significant, what has been the effect of Arden's political conversion to radical Marxism around 1970 on his recent development as a playwright?

Instead of trying to answer the questions posed above by beginning with Arden's early works and attempting to survey his prolific career over the past two decades, I will instead begin by focusing on the play which is the watershed in his development, and represents in a series of dreams, the playwright's own attempt at fashioning a compromise between the need for detachment, and a life of political activism. Although the patchwork compromise which Arden constructed for himself at the end of the play came apart as early as the following year, in his autobiographical play, *The Bagman or The Impromptu of Muswell Hill* (1969), the conflict within Arden is revealed with great clarity.

The Bagman begins naturalistically amid wind, rain and traffic as the Narrator searches for a newspaper along Muswell Hill Road. Unable to find one, he turns within himself and immediately reveals the undisguised autobiographical nature of this work about the artist's vocation:

> So who was I, where was I,
> What was I for? ...
> John Arden (thirty-eight) of ancient family,
> Writer of plays for all to see,
> To see, and pay for, and to denigrate:
> Such was my work since 1958 ...
> If, on this soggy Thursday, I should fall down dead
> What of my life and death would then be said?
> 'He covered sheets of paper with his babble,
> He covered yards of stage cloth with invented people,
> He worked alone for years yet was not able
> To chase one little rat from underneath the table.'³

In those opening lines Arden raises the play's central theme: the guilt of the solitary artist who is incapable of action in the "real" world.

The traffic noises recede and the Narrator falls asleep on a park bench. In his dream he meets an old woman who sells him a canvas bag, suggesting it might hold an "elegant soft young woman." But before he has a chance to open it, he is disturbed and forced to leave. Slinging the bag over his shoulder, he begins his journey, having left the world of reality behind.

Entering a dream world, the Narrator is attacked by a band of frenzied women driven mad by poverty and starvation:

> There he has it
> There he has food in his bag
> Tear it down from him
> Tear it and grab it and drag ...
> For what he has got we can eat ... (pp. 44–45)

He is rescued by a patrol of mounted policemen who brutally disperse the tattered women and escort him into town. Thus the dream vision shapes itself immediately into a spectacle of class conflict, where, according to the policeman, "those who deserve to eat, eat." The horror of this vision is dramatized still further as they near the town and see a man nailed to a leafless tree, screaming, "For the freedom of the people—oh the starving men will live and the well-fed men will rot among maggots of their own engendering" (p. 47). But the poet is unaware of the realities of political life and rides by unconcerned. Entering the town whose inhabitants are well-fed and prosperous (but whose streets are filthy), the Narrator comes upon a crowd of people watching an erotic theatrical entertainment. Having been amused by a Popular Minister who gives the people what they wa:t, an Unpopular Minister stands up "to inform you of the truth about yourselves" and introduces the Narrator to the crowd, obliging him to open up the contents of his bag to the multitude. Despite his fear of the mob, the stranger opens up the sack and dozens of tiny little men and women come tumbling out onto the platform, while the Narrator addresses the crowd in a "strange, distorted voice":

> My little people in a row
> Sit on the stage and watch the show.
> The show they watch is rows and rows
> Of people watching them. Who knows
> Which is more alive than which? ...
> And then you sit and watch my little men
> And you will know yourselves again ... (pp. 58–59)

The spectacle which the tiny figures enact is once again the class struggle ("there was a small group ... in rich costumes, and a large group made up of the ragged and ill-favoured", in which the poor managed to overthrow the rich but finally are themselves defeated through their own dissension. The Popular and Unpopular Ministers disagree as to the play's significance, the former optimistically pointing to the failure of the rebellion, the latter to the image of the violent overthrow of the privileged classes it has depicted. The Narrator himself, however, is unconcerned; "all I could think about was the power of my little men, so newly revealed to me, so manifold in possibility ... " (p. 65). Despite the revolutionary potential suggested by his art, the artist remains entranced by his tools, not the purpose to which they might be applied.

Having been shown to a room, the Narrator again falls asleep, and a young woman comes to seduce him. Instead, however, she reminds him of the masses of starving people outside the walls of the town, of the systematic exploitation of the poor on which the town's economy thrives and of the capacity of art to alter that balance of power, "you send us more remembrances like that, little man, there will be no protection left, no security, no good dinners, nothing but the truth" (p. 71).

Horrified by what he has heard, the Narrator seeks escape from his dream in "reality," which for the artist is found in art; "I will awake from them and work as is my custom upon a clean piece of white paper" (p. 72). However he is captured and taken before an Ambassador "with a face like a bucket of blood" and surrounded by life-size pictures of soldiers with tusks and faces like wild animals. This grotesque projection of authority begins his interrogation by announcing; "Quiet. I am the enormous Ambassador. I eat eggs and they make me fat. What do you do?" (p. 74). Overwhelmed by the Ambassador, the Narrator submissively agrees to shake hands, only to find an egg concealed there which cracks open and splashes yolk on his sleeve, leaving a yellow stain—suggestive of cowardice and capitulation:

> Eggs are full of gold
> They stink when they are old.
> Scramble boil or poach or fry—
> Long and hard oh you may try
> You'll never wipe away the stain—
> The egg is mine and you are mine. (p. 76)

He leaves the Ambassador and is sent before the King and Queen to have his little men perform at court. This time, however, the result is not revolution but eroticism (reminding us of the earlier spectacle presented by the Popular Minister); "And there was no fighting in the story. Nothing but extraordinary variations of erotic postures and intrigues" (p. 78). The artist's vision has been compromised and rendered inoffensive.

Having been bought by society, the Narrator lives a life of luxury, eating well and enjoying the palace gardens and its women. Suddenly the Young Woman enters breaking off the dream of indolence to which the artist has succumbed. She warns him of his corruption, "Within your dream you fell asleep again" (p. 80), and urges him to escape by putting his hand (significantly enough) "out to the left" and lifting up a flagstone which will take them both to the headquarters of the revolutionary underground. He follows her but is slowed down by the bag he carries with him. The message is clear: the artist is tempted by the call to revolutionary politics but his art is an impediment to his commitment; " ... would you leave that bloody bag behind you—you're going to get stuck in the passageways or goodness knows what—as it is you've nearly got both of us caught with it!" (p. 83).

Although they manage to escape to the revolutionaries, "outlandish men, who rise in anger/Against the tyrant and oppressor," the Narrator refuses to abandon his collection of little men and, despite being warned, "Your burden is no good to us/Throw it down—take up a weapon" (p. 85), he decides to dedicate his art to the revolution and tears open the sack. Instead of obeying him, the tiny wooden figures suddenly resist their owner:

> Men of war do not require
> To see themselves in a truthful mirror

> All that they need to spur them to action
> Is their own most bloody reflection
> In the white eyeballs of their foe.
> We are neat and well-considered little people —
> If you bring us into battle
> You bring us only unto grief and woe
> Fracture and breakage that we cannot repair
> They will snap our wooden joints
> Please let us please let us get back into the sack
> When the battle has been won
> We can peep out again and creep back. (p. 86)

Having been betrayed by the craftsman, his tools revolt against him. At this moment the soldiers arrive and in the ensuing battle the Narrator is pushed aside by a soldier and falls down upon the "squirming heap of my terrified little men." The dream ends with the Narrator having betrayed both the revolutionaries and his little men. He awakens in an underground station holding an empty bag where he again meets the Old Woman who tells him of his inability to decide between politics and art:

> You did not find what you expected
> What you found you did not use
> What you saw you did not look at
> When you looked at it you would not choose! (p. 87)

The play concludes with the Narrator reflecting on the implications of the decision of his little men to remain aloof from the conflict and their attempt to crawl back into the protective sack; although he would have liked to help with the revolution ("It would have been easy it would have been good/To have carried a bag full of solid food/And fed the thin men"), he finally accepts the fact that the vocation of the artist is to remain always apart from direct action:

> But such is not the nature of these bags
> That are given away by old woman in rags.
> Such is not my nature, nor will be.
> All I can do is to look at what I see ... (p. 88)

Although at the end of the allegory, the artist has (however guiltily) accepted his role as an observer, within months of its completion Arden suddenly went to the opposite extreme and committed himself to revolutionary politics. After finishing *The Bagman* in the spring of 1969, Arden and his wife travelled to India. During their visit, Arden (who had been Honorary Chairman of *Peace News*) grew disillusioned with Western style liberalism and non-violence and became influenced by both the ideology and tactics of the Indian revolutionaries he met.[4] It was this experience more than anything else that established Arden's future course. As a result of his sympathies with the Indian guerrillas ("'Murder' is the wrong word—the Naxalites [Maoist revolutionaries of Calcutta] say 'Execution' or 'An act of war.' I agree with them," p. 15) Arden determined, as he said in a lecture at Bradford University, that whenever he wrote anything in future he would be asking himself "how it would look through the eyes of an Indian revolutionary."[5]

By the time of the publication of *The Bagman* in 1971, Arden had completely reversed his position with regard to the artist's role in society, specifically with regard to his political responsibilities. As a result, the ending of the play was no longer valid for him, and in the Preface, written for the published version, the author clearly dissociates himself from his earlier stand, stating bluntly that "The attitude of the central character at the end of the story is reprehensible, cowardly, and not to be imitated." Curiously, in a study of Arden published in 1974, Albert Hunt maintains that the ending of *The Bagman* was intended to be ironical, a contention which seems particularly untenable in the light of the author's statement in the Preface that the play reflected "the state of my mind in the spring of 1969" (p. 16).

The Bagman is not so much a typical Arden play as it is a self-analytical critique of his entire career as a playwright. As such, it offers the opportunity of illustrating many of the features and thematic preoccupations of his work until 1969. When, for example, the Narrator empties his bag for the first time, the tiny figures put on a performance which, not surprisingly, has much in common with Arden's own plays. As soon as they are spilled out of their bag, the people arrange themselves into two groups, the rich and the poor. Although for a while the ragged group seems to gain the upper hand, in the end they are defeated. Roughly the same scenario is followed in nearly all of Arden's plays from *The Waters of Babylon* (1957) through *The Hero Rises Up* (1968). Despite the variety of dramatic conventions employed (and few have attempted more: Arden has written comedy, absurdist farce, mime, community drama, ballad opera, period problem play, epic chronicle, melodrama and autobiographical allegory), nearly all of Arden's plays are built around a central conflict between two polarized positions, which might loosely be described as individualistic *vs.* collective, anarchic *vs.* orderly, primitive *vs.* civilized, or as Arden himself put it in his Preface to *The Hero Rises Up*, his play about Lord Nelson, curvilinear *vs.* rectilinear:

> This play is about a man who was, by accident of birth and rearing, committed to a career governed by the old Roman "rectilinear" principles. He himself was of a symmetrical "curvilinear" temperament to an unusually passionate degree.[6]

In *Live Like Pigs* (1958), the central conflict is between the nomadic gypsy-like Sawneys who have been given government subsidized housing, and the lower-middle class Jackson family who are their neighbors. Although it is likely that Arden's personal sympathies are with the vagrants who have first been evicted from their tram-car dwelling by a well-meaning government, then removed from their middle-class house for not conforming to bourgeois standards of morality and cleanliness they have had thrust on them, he conceals his sympathies so cleverly that it is extremely difficult to pinpoint his exact position. In his Introductory Note to the published version of the play, Arden explained that he was accused by the Left for attacking the Welfare State while the play on the other hand was seen as a defence of anarchy and amorality: "So perhaps I had better declare myself. I approve outright neither of the Sawneys nor of the Jacksons. Both groups uphold standards of conduct that are incompatible, but which are both valid in their correct context."[7]

This, then, is the position taken by Arden again and again in his early plays, a position he was later to disparage as "a classic piece of Fence-Sitting" in the Preface to *The Bagman.*

But is "fence-sitting" a fair judgment? Only if one presupposes that the playwright's task is to proselytize his audience instead of provoking it to think. In a statement concerning the play *The Workhouse Donkey* (1963), it would seem as though Arden had already anticipated his own later objections:

> I don't want in the play to persuade the public. I merely want to show these two opposites set up and come into conflict. My presentation of this is obviously coloured by my own view on the subject, but I'm not out to make propaganda for that view. I'm simply out to do what I think is the playwright's primary job—to dramatise the clash of temperaments ... [8]

In this same interview Arden praises Brecht's *Galileo* by saying that "It is a great play because at the end of the play you still don't know where you are." And one is repeatedly reminded of Brecht in reading these early plays of Arden, not only because of their mutual indebtedness to the English ballad tradition, their use of history to illuminate contemporary problems, and the importance given to songs and verse, but because of the value placed on reason, forcing the audience to a heightened pitch of intellectual awareness. As Brecht himself said: "The essential point of the epic theatre is perhaps that it appeals less to the feelings than to the spectator's reason. Instead of sharing an experience the spectator must come to grips with things. At the same time it would be wrong to try and deny emotion to this kind of theatre."[9] By turning the spectator into an observer, both Brecht and Arden force us to examine ideas according to their complexity, instead of offering convenient pigeon-holes or superficial labels.

In an essay on the Icelandic Sagas, W. H. Auden describes the "social realism" (not Socialist Realism) of these epics, and the relationship between the author and his characters in a way which corresponds precisely to the method used by both Brecht and Arden:

> The social realist writer... must exclude himself from his narrative, he must never pass judgment on his characters, but leave them to judge one another; he must restrict his account of human nature to external signs. His heroes and villains must lie within real-life limits (so that their bravery, for instance, has to have an element of cowardice), and their speech has to be in more or less natural terms.[10]

John Arden's attitude towards his fictional creations is almost identical. He is not particularly interested in detailed psychological portraiture or the inner motivation of his characters; rather they are important chiefly as representatives of clashing points of view, neither of which is unambiguously right or wrong. In his early plays at least it follows that Arden's characters have mixtures of qualities we might conventionally consider good and bad; as in Brecht, we are never allowed to identify with Arden's protagonists:

> So far as my attitude to my characters is concerned, it is the attitude of a creator ... And if a character starts off by being sympathetic and then turns off in a direction that people don't like, that is in fact what often happens with people that one knows in life. I don't understand this assumption that some people have that you have to present the audience with people they can identify with ... I never write a scene so that the audience can identify with any particular character ... "

In practice this means that all of Arden's early creations refuse easy labels; all the characters who seem to possess the attributes of heroism are severely flawed, while the characters who seem to be associated with evil have redeeming aspects. Thus in Arden's Christmas Play, *The Business of Good Government* (1960), Herod is not depicted as a gruesome monster but as a contemporary leader, harried by the pressure of political events into ordering the Massacre of the Innocents. These pressures on Herod are visible even in his opening speech:

> Herod the King. Herod the Great. Ruler of Judaea. To the west, the Roman Empire. To the east, the Persian Empire. In the middle a small country in a very dangerous position. If I lean

towards the east, I am afraid of invasion from Rome: if I lean towards Rome, then I shall be called upon to fight Persia. I would prefer to choose neither. But I had to choose Rome, because Rome rules Egypt, and it is from Egypt that we buy our corn. We are not self-supporting. *I* am not self-supporting. I have Roman officers in my army, Roman advisers in my palace, Roman spies in every department of state ... [12]

In an essay on cinema, "Pasolini and Penn" (1967), Arden's remarks about the leading characters in the former's *Gospel According to St. Matthew* and the latter's *Bonnie and Clyde* have particular relevance to his own methods of characterization:

To me, ... as a dramatist, the most striking feature of these movies is the way in which they combine a scrupulous regard for what is said to have actually happened with a clearly conveyed knowledge of what the dramatis personae would have liked to have happened. Clyde is both a sexually impotent killer *and* a romantic hero: Jesus is both a village carpenter gone round-the-bend *and* the Son of God ... Bonnie with a machine-gun burst ripping down her body is both a lump of bloody human meat *and* a sister to Cleopatra, Mary Queen of Scots or Barbara Allen. [13]

If we apply this attitude to Arden's own plays it is clear why so many of his central figures combine apparently contradictory qualities. Krank, in *The Waters of Babylon* (1957) is an architect, a pimp, a slum landlord, and a former concentration camp guard, who nonetheless (like Brecht's Mother Courage) retains our sympathy through his very ability to survive.

In plays such as *Ironhand* (1963) Arden's adaptation of Goethe's *Goetz von Berlichingen, The Workhouse Donkey* (1963), *Armstrong's Last Goodnight* (1965), and *The Hero Rises Up* (1968), Arden's major protagonists are all men who suggest the attractions of an anarchic individualist temperament in a conformist world, yet in each play Arden reveals his heroes as either deeply flawed, anachronistic or corrupt. In *The Workhouse Donkey,* Alderman Charlie Butterthwaite "sees himself as representing the true spirit of socialism, but he has in fact forgotten what it really means, and is relishing just his personal power." [14] Nevertheless, the eccentric individualist Butterthwaite, however corrupt, when pitted against the dehumanized and sterile integrity of the Chief Constable Feng, has considerable charm, and perhaps even represents a less dangerous alternative to society in the long run.

Analogously, Arden's Goetz is a champion of democracy and freedom, but has put himself outside the law; in doing so he has denied freedom to others and is eventually crushed by the representative of order in the play,

Weislingen. This conflict between freedom and order is made explicit in Goetz's dying speech, and indicates precisely what must have attracted Arden to Goethe's play:

> All I said was freedom: all Weislingen said was some sort of order. To put the two together: all the world is broken up, and yet we must break it and break it and break it... After I am dead, should I expect my freedom then? But I inhibited the freedom of other good men and gave them no order. So what do I deserve?...[15]

Again and again in these early plays the forces of order come into conflict with the forces of liberty, and in nearly all instances, despite Arden's liberal views, the latter is defeated.

It is only in *The Happy Haven* (1960) Arden's early collaborative effort with Margaretta D'Arcy, that the forces of revolt are victorious. In this play the inhabitants of a hospital for the aged rise up and defeat Dr. Copperthwaite who wants to forcibly administer an elixir of life, without the patients' consent, to further his own scientific aspirations. Instead he is himself injected and appears at the end of the play wearing a baby's mask and sucking a lollipop. However, this play, written in a vein of absurdist farce with the characters wearing Commedia dell'arte masks, is in marked contrast to the majority of Arden's plays in which the forces of revolt are crushed.

Perhaps *Serjeant Musgrave's Dance* (1959), Arden's most well known play, can best serve as a model for his early style based on the balancing of opposites, although in Black Jack Musgrave, Arden has combined the contradictory principles of anarchy and order in a single figure.

Musgrave, because of his desertion from the army and his disgust with killing, is representative of Arden's large collection of outsiders, rebels and curvilinear personalities such as Krank, Goetz and Gilnockie (in *Armstrong's Last Good-Night*); yet at the same time Musgrave's disillusionment with war is combined with a logical temperament which is militaristic, fanatical and rectilinear, as is found in Colonel Feng, Weislingen and Dr. Copperthwaite. The result of Musgrave's hatred of war is, therefore, not its antithesis but its logical extension, indiscriminate mass murder, justified by the solemn ratio of five to one, calculated on the basis of the five killings made in reprisal for the death of one soldier:

> One man, and for him five. Therefore for five of them we multiply out, *and* we find it five-and-twenty... So, as I understand logic and logic to me is the mechanism of God — that means that today there's twenty-five persons will have to be —[16]

But if the plays of Arden were delicately suspended in equipoise between revolt and order, since his return from India his works have more and more explicitly championed the overthrow of Capitalist-Imperialist society by revolutionary means: "Twelve years ago I looked on at people's struggles and wrote about them for the stage, sympathetically, but as an onlooker. Without consciously intending it, I have become a participant."[17]

The first of the three works written since *The Bagman* is the lengthy and complex trilogy *The Island of the Mighty* (1972). In a sense it is a transitional work between the "old" and the "new" Arden, since it was originally conceived as early as 1953 as a play about the defeat and death of King Arthur, was revised between 1966–69 as a trilogy for BBC television, and following a breakdown in negotiations, was rewritten, after the Ardens' Indian experience, in collaboration with Margaretta D'Arcy, who tried to inject into Arden's originally more picturesque, historical drama a "sense of precise sociological realism" which would emphasize the peasant background against which the figures in the Arthurian legend act. As Arden himself put it, "The true voice of liberty is more likely to be heard today from the kind of men and women who have little part to play in the traditional tales: I mean the ones who did the work, who fed and housed the noble warriors, and equipped them for the fight."[18] The result of this altered conception is that the play occasionally seems split between Arden's earlier, more objective conception, and his more recent partisanship.

Possibly to offset this tendency, the Production Notes suggest presenting "the narratives in as athletic and rapid and light a style as possible" with emblematic backcloths which are "not to be taken as realistic scenery."[19] However, this "extrovert, circus-like quality" which, as Albert Hunt argues, would have accentuated Arthur's ludicrousness and posturing (instead of his pathos) did not come off in the Royal Shakespeare Company production which was actually picketed by the playwrights themselves.[20] But one may wonder how any production of this extremely long and involuted text in which "the subject matter lies so thick on the ground that it is difficult to entangle all the strands" could have been rendered with the light touch that Arden and D'Arcy wished to achieve.[21] Historical pageant and cabaret do not mix especially well.

The first two parts of the trilogy deal with the decline and fall of King Arthur, while the third part returns to the central theme found in *The Bagman*, that of the relationship between the artist and society, concentrating on the figure of Merlin who has gone mad after Arthur's defeat at the end of Part Two. As in Arden's earlier plays, one of the trilogy's central themes is order vs. revolution. But instead of showing the two forces balanced evenly against one another, Arden is concerned with showing the inevitable collapse of the Roman and Christian civilization represented by King Arthur, as Merlin's description of him makes clear:

> My General is a Roman as far as his methods of war are concerned. In his lineage he is both Roman and Briton. By religion he is Christian, and his work is to defend civility and Christianity from one end of the Island to the other. (p. 38)

In this context as representative of a collapsing world order, the fact that King Arthur is lame has obvious symbolic connotations, a fact that is fully exploited visually in the stage directions: *"Enter Arthur in a huge purple gown and plumed fur hat. His sword is slung around him, loose enough for him to lean on like a walking stick"* (p. 123). Thus, the lame king who has turned his back on his primitive origins and turned himself into a "cool-headed Roman" is an image of repressive authoritarianism. Arthur has in fact concealed the true reason for his laming, which we only much later discover was a part of the primitive, incestuous ritual by which he became king:

> Yes, my own sister had me creep into her bed, because Morgan told us it was needful—for the security of the land ... I was marked upon my head, I was made lame by a strange ceremony. (p. 168)

In Arthur, who has renounced his primitive origins in favour of a life based on the defence of order, we are reminded of Arden's major theme, the conflict between (Roman) symmetry and (Celtic) asymmetry; in the "Asymmetrical Author's Preface" to *The Hero Rises Up*, the Ardens' play about Lord Nelson, the authors describe English pre-history in a way which has great relevance to *The Island of the Mighty:*

> When the Romans came to Britain, they came as a determinedly 'rectilinear' people of very *progressive* inclinations. Everything in this *conservative* 'curvilinear' island was to be IMPROVED: and the improvement... was to be carried out with symmetry and efficiency, and above all, *done properly*. The native Celts never entirely submitted. Then the Romans left us: and the English arrived. They found the military virtues of the Celts had been sufficiently smothered by the Romans and eventually they conquered these natives, despising them for their comparative lack of power, and—by extension—for their 'curvilinear' asymmetry.[22]

The true facts about Arthur's laming, revealed at the end of Part Two, mirror the central plot of Part One, "Two Wild Young Noblemen," the story of the twins Balin and Balan. In his account, whose source is Malory's *Morte d'Arthur,* Arden tells how Balan is taken to an island by a wild tribe of Picts and forced to fight a lame king, whom he kills. As a result he is himself crowned and lamed, and within a year forced to fight another stranger—who turns out to be his brother Balin. The two brothers fight and kill each other. Arden interweaves the death of Arthur and the story of the two brothers to suggest, through the overlapping images of lameness and meaningless slaughter, the futility of all authority.

The third part of *The Island of the Mighty* has as its theme the role of the poet in society and may be related to Arden's change of position following the completion of *The Bagman.* Merlin, Arthur's Chief Poet, is Arden's embodiment of the artist compromised by the demands of society. Merlin, then, is the "liberal intellectual who no longer knows what is liberality and what is tyranny, who is unable to draw a distinction between poetic ambiguity and political dishonesty" (p. 14). In short, Merlin is Arden the *un*committed playwright from the standpoint of Arden after 1970.

Before Arthur's death at the battle of Camlann, Merlin's role is to praise in high flown rhetoric Arthur's political and military exploits, taking no responsibility for the slaughter his words may glorify and perpetuate:

> I am the General's Poet—I make
> The words that make him famous in his age—
>> War must he wage
>> Poetry must praise
>> Such war until he wins
>> How can he ever win
>> Without blemish of sin?
>> Dead men are carried in
>> Praise the death and the killing
>> My words are ever willing
> In the service of his sword— (p. 86)

Following Arthur's death, Merlin goes mad, and in his madness imagines himself a bird. Cured of his madness by Morgan, he remains in his unadorned state, living in the wild wood, naked and free. Like King Lear, stripped of all external encumbrances, Merlin acquires self-knowledge and dignity:

> Oh why and when did Merlin ever dream
> That men of power and progress and authoritative domain
> Would keep his pale blood warmer
> Than a little green plant that grows in the running stream?
>> (p. 198)

As he realizes that previously "I but *appeared* to be a Chief Poet. Inside myself: what was I?", Merlin gradually leaves his isolation, not to be of use to any ruler ("He has been used by far too many for too long") but to sing songs to a cowherd's wife who has given him milk. His death (he is killed by the woman's jealous husband) comes only after Merlin has resumed his poetic art in a simple song to a peasant woman, and thus has gone to the opposite extreme of his poetry glorifying Arthur.

Merlin's role as Arthur's official voice in the early parts of the trilogy is contrasted with that of Aneurin, a young poet who is an outcast among the various Chief Poets in the play, and who represents Arden's own artistic ideals. As Merlin realizes only much later, Aneurin has "remained constant from the day of his birth/To the wild forest and the rain-soaked earth" (p. 227).

At the end of the play it is Aneurin who raises the banner of Arden's own (post-1970) vision of art as being at the service of the aims of the people:

> The poet without the people is nothing. The people without the poet will still be the people... All that we can do is to make loud and to make clear their own proper voice. They have so much to say ... (p. 232)

The Island of the Mighty reveals Arden's altered perspective on the social order by suggesting the necessity of the madness of the wild wood and the overthrow of the established and reactionary. The play begins with Arthur in power and ends with his crushing defeat and the true voice of the poet having emerged in Aneurin's hymn to the power of the people. Indeed the play's opening speech spoken by Merlin in official dress, clearly foreshadows the coming revolution:

> The wall fell down, the wild men
> Did jump across it and then ran
> Down every road that led to Rome—
> They broke to bits the Emperor's golden crown
> Kicked over his throne. (p. 32)

It should be noted that Arden has been attracted to such "wild men" from the very beginning of his career as a dramatist. The Sawneys in *Live Like Pigs,* for example, are the "direct descendents of the 'sturdy beggars' of the sixteenth century, and the apparent chaos of their lives becomes an ordered pattern when seen in terms of a wild countryside and a nomadic existence."[23] But whereas previously he saw these wild men as part of a losing battle between freedom and the restrictions of modern life, Arden now sees them as embodiments of a coming revolution against capitalist society.

The next play written by Arden and D'Arcy, *The Ballygombeen Bequest* (1972), was actually staged six months before *The Island of the Mighty*; nevertheless stylistically it belongs to Arden's latest phase. Whereas *The Island of The Mighty* was essentially equivocal on the theme of armed struggle, suggesting in Parts One and Two the futility of all authority and indicating only in Part Three Arden's new vision of the poet's role as the voice of the people, *The Ballygombeen Bequest* is the first play in which an unambiguously Marxist position is taken.

The staging is also characteristic of the Ardens' most recent work with its insistence on fast-paced presentation, no scenery except for a backcloth "which should feature blownup photographs and newspaper headlines illustrating the Northern Irish troubles,"[24] musical accompaniment throughout and stylized makeup and costumes. The tendency towards a new, partisan approach to playwriting is also made clear by the fact that in contrast to so many of Arden's plays which are set in a remote historical past, "the main events, social circumstances and political relationships set out in the play are founded upon current and observed fact," and it reflects too that since their return from India the Ardens have lived in the west of Ireland.

The subject of the play is the systematic exploitation of a poor Irish family by their absentee English landlord; but for the Ardens the sectarian conflict between Ireland and England, however significant, is only a manifestation of the larger class struggle between rich and poor:

> From nineteen-fifty-seven
> To nineteen-sixty-eight
> The fat men of the fat-half world
> Had food on every plate.
> The lean men of the naked world
> Grew leaner everyday
> And if they put their faces up
> Their teeth were kicked away. (p. 25)

The conflict between the forces of order and liberty which were balanced so delicately in Arden's earlier plays is now metamorphosed into the struggle between capitalism and the working class; the resolve of the poet to lend his voice to the people in *The Island of the Mighty* is now programmatically converted into practice.

The plot of the play concerns the swindling of the O'Leary family by the Englishman Hollidey-Cheape who uses the bungalow he has inherited to put up wealthy tourists, while the O'Learys act as caretakers. ("Ballygombeen" is the name of the lodge, but bally gombeen would also mean "bloody usurer" in Irish). After depriving them of their possible rights of ownership (the O'Learys have been living there for centuries) Hollidey-

Cheape then orders the family off the property when Seamus O'Leary is too old to be of further use. Although at the beginning of the play the Englishman's attitude toward the O'Learys is tentative and patronizing ("It's like training a nervous bitch—you keep the stick in reserve..." p. 15) his character gradually hardens into a stereotype of the capitalist exploiter:

> 'Tis the Man with the Long Purse
> Spreads his feet across this land
> His boots that leave no room for the tread of anyone else.
> He opens his purse and he dips in his hand:
> He pulls it out tight clenched
> It is full to the bend of his thumb
> But those few for whom he opens it
> Are the same few every time. (p. 28)

After old Seamus' death, his son resists their eviction. Unlike his father who falls prey to the Irish weakness for whiskey (with which Hollidey-Cheape plies him to get him to sign away his rights), Padraic O'Leary has studied the teachings of Lenin and learned the "Concept of Mass Support and the solidarity of the Working Class!" (p. 29). Padraic calls upon the official I.R.A. for help; but is betrayed by Hollidey-Cheape and Hagan, an Irish contractor who serves to demonstrate the play's thesis that the true enemy of the Irish poor is not merely the English, but the capitalist:

> But Padraic O'Leary is a threat of a different size.
> Educate, Agitate—and bloody well organize...
> He would drive down the rich and bring up the poor:
> I don't want that class of beggar come battering at my door!
> He must himself be driven down— (p. 41)

Padraic is intercepted by the military in Northern Ireland and dies under questioning, his death attributed to internecine conflicts within the I.R.A. The play seems to conclude with Hollidey-Cheape selling his property cheaply to Hagan, the latter claiming that it is now nearly worthless since the I.R.A. has put its mark on the land by blowing up the cottage. However, the dispute between Hagan and Hollidey-Cheape is done as slapstick farce with the pair of capitalists grotesquely wrangling over a wad of bills and hurling custard pies at one another. As Hollidey-Cheape leaves the stage, the dead Padraic, who has already risen from his bier, slips a pie under his foot and sings the play's final lines:

> When you act in a play it is easy to say
> That we shall win and never be defeated
> When you go from here it is not so clear

That power for the people is predestined —
Giddy —i —aye tiddle —iddle —oo
There are more of us than them ... (p. 50)

It is impossible to apply the same criteria to understand *The Ballygombeen Bequest* that we have applied to Arden's previous work. Can one criticize a piece of blatant theatrical propaganda for not successfully offering both sides of the question? Can one criticize Arden's use of stereotyped caricatures of rich and poor without shifting the focus of this essay from the domain of art to that of politics? A play which begins with the following epigraph surely leaves no room for delicate shading and subtlety:

One of these slave birthmarks is a belief in the capitalist system of society; the Irishman frees himself from such a mark of slavery when he realizes the truth that the capitalist system is the most foreign thing in Ireland ... —James Connolly (p. 5)

What the Ardens have created in *The Ballygombeen Bequest* is a revival of agitprop theatre, having exchanged the Brechtian tradition of intellectual paradox (recalling Arden's comment that *Galileo* is "a great play because at the end ... you still don't know where you are") for the Brechtian tradition of the *Lehrstück*, which, like *The Ballygombeen Bequest*, was intended to "teach the tactics of the class war":

Agitprop meant vigorous caricature and denunciation of the class enemy ... It required few actors and often they could be near-amateurs ... The cartoon-like depictions of capitalists with their lackeys, and of workers and minority peoples in their awakening and struggle, could have memorable force. Subtlety? Not desired, any more than primitive peoples strive for fine nuance in a fertility dance or a warpath rite.[25]

The settings for Brecht's *Lehrstücke* were, like the Ardens', minimal. Caspar Nehr's set for the 1932 performance of *Die Mutter,* for example, consisted of canvas stretched on a metal frame, while at the back was a screen for the projection of photographs, sub-titles and slogans. The production was likewise fast-paced and punctuated with music and songs.

Brecht's interest in the *Lehrstück* in the period 1929–36 corresponded with "a decision to desert all audiences but the workers and youth."[26] Here again the analogy with Arden is revealing, since the latter's interest in radical theatre must have been partly motivated by frustration from the fact that his work has never had more than minority appeal, and that among intellectuals. This forced Arden to admit in 1966 that his two community dramas (written in collaboration with his wife), *The Business of Good*

Government (1960) and *Ars Longa, Vita Brevis* (1964) were the two most popular plays he had written. Thus Arden's recent interest in agitprop may reflect a playwright in search of a wider audience as much as purely political considerations.

During the late 1960's and early 1970's, the original distinction between "community" and "professional" drama has gradually disappeared from the Ardens' work, and their activities have included a Vietnam War Carnival at New York University (1967) and a labor drama performed in a working-class neighborhood in London (1971). The final break with established theatre was perhaps symbolized by the disastrous Royal Shakespeare Company production of *The Island of the Mighty* in 1972, which, as has been noted, was picketed by the playwrights themselves.

The Ballygombeen Bequest, though lightweight compared with most of Arden's other work, is largely successful as agitprop theatre. Its scope is carefully defined and strictly limited to a specific event (although with obvious reference to the Irish problem as a whole), and a light touch prevents the thesis from overwhelming the work as theatre. Although Albert Hunt's remark that the play is not used for "repeating familiar propaganda slogans, but for teaching people . . . to understand more clearly the complexities and contradictions and underlying realities of their situation,"[27] is surely an exaggeration, since a work of art that cuts through moral ambiguities with caricatures and pat answers can hardly be said to be interested in scrupulously offering contradictions and complexities; given the limitations of the genre, the play is effective as political theatre.

In Margaretta D'Arcy and John Arden's latest play, *The Non-Stop Connolly Show* (and it is significant that for the first time their names are reversed on the title-page), the Ardens continue the direction of using the theatre as a platform for their stand on the Irish question in particular, and on the necessity for Marxist revolution in general. Unlike *The Ballygombeen Bequest,* however, which was one of their shortest works, *The Non-Stop Connolly Show* lasted twenty-six and a half hours in its only complete performance, from noon on Saturday until Sunday afternoon, March 29–30, 1975, in Liberty Hall, the headquarters of the Irish Transport and General Workers Union in Dublin, the building from which James Connolly marched to start the Easter Uprising in 1916.

The play, which was originally conceived by Margaretta D'Arcy as part of a "giant 'Pop Festival' for the Left," represents the Ardens' final step away from the "fence-sitting" of Arden's early plays towards an attempted unification of community theatre, political commitment, and artistic endeavor. This conception of the theatre is not as wholly new to Arden as it may seem. As early as 1964 in the Preface to *The Workhouse Donkey,* Arden suggested that:

... I would have been happy had it been possible for *The Workhouse Donkey* to have lasted say six or seven or thirteen hours (excluding intervals), and for the audience to come and go throughout the performance, assisted perhaps by a printed synopsis of the play from which they could deduce those scenes or episodes which would interest them particularly, and those which they could afford to miss. A theatre presenting such an entertainment would, of course, need to offer rival attractions as well, and would in fact take on some of the characteristics of a fairground or amusement park; with restaurants, bars, sideshows, bandstands and so forth, all grouped round a central playhouse.[28]

This notion of the theatre as amusement park places, of course, certain obvious restrictions on the dramatist. A play in which the audience may be expected to leave for stretches at a time must be lively, emphasize visual action, and not be too intellectually demanding or dependent on a complicated plot

In rejecting their original idea, a three-act play about Connolly's role in the Easter Uprising, in favor of a "six-play cycle of continuous struggle" lasting over 450 pages in print, describing the life of Connolly from his boyhood in Edinburgh to his death by a British firing squad, the Ardens felt that the life of Connolly should be "built on a traditionally heroic scale" which could not be divorced from other events of importance outside Ireland; "The Paris Commune of 1871, the Boer War, the 1905 Rumanian Revolution, the expansion of the USA into Latin America and the West Pacific, the militant unionization of the Colorado Miners, the ebb and flow of the Socialist International ..."[29]

At the same time, however, the Ardens wished to convey a dramatic picture of Connolly's life, a life which was essentially undramatic except for the last few days in which he led the Irish Citizen Army in the unsuccessful occupation of a Dublin Post Office in the attempt to establish a Provisional Government. As a result, the Ardens decided to present to the audience "the very tediousness and seeming hopelessness of the eternal wrangling which was in itself so essential a part of the life-pattern of any Revolutionist," since if omitted, they would be "distorting our work into spectacular 'high-theatre' at the expense of the long-drawn 'continuous struggle' which inevitably precedes the actual outbreak of revolution" (p. 99).

This last comment in defence of tediousness, is a remarkable admission for any dramatist to make with regard to any play, the more so when the play lasts for twenty-six hours. More than anything else, this comment pinpoints the play's failed compromise between art and political propaganda. Despite having lamented the fact at the beginning of their essay, "A Socialist Hero on the Stage," that Socialist Realism tends to be criticized by different standards from an ordinary play and that "the Principles of drama are all the same, whatever the material involved" (p. 95), the Ardens' interest in a dogmatic approach to Connolly's life clearly outweighs their concern for the spectacle as a work of art or even as effective theatrical propaganda.

Judged by the standards of conventional drama, the plays rely almost entirely on caricature, cliché and slogan to make their principal point of the necessity for a socialist revolution. Thus capitalism is represented by a 'demon king,' Mr. Grabitall, a personification of evil who wears the same mask throughout the six plays; "By disposition of paper and gold . . . I hold my domination over all the world."[30] However, as Connolly's adversaries change, the personification of capitalist evil takes on a new name: in Part Three he is the Lord Lieutenant of Ireland, in Part Four (when Connolly is in the United States) he is J. Pierpont Morgan, and in Parts Five and Six he is William Martin Murphy (the chairman of the Employer's Federation, who organized the Dublin Lock-Out of 1913). Grabitall (whose name was borrowed from an American cartoon figure) is accompanied by three similarly masked henchman, the Employers, who likewise change names and nationality to suit the required adversary; and military, church, judiciary and "bourgeois-political" leaders are handled in the same way. It goes almost without saying that members of the proletariat although not really individualized as characters either, are not masked.

Connolly himself is the only character in the plays with any shred of individuality, but even this is minimal since the Ardens were not interested in anything which might tarnish his image as a "Socialist Hero." This leads to occasional inconsistencies, such as the fact that although Connolly stammered in life, his stammer is only illustrated in the scene where he overcomes his difficulty and delivers a brilliant impromptu speech. Similarly, little or no mention is made of Connolly's repeated belief "that one could be a Marxist in politics and a Catholic in religion without any question of conflict," or that as a good Catholic he sent for a Capuchin friar shortly before his execution.[31]

In the creation of a Socialist Hero who is essentially perfect, Arden has completely repudiated his belief in the complex, flawed heroes who populate his earlier plays ("We were not interested in dealing with him 'negatively'"), going so far as to claim that "the 'flawed hero' in fact is a symptom of a social order in which all power grows out of the strongbox of a bank" (p. 102). The contrast between Arden's work then and now is further heightened by his comment that "the whole story of Connolly was a kind of inside-out version of my invented Black Jack Musgrave" (p. 155).

Whereas *Serjeant Musgrave's Dance* concerned an old soldier who has deserted and attempts to strike a misconceived blow against his masters, but "by his inability to understand the political implications of the labour movement (the striking pitmen), he fails, and is executed," Connolly deserts from the Irish army (at the end of Part One) and devotes the rest of his life to the revolutionary struggle of International Labour. Although Connolly, like Musgrave, is finally executed at the end of the plays, his revolt has not been in vain:

> At Easter nineteen hundred and sixteen —
> We were the first to roll away the stone
> From the leprous wall of the whitened tomb.[32]

The Ardens' play never asks the question that makes Yeats' "Easter 1916" such a great poem about the nature of political commitment; "What if excess of love bewildered them [the revolutionaries] till they died?" Such doubts have no place in propaganda. But considered on its own terms as agitprop, the use of stereotypes and Marxist slogans need not necessarily be seen as objectionable. After all, not only Brecht's *Lehrstücke,* but the Ardens' own *Ballygombeen Bequest* were effective theatrically, regardless of the flatness of characterization or the emphasis on clear-cut Marxist solutions. But where Brecht's didactic plays and the Ardens' earlier work operate generally through simplicity and economy, *The Non-Stop Connolly Show* belabors its audience with ponderous and lengthy debates which cripple the play's effectiveness not only as theatre but as propaganda as well. As Paddy Marsh, who reviewed the Liberty Hall performance in *Theatre Quarterly* wrote:

> ...anyone who did not have a detailed knowledge of Connolly's life would find it very difficult to pick up the story on his return to the dense undergrowth of political discussion and argument that obscured the paths of the play... Such passages of the play were far too lengthy and tedious. There was little attempt to enliven the proceedings visually... This had a deadening effect on the whole proceedings.[33]

Although the Ardens avowedly wrote the plays to appeal to a working-class audience, it is difficult to imagine such an audience maintaining its enthusiasm over long stretches of discussion of socialist tactics, including speeches like the following by the American socialist Daniel de Leon in Part Four:

> Moreover, this new body will not confine itself to existing unions. We intend to create out of it an entire syndicate of the dispossessed: to include beneath the panoply of its united na-

tional strength all those millions and millions of unorganised migrant labourers who at present are protected by no organisation, and who likewise are affected by no political doctrine, save the deeply felt bitterness of their miserable exploitation. In the Industrial Workers of the World, the one party involved that possesses a precise doctrine will be the one ... to achieve the allegiance of this hitherto amorphous mass.[34]

It is hardly surprising that, according to several reviews, the audience was largely made up of members from the middle classes, and that despite the Ardens' recent emphasis on fast-paced production accompanied by music, the effect of the interminable bombardment of long speeches was to render the audience insensible rather than ready to start the revolution. As one reviewer put it, "Propaganda, to be effective, ... must rely on impact, not pedantry."[35]

All of John Arden's work is constructed on the principle of conflict. In his early plays the conflict was left unresolved, and audiences left the theatre discontented with received beliefs and forced to question themselves. This was not merely an intellectual game or "Sitting on the Fence" but a sincere statement that easy solutions in life are not easy to find. But somewhere along the line Arden decided that simply posing the problems without the answers was not enough. To write about politics one must be committed, mustn't one, and so Arden's recent plays take a partisan stance and the "wild man of the wood," always restrained or defeated in his early plays, finally takes command. This aim of bringing the wild man into the theatre (at the expense of craftsmanship) was expressed in the Preface to *The Hero Rises Up*:

We hoped to write a play which need not be *done properly*. That is to say: we wanted to produce it ourselves so that it would present the audience with an experience akin to that of running up in a crowded wet street on Saturday night against a drunken red-nosed man with a hump on his back dancing in a puddle, his arms around a pair of bright-eyed laughing girls, his mouth full of inexplicable loud noises... You don't at once forget him: and although you know nothing about him, he has become some sort of *circumstance* in your life.[36]

But despite his eagerness to haul Dionysus into the theatre, Arden himself remains a solitary intellectual "Bagman" at heart ("I rarely stick my neck out unless goaded to it by someone for whose opinion I have respect"), who has increasingly grown ashamed of his own intellect. As a result, his conversion to radical Marxism has produced not vital popular spectacle but "a pedant's idea of popular theatre."[37]

Like the Narrator in *The Bagman* whose little people rebel against him ("If you bring us into battle you bring us only onto grief and woe"), Arden's excursions into agitprop theatre have compromised his art rather than making his politics uncompromising. As Robert Brustein said of Brecht, "[his] agitprop plays seem like the 'Aves' of a novitiate, paying penance for a recurrent sin."[38] But Brecht went on after the period of his *Lehrstücke* (1929–36) to create his finest works; perhaps the same may yet be said of Arden if he can learn to accept not only his limitations, but his abilities.

NOTES

1. John Arden, "On Comedy," *Encore*, 12, No. 5 (1965), p. 16.
2. Arden, *To Present the Pretence* (London: Eyre Methuen, 1977), p. 137.
3. Arden, *The Bagman or The Impromptu of Muswell Mill* in *Two Autobiographical Plays* (London: Methuen, 1971), pp. 37–38. Subsequent references to this work appear in the text.
4. These views were enthusiastically shared by Margaretta D'Arcy, who has steadily encouraged Arden's political conversion. It would also not be misconceived to identify the Young Woman who leads the Narrator in *The Bagman* towards the revolution, with his wife, who is described in the dedication to the play as "Irish and most radical . . . /she/might well keep guns along with love wrapped up in bed . . . ," p. 10.
5. Albert Hunt, *Arden* (London: Methuen, 1974), p. 153.
6. Arden and Margaretta D'Arcy, *The Hero Rises Up* (London: Methuen, 1969), p. 5.
7. Arden, *Live Like Pigs* in *Three Plays* (Harmondsworth: Penguin, 1964), p. 101.
8. "On Comedy," p. 16.
9. Quoted in John Willett, *The Theatre of Bertolt Brecht* (London: Methuen, 1977), p. 168.
10. *The Theatre of Bertholdt Brecht*, p. 217.
11. "On Comedy," p. 15.
12. Arden and D'Arcy, *The Business of Good Government* (London: Methuen, 1963), p. 18.
13. *To Present the Pretence*, p. 19.
14. "On Comedy," p. 15.
15. Arden, *Ironhand* (London: Methuen, 1965), p. 156.
16. Arden, *Serjeant Musgrave's Dance* (London: Methuen, 1960), p. 91.
17. *To Present the Pretence*, p. 158.

18. Hunt, p. 158.

19. Arden and D'Arcy, *The Island of the Mighty* (London: Methuen, 1974), p. 23. Subsequent references to this work appear in the text.

20. See Arden and D'Arcy's essay "Playwrights on Picket" in *To Present the Pretence*, pp. 159–172.

21. Michael Anderson, *Anger and Detachment* (London: Pitman, 1976), p. 74.

22. *The Hero Rises Up,* p. 5.

23. *Live Like Pigs,* p. 101.

24. Arden and D'Arcy, *The Ballygombeen Bequest,* in *Scripts* 1, No. 9 (1972), p. 5. Subsequent references to this work appear in the text.

25. Lee Baxandall, Introd., *The Mother,* by Bertholt Brecht (New York: Grove Press, 1965), p. 30.

26. Baxandall, p. 26.

27. Hunt, p. 156.

28. Arden, *The Workhouse Donkey* (London: Methuen, 1966), p. 8.

29. "A Socialist Hero on the Stage," in *To Present the Pretence*, p. 111. Subsequent references to this work will appear in the text.

30. D'Arcy and Arden, *The Non-Stop Connolly Show* (London: Pluto Press, 1977), p. 1.

31. P. Berresford Ellis, Introd., *James Connolly: Selected Writings* (Harmondsworth: Penguin, 1973), p. 32.

32. *The Non-Stop Connolly Show,* Part Six, p. 106.

33. Paddy Marsh, "Easter at Liberty Hall: the Ardens' Non-Stop Connolly Show," *Theatre Quarterly,* 5, No. 19 (1975), p. 141.

34. *The Non-Stop Connolly Show,* pp. 22–23.

35. Harriet Cooke, "The Non-Stop Connolly Show," *Theatre Quarterly,* 5, No. 19 (1975), p. 141.

36. *The Hero Rises Up,* pp. 5–6.

37. Irving Wardle, "Salute to Nelson," *The Times,* 8 Nov. 1968, p. 13a.

38. Robert Brustein, *The Theatre of Revolt* (Boston, Toronto: Little, Brown and Co., 1964), p. 251.

Joe Orton

JOHN BULL AND FRANCES GRAY

Joe Orton died between 2.00 and 4.00 on the night of the 9th of August 1967. He was thirty-four years old, and on the brink of the recognition and financial success as a playwright that had eluded him since he had left R.A.D.A. in 1953. He was found in bed with his entire skull smashed in, the result of nine manic blows with the hammer that had been placed neatly on the bed-cover on his chest. The blows had been struck by his friend, Kenneth Halliwell, with whom he had lived for 15 years. Halliwell was naked on the floor, a glass and a can of grapefruit-juice by his side. The twenty-two Nembutal tablets that he had swallowed had killed him considerably quicker than Orton.

Orton's funeral took place at the Golder's Green Crematorium on the 18th August. The two dozen mourners watched the coffin being carried down the aisle to the accompaniment of a tape-recording of the Beatles' song *A Day in the Life* (from the *Sergeant Pepper's Lonely Heart's Club Band* album), from which the drug references had been tastefully removed. One of the mourners suggested to Joe Orton's brother, Douglas, that the ashes should be mixed with those of Halliwell who had been cremated at Enfield the previous day. He thought hard before agreeing; "Well," he said, "as long as nobody hears about it in Leicester."[1]

At the time of his death Orton must have appeared to the public as a complete embodiment of the 1960's London scene. His exploits were those of an outrageous social non-conformist. He was colourfully and promiscuously gay, a constant experimenter with drugs, possessed of a demonic sense of humour—at the time of his first London production he had written to the press complaining about the obscenity in his own play, under the pseudonym of a 'Mary Whitehouse' figure, Edna Wellthorpe (Mrs)—and in receipt of the ultimate fashionable accolade for a 60's writer, a commission to write the screenplay for a Beatles' film. Increasingly his plays reflected his involvement in this world, but always he wrote with a bleak awareness of his past as an inescapable spectre. Douglas was not alone in worrying what Leicester thought about it all.

Orton's death and his funeral were in perfect keeping with the facts of his London life, a bizarre episode that could not have been better calculated to appeal to a popular English press intent on the creation of the myth of an exciting but dangerous 'alternative' society. But there is an uncanny link with the plot of one of his major plays, *Loot,* which is concerned with the macabre events surrounding the funeral of the wife of a Mr McLeavy whose attitudes and obsessions are very like those of Orton's own father, William. Early in the play, the son, Hal, tells his father that another wreath has arrived, and McLeavy goes off to check the contents. The nurse, Fay, who plans to marry the widower in the seventh of her suspiciously brief unions, is left alone with Hal.

FAY: I sometimes think your father has a sentimental attachment to roses.
HAL: Do you know what his only comment was on my mother's death?
FAY: Something suitable, I'm sure.
HAL: He said he was glad she'd died at the right season for roses. He's been up half the night cataloguing the varieties on the crosses. You should have seen him when that harp arrived. Sniffing the petals, checking, arguing with the man who brought it. They almost came to blows over the pronunciation. If she'd played her cards right, my mother could've cited the Rose Grower's Annual as co-respondent.
FAY: The Vatican would never grant an annulment. Not unless he'd produced a hybrid. (p. 198/9)[2]

William Orton was a refugee from the modern world. He had retreated early into a peaceful world of modest horticultural activity, into his own brand of suburban pastoral. After a series of false-starts he had settled for 35 years as a gardener for Leicester City Council, and in addition devoted most of his leisure-time to the allotment and greenhouse to which he cycled 15 miles most mornings before work. Evenings and weekends were spent in this quiet refuge, away from the inarticulate demands of an unsatisfied and embittered wife, and from the growing family with whom he had little contact. "Gardening kept you busy. You always looked forward to something coming up, you see. It was exciting to see if they came up and see how they were doing every year."[3] William Orton was the model for the succession of weak father-figures that inhabit his son's plays. McLeavy's sole ambition on the death of his wife is to construct a Rose Garden; in *Loot* the roses celebrate death, not life or love: "I've ordered four hundred roses to help keep memory green. On a site, only a stone's throw from the church. I intend to found the 'Mrs Mary McLeavy Memorial Rose Garden.' It will put Paradise to shame" (p. 217). Orton had a total contempt for his father, presenting him not only as weak but as the representative suburban man, timorous, dutiful and completely shackled by conformity. In *Loot,* McLeavy is rewarded for his honest and dull citizenship by being the only character to be punished by the due processes of the law he so reveres; while in the earlier television play, *The Good and Faithful Servant* he had appeared as Buchanan, the unquestioning employee who retires from his firm after fifty years employment, with an electric clock and an electric toaster, both of which immediately cease to function. When he learns that his newly discovered grandson, Ray, has never worked, he sets out to make him see the error of his ways:

BUCHANAN:	Not work! What do you do then?
RAY:	I enjoy myself.
BUCHANAN:	That's a terrible thing to do. I'm bowled over by this, I can tell you. It's my turn to be shocked now. You ought to have a steady job.
EDITH:	Two perhaps. (p. 167)

Still haunted by Leicester, Orton has Ray succumb to marriage, work and respectable domesticity—at which point Buchanan immediately dies, the continuity having been established; in his later plays, Orton would increasingly move away from the savage presentation of his past to a riotously threatening version of the alternatives. The other side of Ray—"I enjoy myself"—came to preoccupy Orton more and more. But Orton never really escaped.

In the final, unrevised play, *What the Butler Saw*, Geraldine declares, "I lived in a normal family. I had no love for my father" (p. 382), a remark which owes as much to his own memories as it does to the character's denial of unnatural practices around which so much of the action of the play revolves. The married couple in this play become as farcically obsessed with the significance of a vase of roses as McLeavy had been with his flowers in *Loot*. Having persuaded his prospective secretary, Geraldine, to undress, under the pretext of giving her a medical examination, the psychiatrist, Prentice, is thwarted in his attempt at seduction by the unexpected return of his wife. He crams Geraldine's underwear into the vase and presents a surprised Mrs Prentice with the roses. Later he trims the stems to fit them on top of the concealed clothing. The visual joke is of course reinforced by the fact that the roses—which are, as the visiting psychiatrist, Rance, points out, a 'poetically' Jungian symbol of woman— are presented, and then mutilated, to hide a rather more prosaic symbol, the unfortunate Geraldine's knickers. Much of the verbal humour of *What the Butler Saw* derives from the absurd attempts of the supposed expert on human behaviour, Rance, to explain, in an anarchic parody of psy-choanalytical terminology, the farcical results that follow Prentice's concealment of the attempted seduction; the intellectual complexity of the explanation is always at war with the physical simplicity of the cause. But the parody has a perfectly serious side for Orton. What is being parodied takes us away from the chaotic celebration of 60's excess—when Mrs Prentice believes her husband to have become a transvestite, she tells him "I'd no idea our marriage teetered on the edge of fashion"—and back into the articulated traumas of his early life.

The connection between Orton's upbringing and his plays is impor-tant, more important than for any other English playwright. He is the least impersonal of the modern dramatists. Had he lived, doubtless the connec-tions would have become less vital; indeed in *What the Butler Saw,* there is strong evidence that Orton was beginning to move towards a more generalised analysis of his world. But most of his earlier writing is a straightforward attempt to exorcise through comedy the ghosts of his past; so that it is very easy to make direct links between his plots and characters, and the life of his pre-R.A.D.A. days. This obsessional re-working of his life gives the plays much of their energy, but it also points to essential weaknesses. For instance, the original version of *The Erpingham Camp* was as a television play for Rediffusion in 1966. It is a free-wheeling attack on the British Holiday Camp, complete with regimented fun, and grotesque competition:

> ERPINGHAM: The Mother and Child competition resulted in a dead heat. Mrs J M Nash of Palmers Green and Mrs Susanne Mitchell of Southampton both win cash prizes ... Our disability bonus was won by Mr Laurie Russell of Market Harborough. Both Laurie's legs were cer-tified 'absolutely useless' by our Resident Medical Officer. Yet he performed the Twist and the Bossa Nova to the tune specified on the entrance form.
> TED: He fell over, though. Twice.
> LOU: They help them a lot, don't they? That blind woman would've never found the diving-board if the audience hadn't shouted out. (p. 283)

As a television play it is moderately successful; the problem is that the severe limitations of the selected locale make the targets too easy. It is a play rather obviously aimed at the television viewers of the Ortons' Coun-

cil Estate, at a Mrs McLeavy who included among her wreaths one from
"the Friends of Bingo." Orton attempts to widen the scope of the play with
the abortive revolt of the holiday-makers, but the overall mood is patronis-
ing rather than anarchic in the sense of using the Camp to question larger
issues. Its limitations were made apparent when, in a revised version, it
was produced at the Royal Court the following year. It was too obviously
playing at the wrong audience. *"The Erpingham Camp* has the advantage
of being an assault on holiday-camps intended to provoke those who attend
them, rather than a sneer to flatter those who wouldn't be seen dead in one;
but it retains the mealy-mouthed obviousness of the small screen, and is not
yet ready to be shown to the elite."[4]

Much of the intended impact of Orton's plays derives from an insistent
assault on a series of such British institutions as the Holiday Camp, the
monarchy, the church, the mysterious workings of the public bureaucracy
of police, water-board and the like. They are on the whole, in post—
'Beyond the Fringe' days, fairly safe targets whose comic demolition is
unlikely to surprise, let alone offend, an even casually enlightened
theatre-goer. It is difficult not to feel that, when mounting such attacks,
Orton was still looking back over his shoulder at Leicester. They are at
their most effective, particularly in *Loot,* when they are presented as a
confused, almost surrealistic, collage of attitudes; as when Inspector Truscott finally discovers the stolen bank-notes in the coffin. The absurd moral
outrage is even more comic when we realise that Truscott's distaste is
simply a preamble to allowing himself to be bribed:

TRUSCOTT:	Who is responsible for this disgraceful state of affairs?
HAL:	I am.
TRUSCOTT:	*(stoops and picks up a bundle of notes)* Would you have stood by and allowed this money to be buried in holy ground?
HAL:	Yes.
TRUSCOTT:	How dare you involve me in a situation for which no memo has been issued. *(He turns the notes over)* In all my experience I've never come across a case like it. Every one of these fivers bears a portrait of the Queen. It's dreadful to contemplate the issues raised. Twenty thousand tiaras and twenty thousand smiles buried alive! She's a constitutional monarch you know. She can't answer back... *(He picks up another bundle and stares at them)*

McLEAVY:	Well, Inspector, you've found the money and unmasked the criminals. You must do your duty and arrest them. I shall do mine and appear as witness for the prosecution.
HAL:	Are you married, Inspector?
TRUSCOTT:	Yes.
HAL:	Does your wife never yearn for excitement?
TRUS:	She did once express a wish to see the wind-mills and tulip fields of Holland.
HAL:	With such an intelligent wife you need a larger income . . .
TRUS:	Where is this Jesuitical twittering leading us?
HAL:	I'm about to suggest bribery. *(TRUSCOTT removes his pipe, no one speaks)*
TRUS:	How much?
HAL:	Twenty per cent.
TRUS:	Twenty-five per cent. Or a full report of this case appears on my superior's desk in the morning.
HAL:	Twenty-five it is.
TRUS:	*(shaking hands)* Done.
DENNIS:	*(to TRUSCOTT)* May I help you to replace the money in the casket?
TRUS:	Thank you, lad. Most kind of you. (p. 270/71)

Here, the pious platitudes of the Inspector are not left hanging in the air for a quick and obvious laugh; they are a surface beneath which Orton carefully reveals the face of unlicensed authority—in this instance comically corrupt, but elsewhere genuinely threatening:

TRUS:	Understand this, lad. You can't get away with cheek. Kids nowadays treat any kind of authority as a challenge. We'll challenge you. If you oppose me in my duty, I'll kick those teeth through the back of your head. Is that clear?
HAL:	Yes. *(Door chimes)*
FAY:	Would you excuse me, Inspector?
TRUS:	*(wiping his brow)* You're at liberty to answer your own doorbell, miss. That is how we tell whether or not we live in a free country. *(standing over HAL)* Where's the money?
HAL:	In church. *(TRUSCOTT kicks HAL violently. HAL cries out in terror and pain)*

TRUS:	Don't lie to me!
HAL:	I'm not lying. It's in church!
TRUS:	*(shouting, knocking HAL to the floor)* Under any other political system I'd have you on the floor in tears!
HAL:	*(crying)* You've got me on the floor in tears. (p. 235)

The comic policeman draws real blood. Truscott is Orton's most successfully realised character; the false logic of his bureaucratic mind takes us back to a real world and not away from it. He owes much to Orton's own experiences at the hands of the legal machinery when he and Halliwell were arrested, fined and imprisoned for defacing Public Library books. "'I wasn't actually beaten up,' he said. 'But they hovered around ... I found that the best thing was to be as nice as possible because it was no use standing on your rights once they've got you in their power.' Privately, Orton contended that their severe sentence was 'because we were queers.'"[5] The comically outrageous defacement of the collection of the Islington Borough Council Library thus brought Orton suddenly in conflict with the establishment in two related 'outsider' roles, as criminal and as homosexual. In the original production of *Loot,* Kenneth Williams tried with some success to combine Truscott's comic potential with the real violence that Orton had written into the part. In the more successful revival, Michael Bates turned Truscott into a harmless funny copper, and totally lost the desired effect.

The character of Truscott which came to dominate *Loot,* at the expense of Fay who is clearly intended at first to be the major figure, moved Orton away from the limitations of his usual source material. His is, played properly, not a two-dimensional part; he is paranoia made flesh. This brilliant creation is a possible indication of the way in which Orton might have developed beyond a witty, but essentially superficial, analysis of the contemporary world, to suggest the real horror that lies beneath the skin. As it is, Orton is at his best when he makes play with family archetypes. His mother's confusion of sexual energy and Council Estate propriety is captured in Kath in *Entertaining Mr Sloane;* as Orton's sister, Leonie, recognized immediately when she saw the 1975 Royal Court revival of the play: "That's my mum! That's her! Its like seeing a ghost. She was always over-dressing. Once she got dressed in gold lamé and painted her shoes gold just to go to the pub. The paint cracked when she walked. There were gold flakes all the way to the City Arms."[6] Kath's attitude to Sloane is that of mother as well as lover; in both roles Orton makes it clear that Ed and Sloane find her physically repellant:

KATH:	*(to SLOANE)* Baby, my little boy ... mamma forgives you.

ED:	What have you got to offer? You're fat and the crowsfeet under your eyes would make you an object of terror. Pack it in. I tell you. Sawdust up to the naval? You've nothing to lure any man.
KATH:	Is that the truth, Mr Sloane?
SLOANE:	More or less...
KATH:	Mr Sloane, I believed you were a good boy. I find you've deceived me.
SLOANE:	You've deceived yourself. (p. 143)

Whilst even during her initial seduction of Sloane, a certain maternal propriety is in order: "I don't think the fastening on this thing I'm wearing will last much longer...*(Pause: he attempts to move; she is almost on top of him)* Mr Sloane...*(Rolls on to him)* you should wear more clothes, Mr Sloane.... I believe you're as naked as me. And there's no excuse for it. *(Silence)* I'll be you mamma. I need to be loved. Gently. Oh! I shall be so ashamed in the morning. *(Switches off the light)* What a big heavy baby you are. Such a big heavy baby." In Sloane, Orton created a role for himself in a rearranged 'family,' first killing off the unwanted 'Dadda,' and then being willingly co-erced into servicing both the handsome Ed and his sister, the peculiar mixture of spinsterly lust and maternal coyness.

There is much of Orton in Wilson, the intruder from Mike's homosexual past, who disturbs his and Joyce's unmarried domesticity, in the earlier *The Ruffian on the Stair;* but above all it is in *Loot,* with the character of Hal, the son who, unlike Orton, has not learnt to lie, that Orton comes nearest to confronting his past. The mother is dead before the play begins, but her body carries the burden of the farcical action of the play. Hal removes the corpse from the coffin, and places it upside-down in a cupboard, so that he and his bi-sexual lover, Dennis, can utilize the container to smuggle out the proceeds of their bank raid. Initially, only Dennis has scruples:

HAL:	Has anybody ever hidden money in a coffin?...
DENNIS:	Think of your mum. Your lovely old mum. She gave you birth.
HAL:	I should thank anybody for that?
DENNIS:	Cared for you. Washed your nappies. You'd be some kind of monster. *(HAL takes the lid off the coffin)*
HAL:	Think what's at stake. *(He goes to wardrobe and unlocks it)* Money.

However, when, faced with the potential problem of getting rid of the body, Dennis argues that it will be safer to undress it, Hal is for the first time perturbed:

HAL: *(pause)* Take her clothes off?
DENNIS: In order to avoid detection should her remains
              be discovered.
HAL: Bury her naked? My own mum? *(He goes to the
              mirror and combs his hair)* It's a Freudian
              nightmare. (p. 208/9)

By a curious coincidence, Orton's mother died whilst the first production of *Loot* was in rehearsal. Orton described his plans in his diary: "I'll have to send a telegram to find out details of my mother's funeral. I can't go home if there's nowhere to stay. And I don't fancy spending the night in the house with the corpse. A little too near the Freudian bone for comfort." His description of events is almost indistinguishable in content from the dialogue of the play. "As the corpse is downstairs in the main living room it means going out or watching television with death at one's elbow. My father, fumbling out of bed in the middle of the night, bumped into the coffin and almost had the corpse on the floor."[7] What is different, however, is the tone. Whether he is describing a casual sexual encounter, or the sleeping arrangements during the funeral, the diary entries are objective and dispassionate, though never without humour. Orton's energy and his displays of subjective emotion were reserved for the plays. Orton wrote at length about the funeral in his diary; it was clearly an important event, representing the removal of the last ambivalent tie to his previous existence. And certainly his female characters, never very attractively presented, become in subsequent plays the victims of a no longer thinly disguised sexual disgust on Orton's part:

SGT. MATCH: Only women are permitted to examine
                female suspects.
PRENTICE: Doesn't that breed discontent in the force?
SGT. MATCH: Among the single men there's a certain
                amount of bitterness. Married men who
                are familiar with the country are glad to be
                let off extra map-reading.
                        (What the Butler Saw, p. 406)

Orton took back to London with him one memento of his mother, a memento that emphasises the reality that the world of *Loot* was for him. "Leonie and I spent part of the afternoon throwing out cupboards full of junk collected over the years; magazines, photographs, Christmas cards. I found a cup containing a pair of false teeth and threw it in a dustbin. Then I discovered they belonged to my father. I had to rescue them. I found my mother's teeth in a drawer. I kept them. To amaze the cast of *Loot*."[8] This strange legacy—their falsity and their appetite, Rance, in *What the Butler Saw*, might well argue, representing the sexual duality of Orton's mother—was a deliberately coarse affront to finer sensibilities, a head-on collision between his old world and his new. The urge to shock is apparent in all Orton's work, but it is not until the final, unrevised play, *What the Butler Saw*, that he really begins to concentrate his attention on a 60's London audience without a backward glance at Leicester. "I'm from the gutter," Orton once told Peggy Ramsay, his agent, "and don't you ever forget it because I won't."[9]

Orton was not a great structural innovator. In general he used and abused the theatrical models that were to hand, and most of his recorded comments on his own dramatic techniques give the feeling of being written after the event, of being rationalisations rather than pointing towards any cohesive theory. The plotting of plays perplexed rather than interested him, and he would frequently make major changes up to and beyond the first night. Kenneth Williams was reduced to despair as the opening of *Loot* approached: "I'm now worried about the play—it seems a random collection of bits with no sense of wholeness... I can't see any sense of construction in the piece."[10] What was happening in this instance was that Orton's increasing fascination with the figure of Truscott altered the balance of the plot almost daily; and this obsessive rewriting, in particular involving radical changes of the plays' endings, assumed ever larger proportions as his career developed. The problem was, in essence, that he was far more interested in the first part of the comic game, turning the world upside-down in a festive interlude, than he was in its traditional counterpart, putting the pieces together again at the end. Orton's fascination with the anarchic potential of human behaviour made any firm resolution of the plot narrative difficult. There is a plot which must be resolved, but it does not appear that it matters much what the conclusion is, as long as it brings the particular events to a point of *stasis*. Orton does not wish us to see his plays as moral structures, still less in terms of a process of discovery about the characters and their motivations. The plot is simply a convenient peg on which to hang his own obsessions.

The point is emphasised if we consider the two main areas that Orton turned to for his dramatic models. They are, chiefly for his early work, the plays of the European and, to some extent, the English 'Absurdists,' and above all to the first produced plays of Harold Pinter; and, in his later work, a broad tradition of farce. Orton's first productions, *The Ruffian on the*

Stair and *Entertaining Mr Sloane* (1964) owe much to Pinter's *The Birth-day Party* (1958) and *The Room* (1960); indeed the opening of the original radio version of *The Ruffian* is taken almost word for word from that of Pinter's first play,[11] and the format of the room taken over by sinister intruders is broadly that of Orton's first two plays. However, it is likely that Pinter, at the beginning of *The Birthday Party,* is himself evoking the opening of Ionesco's *The Bald Prima-Donna* (1956), which opens with the middle-class Mr and Mrs Smith discussing their supper: "Goodness! Nine o'clock! This evening for supper we had soup, fish, cold ham and mashed potatoes and a good English salad, and we had English beer to drink. The children drank English water. We had a very good meal this evening. And that's because we are English, because we live in a suburb of London and because our name is Smith."[12] Certainly the supposedly logical way that Truscott establishes Fay's guilt in *Loot* is reminiscent of Mr and Mrs Martin's tortuous process of deduction later in the play by which they conclude that they must be married to each other. It is not important to establish particular links: from 1956 onward, the French and European 'Absurdists' were beginning to be produced in London, and there are many examples of the absurd deflation of suburban life that were available to both Pinter and Orton.[13]

The most significant one is probably Max Frisch's *The Fire-Raisers* (1961 at the Royal Court), a play in which the respectable burghers invite the mysterious arsonists to share their house, keeping up their respectable life in spite of their certain knowledge of the consequences of their invitation. The connections with Pinter's contemporaneous work are obvious enough: "The world is full of surprises. A door can open at any moment and someone will come in. We'd love to know who it is, we'd love to know exactly what he has on his mind and why he comes in, but how often do we."[14] But the intrusion into the room in Orton's plays is not into a world that could be remotely described as respectable, suburban or middle-class, nor is there any attempt, as in Pinter, to cloak the motives of the intruders in mystery. Orton stressed the point in his production notes to the Royal Court when the revised *Ruffian* was being staged: "The play is not written naturalistically, but it must be directed and acted with absolute *realism* ... Unless it's real it won't be funny. Everything the characters say is true. MIKE has murdered the boy's brother, JOYCE is an ex-call girl, WILSON has an incestuous relationship with his brother, WILSON does provoke MIKE into murdering him. The play mustn't be presented as an example of the now out-dated 'mystery' school—*vide* early Pinter. Everything is as clear as the most reactionary *Telegraph* reader could wish. There is a beginning, a middle and an end."[15] Orton's use of the model rejects the idea of the settled norm being invaded by a sinister abnorm; disorder, in conventional societal terms, is already present, and the doors open, as they do increasingly regularly, on clearly articulated explanations.

Given this, it is not surprising that the 'invaded room' model, which is to some extent still in evidence in *What the Butler Saw* (1969), would be further modified towards farce—the ridiculous mechanics of plot moving the audience away from any possibility of a moral evaluation of the characters' acts or motivations. On his first entrance in the last play, Rance asks, "Why are there so many doors. Was the house designed by a lunatic?" (p. 376). It is a question which not only emphasises the function of the psychiatric clinic in the play—a mad-house with doors for all tastes; it takes us back to the play's epigram, from Tourneur's *The Revenger's Tragedy*: "Surely we're all mad people, and they /Whom we think, are not." Farce, as Orton understood it, was a perfect medium. It allowed for a complete abandonment of a naturalistic paraphernalia of plot and character— although he continued to insist that the plays should be performed naturalistically—in favour of a world in which the repressions and sublimations of life are allowed fully-articulated play. The world that he first presented in *What the Butler Saw* is a true Freudian nightmare of unleashed sexual repression, free from the burdens of respectability or convention. It is civilisation without its clothes. Indeed it is Dr Prentice's inability to admit to his attempt at the only comparatively straightforward heterosexual act in the play that sets things in motion. The wife he would deceive has just returned from a meeting of a club "primarily for lesbians," during the proceedings of which she has availed herself of the body of the hotel porter, Nicholas Beckett, who is about to demand money from her for photographs taken during the event; having himself spent a large part of the previous evening molesting an entire hotel corridor of school-girls. Normality is never the norm in this play; as in the brothel in Genet's *The Balcony,* the clinic converts hidden fantasy into living reality. "Marriage excuses no one the freaks' roll-call," the policeman, Match, assures Prentice when he protests his status as a proof of his innocence (p. 409). What follows is a sort of sexual *Bartholomew Fair* in which clothing is first removed and then redistributed in a confusion of sexual roles—the whole business being presided over by a lunatic bureaucrat, Rance, who offers a succession of psychoanalytical explanations of the characters' behaviour, the unlikelihood of which is only outreached by the truths of the case.

What the Butler Saw is a flawed play. It needs, and would certainly have received, considerable rewriting—in particular, the tedious running gag about the lost penis from the statue of Winston Churchill which is eventually used to bring proceedings to a halt, takes us back to the world of sacred cows, and could easily be removed. However, what it promises is a redefinition of farce, a complete liberation of *libido* in a glorious celebration of chaos and *fin-de-civilisation*. " 'It's the only way to smash the wretched civilisation,' I said, making a mental note to hot-up *What the Butler Saw* when I came to re-write... Yes. Sex is the only way to infuriate them. Much more fucking and they'll be screaming hysterics in next to no time."[16] But sex is both the subject of the play and the vehicle which suggests potentially more serious matters. The tradition of farce which Orton had inherited was diluted and trivial; it confirmed rather than questioned the assumptions of its audience. Orton's unusually perceptive analysis of the situation suggests that, given time, he might well have developed into a major dramatist.

> "I am a great admirer of Ben Travers, in particular, but the boundaries he set to present-day farce are really very narrow. As I understand it, farce originally was very close to tragedy, and differed only in the *treatment* of its themes—themes like rape, bastardy, prostitution. But you can't have farce about rape any longer. French farce goes as far as adultery, but by Ben Travers time it was only *suspected* adultery, which turned out to have been innocuous after all... A lot of farces today are still based on the preconceptions of half a century ago. But we must now accept the fact that, for instance, people *do* have sexual relations outside marriage: a 30's farce is still acceptable because it is distanced by its period, but a modern farce which merely nurses the old outworn assumptions is cushioning people against reality. And this, of course, is just what the commercial theatre usually does. In theory there is no subject which could *not* be treated farcically—just as the Greeks were prepared to treat any subject farcically. But in practice farce has become a very restricted form indeed."

Orton's awareness of the proximity of farce and tragedy, both as theatrical modes and as mirrors of psychological reaction to chaos, points to what he was attempting in *What the Butler Saw*; but it also highlights the structural weakness, in particular its lack of any resolve. Orton seems only fascinated by the chaos and with a sense of personal liberation achieved by its embracement. Whilst the plays of such as Tourneur and Webster move easily from farce to tragedy, the presentation of chaos counterpointed by a sense of moral order, in Orton's work the possible transition to a tragic sense of farce is never a possibility. The characters do end the play bloodied, if unbowed, but that transition is purely mechanical. As Orton argues, farce has become a purely escapist medium, on the run from precisely that which it had originally presented—the disturbing manifestations of the human consciousness which threaten the stability of the social order. Farce, from the 30's through Brian Rix's Whitehall antics, no longer really explored the subconscious fears of public self-revelation; it provided a safety-valve, allowing the audience to laugh off nothing more important than losing one's trousers in public. Thematically, Orton moves farce towards a properly Freudian consideration of its roots, but the connection between plot and character is never satisfactorily made. In the end, we cannot take any of it very seriously. It may offend, it may amuse, but it does not involve. Orton has frequently been compared to Wilde,[18] and it is an instructive comparison. In one respect at least he is completely different. Where Wilde invites us to see beyond the brittle and studied brilliance of his characters' dialogue, the hollowness underneath, Orton presents all his cards directly at the audience. What we are being shown is the underneath. What Orton is moving towards is the presentation of a pre-civilised world in which the awakened subconscious at large in a decadent society makes each individual a 'minority group.' The problem is that the action takes place entirely on the surface, and it is as a manipulator of the restricted codes of opposing languages of ordinary discourse that Orton, on what he has left us, has finally to be measured.

II

'Leggo!
Geroff!
Yaroo!'
And then of course;
'These stentorian cries echoed down the corridor of the Upper Shell.' The novice should begin every school story with exactly those words. In the next sentence he must introduce his principal characters, a bunch of bold, breathless, exclamatory, ink-stained, beastly, Dickensian-surnamed boys with their caps awry, their lines undone, pets in their desks, paper pellets in their pockets, and barbarous though innocuous oaths on their unrazored lips.
But let us introduce a new element:
'Leggo!
Geroff!
Yaroo!
These stentorian cries echoed down the corridor of the Upper Shell as Tom Happy and his inseparables, known to all Owlhurst as 'The Filthy Five,' lurched arm-in-arm out of Mrs. Motherwell's fully licensed tuckshop.'
There you have a beginning at once conventional and startling. The reader is at your mercy. And you can continue, within the

accepted framework and using only the loudest, minutest and most formal vocabulary, to describe such going-on as the formation, by Tom Happy, of the Owlhurst suicide club and the setting-up of a hookah in the boothole.

(Dylan Thomas, *How to begin a short story.*)

'Conventional and startling' is an apt description of the linguistic antics of Joe Orton, as is 'formal.' But Dylan Thomas is deceiving his readers as to the flexibility of a formal and conventional mode of speech; his choice of 'goings-on' sounds random enough, a mere example of the total license possible to the author who can train his audience to respond to certain conventions. In fact, suicide clubs and hookahs sneak, via Robert Louis Stevenson and *The Arabian Nights,* into most schoolboy sensibilities, even perhaps the relatively infantile ones of Tom Happy addicts. But substitute 'bourgeois revolution,' 'primal therapy' or indeed any activity which carries with it its own linguistic conventions and it becomes clear just how limited Tom Happy's prospects are.

Orton is similarly deceptive. Although his plays incensed conservative theatre-goers by their 'permissiveness,' they in fact present a world in which activity is rigidly restricted and often incomprehensible to the participants because they lack a rational vocabulary in which to discuss their behaviour. Orton himself came from a background which was cruelly circumscribed and linguistically deprived. At school he could barely frame a coherent sentence. "He couldn't express himself. He'd get so far in talking with you and then, if you didn't understand immediately, he would become impatient. He would close up, move away, go back into his world" reports one of his teachers.[19] One might predict from this, the violence of Orton's plays and of his life, but his elaborate language, instead of betraying an inarticulate frustration, stands apart from this linguistic deprivation and satirises it. He made malicious use of the pretension that, in his mother's case, ran alongside the deprivation; from his education at Clark's College he learned the rococo language of commerce and the limits imposed by linguistic convention.

This discovery is explored in his early work; compare the first, radio version of *The Ruffian on the Stair* with its most apparent source, Pinter's *The Birthday Party:*

MEG: I've got your cornflakes ready. *(SHE DISAPPEARS AND REAPPEARS.)*
Here's your cornflakes.
(HE RISES AND TAKES THE PLATE FROM HER, SITS AT THE TABLE, PROPS UP THE PAPER AND BEGINS TO EAT. MEG ENTERS BY THE KITCHEN DOOR)
Are they nice?

PETEY: Very nice.
MEG: I thought they'd be nice.

SCENE ONE. A ROOM.
JOYCE: Did you enjoy your breakfast?
MIKE: What?
JOYCE: Did you enjoy your breakfast? The egg was nice wasn't it? The eggs are perfect now I have the timer. Have you noticed? (PAUSE) The marmalade was nice. Did it go down well?
MIKE: The egg was nice.
JOYCE: (SHARPLY) That's what I said. (PAUSE) That marmalade was your favourite brand. Are you still collecting the Gollies?[20]

Orton later rewrote the play to remove the more obvious echoes of Pinter. Even here, however, it is plain that the difference between the extracts goes deeper than the menu. The Pinter extract moves slowly. Complex actions take place, during which nothing is spoken. This in itself sets up a tension between the banal content of the words and the emotional forces which underlie them. If we are aware of the dullness and boredom of Meg and Petey's existence, we are also aware of their mutual concern, and, in the solicitous repetition of the talismanic 'nice,' of Meg's role as mother-figure which will be developed later in all its strengths and limitations. The play depends throughout upon subtext.

Orton, by contrast, has changed the pace of his very similar exchanges simply by putting them in a different medium. Radio cannot support the dead air time required to exchange plates, set up a defensive newspaper, leave and enter rooms. With the sharper pace the sense of trouble taken on another's behalf disappears and Joyce's repeated question, which Mike can't be bothered to listen to, becomes harassment. In place of the timeless assertions of 'niceness,' Orton puts phrases which locate Joyce precisely in a defined world. The query 'did it go down well?' strikes an accurate note of lower middle class pseudo-gentility; as Nancy Mitford would put it, it is non-U, a term which might be inscribed over the door of the Orton inferno. The placing is not one of class. "The eggs are perfect now I have the timer. Have you noticed" has the aggressively joyful domesticity of a TV commercial, a note reinforced by the 'Gollies,' which suggest not only the brand of marmalade Joyce buys but also the exact quality of emptiness her life possesses. No Pinter character, however bored, collects paper golliwogs from jam jars; his creations are closer to basic things; food, sleep, survival are what preoccupy them, however physically comfortable their circumstance. A kind of spiritual levelling takes place in a Pinter play, and we are not primarily aware of, say, Davies as a tramp or of the married couple in *A Slight Ache* as well-off. Orton's characters have a specific kind of poverty, symbolised by the 'Gollies'; they live out their lives surrounded by cheap trash—Kath's sexy nightdress or her Bombay vase; the tasteless wreaths of *Loot*. That Orton felt poverty resided in possessions as much as in the lack of them is plain from *The Good and Faithful Servant,* in which the stopping clock and disintegrating toaster are constant reminders of the crushing dehumanisation of an industry that throws its workers away like disposable tissues.

Objects are an integral part of the Orton vocabulary. Macabre props such as the late Mrs McLeavy, George Buchanan's false arm or the pieces of assorted corpses in *Funeral Games* have a speaking presence as well as a function in the plot; they serve to bring people and things down to the same level; Buchanan is an object to his firm, and they fit him with a new arm as if he were a machine needing a spare part. The money in *Loot* becomes, by its contact and identification with the body, a person of sorts; the statue of Churchill and Geraldine's step-mother are inextricably mixed, bronze and flesh together. It is curious, too, that for all their meanness of spirit, Orton's characters are always proffering gifts, or at least bribes—the slippers trimmed with Leeds fluff that Fay appropriates on Mrs McLeavy's death prior to stepping more metaphorically into her shoes; the white brushed nylon T-shirt Ed offers Sloane as an inducement to enter his service; or the more abstract 'post-sponge attentions' Tessa renders McCorquodale in *Funeral Games*. Gifts provide the characters with a means of communication not unlike their verbal methods—highly artificial, even elaborate, and with a sort of seedy sensuality; but for all their pretensions, it is clear enough what the gifts are about.

> HAL: Twenty per cent.
> FAY: Thirty three and a third.
> HAL: You can keep her wedding ring.
> FAY: Is it valuable?
> HAL: Very.
> FAY: I'll add it to my collection. I already have seven by right of conquest. Thirty three and a third and the wedding ring. (p. 225)

In Orton, all is spoken; ambiguity rarely enters into the texture of his work. This is not, of course, to imply that his characters 'mean what they say' in the way that, say, Osborne's do. In Osborne's diatribes we are always aware of a belief behind the words, a commitment to what is being said, and indeed to the process of saying it; Left or Right, Jimmy Porter and Pamela Orme feel that what they say matters, that other people may, and they certainly do, need their rhetoric. Orton's characters rarely speak from a powerful impulse; occasionally they will perform an action as if driven by intolerable pressure, such as Buchanan's smashing of the clock and toaster. Generally though, even the most violent and extraordinary acts are performed as if they required little internal reflection. Sloane's murder of Kemp is counterpointed by the calm words, "You bring this upon yourself. All this could've been avoided" (p. 126). "Bury her naked? My own mum?" says Hal, "It's a Freudian nightmare" (p. 209). Lest there be any doubt of the tone of voice required, Orton adds a stage-direction: "HE GOES TO THE MIRROR AND COMBS HIS HAIR." The delivery does not neutralise the horror, but it stresses the paradox and makes laughter possible. This kind of delivery is virtually demanded by many lines, despite Orton's insistence that *Loot* be played as naturalistically as possible. Like Sheridan or Congreve or Wilde, all the dynamics of Orton's dialogue are too near the surface for naturalism; the impulse to speak comes not from underlying emotional rhythms but from the sentence structure.

That structure is something unique in English comedy. The most noted exponents of artificial comedy grounded their outrageousness in the purest syntax:

> *GWENDOLEN:* Ernest, we may never be married. From the expression on Mama's face I fear we never shall. Few parents nowadays pay any regard to what their children say to them. The old-fashioned respect for the young is fast dying out. Whatever influence I ever had over Mama, I lost at the age of three. But although she may prevent us from becoming man and wife, and I may marry someone else, and marry often, nothing that she can possibly do can alter my eternal devotion to you.[21]

This is English as it is never spoken, so perfect is its structure. Each clause is clear and distinct, allowing the voice to inflect upwards so that we lose no part of the build-up to the final punch of the sentence. The eccentricity lies only in what is being said, in the reversal of expectation (for we are all used to these sentiments used by the old of the young) and in the precise placing of 'and marry often' to extract maximum piquancy from the idea. One is not aware, when listening to this speech for the first time, how its effect is achieved; the syntax, remarkable only for its obedience to textbook norms, is a filter through which the joke is transmitted; it never calls attention to itself, never varies between characters; even Wilde's servants speak in the same style:

| ALGERNON: | Why is it that at a bachelor's establishment the servants invariably drink the champagne: I ask merely for information. |
| LANE: | I attribute it to the superior quality of the wine, sir. I have often observed that in married households the champagne is rarely of a first-rate brand.[22] |

While this language is artificial, Orton's is synthetic, a composite of several idiosyncratic styles. The term Orton favoured was 'collage':

> It does have a collage quality. Shakespeare and the Elizabethans did the same thing, I mean you have absolute realism and then you get high poetry, its just language. I think you should use the language of your own age and every bit of it. They always go on about poetic drama and they think you have to go off on some high flown fantasy, but it isn't poetic drama, it's everything, it's the language is use at the time. I have to be very careful in the way that I write, not to let it become sort of a mannerism, it could very easily become a mannerism.[23]

The synthetic quality of the dialogue is shared by most of his characters; with the possible exception of Sloane, who is a disturbingly amoral force, a kind of animated instinct, they lack spontaneity; they are put together on an assembly line of trends and unquestioningly accepted social values; amalgams rather than personalities, whose constituent parts are easily traceable.

Large portions of their speech and their natures are glued together from the popular press. "We were refused permission to wed" yell the couple from *The Erpingham Camp.* "We defied the ban on our love" (p. 302). They are not only stating a fact, they are defining themselves, and by using the language of the 'News of the World' asserting their value and superiority. The Sunday paper tendency is most marked in the areas one might expect, sex and crime. To the cheap press of the fifties and sixties, as to the Edgar Lustgarten B-movies Orton also evokes, crime meant a specific approach—that is, via the police. "You have before you a man who is quite a personage in his way—Truscott of the Yard. Have you never heard of Truscott? The man who tracked down the limbless girl killer? Or was that sensation before your time?" (p. 250). The television series *Fabian of Scotland Yard* crystallised an already existing tendency among British police memoirs: no autobiographically minded officer of the period worth his salt would not be 'of the Yard' for the Sunday press. The phrase is a perfect combination for the creation of an image—the 'of' implying romance, shades of Lawrence of Arabia or Gordon of Khartoum, while the homely 'yard' gives a reassuringly cosy touch which suggests that, for all his glamour, the policeman is still the guardian of our domestic bliss. The newspapers' orientation towards the police in crime reporting meant two things. First, there was a heavy concentration on the act of detection rather than on the crime and its causes, a tendency Orton parodies here, where the most obviously interesting fact of the case is passed over for some police jargon:

HAL:	Who would kill a limbless girl?
TRUSCOTT:	She was the killer.
HAL:	How did she do it if she was limbless?
TRUSCOTT:	I'm not prepared to answer that to anyone outside the profession. (p. 250)

Truscott discusses his deductive powers in the newspaper clichés that spring ultimately from Conan Doyle: "My methods of deduction can be learned by anyone with a keen eye and a quick brain. When I shook your hand I felt a roughness on one of your wedding rings. A roughness I associate with powder burns and salt. The two together spell a gun and sea air. When found on a wedding ring only one solution is possible" (p. 214). Sherlock Holmes, however, invariably announced his conclusions by asking questions and eliciting answers or providing them himself after a suitable interval. The cheap press substituted words like 'associate' and 'spell' which mean that the reader arrives at the solution more quickly, and this casts its reflected glory upon the actual speed of the deduction. When the words are spoken on stage the speed becomes that of parody, a patent image-boosting device by Truscott. The second result of the police-geared report is a curious detachment achieved by retaining the first person for an account of the deductive process, while the actual arrest and events surrounding it 'adopt' a protagonist such as 'the law'; or employ a royal plural, which Orton allows to slip when Truscott is carried away by his personal delight in violence: "Understand this, lad. You can't get away with cheek. Kids nowadays treat any kind of authority as a challenge. If you oppose me in my duty, I'll kick those teeth through the back of your head" (p. 235). Orton parodies the allusions to Duty, Law, Authority: "The water board doesn't need a warrant to enter private houses. And so I availed myself of this loophole in the law" (p. 251), as he parodies the detached use of the passive voice to evade personal responsibility:

TRUSCOTT:	There's more to this than meets the eye. I'm tempted to believe that you did have a hand in the bank job. Yes. I shall inform my superior officer. He will take whatever steps he thinks fit. I may be required to make an arrest.

FAY:	The water board can't arrest people.
TRUSCOTT:	They can in certain circumstances.
FAY:	What circumstances?
TRUSCOTT:	I'm not prepared to reveal the inner secrets of the water board to a member of the general public. (p. 234)

It would be a mild joke, no more, simply to substitute the words 'water board' for 'police' rather as Huxley uses the term 'Ford' for 'Lord' in *Brave New World*. What gives the comedy its bite is the fact that Truscott's moralising stance is possible for him while conducting a piece of unethical deception; he clearly spends his time creating loopholes rather than finding them. The glamour that obfuscated police cases in the press was anathema to Orton: "I think it's very unhealthy for a society to love the police the way the English do. When you have that kind of affection for authority, you begin to have the makings of a police state."[24] The lovingly gilded parody is often shot through with real violence. As he rewrote *Loot,* Orton became obsessed with the exploits of Detective Sergeant Harold Challenor; Challenor became the subject of the first Police enquiry into Police behaviour under the terms of the 1964 Police Act; his evident lunacy was chronicled week by week in the same papers that had employed a Truscottesque vocabulary in his praise; crime reporting was never to be quite the same again. Phrases actually uttered by Challenor found their way into *Loot.* "You're fucking nicked, my old beauty" says Truscott to McLeavy (p. 273). Naturally, it was to an innocent man that Challenor used these words, a demonstrator on whom he had planted a brick. The extra dimension of violence this added to the character made it possible for Truscott to swing in seconds from officialese spiced with mild wit—"The theft of an article of clothing is excusable. But policeman, like red squirrels, must be protected" (p. 244)—to an overt threat of physical force: "If I ever hear you accuse the police of using violence on a prisoner in custody again, I'll take you down to the station and beat the eyes out of your head" (p. 246). The sudden descent from formal speech has frightening implications. In the Wilde extract quoted earlier, there may be no emotional subtext, but there are unspoken rules—about marriage, about society—which the content, not the form, of the speech questions. Here the rules have in themselves a violence which breaks the form to reveal itself; it suggests that the crime-writers' normal 'Yard' jargon endorses concealment and hypocrisy, that the 'rules' will never change.

Much of the sexual language of the fifties' and sixties' cheap press had the same function of preserving the status quo. Magazines peddled a selection of genteel euphemisms which served to give the illusion that crumbling sexual taboos were still stable. "A girl is more likely to lose a boy than keep him if she lets him have his way: she begins by losing her own self-respect and ends up by losing him too" pontificated the teenage magazine *Honey* in 1963, when Orton was already at work on *Sloane*; despite articles on 'how to get a man' it implied that the getting involved some danger, warning that one must not go too far for "It is one of the deepest instincts to want purity in a bride." Kath subscribes to the simpering doublethink, rousing Sloane while pretending to herself that he is the one with the uncontrollable urges, which must be prevented: "You're all the same. I must be careful of you. Have me naked on the floor if I give you a chance. If my brother was to know ... he's such a possessive man. Would you like to go to bed?" (p. 79). The ambiguity of the whole speech—is 'have me naked' abbreviated from 'you would have me naked,' or is the verb imperative?—captures perfectly the double standard of the agony column. As Truscott slides from rulebook formality to threats, Kath skids from the lush, torrid prose of the paperback romance (in which the heroine is always a virgin and the hero never is)—"He too was handsome and in the prime of manhood. Can you wonder I fell." (p. 94), and "He sent me the letter I treasure" (p. 108)—to what one could describe as coarseness at one remove, euphemisms which have no actual concealment value but relegate sex to the nursery: "I'm in the rude under this dress ... you wanted to see if my titties were all my own" (p. 78–9). Orton satirises, too, a tendency to infantilism found in the magazine-morality that curiously equates sex and intelligence. Edith, in *The Good and Faithful Servant,* tells Ray, "I was very silly, and Mr. Buchanan behaved badly" (p. 165). The avoidance of sexual terms at all costs reaches the nadir of bathos in Buchanan's definition of it as a 'group activity' which could easily be replaced by Ludo (p. 176). It is debatable whether the *words* used by Orton's characters actually shape their morals or whether their woolly moral thinking leads to their attenuated vocabularies. Ed uses a classic phrase of the lazy reviewer when he rebukes Sloane's attack on Kath with "this is gratuitous violence" (p. 146), but the remark has a sinister double edge; Ed is not altogether averse to violence, and uses the term 'gratuitous' in a sense far more literal than is common these days.

The attitudes Orton enshrines in his sexual collages are often termed 'middle-class,' but it must be made clear that this is a useful adjective rather than a precise social location. At the time Orton was writing, lip service was paid to the values he satirised at all levels, and public figures went into considerable contortions to make this apparent. There are times when Orton's mandarin prose sounds like the purest realism:

Q: And it does not finish there, because if we can go on to the next page almost at the end of the first long paragraph 'womb' appears?

A: Yes.

Q: Then a little bit further down page 141, towards the bottom, at the end of the longish paragraph, the two words 'womb' and 'bowels' appear again?

A: Yes.

Q: Is that really what you would call expert, artistic writing?

It would not come as a stylistic shock if Rance's rejoinder to Prentice's assertion of his heterosexuality—"I do wish you wouldn't use those Chaucerian words" (p. 411)—were to appear in this physiological/literary analysis, but the quotation comes from the trial of D. H. Lawrence's *Lady Chatterley's Lover* in 1960, which took some weeks to decide that the words 'womb' and 'bowels' were indeed suitable for the public at large to read, and might even, like Sloane, be 'cultured' or artistic.' It is possible to track down other sources for Orton's 'collages'; much of *The Good and Faithful Servant,* for instance, originates from works' magazines using their jargon about 'the eve of a well-earned rest' to convey the unattractive aspects of retirement; or the retirement speech notable chiefly for its formulaic applicability to anyone over 65: "He quickly became known for his speed and intolerance of any work which was the least 'slip-shod' ... George has had his share of life's tragedies ... his cheery laugh echoed once again through the canteen ... " (p. 159–60). Or one might cite the heavily parodied dialect of the Catholic Church which pervades *Loot,* largely in the persons of various imaginary organisations like the Fraternity of the Little Sisters and the Knights of the Order of Saint Gregory. Basically, however, all these sources have a common factor, the desire to preclude questions. They laud the *status quo,* whether legal, religious or social; they imply, some actively stress, the need for obedience to authority to preserve it; and, by employing a highly specific vocabulary, they make their assertions difficult to refute. It is hard to explode even the most ill-founded point made within a closed linguistic system; terms have to be defined, new concepts introduced, which need words from outside the normal vocabulary of that system; and, of course, among Orton's characters there are few who are linguistically aware. This means that few possibilities for action are open to them; even fewer possibilities, for actions which they can commit without hypocrisy. They may be morally corrupt, but they are not permissive because their word-systems do not permit them to be. They are trapped in a web of pseudo-genteel language which makes it impossible for them to look their own actions in the face. Kath can accept the murder of 'Dadda' and the sharing of Sloane's body as long as she can phrase it appropriately to herself. "See, Ed, he hasn't lost respect for me," she says of Sloane (p. 147). This not only reduces the moral aspect of the situation to one area, the sexual, but substitutes a conveniently vague term like 'respect' for a more precise one like 'marriage,' 'adultery' or even 'love'; respect can mean whatever she wants it to mean, and so the state of affairs at the end of *Sloane* can perpetuate itself without the need to ask questions, as long as she can stretch the term 'respect' to provide a moral blanket. Fay and Hal plan the eventual murder of McLeavy behind a marzipan coat of religious sentiment. "We'll bury your father with your mother. That'll be nice for him, won't it?" (p. 275). The future tense is chilling, but hardly noticeable, so easily does it roll off Fay's lips. Time and again the characters stress the need to keep up appearances—it is the last statement made in *Loot*. It might seem crude and obvious if it were not for one fact, that Orton's characters are paradoxically sincere in their hypocrisy. Another strain runs through the plays, as obsessive as the need to keep up appearances—the need for truth. *Funeral Games* is concerned with the attempt to bring fact in line with fiction, even to the extent of murdering someone because the lie runs that way. Hal in *Loot* cannot tell a lie. "It's against my nature" (p. 207)—he tells Dennis, cheerfully jeopardising the whole plot in the interests of truth. *What the Butler Saw* abounds in references to confession and confidentiality. "I have to ask you a question which may cause you embarrassment. Please remember that I'm a doctor," preface an enquiry as to Geraldine's shorthand speeds (p. 365). "I'm going to speak frankly and with complete candour," says Mrs. Prentice before relating the linen-cupboard episode (p. 374). These efforts at honesty, combined irresistibly with the urge to euphemism and evasion, suggest that for Orton's characters, words have the same concealing intent as the many doors of more orthodox farce; they lurk behind secondhand phrases as Brian Rix lurks in cupboards, aware that they are hiding something but never noticing how deep the deception actually does go. This is perhaps the major difference between Orton and Wilde. In both cases the dialogue lacks psychological depth, but Wilde's characters are aware of their own wit. They will never change, for they do not develop, but it is not especially desirable that they should; Orton's characters don't know they are ridiculous; although questions of style sometimes obsess them, the reasons for the obsession are different. "Your style is simple and direct," says Truscott to Fay. "It's a theme which less skillfully handled could've given offence" (p. 255). Miss Prism opted for style rather than sincerity every time, but here the genteel has been elevated to the status of a Great Tradition. Fay deserved the praise for a confession that exploits every traditional trope of the True Confessions magazines—"I have had nothing but heartache ever since....I am sorry for my dreadful crime."

It is precisely the closed linguistic system that makes Orton's plays work, but they work in a way which generally belies the 'permissive' label. To Orton's detractors permissiveness meant immorality, to his admirers—who tend to employ words like 'Dionysiac' and 'rambunctious' it meant freedom—but this is to ignore what is the essential quality of all his plays except, possibly, *What the Butler Saw*. Dionysus is, after all, the harbinger of freedom, and Orton's characters are in cages. One might as well call Emma Bovary Dionysiac. Perhaps in *What the Butler Saw* he does, for the first time, make a comedy of liberation rather than restriction, and here, significantly, the dialogue leans less heavily upon collage. Much of it is stylised and formal, but it is not especially allusive. "Despite all appearances to the contrary, Mrs. Prentice is harder to get into than the reading room at the British Museum" (p. 396), is a line which has the grammatical purity of Wilde, and a similar dependence upon ludicrous verbal juxtaposition. What jargon there is satirises the discipline of psychiatry, whether Laingian—permissive—"The purpose of my husband's clinic isn't to cure, but to liberate and exploit madness" (p. 388)—or Jungian-interpretive—"You're aware of the plant allegory? the rose is a common cipher for a woman" (p. 431). But the fact that there is a choice of psychiatric jargon is in itself more liberating than the strait-jacket terminology of the Church in *Loot*, or the factory in *The Good and Faithful Servant*. The only full-blown collage user in the group is, of course, Dr. Rance, whose style is a maelstrom of professional jargon and Gothic novel lushness: "Lunatics are melodramatic. The subtleties of drama are wasted on them. The ugly shadow of Anti-Christ stalks this house. Having discovered her Father/Lover in Dr. Prentice, the patient replaces him in a psychological reshuffle by the archetypal Father-figure—the Devil himself. Everything is now clear. The final chapters of my book are knitting together: incest, buggery, outrageous women and strange love-cults catering for depraved appetites" (p. 427). This semi-conscious literariness stands out here as it would not in earlier plays. And Rance, of course, is deflated at the end in a way unprecedented in Orton's plays. Having preserved all along the illusion of control over his environment, he finds that all his diagnoses are right, but that they do not lead to the expected tragedies. The characters are delighted to find that they have committed incest and rape as long as it brings them together. At the end of *Butler* we are confronted for the first time in Orton's world with a truly topsy-turvy world. What he would have written subsequently might have continued to employ jargon and collage. But the closed system of the earlier plays could well have opened to a richer, less restricted world which gained in compassion while losing none of its anger.

NOTES

N.B. Dates of plays are for first performance in England.

1. We acknowledge, as any work on Orton must, a general debt for biographical information to John Lahr's invaluable *Prick up Your Ears*, (London: Allen Lane, 1978).

2. All references to Orton's work are page-referenced to Orton, *The Complete Plays* (London: Methuen, 1976), unless otherwise stated.

3. Lahr, p. 48.

4. D.A.N. Jones, 'Common Indecencies,' *New Statesman*, 16 June 1967, p. 854.

5. Lahr, p. 100.

6. Lahr, p. 190.

7. Lahr, p. 61.

8. Lahr, p. 64.

9. Lahr, p. 43.

10. Lahr, p. 240.

11. C.f. Lahr, pp. 158–9 and p. 81 of this article.

12. Eugene Ionesco, *Plays I* (London: Calder & Boyars, 1960), p. 86.

13. A typical example might be Giles Cooper's *Everything in the Garden*.

14. Quoted in Marin Esslin, *The Peopled Wound*, (London: Methuen, 1970).

15. Lahr, p. 157.

16. Lahr, p. 136.

17. Lahr, pp. 225–6.

18. C.f., for instance, D.A.N. Jones, *op. cit.*, p. 853.

19. Lahr, p. 57.

20. (ed.) Bennett Maxwell, *New Radio Drama*, BBC, 1966, p. 197.

21. From Oscar Wilde, *The Importance of Being Earnest*.

22. *Ibid.*

23. Lahr, p. 185.

24. Lahr, pp. 237–8.

Peter Barnes

BERNARD F. DUKORE

In his Introduction to Peter Barnes's *The Ruling Class,* Harold Hobson, then theatre critic of London's *Sunday Times,* declares, "The most exciting thing that can happen to a dramatic critic is when he is suddenly and unexpectedly faced with the explosive blaze of an entirely new talent of a very high order." Such an event, he adds, may "prove a turning point in the drama. . . . "[1] In twenty years, only four playwrights unexpectedly excited him: Samuel Beckett, with *Waiting for Godot;* John Osborne, with *Look Back in Anger;* Harold Pinter, with *The Birthday Party;* and Peter Barnes, with *The Ruling Class.*

Time and critical consensus have confirmed Hobson's assessment of Beckett, who is Irish and more than a generation older than the rest, who are English and of the same generation: born 1929, 1930, and 1931, respectively. Today, Osborne's early promise seems largely unfulfilled and despite the historical importance of *Look Back In Anger,* he appears less prominent than he used to; but Hobson's judgment of Pinter and Barnes remains valid and both have grown in stature. In originality, distinctiveness, theatrical and intellectual power, they tower above all other contemporary English dramatists.

Yet how different they are. Whereas Pinter's drama is not politically orientated, class hatred and a loathing of social, economic, and religious bastions of Western society permeate Barnes's. While both are theatrical, their use of the stage differs. Pinter's art is intense and contractive, like that of Beckett, whom he reveres. Barnes's is full-blown and expansive, like that of Ben Jonson, whom he reveres. Pinter's proscenium-arch stage is an enclosed, confined space, often like a tomb. Barnes's is a show-place, evocative of the amusement-park atmosphere of the pier at the seaside resort Clacton-on-Sea, where he spent most of his youth.[2]

The Ruling Class (1968)[3] did not spring Minerva-like from the head of an Olympian author. Barnes began his writing career in the early 1950s as a film critic, became a story editor for Warwick Films in 1956, and started to write for movies and TV in 1959. Such drama he regards as "assignment work, craft work." Because the writer usually has less influence than the director, producer, or star in these media, he turned to the stage, where he could express his ideas with integrity. After he did so, he realized that the theatre was his true medium, for he thought in theatrical terms. *The Time of the Barracudas* (California, 1963), *Sclerosis* (Edinburgh, 1965), and *Clap Hands, Here Comes Charlie* (written 1966) are apprentice pieces, whose publication he has not permitted. With *The Ruling Class,* he advanced to master.

In addition to composing original plays, Barnes has prepared acting editions of Ben Jonson's comedies, including *The Alchemist* (1970; re-worked, 1977) and *Bartholomew Fair* (1978). Are not the originals "acting editions"? With the passage of time, he points out, words and passages lose their meanings. As editor, he tries—like directors, who do not announce it—"to make the meaning clear to a contemporary audience, but to make the changes as vivid and as poetic as the original. As I've dealt mainly with comedy, it's important that the jokes are funny and you understand them as they're being said, not with a glossary afterwards. I attempt to bring the footnotes into the text." With plays he considers flawed, he extends his role as editor into collaborator, and has adapted such works as *The Devil is an Ass* (1973; reworked 1977) and *Eastward Ho!* (1973). His adaptations also include drama not written in English, notably Wedekind's *Lulu* (which combines *Earth Spirit* and *Pandora's Box,* 1970) and *Frontiers of Farce* (Feydeau's *The Purging* and Wedekind's *The Singer,* 1976).

What have the Jacobeans, Wedekind, and Feydeau in common? Barnes's response describes his own plays too: "Extreme theatricality. They have huge size, passion, and extremes of emotion." Like some of his critics, he calls himself Jacobean. Opposed to naturalism, he regards Jacobean drama as "a strong tradition in English literature. But we lost the golden pathway, which is theatrical, poetic—theatrically poetic—and richly textured. When we see it, we recognize it in an enlarged, inflamed, and glorious way, touching us, but not actually a photographic reproduction of the life we lead."

Such affinities notwithstanding, Barnes's plays are *sui generis*. Let us examine them individually, then in terms of their distinctive theatrical style.

Their titles indicate their subject matter. *The Ruling Class* dramatizes the nature of that class, its values and viciousness, its perversions and pernicious charm. The existence of a privileged, ruling class depends upon the existence of unprivileged, ruled classes; authority requires submission and the maintenance of the status quo. Is not such a society lunatic? In the play, its leading exponent is insane. Does it not pervert humanity? The madman's father relaxes by wearing a tutu ballet skirt, a three-cornered hat, and a sword, then obtains sexual thrills by pretending to hang himself (he accidentally succeeds). Are the words it uses to impose upon the masses and bolster its own self-esteem gibberish? Barnes has members of the ruling class misquote Shakespeare and recite a popular nonsense song ("Mairzy Doats"). Does its perpetuation intimidate and kill members of the lower classes, and subdue possible revolt? The play's peers do so.

The Ruling Class revolves around the fourteenth Earl of Gurney, who on an August 25th (the birthday, Barnes knows, of mad Ludwig of Bavaria) received the revelation that he was God. As his psychiatrist, Dr. Herder, explains, he has delusions of grandeur, and since he belongs to England's ruling class, the only being he considers grander is God. Disliking his name, Jack, he substitutes such titles as "My lordship," "the Naz," and "J. C." (18, 24). Although the ruling class employs religion to maintain its powers, his relatives —including a bishop—fear he may take seriously the teachings of Jesus. "Pomp and riches, pride and property will have to be lopped off," says J. C. "All men are brothers. Love makes all equal. The mighty must bow down before the pricks of the louse-ridden rogues." Such a declaration upsets Sir Charles Gurney more than Jack's belief that he is God. To call for the destruction of property and the equality of all men is proof that "he's not only *mad,* he's *Bolshie!*" (24–25). No matter that J. C. calls the lower classes "louse-ridden rogues," no matter that he continues to employ a butler, Tucker, who brings him tea while he meditates on a huge cross—both revelatory of his essentially aristocratic nature—to consider social equality is subversive.

Serving the interests of the ruling class, for he aims to make people adjust to society, Herder cures J. C.'s delusion that our world is based on the idea that God is love. Because two people cannot be God, Herder confronts him with a rival madman, McKyle, who considers himself to be the Old Testament God of vengeance. McKyle rids J. C. of the belief that he is God.

But Jack, a name he now accepts, substitutes one form of madness for another. When he jokingly remarks that a cousin who thought he was Christ would not be a political asset to Dinsdale, who hopes to win a seat in the House of Commons, Dinsdale —referring to Edward Heath—responds, "I don't know. The Tory Leader's the son of a carpenter, after all." Jack is surprised: "Lord Salisbury's a carpenter's son?" (75). His reference to a Conservative Prime Minister of the previous century hints what he soon confirms, that he believes he lives in 1888, when the ruling class held great power. He thinks he is Jack the Ripper. Jack apostrophizes the class system, wins the admiration of those he appalled when he called for love, subdues subversion (he frames the secret radical Tucker for a crime he himself committed), inspires the devotion of the police who serve his interests, delivers a rousing speech in behalf of his class's values, and kills his lower-class wife, who had done her job (provided a male heir).

Although Jack is mad, he is not essentially different from the other peers. The play is named after his class, not him. His skirt-wearing father is also looney. As Tucker says, Jack is "a nut-case all right, but then so are most of these titled flea-bags" (37). While Jack's final speech—which calls for the restoration of flogging and hanging the lower classes when the social order requires such measures—is shocking, other lords express similar views and the basis of Dinsdale's electoral campaign is "the reintroduction of the death penalty" (89). He and Jack, in the House of Lords, will "work as a team," for "We think alike on lots of things" (108). The main concern of the former Etonian who certifies Jack's sanity is "property and its proper administration" (82).

Whereas *The Ruling Class* provides a view of the top, *Leonardo's Last Supper* (1969) offers one further down. Property and authority concern not only the ruling class, which has them, but also the middle class, which wants them.

In *Leonardo,* the painter of "The Last Supper" has a last supper—though it occurs after, not before, his resurrection. Like Jesus, he is betrayed by his own people, fellow Florentines. Jesus's supper celebrated Passover, named to commemorate the night before the Israelites departed from slavery in Egypt into the promised land, when the Angel of Death slew firstborn Egyptian children but passed over the Israelites' homes. In *Leonardo*, no Angel flies over the Ambois charnel house that is the play's set, but one resides within, *Angelo* Lasca, who with his wife and son kill Leonardo for money to return to Florence, which to them is a promised land and a deliverance from the poverty that enslaves them.

Commissioned to bury Leonardo, the Lascas delight at their fee and the prospect of increased trade once it becomes known whom they buried. When his death turns out to have been a mistaken diagnosis, they demand payment for both the burial and loss of trade. Lasca regards the gratitude of future generations as insufficient. Plunging Leonardo headfirst into a bucket of excrement, urine, and vomit, they drown him.

At the play's start, a voice hails the Renaissance: "In an extraordinary burst of intellectual energy the human spirit recovered its freedom after centuries of political and spiritual oppression. ... The Gothic night dissolved, making way for the birth of modern man and the achievements of our age" (3). But the Renaissance also hastened the rise of capitalism. It was a time when Leonardo painted the "Virgin of the Rock" and "a time for the man o' business. For the only question asked was 'how does it profit me?' It was...Lasca time" (18). The Gothic night did not entirely dissolve. Concurrent with a "burst of intellectual energy," Lasca bottled excrement, whose smell, people believed, warded off the plague. If it did not, he profited by burying them. Among our age's achievements derived from the Renaissance are merchandising techniques. "'Lasca's Excremental Goodness' came in three sizes," says he. "'Lady's Own' was a tiny bottle most beautifully engraved with signs o' the Zodiac and attached to a gold necklace. 'Man Size' was flat and decorated with the figure o' Hercules strangling a lion; it sold at six florins. Our 'Jumbo Family Jar' cost all o' ten florins, but it lasted weeks....I o'ertopped those learned Alchemists. They only turned *lead* into gold" (19–20).

At the dawn of the modern age, the solitary artistic and intellectual genius confronts a money-grubbing family. "I'm the future," says the son, accurately. "We're needed. You're a luxury. We're the new men you scholars prate on about. You put us in the centre o' the Universe. Men o' trade, o' money, we'll build a new heaven and a new earth by helping ourselves.... You're our meat, you belong to us" (26 27). After they kill him, they sing "Mona Lisa." All Leonardo means to the future Lascas of the world is a machine-made hit song that trivializes a work of genius and profits those who market it as Lasca did his "Excremental Goodness." To them, Leonardo's painting might be, as the song's and the play's last line says, *just* a work of art. Leonardo's legacy is in the hands of the Lascas, whose name derives from *lascito,* legacy.

Written as part of a double-bill with *Leonardo, Noonday Demons* (1969) takes place in the fourth century. "Still the Devil stirs at noon," says the hermit St. Eusebius (34). At that time of day, demonic powers are highest. To Eusebius, who has lived in a cave, chained, on a daily diet of seven olives and muddy water, the demon arrives punctually. "It's Temptation Time, folks!" he announces (36), and projects onto a pile of excrement the lures of money, lust, and power. The play also suggests that saintliness and religion are themselves demonic. The devil is not a separate character but resides within the holy hermit, who changes his voice to tempt himself. When a rival saint, Pior, claims the cave as his own, each becomes convinced that the other is a demon sent to corrupt him. Wrapping their chains around their right fists, they fight and cry, "Kill, kill, kill for Christ!" (57). Atop a mound of excrement, Eusebius strangles Pior and sings "Gloria in Excelsis." Murder results from extreme devotion to God.

The conclusion of *Noonday Demons* parallels that of *Leonardo*. Early in the play, the tempter tells Eusebius that all his privations, humiliations, and attempts to reach God are meaningless, incapable of accomplishing good. "You'll be resurrected in the second half o' the twentieth century as a stage freak. Your agonising abstinence'll be treated as a subject for laughter. ... 'Noonday Demons' by Peter Barnes" (39). At the end, Eusebius sees the future. After he kills Pior, a duplicate Eusebius joins Pior in a curtain call. Shaking with fear, the first Eusebius pleads to God for mercy. Instead, he gets applause. Like "Mona Lisa," he becomes show biz entertainment.

Dramatized in earlier plays, such themes as a ruling class, profit, murder in the name of religion, and show biz reappear in new form in *The Bewitched* (1974). True to its title, it concerns people bewitched by secular and religious authority, which employs murder, torture, intimidation, and entertainment for the purpose of bewitchment. It even employs murder, torture, and intimidation *as* entertainment. Insidiously, those who bewitch are themselves bewitched.

The play revolves around Carlos II, seventeenth-century King of Spain, last of the Hapsburgs, whose failure to beget an heir resulted in the War of the Spanish Succession, which left millions dead and wounded. In this play, church and state join to help an exemplar of absolute authority procreate. What is the person who would reproduce himself? Reigning by divine right, he believes, his empire administered by churchmen and statesmen, the King is a stuttering, slobbering, vomiting, pants-wetting, impotent, spastic epileptic. This is authority. As Carlos's limbs jerk spastically, he cries, "III aaaaam Spain" (40). Referring to Carlos's penis, a courtier genuflects: "Like Atlas, Sire, you balance our world on 'ts tip" (23). So he does. For the future of Europe to depend on a grotesque lunatic's erection and potency is both symptom and symbol of authority's bewitchment.

The play's action consists of attempts to obtain a successor. Since Carlos cannot create one in the conventional manner, his wife and mother vie with each other to persuade him to name their choice. To stimulate his virility, and provide entertainment for the exploited populace, the church stages a massive auto-da-fé. Unwilling to believe the royal Carlos is naturally impotent, his confessor attributes the deficiency to diabolical influences. To cure his impotence, the Inquisition overcrowds dungeons with people suspected of witchcraft. Their torture and murder fail to give Spain a prince.

Yet the bewitched victims of authority reject neither the cause of their sufferings nor the established rituals which maintain them. Visiting the torture chamber, Carlos accidentally moves the rack handle. A prisoner screams in pain and gasps, "Twas a great honour, Your Majesty" (73). A tortured nobleman appreciates that "E'en in the House o' Pain my rank and privileges were observed. My body's fire-wracked, my mouth blood-filled, but I cry out, 'God save the King!'" (139).

One reason they submit is that authority relieves them of choice and provides certainty. In a moment of post-epileptic lucidity, Carlos perceives, "Authority's the Basilisk" and as long as one man commands and another obeys, it will ruin the world (138). But when he offers to renounce his crown, his subjects cry in terror and flee. Without authority, the bewitched believe, "Blind chance rules the world!" (115).

However, it is authority which creates chaos, not its absence. At the play's end, Carlos acts upon the logic of authority and the status quo, not rational skepticism and humanity. Although he and his councillors recognize that to name Philip of France as his heir will plunge Europe into a ruinous, bloody war, he names him, for "Only France's strong enough t' hold our Empire together." When Carlos says he is Spain, he is right. This cretin's sole logical choice derives from and aims to maintain what he incarnates. Its logic "makes all that's gone afore meaningless" (145).

Carlos is exemplary, not unique. According to the Queen's brother, "all the Catholic crowned heads o' Europe've been possessed f' years" (133). The Epilogue shows Carlos's Bourbon successor to be *"another freak, with massive legs and arms, bloated stomach and a small elephant's trunk hanging down over his chest in place of a nose."* His face is that of a grinning imbecile. Although a voice calls Philip's ascension the hopeful light of the Age of Reason, the sight of a monstrosity even more grotesque than Carlos derides this assertion. As subjects cry, "God save the King" (149), Barnes makes clear that the generations after Carlos's are as bewitched as his.

Laughter! (1978) gives major emphasis to a theme treated less prominently in earlier plays. In particular, it links to the torture scenes of *The Bewitched,* which draw laughs from suffering. In *Laughter!* Barnes also prods the audience into recognizing why they should not have laughed. *Laughter!* is about the nature of its title. Framing two one-act plays, "Tsar" and "Auschwitz," is a Prologue—a comic attack on laughter by a character called the Author—and an Epilogue—the murder, both comic and horrifying, of two comedians who are concentration camp inmates.

According to the Author, laughter is "no remedy for evil. . . . It softens our hatred. An excuse to change nothing, for nothing needs changing when it's all a joke." He demands we "root out comedy" (2). During his impassioned jeremiad, a custard pie hits his face and his pants fall down. The slapstick comedy demonstrates how laughter diverts us from ideas that should engage our attention. The Author's statement, less a thematic summary than a challenge based on a recognition of the limitations of the satirist's art, is more extreme than Barnes's own view. Through the Author, Barnes raises questions rather than provides answers.

Laughter! dramatizes themes of earlier plays in an entirely new manner. In "Tsar," Ivan the Terrible embodies the authority of a ruling class. In "Auschwitz," the Nazis do. The subjects of both are bewitched. Shibanov, whose foot Ivan has speared to the floor, tells why he worships him: "You're God's anointed. You've the authority o' blood, Sire, authority that rests on the past. It gi'es our world a permanence which men need. . . . You gi'e us certainty, Sire, which is better than goodness" (10). As in *Demons* and *The Bewitched,* "Tsar" derides the value of suffering for God. Religion serves the state. "Christ's crucified's a pledge o' God's pardon," says Ivan, who notes, "his hands nailed flat casn't strike me" (3). At the end of "Tsar," Ivan's voice explains, "The title 'Terrible' was due to an unfortunate mistranslation; it was more accurately 'Ivan the Awe-Inspiring'" (26). Barnes's point is not academic. Both translations are appropriate, for Ivan's terrors inspire awe.

Whereas "Tsar" derives comedy from individual despotism, "Auschwitz" focuses on impersonal slaughter. "In the coming years," Death tells Ivan in a transitional scene between the plays, "they'll institutionalize [death], take the passion out of killing, turn men into numbers and the slaughter'll be so vast no one mind'll grasp it, no heart'll break 'cause of it" (23–24).

"Auschwitz" is the German concentration camp and also a symbol of how most people blind themselves to and thereby perpetuate other horrors. Audaciously, Barnes manipulates spectators' responses to make them recognize their kinship to functionaries at Auschwitz. A group of civil servants, who tell jokes to help them bear (not change) their lot, engage in bureaucratic rivalry with Gottleb, the quintessential Nazi. As Gottleb goads his rival Cranach to tell an anti-Hitler joke, and tries to turn Cranach's co-workers against him, spectators sympathize with the functionaries, people like themselves, and become hostile to the ruthless Nazi zealot. At the start, they laugh at Cranach's bureaucratic jargon: "Component CP3 (m) described in regulation E(5) serving as Class I or Class II appliances and so constructed as to comply with relevant requirements of regulations L2(4) and (6), L8(4) and (7)" (28). After Gottleb fails to enlist Cranach's co-workers, he makes them face the reality behind the jargon, which refers to the concrete chimneys of the crematoria. While he does so, spectators see what they have laughed at. In reality, the civil servants know: "Deaths and paragraph fifteen isn't any of our business" (38). To close their minds to their knowledge, they replace descriptive language with neutral. Gottleb, our enemy as well as theirs, employs description to open their—and our—minds to Auschwitz's atrocities. The functionaries protest their inability to prevent them: "I can't fight 'em. . . .

This isn't the time to say 'no.' I've just taken out a second mortgage!'' ''But what can I do? I'm only one woman.'' ''You can't expect me to say 'no.'... I'm retiring next year'' (64–65). Having previously manipulated our sympathies toward ordinary people at the mercy of a Nazi beast, Barnes turns us against them. Fighting Gottleb with bureaucratese, which divorces meaning from words, they shut their minds to Auschwitz's horrors. They exult in their victory over the Nazi fanatic: ''We may not be much, but we're better than Gottleb. This time it didn't end with the worst in human nature triumphant, meanness exalted, goodness mocked.'' Cranach proudly prophesies that Gottleb's defeat will make future generations recognize that those who really ran Auschwitz were ''ordinary people, people who liked people, people like them, you, me, us'' (68). With this statement, Barnes convicts the audience. Those with whom we empathized are worse than the Nazi Gottleb, who does not blind himself to the truth about Auschwitz, as people ''like... us'' have done, as we ''like them'' still do.

In an Epilogue, two hollow-eyed concentration camp inmates do a dance and patter number, with such gags as: ''According to the latest statistics, one man dies in this camp everytime I breathe.'' ''Have you tried toothpaste?'' (69). Gassed during their act, they die while telling jokes. As they expire, one recalls the words of the Author in the Prologue: ''In the face of... Ivan the Terrible... or Auschwitz, what good is laughter?!'' (2).

Red Noses, Black Death (written 1978)—to date, Barnes's greatest and most complex work represents both the culmination of his previous original plays and a new direction, in that it suggests the basis of positive action to eliminate the social evils he satirizes. Chiefly, according to Barnes, it derives from the Prologue to its immediate predecessor, *Laughter!* ''It dramatizes a situation in which people use laughter. Does it help to alleviate the suffering that goes on around them, or does it make it worse?'' In *Red Noses, Black Death,* Barnes makes theatre people his central figures. Although one should be careful not to identify a dramatist too closely with a character, even—as in *Laughter!*—a character called the Author, Father Flote, the protagonist of *Red Noses,* comes by the end of the play to a realization similar to that of Barnes, who admits, ''A lot of what he goes through is a progress I have undergone in writing comedy. I've theorized about it, but he lives it as a created character.''

The fourteenth century was a time of death on a vast scale. ''One-third of Christendom lies under sod,'' says Flote well before the plague ends (Prologue). It was a time of chaos and anarchy, for death struck randomly. Goodness, wealth, and trappings of power were no proof against it. From Pope to peasant, everyone was terrified. ''Men've seen death treat all men equal,'' says an archbishop. ''Authority's gone, no place for Christ'' (I,3).

BERNARD F. DUKORE

With the perceptions that the Black Death levelled all human beings and that conventional authority was powerless, it was a time of enormous revolutionary potential.

Three groups contend to influence the populace. Although each is necessary, each is insufficient as a force for social improvement.

Lamenting that "Men can't live in this misery, die in this despair" (Prologue), Flote forms the Red Noses, a religious "brotherhood of joy, Christ's Clowns, God's zanies," designed to "cheer the hearts of men with gibs, jibes, and jabber jinks; masques and other merriments" (I,3). Each member wears a symbol of the order, a clown's red nose. Trying to lighten the dying moments of a plague-striken woman, the red-nosed priest jokes, "Old Dubois told the marriage broker he wouldn't marry the girl without a sample of her sexual powers. 'No samples,' said the girl, 'but references he can have!' (I, 1). The woman smiles and dies. Believing that laughter is more apt to discourage than encourage rebellion, Pope Clement VI blesses the order.

The Red Noses' compassionate mirth diverts people from such facts as "Ten percent of the population of Auxerre dies of starvation every year without plague help" and "Free men're made bondsmen, dress in tatters, whilst [their] fields're enclosed and stolen by landlords" (I,5). Thus, the Red Noses perpetuate social conditions which constitute a plague comparable to the Black Death.

Opposing them are the Black Ravens, former galley slaves freed to bury corpses, whose possessions they loot. Nihilistic, they seek destruction of the existing order and ask the poor to join them in killing the rich, but they understand only hatred, not how to implement their egalitarian vision. As one of them later confesses, "I broke the eggs but I didn't know how to make the omelette" (II,5).

The Flagellants, who seek salvation through suffering, are evangelical proto-Protestants. Calling the Pope "a sucking dog-leech" who sells religion for profit, they aim to "appeal to God direct. We need no mitred prelates to intercede for us. No man needs to go to Avignon [where the papal seat has moved] nor Hell to find Pope or Devil. Both lodge in his own breast!" (I,6). But its leader afterward recognizes, "We Flagellants embraced pain when we should've been trying to eliminate it" (II,6).

Individually, each has something of value: the Red Noses, the joy and laughter that should be cornerstones of a new world, in contrast to the misery and pain of the old, and the ability to influence the masses; the Black Ravens, the conception that the populace should overthrow the ruling classes and seize power; the Flagellants, the idea that within each human being is divinity. In a climactic scene, they recognize that only together can they hope to create a better world, and they join in fraternal communion.

But they act too late. At the scene's end comes the announcement that the plague is over. The Black Ravens' egalitarian ideas threaten authority and the Flagellants endanger the church's revenue: "what's to become of the most profitable function of the Holy Office — selling salvation, if men can cleanse themselves of sin by self-inflicted penances?" With the normal order restored, church and state join to isolate and crush them. Still, Clement VI sanctions Flote's Red Noses. "He's helped keep unrest down to a minimum, made men more readily accept their miserable lot. ... A revolution never returns" (II,4). But the laughter of the radicalized Flote now serves revolution, not the status quo. He creates an acronym for social reform through moderation: "Slow, Lawful, Orthodox Progress: S-L-O-P, SLOP" (II,5). The Pope has the Red Noses killed.

Barnes's position in *Red Noses* differs from that of the Author in *Laughter!* Laughter need not be only for losers. The later play proposes a socially productive type of laughter, and it contrasts both types. Exemplifying them are two plays-within-a-play, twin climaxes of the play's two acts. In the first act, a parody of *Everyman* demonstrates the laughter that is for losers. In the second, a parody of a nativity play shows revolutionary laughter.

The *Everyman* parody diverts people's minds from the reality of death. Everyman's baby throws a spoonful of porridge in Death's face and Death agrees to let Everyman bring a companion "if you can find a friend dumb 'nough" (I,11). Members of the onstage audience laugh, then die. By contrast, the nativity parody derides secular and religious authority. "What do you do?" asks Herod. The answer: "Nothing. I'm a nobleman." One of the three kings tells the infant Jesus, "remember in Thy coming years of triumph KINGS paid you tribute. We bend knee to you so your followers'll bend knee to us after." Mary declares, "I *have* been a virgin and a mother. Not both at once, of course." A character announces, "In a stable the infant Jesus chose to lie. Amongst the poor who never die. How can they die, they've never lived" (II,9). Such jokes, subversive of authority, are potentially revolutionary.

The stage spectators' responses to the parodies — which, in a play-within-a-play, cue the real spectators' responses — differ. Of the *Everyman* parody, a Black Raven complains, "They haven't shown the world as 'tis or how we can change it. 'Tisn't real enough." The audience boos him and a prostitute cries, "let 'em play" (I, 11). Of the nativity parody, an archbishop complains, "We were promised soothing syrup and see what they give us!" This time, she concurs, "It isn't funny!" To the targets of his revolutionary jokes, Flote agrees, the nativity play is not comic: "'Tisn't funny now inequality's in the world, naming rich and poor, mine and thine. 'Tisn't funny when power rules. 'Tisn't funny till we throw out the old rubbish and gold and silver rust. Then it'll be funny" (II,9). After the *Everyman* parody, nature's plague comes — as Death does in the play — for one actor. After the nativity parody, the Pope, who represents the plague of secular and religious authority, slaughters — as Herod does the innocents — all the actors.

Because unsympathetic forces of reaction destroy sympathetic characters who exemplify progress, the play contains a note of despair. But *Red Noses* is a composition of more notes than one. The nativity performance and the actors' defiance of authority after it constitute hopeful notes. So does an Epilogue, in which voices of the dead Red Noses echo passages from earlier scenes — not only quips but also thematic statements, such as "I see hatred of authority as our first duty" and "Every jest should be a small revolution. We come to ding down dignity and make a new world. All forms of rebellion must come together." As they prepare to meet their maker, they declare, "God's up for judgment." Revolutionists die, but the idea of revolution lives, joined by laughter.

"Every play is a problem of language," says Barnes in his Introduction to *Leonardo* and *Demons*. For them, he sought "a live theatrical language," an "artificial vernacular" with "historical weight yet ... flexible enough to incorporate modern songs and jokes. For such deliberate anachronisms can only work fully if they spring out of an acceptable period texture. So I pillaged; everything from Elizabethan argot to the Bible" (ix). In *Leonardo,* Lasca remembers, "Those gotch-gutted curs drove me out o' Florence" (4). In *Demons,* with an authentic-sounding texture of a different period, Pior recalls, "A grimliche country; petrified like my heart, dead like my body" (44). Barnes's language is invented, different for each play and character. The "gotch-gutted curs" of Lasca would be as inappropriate in the mouth of Pior as his "grimliche" would be in Lasca's, or as either would be in anyone's in *Red Noses*. There, he pillages such period sources as a traditional flagellant's hymn, "Pain, pain, pain" (II,2), Chaucer's *Canterbury Tales*, "a very perfect gentle knight" (II,3), and mystery plays, as when Mary says of the infant Jesus, "Lookee, look how he merrys, my sweeting laughs. Oh, he's a prince, divine" (II,9).

The "artificial vernacular" of a playwright immersed in Jacobean drama has a Jacobean flavor — even in plays set in modern times — with striking imagery and bold extravagance. "You'll be nicked down to your bloody membrane, Mary. ... You want two seconds of DRIPPING sin to fertilize sodomized idiots" (*Ruling Class,* 94). "Lord, I suppeth up sin as 't were water. My lust corrupts the age. Troops o' virgins passed under me;

ripe lips bathed in rancid grease, pink bodies smelling o' perfume and sweet waters t' cover the stench from their wrinkled thighs and armpits" (*Bewitched*, 4–5).

Into his period texture, as he says, he inserts modern jokes. In *Demons*, the tempter says Eusebius has "B.O." (36). In *The Bewitched*, a parrot screeches, "Jesus saves but Moses invests" (32). In *Red Noses*, an actor punningly calms an actress with stage fright, "you'll get a warm hand on your opening" (I,11). He also inserts meaningless words and phrases of his own invention, such as "Must get my grunch thoughts in order" (*Ruling Class*, 111), the adjective suggestive of crunching grunts; "rabbit suckers" (*Leonardo*, 69), connotative of an archaic expletive; and "Cow-elephants kneel" (*Bewitched*, 138), evocative of bulky, mighty beings in obeisance.

Barnes's linguistic thefts conform to his themes and situations. Largely because of the apt and original use to which he puts his plunder, of both literature and pop culture, he transforms it into his own property. First, his literary allusions.

At the start of *The Ruling Class*, he parodies, misquotes, jumbles the order, and thereby transforms John of Gaunt's famous praise of England (*Richard II*) into a condemnation—unintended by the speaker—of the basis of English society: a "teeming womb of privilege" (not "of royal kings"), still "a feudal state," beating back "foreign anarchy" (not "envious siege")—no doubt the revolutions of 1789 and 1917 (3). Important too, these lines derive from Gaunt's *dying* words, since the entire Prologue — which ends in death—is a compendium of allusions associated with death, including the last words of Sidney Carton in Dickens's *A Tale of Two Cities* ("It is a far, far better thing," etc.), a paraphrase of Claudius after he discovers Hamlet has killed Polonius ("Desperate diseases need desperate remedies"), and the last words of Viscount Palmerston in 1865 ("Die my dear doctor? That's the last thing I shall do") (6–7). Even if one recognizes none of these sources, the archaic mode of some passages suggests moribund tradition (Gaunt); death is sometimes implicit (Claudius), sometimes explicit (the Viscount), sometimes visualized (the speaker climbs steps to a noose before he quotes Dickens).

Literary and Biblical allusions pepper *The Bewitched*. Diseased and dying, Philip IV tries to engender a legitimate heir. In order to achieve an erection, he conjures in his imagination a beautiful, young, scantily clad former mistress, who erotically stimulates him. Soon, he observes, *"It quivers. 'Tis not as hard as a ram's horn, nor as stout as Hercules but 'twill serve"* (6). Whether or not one recognizes the allusion to *Romeo and Juliet* (Mercutio's comment on his death wound, " 'tis not so deep as a well, nor so wide as a church-door; but 'tis enough, 'twill serve"), the statement is funny. Also, it is both ironic and appropriate. Romeo and Juliet are young, romantic lovers, whereas Philip is decrepit and unromantic; and by the end of the scene—which begins with a funeral bell—Philip will be, in Mercutio's words, "a grave man." The Queen's parrot cries, "O impotence, where is thy sting?" (85), which parodies "O death," etc. (I *Corinthians*, 15:55). Though ironic—the parrot addresses the absence of *le petit mort* in words evocative of *le grand mort*—the allusion becomes apt at the close of the scene, when the Queen Mother strangles the parrot.

In "The Second Coming," Yeats writes, "Things fall apart; the center cannot hold." In *Red Noses*, a character observes that with the plague more than the center cannot hold: "The rim and centre's breaking" (I,3). During the Black Death, prostitutes raised prices, for money was valueless to those who might die and death decreased supply while it increased demand. When the plague ends, prostitutes—about to marry and give what they once sold—lament, "we've dwindled to wives" (II,5). The allusion is to Congreve's *The Way of the World*, where Millamant, having set forth conditions under which she would marry Mirabell, says, "I may by degrees dwindle into a wife." In one respect, the reference is ironic. Whereas Millamant will retain her independence, the prostitutes will lose theirs. As they recognize, they are rushing to their chains. In another respect, the allusion is apt. *This*, Barnes hints, and not Millamant's contract, is the way of the world.

While most of Barnes's references to pop culture are anachronistic— only *The Ruling Class* is set in the present—they are what Bernard Shaw, in his notes to *Caesar and Cleopatra*, calls *apparent* anachronisms, for they mock the notion that mankind has progressed since the play's historical period.

In *Demons*, fourth-century hermits sing "Monks," a parody of "Kids," from the musical *Bye Bye Birdie*. Barnes's changes are appropriate to the saints, each of whom believes the other is less worthy than himself, and to the play's anti-religious theme. Whereas the musical's father complains that no one can *understand* anything kids say, the hermits sing that no one can *believe* anything monks say. Whereas kids "do just what they want to do," monks "say anything—even if it isn't true!" (48). In the Epilogue to *Laughter!* the song to which the dying Auschwitz inmates dance, as they tell jokes, is "The Sunny Side of the Street," which is more apt than might first appear. In death, these victims of Nazism will leave their worries on the doorstep, and conditions will be sweeter on the other side of life's street. In *Red Noses*, Flote sings "Life Is Just a Bowl of Cherries" to people dying of the plague. True to the Red Noses' job, to take people's minds off serious matters, it urges them not to take life seriously and it tells the poor that they cannot lose what they never owned.

Not every pop reference is to a song. J. C.'s concern extends unto the least of mankind, including Mr. Moto and the Cisco Kid, of Hollywood B-movies. In *The Bewitched,* the advice of court-jester father to court-jester son—"Thy only call is t' entertain.... If thou has a message, send 't by messenger" (14)—derives from advice attributed to comic playwright George S. Kaufman, "If you have a message, use Western Union." The terrified Le Grue, a blind Red Nose, adopts the exit line of B-movie star Mantan Moreland, whose roles included that of Charlie Chan's chauffeur, "Feet, do your stuff" (II,9): Moreland's actual line began "Feets."

Language is only part of the extravagant theatricality of Barnes's plays. As Ivan unsuccessfully tries to persuade Semeon to remain Tsar, an invisible force pulls Semeon backward, until he is spreadeagled against an upstage wall, which sucks him in and swallows him. In the first-act climax of *The Bewitched,* sounds of whipping and moans accompany an onstage strangulation and red-lighted stakes; while the red wax of an effigy bubbles and flows like blood, a choir sings a hymn, an immense phallus sprouts from between Carlos's legs, grows eight feet, and—carried by a priest— impales the Queen. A superbly theatrical tour-de-force in *Red Noses* combines language, sounds, song, banners, and the movement of objects. Rather than kill each other, the Black Ravens, Flagellants, and Red Noses let God determine the victor. The Ravens unfold their banner, a black raven against a red background; the Flagellants theirs, a crucified Christ; the Noses theirs, an angel and St. Genesius, patron saint of actors. Releasing a black balloon, a Raven cries *"Caw-caw-caw"* and enunciates his creed. Releasing a red one, a Flagellant cries *"Ahhh-ahhh-ahhh"* and declares his. Releasing a blue one, Flote laughs *"Haaa-haaa-haaa"* and states his. Boos from the flies follow each speech. Then, Flote recognizes that jokes should be revolutionary and that the three groups should join to create a better world. As the leaders link hands, the black, red, and blue balloons— now tied together—descend, accompanied by applause from the flies. Everyone sings, "Join together, that's the plan. It's the secret. Man helps man.... Join together. Go, go, go. Change conditions. Here below" (II,3).

Expressionism is among Barnes's theatricalist devices. Instead of explaining that the ruling class is outmoded and monstrous, Barnes shows members of the House of Lords to be skull-faced, cobweb-covered, bloated-bellied, goitered people smothered in dust, seated beside a skeleton. In *The Bewitched,* to express that Ana is not pregnant, he has a patriarch, during her account of a dream about her baptised child, pour blood over her and a baby in christening clothes.

Barnes, who acknowledges his debt to Artaud, makes language approximate cries or screams, and become inarticulate sounds that convey meaning. Ivan the Terrible says and does as much: "Suffering beyond the reach o' language. *KK arrrxx ccrrrrr aaaaakk AAAARRR"* (21–22). An entire scene of *The Ruling Class* expresses emotion through inarticulate sounds (112). Unlike Artaud, however, Barnes is a comic writer who parodies his own technique, as in *Demons*: "And I, I spake unto them, sweetly in the language o' angels. 'Eeeeeepphh-Singggeeee-Yaaaanngg' I said. And they answered, 'Eeeeeepphh-Singggeeee-Yaaaanngg' to you too" (35).

Like Artaud, Barnes's theatre visually and aurally depicts the cruelty of existence. In *The Bewitched*, characters inflict bodily injury through force of will: "PONTOCARRERO *lets out a grunt of pain and* MOTIL-LA's *face contorts in agony. Neck muscles tighten, faces turn white with strain,"* until: *"Suddenly blood pours from* MOTILLA's *mouth and nose. It gushes down the front of his white habbit, but he never takes his eyes off* PONTOCARRERO. *There is a sickening 'crack' as a bone snaps and* PONTOCARRERO's *arm is broken. It is quickly followed by another 'crack' as his right leg is smashed too"* (102). In "Auschwitz," a Nazi's pincers tear at the mouth of a corpse, *"accompanied by a loud, wrenching sound."* He and another *"rip, slice and gouge with increasing frenzy amid the noise of breaking bones and tearing flesh"* (64). Again unlike Artaud, the comic Barnes mocks cruelty. In a torture scene of *The Bewitched*, the chief torturer reprimands a prisoner: "You've been *bleeding* again! We spend the night cleaning up your mess and you start t' bleed all over the place. (*The* PRISONER *groans.*) That's no excuse" (68–69).

Like Brecht—whose influence, Barnes asserts, pervades contemporary drama—he writes in order to change the world. He paraphrases Brecht (*Saint Joan of the Stockyards*): "The phrase 'when you leave, leave a better world behind you' I think is very apposite for any artist." Although he distrusts parties of both right and left, he inclines toward socialism and anarchism. Class distinctions and extreme inequality of money constitute "barriers between people. Permanent authority is a canker for the leader and the led."

As the analysis of his plays indicates, Barnes opposes class stratification, exploitation, and capitalism. The very title *The Ruling Class* tells which side he is on. In *Leonardo*, Maria calls poverty a disease worse than the plague. In *The Bewitched*, a Spanish grandee sees the fall of Barcelona in terms of money—"My Government bonds! 'Tis the dark night o' the soul" (95)—and Barnes shows what underlies the trappings of wealth. "I've the most exquisite taste in Europe," says an archbishop, whereupon *"The rich wall-drapes are pulled down to reveal grey panels covered with filth and graffiti"* (100). Paraphrasing Biblical passages—the same Brecht does in *Saint Joan of the Stockyards* (*Matthew*, 13:12, 25:29; *Mark*, 4:25; *Luke*, 8:18, 19:26)—and thereby turning them to his own use, which resembles Brecht's, he has Ivan declare, " 'Tis nature's iron law: those that have shall be gi'en" (13). In *Red Noses,* a gold merchant recites his guild's motto: "We live by the golden rule, those that have the gold make the rules" (I,6); Flote calls Christianity "the triumph of hope over experience" (I,8); and the Pope admits the church's important work is to collect taxes and draft laws.

Like Brecht, Barnes writes on a panoramic scale, and his disorientation techniques resemble Brecht's *Verfremdungseffekt.* Their chief differences are that Barnes makes more frequent use of jokes to disorient and permit social evaluation, and that his transformational techniques operate swiftly, usually as comic diversion, so that the spectator evaluates just after the sudden, frequently comic shift in theatrical mode, rather than —as with Brecht—prepares to examine as a new mode is introduced.

In *The Ruling Class,* immediately after Jack brutally stabs Claire, the butler enters, singing "Come Into the Garden, Maud," sees the corpse, and shouts, "*(Gleefully)* One less! One less! Praise the Lord. *Hallelujah*" (95). "Oh Lord I can't think o' all the suffering in the world," says Ivan the Terrible, and he adds, "so I don't" (18). In *Red Noses,* when the Master Flagellant recognizes that he and his followers should have tried to eliminate pain, not embrace it, one of them comments, "Now he tells us!" (II,6). Like Brecht, Barnes disorients to maintain objectivity. When the butler is about to be arrested for the murder Jack committed, he is frightened and cries. *"As he takes out a handkerchief to wipe his eyes, a half dozen spoons fall out of his pocket with a clatter"* (102). About to be shot by a crossbow, Flote stands on his head for his execution.

Barnes's most distinctive artistic signature, which previous examinations of language and of Brecht-related disorientation suggest, consists of disorientating transformations from one theatrical mode to another.[4] Swiftly and lightly, actors switch from intellectual discourse, to period argot, to poetry, to modern slang, to rhetoric, to musical comedy, to ritual, to dance, to opera, to slapstick. Entertainingly, Barnes juggles the audience's moods and enables them to examine critically, detached and with a smile, the social values and attitudes he scrutinizes. Perhaps in homage to Ben Jonson, he refers to this style not as Barnesian but as "Barnesonian" (Introduction, *Leonardo,* x).

In *Leonardo,* the revived da Vinci goes within seconds from today's slang ("The verdict is in. I'm alive."), to prayer ("Jesu, I'm alive."), to a jig and a whoop of joy, to intellectual discourse ("The evidence proves I'm in the land of the living in the bosom of a natural family. I recognize the species: genus homo sapiens. Bipedal primate mammals. Erect bodies, short arms, large thumbs, developed brains with a capacity for articulate speech and abstract reasoning."), to a parody of "Molly Malone"

("Alive-alive O, alive-alive O, singing pasta and pizza alive-alive O.") (22). In "Tsar," Ivan—within three pages—dances Cossack-style, jumping and écarting with joyful cries; speaks in archaic diction ("My leming lufsom boy. I leif you more than life"); hears the screams of a skeleton of a man he tortured and killed, and cracks a joke in modern diction ("They don't write songs like that anymore"); goes into convulsions as he tries to strangle himself; delivers a running joke to the audience ("Root it out!"); murders his son by repeatedly spearing him; employs inarticulate sounds to convey emotion; and sings two arias from Gluck's opera *Orfeo and Eurydice* (20–22).

A major reason for the success of so daring a mixture of modes is their analogical appropriateness. Since rational discourse is insufficient to express Leonardo's delight at being alive, he bursts into song, whose lyrics celebrate life. Ivan derives pleasure from the "songs" or cries of his victims, and the world he creates is a hell, perhaps worse than the one into which Orfeo descends in search of Eurydice.

Barnes' transformations reflect our fragmented world, which encompasses and accommodates Rembrandt and Magritte, Vivaldi and Frank Loesser, Seneca and tap dancing. They succeed on stage partly because one is accustomed to them in daily life. Is it unusual to play a record of a Mozart quartet, then of a Broadway musical, on one's own player? Is it unusual to read the comic section of a newspaper during morning coffee, then the *Oresteia*? On TV, a gripping scene in a concentration camp might suddenly shift to an animated tuna fish who recites Shakespeare and is told that the manufacturer wants tunas who taste good, not tunas with good taste. The difference between Barnesonian transformations and diurnal transformations is that the Barnesonians are purposeful and unified, not merely random. In brief, they are art.

NOTES

1. (London, Heinemann, 1969), pp. V, vii. Subsequent quotations from this play will be cited parenthetically in the text. With one exception, quotations from Barnes's other plays, also to be cited in this way, are from Heinemann's London editions: *Leonardo's Last Supper* and *Noonday Demons* (1970), *The Bewitched* (1974), and *Laughter!* (1978). The exception is *Red Noses, Black Death*, not yet published. I quote from the typescript (courtesy Peter Barnes) and cite act and scene.

2. Unless otherwise indicated, such information, as well as quotations and para-phrases of Barnes, derive from conversations with him in October 1978.
3. Unless otherwise indicated, years are of the plays' first productions, in England.
4. Despite their affinity, in this respect, to America's Open Theatre, which flourished in the sixties, Barnes was unfamiliar with this company.

Parody, Travesty, and Politics in the Plays of Tom Stoppard

ENOCH BRATER

Stoppard is that peculiar anomaly—a serious comic writer born in an age of tragicomedy and a renewed interest in theatrical realism. Such deviation from dramatic norms not only marks his original signature on the contemporary English stage, but has sometimes made it difficult for us to determine whether his unique posture of comic detachment has been "good," "bad," or simply "indifferent."[1] "Seriousness compromised by frivolity" is not what we have been trained to value in the important theater of our time. Yet Stoppard's "high comedy of ideas" is a refreshing exception to the rule. Offering us "a funny play," Stoppard's world "makes coherent, in terms of theatre, a fairly complicated intellectual argument."[2] That the argument is worth making, that it is constantly developing and sharpening its focus, and that it always seeks to engage an audience in a continuing dialogue, are the special characteristics of Stoppard's dramatic accomplishment. They are also the features which dignify and ultimately transform the comic tradition to which his work belongs.

It would be convenient to assume that Stoppard's first play, the rewriting of *A Walk on the Water* we now know as *Enter a Free Man,* already demonstrated some clear evidence of that discrete synthesis between "seriousness" and "frivolity" which has become the hallmark of his style. This is not, however, the case. A first play, as Stoppard has discussed, "tends to be the sum of all the plays you have seen of a type you can emulate technically and have admired. So *A Walk on the Water* was in fact *Flowering Death of a Salesman*—though of course I didn't think that when I was doing it."[3] The play's hero, inventor George Riley, is the British cousin to Arthur Miller's Willy Loman. Complete with a long-suffering Linda (the daughter this time—the wife is now a dowdy English Persephone), *Enter a Free Man* tells the story of the generations who will never make it. And Stoppard's play, like Miller's, is meant to be emblematic:

each act opens to the tune of "Rule Britannia," enforcing the idea that the Riley syndrome is not so much eccentric as it is representative. The English hero dreams of sponge principles and re-usable envelopes, but the vacuum cleaner and the shilling-a-day (cribbed from Linda) are his true reality. "Man is born free," quotes Riley in a pub rather shakily from Rousseau, "but everywhere he is in chains." Time, place, and class, as much as his own inner weakness, block the entrance of Stoppard's free man.

But the thematic resemblance to Arthur Miller ends here—this is a *Flowering Death of a Salesman* after all. For the tone of *Enter a Free Man* is tragicomic and links Stoppard very conspicuously to his British contemporaries. This particular blend of outrageous humor in a tragicomic framework has its origins in a respectable tradition quite different from the one Stoppard has himself connected with Arthur Miller and the American drama. *Enter a Free Man,* a fanciful *tour-de-force* along the forget-me-not-lane, reminds us very much of the work of Peter Nichols, Joe Orton and, even earlier than that, N. F. Simpson. Here we see an early Stoppard at his most derivative: this is imitation, but it is good imitation. Stoppard, one-time theater critic in Bristol, has studied very carefully this particular style of playwriting. *Enter a Free Man* is the disciplined work of his apprenticeship and as such its form looks backward rather than forward. This is the play Stoppard wrote and then rewrote to get tragicomedy out of his system.

One must not, however, pass over *Enter a Free Man* too lightly. Though the tragicomic muse cramps the style we will later associate with vintage Stoppard in his other full-length plays, this early work contains in embryo an important element developed with greater precision in the comedy to come. The best moments in *Enter a Free Man* are the long passages of Riley's dialogue, comic verbosities which look ahead to those witty diatribes in *Jumpers* and *Travesties*:

> How can I help being excited! For centuries while the balance of nature has kept flower gardens thriving with alternate sun and rain in the proportions that flowers understand, indoor plants have withered and died on a million cream-painted window-sills, attended by haphazard housewives bearing arbitrary jugs of water. For centuries. Until one day, a man noticing the tobacco-coloured leaves of a dessicated cyclamen, said to himself, what the world needs is indoor rain. Indoor rain of the volume and duration of natural rain. He considered: if for instance, one put a delicately poised sponge on the roof of a house, then that sponge would be just heavy enough to operate a valve, thus allowing the water system of the house to flow

through prepared ducts, *(he demonstrates at the pipes)* and sprinkle itself wherever a flower is positioned. First Watt and the steam engine—now Riley and the Sponge Principle!

Despite this zaniness in George Riley's imaginative life, he remains, nevertheless, a figure forever caught up in a mundane domestic crisis. Persephone is no longer Pluto's mythological consort reigning over the underworld, but a "matronly, plump, plain, nice, vague, usually vaguely distracted... great duster and emptier of ash-trays." The ending of the play amplifies the bittersweet texture of this work: when we hear the raindrops fall, Riley's plants are indeed watered but his home barely escapes inundation. A sadder but wiser Linda has returned to the bosom of family life and with a liberal distribution of buckets and saucepans fends off imminent disaster. The curtain falls on a tragicomic situation bordering perilously close to sentimentality.

The first signs of Stoppard's stylistic breakthrough come with *Rosencrantz and Guildenstern Are Dead.* Here Stoppard discovers an objective comic vehicle which avoids any suggestion of sentimentality. Like *Enter a Free Man,* this play is a revision of an earlier dramatic idea, a one-act "Shakespearian pastiche" in which Rosencrantz and Guildenstern find themselves in an England ruled by King Lear. "The whole thing was unspeakable," admits Stoppard. "But it did contain some of the dialogue which still exists in the play."[4] Turning *Hamlet* inside out gives Stoppard the opportunity to be simultaneously frivolous in conception but dead serious in execution. The heroes are Shakespeare's marginal men caught up in a stage reality of life and death they can never fully comprehend. But the tone here is deliberately cold and detached. It is only in this way that Stoppard can sustain for three acts his analytical perspective on what happens at Elsinore. The accent is on comedy, not psychology. Stoppard has caught us off guard: the surprise curtain raiser features a game of chance in place of Shakespeare's threatening apparition of a ghost. The coins keep landing on heads.

What is at stake here is not only a relaxed view of *Hamlet,* but a new kind of comic writing halfway between parody and travesty. Let us for a moment consider an elementary distinction between the two, for in so doing we may go a long way in explaining the extraordinary appeal *Rosencrantz and Guildenstern* has had on stage. While both parody and travesty closely imitate the style of an author or work for comic effect or ridicule, only the former employs this strategy to make some critical commentary on the original. Travesty, on the other hand, makes no such evaluative claim and harbors no such analytical pretension. A travesty is merely a burlesque whose tactics are gross distortion and incongruity for their own sake. Now what is unusual about Stoppard's work is the way in which it dramatizes a tension between two elements of comedy which have traditionally remained separate and distinct. The conflict in *Rosencrantz and Guildenstern Are Dead* is, then, a stylistic one. Is this parody or travesty, seriousness or frivolity?

Because Stoppard has been so adept at treading a thin line between the two, *Rosencrantz and Guildenstern* keeps us guessing. In certain respects this rewriting of *Hamlet* with Hamlet in a bit part is no mere travesty, but a rather ingenious parody of theatrical style. And Shakespeare is by no means the only butt of the joke. As Andrew Kennedy has pointed out, the play is a "serio-comic parody of *both* the Shakespearean and the modern tragic sense."[5] Stoppard uses *Godot* as often as he relies on *Hamlet:* going conflicts with not-going, games are played to pass the time, the simile of leaves is the subject of considerable commentary, and pants fall down when the belt, not the center, cannot hold. Stoppard breathes new life into Rosencrantz and Guildenstern by making them dramatic ancestors of Beckett's Vladimir and Estragon. Their one-liners are the product of a verbal strategy designed to recycle Gogo and Didi's energetic "little canters." But Stoppard's parody of styles does not end here. Other playwrights will be called upon to strut and fret their hour upon this stage. Stoppard uses the acting troupe of *The Murder of Gonzago,* Shakespeare's play-within-the-play, not only to insinuate the bleak subject of death, but to reflect the essence of tragedy in Pirandello's *teatro dello specchio.* What is theatrical death and what is real death? When does illusion end and reality begin? Are we responsible for our actions or are we merely manipulated stage characters predestined by some offstage hand? More particularly, are Rosencrantz and Guildenstern free to choose their own destiny or are they tied down to an Elizabethan script controlling the ultimate end of their action on the boards? Is Hamlet, too, impaled by the same fate? "There must have been a moment, at the beginning, where we could have said — no. But somehow we missed it," Guildenstern's exit lines, therefore make the irony cut deep. This is Stoppard parodying Shakespeare, Beckett, Pirandello, and existential philosophy all at once. The collage is still not complete. Oscar Wilde, too, must come momentarily out of the closet. A Player confronts us with a bitter paraphrase of Miss Prism's literary theory from *The Importance of Being Earnest*: "The bad end unhappily, the good unluckily. That is what tragedy means.... Positions!"

Suddenly the parody of theatrical styles has created a serious conflict of ideas on stage. Stoppard's technique has been to set in motion "a series of conflicting statements made by conflicting characters," then to let them play "a sort of infinite leap-frog. You know, an argument, a refutation, then a rebuttal of the refutation, then a counter-rebuttal, so that there is never any point in this intellectual leap-frog at which I feel *that* is the speech to stop it on, *that* is the last word."[6] The dramatic impact of such an imaginative "leap-frog" results in a verbal overkill which suggests that everything that can be said about the human condition appears to have already been said and—in the grand style of writers like Shakespeare, Beckett, Pirandello, or Wilde—said most persuasively. The only problem is that we, like Rosencrantz and Guildenstern, don't know which ideas still have a bearing on the present. "What do you read, my Lord?" asks Shakespeare's Polonius. "Words, words...," responds Hamlet. Stoppard's Guildenstern offers the following footnote: "They're all we have to go on." But in this context the "words" of the past turn out to be an especially heavy burden. They fail us when we need them most, for they tell us nothing very much about how to act in a critical moment. "You understand," observes a Player susceptible to epigram, "we are tied down to a language which makes up in obscurity what it lacks in style." Stoppard therefore confronts us with the recognizable dilemma of the man who, having read much, can't be sure of anything. The more possibilities Stoppard's marginal man allows for, the less he understands. This is comedy of a high order, but it is a "comedy of incertitude."[7] The hero of our time is not a romantic Hamlet, but a rather pathetic little fellow who can't even remember whether his name is dear Rosencrantz or gentle Guildenstern. We are all bit players at life. Because Stoppard has avoided giving us any "single, clear statement" in *Rosencrantz and Guildenstern Are Dead*, the determined confusion he fosters in this play succeeds in representing our own unenviable situation.[8] The restraint has earned a crucial dividend. Just when we were having a really good laugh, the comedy has taken a serious turn indeed.

By offering us a conflict of ideas in a realm prior to resolution, *Rosencrantz and Guildenstern Are Dead* therefore establishes Stoppard as a writer of serious comedy which bears his own personal stamp. Having put tragedy as well as tragi-comedy on the shelf, Stoppard replaces them with a high comedy of ideas which speaks to us with immediacy and clarity. Here is the comic form of irreconciliation for which Stoppard has been searching. Parody and travesty alternate, interact, and finally collide in a theatrical flamboyance whose every element of style and substance is under dramatic investigation.

Having hit upon this master plan for marrying "the play of ideas to comedy or farce," Stoppard makes an important distinction between his full-length plays and the shorter pieces for the theater he calls "nuts-and-bolts" comedies.[9] Here, too, seriousness is tempered by frivolity, but in proportions quite different from those we recognize in *Rosencrantz and Guildenstern Are Dead*. In *The Real Inspector Hound* and *After Magritte* the difficulty of knowing precisely what is going on is similarly called into question. In the tradition of Ben Travers' highly successful Aldwych farces, Stoppard's one-acts show us what has happened to the comic-thriller once Shaftesbury Avenue has recovered from its flirtation with the theater of the absurd. A take-off on *The Mousetrap, The Real Inspector Hound* parodies the plot of Agatha Christie in the style of Luigi Pirandello. An establishment critic has unfortunately failed to remove himself from the set once the second act begins and is murdered for this breach of good form in forgetting his place. The distinction between "play" and "play-within-play" becomes as obscure as the obligatory mist surrounding Muldoon Manor. In this frolic, however, Stoppard's focus is on comedy, not ideas. No philosophical burden threatens to encumber the "nuts-and-bolts" of farce and fluff. *After Magritte* is another such comic coup in pure mechanistic terms.[10] This, too, is a mystery play satirizing the genre of the stage thriller, only in this case the cup-and-saucer has a hard time in getting itself going. Stage characters spend the entire one-act trying to extract sense from the bits and pieces of circumstantial evidence which continually elude their fingertips. Minds of inferior lucidity—but of congenital loquaciousness—make a detective's nightmare out of the unreasonableness of reason. In *After Magritte* the comic emphasis is on visual as well as narrative ambiguity: when the curtain goes up the first prop to capture our attention is a light fixture on a counterweight system with a basket of fruit. In this extended parody of surrealist compositional technique, Stoppard takes Magritte out of the Tate and adapts for the stage his "eclectic" tricks with balance and perspective. Yet the special context of this staged Magritte is placed in a frame that makes perfect sense: what appears to be madness proves to be perfectly logical by the time the curtain comes down.

The comic style Stoppard masters in *After Magritte* and *The Real Inspector Hound* is crucial in understanding the strategy he uses to great advantage in his next two full-length plays. *Jumpers* and *Travesties* exploit the same devices of "nuts-and-bolts" comedy in order to sustain entirely different effects. The goal has changed; Stoppard has expanded his repertory. Having employed the punch of comedy and the timing of farce in *The Real Inspector Hound* and *After Magritte*, Stoppard will now use these methods to dramatize what might otherwise be dry philosophical debates. But while the one-acts never defile the purity of good comic romp, the longer plays confront us with more than one level of theatrical experience in more than one dimension of theatrical form. *Jumpers* and *Travesties* are farces *and* high comedies of ideas at one and the same time. In these plays parody and travesty no longer alternate in counterpoint, but rather reverberate in simultaneity. This is no Shavian "comedy" and "philosophy," but a new version of parody working in complicity with travesty.

In *Jumpers,* parody frequently masquerades as travesty. George Moore, professor of ethics, is Stoppard's contribution to the traditional figure of the stage pedant. But the three playing areas—the study, the bedroom, and the hall—are parts of an elaborate simultaneous set which suggests that there is far more here than meets the eye. When we recognize that there is both a comic surface as well as a philosophical depth, the play begins to operate on more than one level. But Stoppard quickly sets out to short-circuit the connections between one level and the next. What appears to be philosophical debate turns into slapstick (Professor Moore will inadvertently crush poor Thumper) and what seems to be music hall innocence (a production number of "Shine on Harvest Moon") proves to be bitterly ironic. *Jumpers,* however, never fixes moral philosophy and muscial comedy in any stable order, hierarchy, or progression. The play therefore implicates us in the process of making decisions. But as we try to distinguish the serious from the comic, the adventure of evaluation becomes far more complicated than we may have initially supposed.

Jumpers has been carefully structured to confuse any safe or comfortable orientation to it. Stoppard situates us in a futuristic yet curiously recognizable world in which all value systems are up for grabs. The "incredible" Radical Library Party has assumed control of the ship of state, an English astronaut has landed on the moon and forfeited the life of his fellow traveller in order to assure the continuation of his own, and a former Minister of Agriculture, an admitted agnostic, has been appointed Archbishop of Canterbury. Society is in rough transition. McFee, George Moore's colleague and philosophical rival, has been found dead in a park, wrapped in a plastic bag. Who killed McFee? Suddenly we are back to the who-done-it of *After Magritte* and *The Real Inspector Hound.* But "unlike mystery novels," as Sir Archibald Jumpers observes near the end of the second act, "life does not guarantee a denoucment." Neither does this play. What it does guarantee is a vigorous confrontation of theatrical styles which avoids any neat system of synchronization. The intellectual debate as well as the comic gymnastics take place in a strange magnetic field whose poles constantly shift. The curtain rises and falls on a confusion which has been staged without the intrusion of reconciliation. Too late for integration or mediation, the world Stoppard portrays in *Jumpers* is beyond synthesis. Everything is out of joint.

George Moore, moralist by profession and inclination, cannot and will not "forget yesterday." He remains tied to the systems of the past. Seeking to reconcile ethical antitheses in a humanistic tradition long out of date, he prepares his lecture on "Man—Good, Bad, or Indifferent" while the world around him is in shambles. But the interrogative "Is God?," in any of its combinations or possible permutations, hardly distinguishes him as the man of the hour. Doomed as he is to life on a verbal trampoline, his situation is no more secure than the human pyramids built by Archie's team of acrobatic Jumpers. His arrow aimed at moral absolutes, George always misses the target of reality. Hoping to illustrate his point about things being only halfway there, he accidentally shoots his arrow into the air; it lands, most conclusively, on a wall in his wife's bedroom. Thinking in this world and being in this world are totally out of sync. As he dictates his lecture on one side of the stage, his wife Dotty cries out vainly for help on the other. In Stoppard's play, however, contraries never meeet in one.

Dotty is as unprepared for facing the music as George is. An incorrigible romantic, this prematurely retired musical comedy star is bogged down by the mythology of the past and the uncertainty of the present. The moon will never be the same again—goodbye Shelley and goodbye Cole Porter: "Goodbye spoony Juney Moon." At the eleventh hour George is still pondering "Zeno Evil, St. Thomas Augustine, Jesus Moore and my late friend the late Herr Thumper who was as innocent as a rainbow," while Dotty sings her swan song astride a spangled crescent moon. But hers is a most unsentimental "Sentimental Journey" ("Heaven how can I believe in heaven?/Just a lying rhyme for seven!"). Even when the lyrics change, the lines of the past provide only cold comfort. As repeated by Dotty and George Moore, T. S. Eliot and Shakespeare ring similarly false. Even Beckett sounds a little tired when lampooned by Archie, the man who believes no problem too great for a plastic bag:

> Do not despair—many are happy much of the time; more eat than starve, more are healthy than sick, more curable than dying; not so many dying as dead; and one of the thieves was saved. Hell's bells and all's well—half the world is at peace with itself, and so is the other half; vast areas are unpolluted; millions of children grow up without suffering deprivation, and millions, while deprived, grow up without suffering cruelties, and millions, while deprived and cruelly treated, none the less grow up. No laughter is sad and many tears are joyful. At the graveside the undertaker doffs his top hat and impregnates the prettiest mourner. Wham, bam, thank you Sam.

Jumpers therefore proclaims an end to innocence without making any quick judgment on its characters' attempts to deal with it. Stoppard's play takes no stand because it sets out to dramatize the situation of not knowing which one to take.

Travesties takes us several steps further in Stoppard's attempt to systematize confusion. In this piece the machinery of play-as-commentary-on-another-play used before in *Rosencrantz and Guildenstern Are Dead* is reassembled in a slightly different form. The tone has been altered to accommodate the levels of theatrical style which help set *Jumpers* in motion. Comedy is once again mismatched with ideology. But in this case Stoppard has us explore a serious relationship between art and revolution. This true history that never happened opens in Zurich and features Lenin, Joyce, and Tristan Tzara as dramatis personae. Each modern hero, however, has his own particular version of what constitutes modern heroism: Lenin's is a hammer and a sickle, Joyce's is art as a fire above all dogma, and Tzara's is a heart that belongs to Dada. Here is Stoppard's three-ring circus of twentieth-century alternatives. Which way should we turn? Where can authenticity be found? Does the artist need to justify himself in political terms? At what point do political realities begin to corrupt human values? When is "revolution" only a code word for crass materialism and bourgeois art? The philosophical debate, however, has been momentarily upstaged by that local aberration known as World War I. With military, ideological, and artistic warfare raging everywhere, the British Consular Office, stiff upper lip as always, opens rehearsals for *The Importance of Being Earnest*. Partisan politics must play second fiddle to drama.

Enter Henry Carr, very marginal man — but the real lead in Stoppard's play. The curtain discovers him as a seedy old man in the Zurich of today "recollecting, perhaps not with entire accuracy," what took place there in 1917–18.[11] Henry Carr is Stoppard's stunt man for recapturing the past. This narrator, however, is not always reliable. From time to time his memory goes on the skids as a scene is repeated with minor variations in a hilarious parody of revisionist psycho-history. The old Marxist Cecily is there to remind her husband of the cold facts, but as an 80-year-old hard-liner, we begin to mistrust her too. Even if he got things right, Carr would never understand the implications of the events he witnessed. For him history is merely the price of a pair of new trousers, his dandified costume for Algernon in *The Importance of Being Earnest*.

Juggling Joyce, Lenin, Tzara, Wilde's play, and Carr's memory, Stoppard counts on what the audience knows of the present to make a running commentary on the spectacle that unfolds in *Travesties*. For Stoppard's audience, no longer innocent, has seen every idea championed in this comedy developed, shortchanged, and frequently prostituted by history. In the name of "art" or "revolution," the idealism expressed in *Travesties* has been seriously compromised by events since 1917. Hence the real impact of Stoppard's play: man can be a revolutionary, man can be an artist, man can even be a revolutionary artist — or man can be, like Henry

Carr, absolutely nothing at all. Given what Stoppard's audience brings with it to the theater concerning the violent history of this century, the latter posture is not necessarily the least attractive.

Travesties therefore surprises us by offering something more than mere "clever nonsense."[12] Making his elements of travesty reverberate with the density of parody, Stoppard tempts us to ask several questions simultaneously. The structure of this play has been carefully arranged to expose its many layers. This is, as the title suggests, a comedy of irreconcilable pluralities. Items which function on one level soon pass on to the next in swift dramatic tempo. Lenin's positive "Da, da," a Russian cry of yes to "revolutsia," is Tzara's nonsense word of artistic rebellion for its own sake and still another linguistic possibility for Joyce to forge in the smithy of his Irish soul. Gwendolen and Cecily move in and out of Wilde's comedy to arrange their experience quite differently in the present play. As the "Appassionata" degenerates absurdly into music-hall contretemps, their famous encounter from *The Importance of Being Earnest* is mocked to the tune of "Mr. Gallagher and Mr. Shean." Such rich allusive texture, however, can be deceptive. Rather than direct us to any one particular course of action, it dooms us instead to an endless circle of parts forever eluding a whole. The vast panorama that unfolds in this play, its scope and its extravagant vitality, has therefore been calculated to place us right in the center of its own fragmentation. Forcing us into a dramatic encounter with uncertainty when we least expected it, Stoppard's comedy rebounds on us.

Travesties, however, is both a beginning and an end. In terms of dramatic form it is the culmination of Stoppard's attempt to "marry" the play of ideas to comedy and farce.[13] But in terms of theme the play demonstrates its author's increasing political consciousness. In questioning the compatability of the revolutionary and artistic temperaments, Stoppard for the first time makes politics a central issue in his work. The subject has certainly been implied before: *Rosencrantz and Guildenstern Are Dead* situates its protagonists in the crossfire of Shakespearean power politics and *Jumpers* abandons its characters on the empty runway of radical liberalism. But wedded simultaneously to so many other considerations, the politics of these plays never succeeds in upstaging the spectacle of possibilities competing for our attention. Though in *Rosencrantz and Guildenstern Are Dead* and *Jumpers* politics makes for some rather strange bedfellows—as it does in the "nuts-and-bolts" of *Dirty Linen*—it commands only secondary interest when shaped by the hand of an accomplished farceur. *Travesties* signals a change, not only a shift in tone, this time in the direction of dramatic intention. With the shock of realism, politics begins to intrude a weary head into a theatrical merry-go-round previously free of any imperatives whatsoever.

When asked in 1977 to discuss the purpose of theater and his feelings about modern man in his own plays, Stoppard admitted that he was being interviewed at a rather transitional moment in his career. But he attempted an answer which ended, ambiguously, with the following poem:

And Apollinaire said, "Come to the edge."
"We'll fall!"
"Come to the edge."
"No, no, we're afraid we'll fall."
"Come to the edge!"
So they came
And he pushed them
And they flew.[14]

The plays which follow are anything but ambiguous. In *Every Good Boy Deserves Favor* Stoppard aims his weapons of parody very heavy-handedly at the K.G.B. and its illegal detention of political prisoners. What saves this play from sliding into propaganda, however, is the ornate preparation for staging.[13] Alexander Ivanov, a victim of Soviet totalitarianism, finds himself in the same cell as another Alexander Ivanov, a genuine lunatic who has fantasies about conducting a symphony orchestra. The Jew's harp has even applied for a visa. Stoppard makes "fantasy" as well as "reality" concrete: when the madman is inspired, the lights go up to reveal a Russian orchestra playing the classical music he alone is supposed to hear. This is, after all, the nation "very good at *Swan Lake* and space technology." Even Lenin, we remember from *Travesties,* had been momentarily struck by a Beethoven Sonata:

I don't know of anything greater than the Appassionata. Amazing, superhuman music. It always makes me feel, perhaps naively, it makes me feel proud of the miracles that human beings can perform. But I can't listen to music often. It affects my nerves, makes me want to say nice stupid things and pat the heads of those people who while living in this vile hell can create such beauty. Nowadays we can't pat heads or we'll get our hands bitten off. We've got to *hit* heads, hit them without mercy, though ideally we're against doing violence to people...

The simultaneous set used in *Jumpers* (which had earlier expanded to incorporate a huge television screen) is now adapted to make musical a grotesque abuse of human rights. Marxism is no longer the same amusing "Da, da" it was in *Travesties.* Yet Stoppard's is no agit-prop theater. What makes *Every Good Boy Deserve Favor* a play and not a political pamphlet is the subservience of ideology to histrionics. In this light and sound show we are so overwhelmed by the extravagance of production that the horror

of repression, Stoppard's real theme, only strikes us as an afterthought—
but one which gnaws at our conscience long after the interludes are over.
Stoppard's elaborate travesty of theatrical propriety turns out to be the
vehicle for sustaining a chilling parody of political brutality. In *Every Good
Boy Deserves Favor* Stoppard's style therefore remains recognizably in-
tact. What has changed—and changed radically—is the use his theater will
now make of it.

Professional Foul is a play for television and as such obeys formal
considerations quite apart from those pertaining to the theatricality of
Every Good Boy Deserves Favor. Though Stoppard says "it was really only
a coincidence that these plays about human rights should have been written
about the same time" and that "there was no sudden conversion on the
road to Damascus," the tone of both plays is more sober, the subject matter
more specific, and the emphasis more political than anything we have seen
in his work before.[16] *Professional Foul* takes place in Prague, where Stoppard has a Philosophical Colloquium coincide with a World Cup Eliminator
soccer match. Even in this "serious response by a writer of comedy,"
Stoppard cannot resist mixing his metaphors.[17] The title of this piece, a
penalty term lifted from European soccer, represents the detachment Professor Anderson risks when an unforseen contact with a young Czech
dissident forces him to violate diplomatic hospitality. Given the platform to
deliver his previously announced paper on "Ethical Fictions and Ethical
Foundations," he speaks out instead on the philosophical basis of human
rights. Anderson, a marginal man like George Moore and "the embodiment of the well-intentioned, mildly distracted, almost totally ineffective
intellectual," surrenders his professorial demeanor but not his dignity:
harsh reality shows him how "ethical foundations" can be a poor excuse
for the "ethical fictions" of political manipulation. He smuggles his former
student's thesis out of the country by hiding it in the unsuspecting Professor
McKendrick's baggage—a most unethical, un-English breach of good
manners but in this instance a most necessary professional foul. Stoppard
has come a long way from the comic frills of *The Real Inspector Hound,* but
the discipline of sustaining dialogue on more than one level and the technique of startling us into recognition with a completely unexpected ending
have remained essentially the same.

Stoppard's recent work has therefore been an attempt to adapt his own
theater style to accommodate social and political issues far more identifi-
able than that motley of opposing values threatening to disturb the comic
surface of his plays. In *Night and Day,* a work which, had it been written
earlier, might have contrasted the lyrics of Cole Porter with the light/dark
imagery of *Richard II* in a sophisticated parody of Noel Coward, Stoppard
turns his attention to trade unionism, the price society must pay to ensure

freedom of the press, and an African nation on the brink of civil war. Kenneth Tynan once called Tom Stoppard "a cool, apolitical stylist" and to illustrate the description quotes the playwright as having said that his favorite line of English drama comes from Christopher Hampton's *The Philanthropist*: "I'm a man of no convictions—at least, I think I am."[19] But Stoppard's recent work displays a darkening tone, a focus on social responsibility, and the necessity—if not the inescapability—of taking a stand. It is impossible to say what role parody and travesty will ultimately take in Stoppard's continuing experimentation or whether they have any future at all in this sudden turn to theatrical naturalism.[20] But what we can say about Tom Stoppard is that, unlike so many other fashionable playwrights, at least he has an authentic style he can develop and perhaps even depart from. In the past Stoppard has given us a new kind of comedy to capture the drama of contemporary ideas. Judging from the quality of his new work, there is no reason to suspect that this serious writer masquerading as a comedian has run out of ammunition. For style in Stoppard has always been a question of substance as well as technique. What he has found in his theater is not only a special way of saying something, but something, at last, that needed very much to be said.

NOTES

1. See the topic of George Moore's lecture on "Man—Good, Bad, or Indifferent?" in *Jumpers* (New York: Grove Press, 1972).

2. Tom Stoppard, "Ambushes for the Audience: Towards a High Comedy of Ideas," *Theatre Quarterly* 14 (1974), pp. 7–8.

3. Ibid., p. 4.

4. Ibid., p. 6.

5. "Old and New in London Now," *Modern Drama* 11 (1968–69), p. 440.

6. "Ambushes for the Audience," pp. 6–7.

7. Allan Rodway discusses comedy in connection with *Rosencrantz and Guildenstern Are Dead* and *Jumpers* in *English Comedy* (London: Chatto & Windus, 1975), pp. 264–72. On Stoppard's use of the "marginal man" to refract the debates in his plays, see C. W. E. Bigsby, "Tom Stoppard" in *Contemporary Dramatists*, ed. James Vinson (New York: Macmillan Company, 1977), pp. 760–63.

8. "Ambushes for the Audience," p. 6.

9. Ibid., pp. 7–8.

10. See John Russell Taylor's chapter on Stoppard in *The Second Wave: British Drama for the Seventies* (London: Methuen, 1971).

11. See Stoppard's note on the real-life Henry Wilfred Carr in the Faber edition of *Travesties* (London: Faber and Faber, 1975), p. 12.

12. *Travesties*, p. 37.

13. "Ambushes for the Audience, " p. 8.

14. "Gleanings from London," *Readers Theatre News* 4, 2 (Spring, 1977), p. 4.

15. The original production of this play integrated the London Symphony Orchestra under the direction of André Previn.

16. Milton Shulman, "The Politicizing of Tom Stoppard," *The New York Times,* April 23, 1978, sec. 2, p. 3. For an elaboration of Stoppard's recent political views and his reaction to the problem of human rights in Czechoslovakia, see Kenneth Tynan, "Profiles: Withdrawing with Style from Chaos," *The New Yorker,* December 19, 1977, pp. 41–111.

17. John O'Connor, "TV: Stoppard's 'Professional Foul' on WNET," *The New York Times,* April 26, 1978, p. 32.

18. Ibid.

19. Shulman, p. 3.

20. Benedict Nightingale, "Have Pinter and Stoppard Turned to Naturalism?" *The New York Times,* December 3, 1978, sec. 2, p. 4.

The Method of Madness: Tom Stoppard's Theatrum Logico-Philosophicum

DIETRICH SCHWANITZ

The theatre is a medium which simulates reality by presenting us with a segment of it. But since Plato it has also been understood and used as a model for the whole of reality, for the world at large. This model has been called the theatrical metaphor or the image of the theatrum mundi and was particularly en vogue during the Renaissance and Baroque periods.[1] Its central statement that 'all the world's a stage, and all the men and women merely players' (As You Like It, II, 7) contains several implications which can be paraphrased as follows:

1) if people are only acting out their lives like parts in a drama they are under the control of a playwright who is responsible for the play, as a rule the author of the play is understood to be God.

2) limited by the narrow perspective allowed by the individual parts, people, like players, cannot grasp the meaning of the whole play; this can only be understood by the spectator and the dramatist (God, the historian, the philosopher).

3) as actors in a drama, people are not part of a fundamental reality; like actors they are not quite real and will be judged from the point of view of a more fundamental, transcendental reality.

If can easily be seen that these implications have led to a number of conclusions that are, by and large, psychologically gratifying: a person cannot be made responsible for the position that is allotted to him; even if the part a person plays is unattractive or looks meaningless, the theatrical analogy contains the assurance that the play as a whole has meaning and that every part, no matter how disagreeable, contributes to the harmony of the whole; it is therefore useless to rebel against a part—the only task is, as Epectetes said, to play it well.

This model of reality has a certain conservative tendency;[2] it is able and is meant to console, and it expresses the conviction that there is a difference between the fictive, transitory reality of the play (and this world) and the fundamental reality of the playwright or spectator (the transcendental reality of God or the reality of immutable laws of the philosopher); and it is able to express (and reconcile the individual with) the feeling of helplessness against some inscrutable power that has prescribed him a part which he is unable to understand but which he is nevertheless forced to play. As one can see, the theatrical metaphor is burdened with a certain ambiguity which, however, has made it all the more attractive as a literary and philosophical commonplace. As such it has been frequently employed by the drama itself, which could put it to the test and to artistic use by applying it to itself. Because of the feeling of resignation and conservative consolation it expressed, it was less frequently employed in the literature of a victorious bourgeoisie, but significantly enough it has been experiencing a comeback in a modified form in the twentieth century.[3] And it is in this context that we have to see the work of Tom Stoppard.

Modern literature and drama exploited this metaphor mainly by dismantling or deforming it in one way or another. Thus it could be shown that the play of life was a joke and a bad one at that, that it was a cruel and fantastic farce 'signifying nothing' as Macbeth already surmised;[4] it could be pointed out that the author of the play was mad, that he did not really exist, that man acted out his part in a void with nobody looking and nobody caring; and it could be demonstrated that man was not content with his part, that he rebelled against it or wanted to write his own part and be his own author. The former attitude corresponds to a surrealist or absurdist point of view, the latter expresses an existentialist stance. Playwrights who, like Stoppard, exploit the theatrical analogy extensively tend to stress dramatic technique; i.e. they use the technique of play-within-the-play, play-outside-the-play and all kinds of play-reality confrontations.[5] And Stoppard is a particularly versatile and inventive technician. There is one further implication of the theatrical anology which I have briefly alluded to: through the differentiation between a dramatic and metadramatic reality, the world compared to a drama is pronounced not quite real. I think that the sense of the reduced character of reality expressed here has become a pervasive and frequently commented upon feeling today. One aspect of it is that the theatrical analogy has invaded sociology where it has been reborn as an elaborate role-theory which in its turn — significantly enough — was accepted and absorbed into the view the general public in Western society has of itself.[6] I think that Stoppard is concerned with this problem and I should like to show that his technique can best be understood from that perspective.

Before analyzing some of his major plays I should like to give a short survey of Stoppard's background and production so far.

Tom Stoppard was born in 1937 in Zlin, Czechoslovakia, the son of Eugene Straussler. Before the German invasion, the family fled to Singapore, but were forced to move again after the Japanese occupation of the city, during which Stoppard's father was killed. In India his mother remarried and the family name became Stoppard. After returning to England, Stoppard attended Prep-School and Boarding Grammar School and in 1954 began his career as a journalist and as a theater reviewer. In 1960 he wrote his first play *A Walk on the Water* which was later produced under the title *Enter a Free Man*. This was the version finally staged in the West End after several revisions including a television adaptation. It is a sort of Ibsenist play about a man with a life-lie who is strongly reminiscent of Willy Loman in Miller's *Death of a Salesman* though more farcical. After three more or less autobiographical stories *Reunion; Life, Times: Fragments* and *The Story,* he wrote two fifteen-minute radio-plays: *The Dissolution of Dominic Boot* later to be expanded and adapted for television, and *'M' is for Moon among Other Things*. These were followed by *The Gamblers,* the first play he considers as his own (produced 1965 by the Bristol University Drama Department). This play deals with the relationship and final reversal of roles between a political prisoner and his executioner on the eve and the morning of the execution. Its principal method lies in contrasting philosophical dialogues with farcical stage business. In 1967 Stoppard won nation-wide recognition after the Old Vic production of *Rosencrantz and Guildenstern Are Dead.* This play originated in a one-act verse burlesque called *Rosencrantz and Guildenstern meet King Lear* which Stoppard wrote in 1964 during a visit to Berlin. Later Stoppard eliminated King Lear, confined himself to the events in Elsinore and re-wrote the play in prose. With his final version Stoppard was immediately recognized and acclaimed as one of the leading playwrights of Great Britain. Since then Stoppard has written for the radio, for television and the stage, not to mention his major novel *Lord Malquist and Mister Moon,* which was published at the same time as *Rosencrantz and Guildenstern Are Dead* was being produced. His radio plays include:

1. *If You're Glad I'll Be Frank.* This is about a bus-driver who has identified his long lost wife Gladys in the voice of the speaking clock; in the seconds snatched from his bus time table he tries but fails to rescue her from the G.P.O.

2. *Albert's Bridge.* To save the expenses for the maintenance of a bridge, a city council switches from a paint lasting two years to one which lasts eight and reduces the crew of four painters to one. Albert, the man hired, is a university graduate who gets fascinated by his detached view of the world below which makes the terrestrial chaos look like order. After 2 years, however, it turns out that in switching from the 2 year to the 8

year-cycle a mistake has been made: Albert has only painted one quarter of the bridge with the new paint when the remaining three quarters covered with the 2-year paint rapidly deteriorates. To save it they send an army of 1800 painters to do the job in one day. Under their military march the bridge collapses.

3. *Where Are They Now?* This depicts an Old Boys' Dinner contrasting the happy memories with flashbacks of the cruel reality of the past. At the end, one of the Old Boys finds out that he is at the wrong reunion.

4. *Artist Descending a Staircase.* This interesting play is an exercise in the reconstruction of relationships and a mysterious death: a young girl fell in love with one of three artist friends at an exhibition of their work before she became blind so that she can identify her lover later only by the picture she thought was his. One of the rejected artists is still in love with her long after she has committed suicide because the other got tired of her, when the third suggests that her identification was a mistake since the picture may very well have belonged to the rejected lover. After this shattering revelation the rejected lover breaks his neck by accidentally falling down the staircase leaving the other two accusing each other of murder. The play shows the reconstruction of these relationships from the time of the accident through five retrogressive flash-backs to a date in 1914 and back through the same stages to the present. Some of the motifs are taken up again in *Travesties.*

For television Stoppard wrote the following pieces:

1. *A Separate Peace.* A man books himself into a nursing home without being ill just because he likes the regimented routine but ends up disconcerting the staff.

2. *Another Moon Called Earth.* While the historian Bone tries to discover the pattern behind history, his wife Penelope takes to bed on the occasion of the first moonlanding rejecting any further responsibility for her acts. As her relationship with her doctor assumes an increasingly ambiguous character she also seems to become instrumental in killing her maid. This play is practically the nucleus version of *Jumpers.*

3. *Neutral Ground.* A television thriller based on Sophocles' *Philoctetes.*

4. *Teeth.* A jealous dentist takes his revenge on his rival in the dentist's chair by staining his teeth green, pulling his front tooth and seducing his wife who is the dentist's nurse.

5. *The Engagement* (the expanded version of *The Dissolution of Dominic Boot).* The hero's efforts to borrow money for a taxi lead him around town running up an enormous fare and end in the loss of his fiancée and his job.

6. *Professional Foul.* A professor of ethics who goes to give a paper at a philosophical congress in Prague (and incidentally to see a football match) gets drawn into politics when a former pupil asks him to smuggle out a paper on human rights (the play was written to mark Amnesty International's Prisoner of Conscience Year 1977).

These short plot summaries may already point to the techniques and problems Stoppard favours: many of the plots are wildly improbable and contain incidents which originate through the blending of two completely different situations; several plays deal with investigation, reconstructions or interpretations of some strange happenings. This shows clearly that Stoppard is not a social realist or committed playwright in the usual sense but, rather, is concerned with the structure and logic of reality. Many of these radio and television plays are preludes and early studies of themes he explores in greater depth in the stage plays. Thus both his novel and the radio play *Another Moon Called Earth* lead up to *Jumpers* while *Travesties* depends on the experience gathered with *Where Are They Now?* and *Artist Descending a Staircase.* This makes it possible to concentrate our analysis on the theatre plays; moreover, TV plays demand much less textual discipline because their main artistic potential consists in the composition of pictures, while Stoppard's extremely skillful handling of the radio play technique deserves a special study.

Among the theatre plays, however, there are some minor pièces d'occasion like *Dogg's Our Pet,* or *Dirty Linen and New-Found Land,* which is a light-weight. *Dogg's Our Pet* is a Wittgensteinian experiment to explore new forms in participatory theatre written for the opening of Interaction's Almost Free Theatre of Ed Berman. *Dirty Linen* (with *New-Found Land* as entr'acte) is a very light piece about the difficulties the members of a committee for the investigation of parliamentary sexual morals are having reconciling their task with their own sins. *Rosencrantz and Guildenstern Are Dead* is by far the best known and certainly the most frequently analysed of Stoppard's plays if for no other reason than that it aroused the interest of Shakespeare critics.[7] It presents the action of *Hamlet* from the point of view of the two well-known attendant lords. The idea of inventing stories which might explain some aspect of a Shakespeare play or throw a new light on it through writing the prehistory of a character is not altogether new and demonstrates the vitality of Shakespeare's plays as modern myths which are known to practically everybody. Thus Gordon Bottomley wrote the prehistory of Macbeth in *Gruach* and of King Lear in *King Lear's Wife*; Hauptmann wrote a play called *Hamlet in Wittenberg* and Gilbert and Sullivan even wrote a burlesque with the title: *Rosencrantz and Guildenstern.* Stoppard's originality in treating this material[8] consists in his confining himself to the little information Shakespeare gives us about the characters and to the few appearances they make within the original which are then quoted in full. The long gaps in between he fills in by showing us the two characters in their confusion and bewilderment, trying to find out what is going on, what their roles are within the action, what Hamlet's motives are and what it all means. Apart from their frantic attempts at interpreting events, Stoppard explores their activity of simply waiting and killing time in playing games, tossing coins, telling jokes and carrying on the conversation. A further level is introduced into this construction by the players of Elsinore who confront them with the kind of action out of which they themselves have sprung: the play.

The many critics who have analyzed the play have largely concentrated on the relation between Shakespeare and Stoppard's play, tracing the structural combination and thematic parallels,[9] and pointing out its indebtedness to the theatre of the absurd, especially to Beckett's *Waiting for Godot,* [10] and to Pirandello and the use of the theatrical metaphor.[11] Few, however, have analyzed the peculiar impression an audience must receive from a play which makes the very relation of some characters to a play its subject.[12] For, as we shall see, the very point of such an arrangement lies in changing the audience's relation to the theatrical event and, incidentally, to its own sense of reality.

Stoppard plays with several intricately connected layers of reality/fiction: the basic level is provided by the theatrical occasion as such in which the audience sees Stoppard's play. *Rosencrantz and Guildenstern* shows two characters reacting to a play we know very well: *Hamlet.* The distinction between the two levels is indicated by the switch from one style (absurdist) to another (Aristotelian Shakespeare). The combination of these three levels produces very sophisticated effects: the position of Rosencrantz and Guildenstern in Shakespeare's play (they get caught in an action they don't understand) justifies their being presented outside the drama in the style developed by the theatre of the absurd (which expresses this predicament). At the same time the two styles exclude each other since traditional Aristotelian drama makes sense, and the audience understands the action of Hamlet (at least much better than the two bewildered lords); but it also understands Rosencrantz and Guildenstern's bewilderment. This paradox combines the limited perspective of the two role players with the better understanding of the uninvolved spectator, thus merging the two complementary perspectives of the theatrical metaphor. This makes it possible for the two characters, whose existential mystification we are supposed to watch, to define their own lives in terms which the audience recognizes as belonging to its own view of the traditional Aristotelian theatre and of Hamlet. Here are some of the statements made by either Rosencrantz or Guildenstern:

> 'All right! We don't question, we don't doubt. We perform.' (78)
> 'Consistency is all I ask!' (28)
> 'Incidents! All we get is incidents! Dear God, is it too much to expect a little sustained action?!' (85)
> 'What a fine persecution—to be kept intrigued without ever quite being enlightened.' (30)[13]

This shows that the two lords have an orthodox artistic taste which is explicitly made clear when Guil says: 'I'd prefer art to mirror life' and 'I want a good story, with a beginning, middle and end.' But their predicament belies this expectation. Stoppard makes this point by introducing a fourth level: the players present the future story of Rosencrantz and Guildenstern in dumb show, but the two lords do not recognize themselves and applaud the acting of their own deaths.[14]

The confusion of theatre and life produces in the audience an oscillation between two perspectives: Rosencrantz and Guildenstern are like spectators (or Shakespeare critics) insofar as they are only partly involved in the action and try to make sense of it; as spectators they have a right to expect consistency in a work of art; but they are also involved as actors in a play whose very consistency demands that their perspective be limited to their parts. Since this limitation is an existential one, they share it with the audience who cannot be sure of the meaning of their own lives; and this in turn proves that the traditional expectation of the drama is all but justified. The logic induced is cyclical, self-defeating, but consistent. Such logic is disastrous since it involves all reality in its destruction. In following it up, Stoppard treads the traditional paths of the theatre of the absurd by questioning the (indeed) basic foundations of reality: identity, memory, time, communication and probability. This then is the basic technique of Stoppard: he confuses two different levels of reality; the resulting mystification produces in the audience the attempt to resolve it; but the confusion is arranged in such a way that any attempt to find a starting point for its solution on any of the levels leads only to a further justification of the confusion: these attempts therefore run in mad cycles. The principle can succinctly be illustrated by the following exchange in which Guil and Ros want to play a game; while Ros still talks about the game, Guil is already playing it, but, at the same time, he is also talking about the game. In principle this is the same kind of confusion which is produced by being inside and outside a play at the same time:

ROS.:	We could play at questions.
GUIL.:	What good would that do?
ROS.:	Practice.
GUIL.:	Statement. One-love.
ROS.:	Cheating!
GUIL.:	How?
ROS.:	I hadn't started yet.
GUIL.:	Statement: Two-love.
ROS.:	Are you counting that?
GUIL.:	What?
ROS.:	Foul! No repetitions. Three-love, First game to ... (30)

In accordance with its cyclical structure this kind of confusion is endless and completely frustrating because it allows no way out. Thus the bewilderment of the two characters in no way indicates a freedom of interpretation. On the contrary, a switch to the other aspect of the theatrical metaphor raises the suspicion that—as in a play—the confusion is planned. Guil shows an awareness of this: 'Because, if we happened, just happened to discover, or even suspect, that our spontaneity was part of their order, we'd know that we were lost.' In saying this he describes the act of playing: the played spontaneity is demanded by the order of the play. In the last resort the cyclical spiral induced through the confusion of reality and fiction reaches the real theatrical situation: everything that Ros and Guil say about themselves using the theatrical metaphor is justified by their being characters played by real actors, in a real theatrical situation watched by a real audience. And everything the First Player says about actors applies to the real actor who plays the First Player. Therefore, the audience is drawn into this process and made aware that they too could be only part of a play—since all the proofs to the contrary have been tested in the play and exploded. They can only believe that they are real and that, too, is all the characters are left with:

> *PLAYER:* ... Everything has to be taken on trust; truth is only that which is taken to be true. It's the awareness of living. There may be nothing behind it, but it doesn't make any difference so long as it is honoured. One acts on assumptions ... (48)

Once this trust is lost, the sense of reality is also lost. Here Stoppard confirms the insight of most psychologists and psychiatrists that there must be a rock-bottom security (Erikson),[15] a sense of ontological security (Laing)[16] as a prerequisite for a sense of reality. Doubt opens a passage into a bottomless pit of unreality. Perhaps this is one aspect of the title's meaning: Rosencrantz and Guildenstern have never been alive. Their

frequent exchanges on death in the play all end in the conviction: 'Death is
... not. Death isn't. You take my meaning.'

Death is the ultimate negative. Not-being. (78)

Therefore Guil thinks that death cannot be acted. However, when the
Player does act it he too is taken in, which proves his point: that what one
can believe in cannot be the ultimate negative, cannot be death. This then is
the final opposition: belief and nothingness. The play leaves it unresolved.

This would also apply to *The Real Inspector Hound* which is equally
intricate though much shorter (it covers only half of a double bill).[17] Two
theatre critics watch a thriller strongly reminiscent of Agatha Christie's
The Mouse Trap. Their comments on the play and their conversations
reveal enough of their situation and respective characters to provide material for a later stage of the play when both critics are drawn into the murder
plot of the play they watch: the telephone keeps ringing on the empty stage
until one of the critics (Moon) can stand it no longer and answers it only to
find out that his colleague's wife wants to talk to her husband (Birdboot).
When one of the characters of the play (Felicity) comes back on stage she
addresses Birdboot with the same dialogue she had previously used with
her lover in the play. And it is in the following conversation that this
dialogue which had sounded very artificial and theatrical the first time
becomes uncannily real against the background of the information we have
about the theatre critic. Gradually the two critics become completely
implicated in the play until they find out that the corpse on the stage belongs
to one of their colleagues. Later, their two empty chairs are occupied by
two of the characters. Moon tries to solve the murder, is himself suspected
and finally shot by the real inspector Hound who turns out to be his rival in
theatre criticism. *The Real Inspector Hound* confronts the spectator with
two levels of reality: one is represented by the thriller being performed, the
other by the critics who watch. Both realities are properly defined by the
usual markers we use to index the respective frames with which we bracket
reality. On the level of solid reality (outside the play) we learn that the critic
Birdboot has been philandering with the girl who plays Felicity and is now
in love with the actress playing Cynthia. Within the play the young lover
Simon throws over Felicity because he too has fallen in love with Cynthia.
He visits Cynthia and is very embarrassed to find Felicity also visiting.
Before he can escape she corners him, thus starting their dialogue. Later in
the play Birdboot steps onto the empty stage and answers the phone.
Before he can escape into his seat Felicity comes back and addresses him
with the same lines with which she addresses Simon. But now the lines take
on a realistic and sinister meaning because they refer to the reality of her
relationship with Birdboot outside the play. The parallel between Birdboot

(the critic) and Simon (the character) is so cleverly arranged that Birdboot's being caught standing on the stage in the middle of the play is just as embarrassing as Simon's being caught by Felicity visiting Cynthia. Both situations are expressed by exactly the same dialogue. When it is spoken for the second time between Felicity and Birdboot the amazed audience gradually realizes that the conversation that had sounded so theatrical the first time seems quite natural and fitting the second time. Through this device the distinction between intra-theatrical fiction and the extra-theatrical reality becomes obliterated. The same statements that were previously limited to the intra-theatrical fiction become also applicable to the outside reality. Through this contamination of reality and fiction, Stoppard very skillfully produces the impression that what we thought was a very conventional and theatrical thriller contains more reality than met the eye; and that what we thought to be solid reality dissolves into any number of tenuous assumptions. The effect is funny but — at the same time — rather unsettling. The audience is led to doubt its own faculty of distinguishing between levels of reality and frames of reference. It may throw a revealing light on Stoppard, who produces this effect in many variations, that this very mystification and confusion has come under scientific scrutiny in such seemingly unrelated fields as logic, interaction theory and psychiatry. In order to show the significance this has for drama and for Stoppard, I shall very briefly indicate how this phenomenon has been explored and explained.[18]

Philosophers and logicians very early came across a kind of paradox that is characterized in the following example: A Cretan says: 'All Cretans are liars.' If this were true the statement must be a lie, and therefore the contrary be valid, which would mean that all Cretans were truthful, which would confirm the statement about the Cretans and so on ad infinitum. This is a so-called semantic paradox which could only be solved in modern times through a derivation of the solution that Bertrand Russell had found for a similar logical-mathematical paradox. Russell had found a fundamental distinction between all possible categories or classifications of things: there were those classes that did not contain themselves (the class of cats is not in itself a cat) and those that did (the class of words is also a word). The division of the universe into self-containing and self-excluding classes is exhaustive, there is no third possibility (tertium non datur). If we call all classes that contain themselves C and all those that do not E, they themselves have to be fitted into this universal opposition. But this turns out to be impossible: if we assume that E contains itself, it does not contain itself, because it is by definition the class that does not contain itself. And if we assume that it does not contain itself it fulfills the condition of self-containing, for it is the distinctive quality of all classes belonging to category E that they do not contain themselves. Russell solved that paradox by formulating the following rule: whatever concerns the whole of a class may not be part of this class. A class is on a higher logical level than any of its elements and therefore a class may not be confronted with any of its elements on the same level. Following Wittgenstein, logical positivists have found out that ordinary language abounds with similar paradoxes. So the word 'liar' in the sentence 'all Cretans are liars' sounds like the word 'miller' or 'grocer.' Nevertheless it belongs to a different category because it does not refer to an object but to language which makes statements about objects. It is not part of object-language; instead it must be seen on the higher level of meta-language, a language which comments on object-language. Many logical positivists have come to the conclusion that traditional metaphysics and its problems are only the result of the confusion between object-language and meta-language, and that once this confusion is cleared up all metaphysical paradoxes will disappear. Unfortunately ordinary language does not make the distinction between object- and meta-language; therefore Wittgenstein even went so far as to maintain that any reasonable statement about language was impossible within the structure of that same language (including this last one). That would indeed make nonsense of all literary criticism and of all scholarship. Without daring to judge this enormous issue, I shall proceed to show that the effect of the unclarified self-reflexiveness of language on the pragmatic level can indeed be disastrous—as interactionists and psychiatrists have found out and as can be seen from the following Jewish numbskull tale: a Russian landlord orders the Orthodox priest and the Rabbi to engage in an intellectual contest by asking each other questions. The first who failed to answer a question was to lose his head. The Rabbi hesitates to take part in such a dangerous exploit until the village idiot offers himself instead under the condition that he is allowed the first question. The priest is content with the arrangement, so the idiot asks the following question: What is the meaning of the Hebrew eineni jodea (I don't know)? The priest who knows Hebrew well answers promptly: 'I don't know' and loses his head. When the delighted Jews asked the idiot how he had hit on that clever ruse he answered: Well, some time ago I asked the Rabbi after the meaning of eineni jodea, and he said: I don't know. So I thought that if our clever Rabbi could not even tell me the meaning of eineni jodea the priest would never be able to do it.[19]

Without knowing it, the idiot had manoeuvered the priest into an impossible position, because the question cannot be answered without having resort to Russell's rule that whatever concerns the structure of a system (the meaning of language) cannot be expressed within that structure. Predicaments of this kind have been called double-binds (self-contradictory orders combined with severe punishments for failure to obey them). Some psychiatrists claim that double-binds of a similar nature can become typical of communication-processes within families. Here they can assume the most diverse forms: a statement can contradict its context (irony), or the emotional form of a statement can be at odds with what is being said, or the form of a statement can contradict its content (like the order: be spontaneous!) etc. Some psychiatrists claim that people exposed to this kind of communication by their mothers or families from early childhood are prevented from developing the faculty of taking part in normal communication, because their ability to distinguish between levels is severely impaired. The confusion thus engendered leads to symptoms that have been observed as part of the syndrome classified as schizophrenia. They include the inability to understand irony, the tendency to take jokes and metaphors literally and the general incapacity to distinguish between the inner and the outer world, the word and the thing, ego and alter ego, and the individual and his role. This is often accompanied by feelings of being controlled by invisible powers and a feeling of derealization and unreality.[20]

I think it has become clear by now that, in the plays hitherto discussed, Stoppard produces this very pattern: he confuses the theatrical fiction which is supposed to be a fictive picture of reality with extra-dramatic reality until the audience finds it impossible to decide whether an action or a dialogue is supposed to be part of a play or of reality.[21] Since the audience is also witnessing a play (albeit by Stoppard) it becomes gradually unsettled about its feeling with regard to this event as well. Once the distinction between reality and play is effectively blurred, the confusion becomes corrosive and there can be no Archimedean point from which to regain the difference.

This confusion can also be attained in the pictorial arts, and one of the painters who specialized in it was the surrealist Magritte. For instance, he painted a picture with a picture in it which, however, was not only a model of the reality shown on the painting but also its direct continuation.[22] It was, simultaneously, a model and a part of reality, thereby violating Russell's theory of types. It is therefore hardly without significance that Stoppard called another play *After Magritte*. This short piece has a completely circular structure: in a very bizarre opening tableau we can see a couple quarreling about an equally bizarre occurrence they have just witnessed after leaving an exhibition of Magritte: when they pulled out of their parking lot near the gallery they saw the puzzling spectacle of a blind, one-legged football player with a white beard hopping through the rain with a stick in one hand and a tortoise under his arm (according to various interpretations). An old lady watches this incident and reports it to Inspector Foot who turns up at the couple's flat in pursuit of what he thinks was a one-legged minstrel making off with the advance takings of the box-office. But it turns out that the mysterious stranger had really been Foot himself; when he was shaving in his pyjamas near the open window he saw a couple (the couple in the play) get into a car and drive off. In order to secure the free parking lot for himself, he grabbed his wife's handbag with the change and the keys and her umbrella and rushed into the street; but he did not get very far because in his haste he had put both feet into the same leg of his pyjama trousers. So the report about himself had been the occasion for the Inspector's pursuit of himself which led him to the couple who had provided the motive for making this bizarre appearance in the first place. With this play Stoppard exemplifies the socio-psychological insight that reality is a product of our respective interpretations. Since one and the same event can give rise to as many different interpretations as there are witnesses, reality becomes dichotomized. The more bizarre an event is, the more likely this is, for there is no end to man's ingenuity in interpretation.[23] And Stoppard goes on to illustrate a rule that was first established by the sociologist W. I. Thomas: if men define a situation as real, it is real in its consequences.[24] In the construction of the plot, Stoppard again blends two levels of reality: the interpretative and the causal connection between people and the event they witness. Since all interpretations leave out this causal connection, the discovery that they themselves were closely connected with the event is somewhat shocking when it dawns on people; for it shows that they do not recognize themselves and that the bizarre interpretations they come up with have to be seen as a form of complete self-alienation. Though *After Magritte* seems rather light it is a very skillful exercise in social philosophy.

It seems that in his more ambitious full-length play *Jumpers*, Stoppard combined the plot of *Another Moon Called Earth* with the central situation of *After Magritte*: in the middle of the play a policeman rings the bell of a front door which is opened by a man holding a bow-and-arrow in one hand and a tortoise in the other, his face covered with shaving-foam. This time the man is George Moore, a professor of moral philosophy who uses the bow-and-arrow and the tortoise to illustrate Zeno's paradox about the impossibility of movement (and Achilles' incapacity to overtake the tortoise and the arrow's to hit the mark)[25] while preparing a lecture in which he attempts to prove the existence of God.[26] The inspector comes to investigate the murder (by all appearances committed by Moore's wife Dotty without her husband's knowledge) of a professor of logic, shot during a performance of acrobatics staged by the university gymnastics team to celebrate the victory of the Liberal Radical Party at the polls. While this technocratic fascistoid movement takes over society, Professor Moore is engrossed in his attempt to prove the existence of God, and his wife takes to bed because a British moon landing has drained her life of meaning. The murder—of which the professor is not aware to the very last, mistaking references to it for remarks about the death of his rabbit—is hushed up through the efficient exertions of the Vice-Chancellor of the university, Sir Archibald Jumper, who also manages to combine with this function the position of coroner, solicitor and loving doctor of Moore's wife. As the epitome of modern secularism, nihilism, pragmatism, relativism and efficiency, he is the antagonist of Moore who in his turn fails to understand and deal with what is going on around him through his preoccupation with metaphysics and even inadvertently kills his pet rabbit and tortoise.

The combination of acrobatics with philosophy ironically takes the ideals of ancient Greece literally and provides a background metaphor for many puns about mental and ethical acrobatics, besides being the source of much of the fun generated by the parody of the very school of philosophy we have mentioned above: Wittgenstein, Russell, Moore, Ayer etc. But precisely with regard to its philosophical content the play suffers from a serious defect: apart from poking fun at the philosophers, Stoppard also tries to be serious by introducing a philosophical correlative to his technical acrobatics through the extensive ramifications of Professor Moore. But—as Moore himself says about another philosopher—Stoppard's technical acrobatics are better than his thinking. As far as I can see, Moore's disquisitions seldom rise above an inept handling of Aquinas, Cantor, Ryle, Wittgenstein and Russell.[27] Nor is his thought—whatever it is worth— vindicated by being functionally important. Its only truly philosophical point is that Moore gets entangled in the by now familiar paradox of trying to prove the existence of God with the very logical method which has dethroned him in the first place. This leads to the same cyclical and mad logic which we have found in the previous plays. Moore's frustration is matched by his wife's disillusionment with the perspective of the earth as seen from the moon. In demonstrating this perspective relativism Stoppard uses many of his usual devices: the murder of the professor, his wife's relation to Sir Archibald and many wildly improbable coincidences which are open to all kinds of interpretations. This may be succinctly illustrated by one of the more philosophical anecdotes that Moore tells about Wittgenstein: Meeting a friend in the corridor, Wittgenstein said, 'Tell me, why do people always say it was natural for men to assume that the sun went round the earth rather than that the earth went round the sun?' His friend said, 'Well, obviously because it just looks as if the sun is going round the earth.' To which the philosopher replied: 'Well, what would it have looked like if it had looked as if the earth was rotating?' (75)

This relativism, however, is not brought home to the audience as forcefully as in many of the other plays because in *Jumpers* Stoppard hardly exploits the medium, that is, the theatrical metaphor. I think it is not going too far to assume that Stoppard falls victim to the same logic which he exploits so skillfully elsewhere: he tries to deal seriously with the relationship of technical acrobatics and philosophical thought within a form defined by this relationship. As a whole, the attempt miscarries.

Fortunately Stoppard's next full-length play, *Travesties,* avoids this mistake. Though it is a play based on historical fact it is almost impossible to summarize.[28] The historical material, however, is extremely meagre even if possibly very significant. During the First World War there lived in Zürich not very far from each other, the following people: James Joyce, destined to revolutionize the world of fiction; Vladimir Ilyich Ulyanov, called Lenin, destined to revolutionize the world of reality; and Tristan Tzara, the leader of the Dadaist movement, who wanted to revolutionize everything. Stoppard brings these people together by drawing on an equally historical if less significant incident: Joyce became the business manager of a theatre company which was supposed to advertise British culture in wartime Switzerland through the performance of Wilde's *The Importance of Being Earnest.*[29] The actor playing Algernon was a minor British consular official by the name of Carr who, after having scored a minor success in this role, entered world literature by suing Joyce for the reimbursement of the cost of the trousers he had bought for the occasion. Joyce won the case and immortalized Carr as the Chauvinist Private Carr who knocks down Stephen Dedalus in the Circe Episode of *Ulysses.*[30] Stoppard in his turn transforms Carr into an elderly gentleman married to the girl he met in the Zürich public library. He recollects his encounters with Lenin, Joyce and Tzara, but his memory being rather erratic, he becomes the consul while the historical consul is degraded to his manservant Bennett. One further result of the erratic nature of Carr's memory is that (as Stoppard explains) 'the story (like a toy train perhaps) occasionally jumps the rails and has to be restarted at the point where it goes wild' (27). As Carr consecutively drops a scene and picks it up again a sequence of cycles is being built up forming a sort of musical pattern of variations on a theme. The theme is the relation of art and politics, or literature and solid, existential and cruel reality. The overall pattern for the composition of these variations is provided by Wilde's *The Importance of Being Earnest.* Thus Stoppard constructs equations between practically all of his characters (except Lenin) and almost all of Wilde's: the young Carr is Algernon, Tzara is Ernest, Gwendolen as Carr's sister types for Joyce who is equated with Aunt Augusta, and Cecily is the Zürich librarian who helps Lenin with his *Imperialism, the Highest Stage of Capitalism.* Just as Gwendolen is an admirer of Joyce, Cecily is a disciple of Lenin. Therefore they allow their respective admirers Tzara and Carr only to pay their addresses if they share their principles. Tristan Tzara, who already has a reputation as a Dadaist, poses as comrade Jack to Cecily, telling her that the notorious Tristan is his profligate brother who has unfortunately succumbed to decadent nihilism. Carr, who in his capacity as consular official has to spy on Lenin to help prevent his return to Russia, impersonates this invented brother. He pinches Tzara's visiting card, meets Cecily in the library and dares her to reform him. Cecily and Gwendolen each test their admirer's principles by having him judge a chapter from the respective manuscripts they have to type. Through a mistake the manuscripts get mixed up so that Tzara, who is supposed to express his reaction to the chapter "Oxen of the Sun" in *Ulysses,* talks about *Imperialism, the Highest Stage of Capitalism* which he finds wanting in grace, style and interest. Correspondingly Carr, who has to judge Lenin's analysis as social critique, finds himself voicing his opinion on an erratic tale remotely connected with midwifery. Out of this confusion of identities and changing of manuscripts one improbable but decisive event emerges: Carr's manservant Bennett who has radical sympathies hands over the consular correspondence to the radicals and Lenin leaves for the Finland Station.

By deriving tone and structure for the treatment of his theme from Wilde's play, Stoppard casts the seemingly weighty subject of art vs. politics into an appropriately inappropriate form (this process, incidentally, is the definition of travesty). Besides Wilde's play, Stoppard finds two further justifications for the freedom which he takes with his material: the more realistic old Carr's defective memory is, the more intrinsically justified is the trend of modern art towards montage and construction. Thus he sprinkles the play with dialogues in limericks, quotations from Shakespeare, travesties of conjuring tricks and Dadaist nonsense, a lengthy parody of Joyce's question-and-answer chapter in *Ulysses,* and parodies of the usual memories-of-the-famous of the type: halfway to the Finland Station with V. I. Lenin (with an allusion to Edmund Wilson's excellent book that Stoppard exploited).[31] This playful mode is structurally juxtaposed with the historical impact of Lenin's politics. And again Stoppard finds in art a forceful metaphor for the accidents, vicissitudes and inherent improbabilities of real life: Lenin's success was just as much an improbable construct as Wilde's play and sometimes even shows aspects almost as surrealistically funny: in order to get safely to Russia, Lenin planned to get hold of two Swedish passports for Zinoviev and himself and then, since neither of them knew any Swedish, to travel as two Swedish deaf mutes.[32] This sounds almost as surrealistic as the idea that the café-conspirators of No. 14 Spiegelgasse were to change the course of world history: 'Social Democrats for Civil War in Europe. Total attendance: four. Ulyanov, Mrs. Ulyanov, Zinoviev and a police spy' (24). As Bennett puts it: 'A betting man would lay odds of about a million to one against Lenin's views prevailing' (32). Through their juxtaposition, art and the deadly reality of war and revolution are made to define each other. Thus being an artist at all is defined as living in Switzerland during a World War. On the other hand, the solidity of real life is dissolved into constructs that have the improbability of dramatic plots. So Carr and Tzara argue about the causes of the First World War (a question which has been the occasion for the spilling of much sweat and ink ever since the imposition of the war guilt clause in the Versailles treaty): what is really behind it all? Patriotism, duty, love of freedom? Well, Tzara says, these concepts are as thoroughly destroyed as a sonnet by a Dadaist revision (which he demonstrates). Instead, war is capitalism with the gloves off. To which Carr replies: 'Why not infantile sexuality in khaki trews? Or the collective unconscious in a tin hat?' Which Tzara in turn tops with the real reason: 'You ended up in the trenches, because on the 28th of June 1900 the heir to the throne of Austro-Hungary married beneath him and found that the wife he loved was never allowed to sit next to him on royal occasions, except when he was acting in his military capacity as Inspector General of the Austro-Hungarian Army—in which capacity he therefore decided to inspect the army in Bosnia, so that at least on their wedding anniversary, the 28th of June 1914, they might ride side by side in an open carriage through the streets of Sarajevo!' (40). In short, as Tzara says, 'everything is chance, including design,' which means, 'my dear Henry, that the causes we know everything about depend on causes we know very little about, which depend on causes we know absolutely nothing about. And it is the duty of the artists to jeer and howl and belch at the delusion that infinite generations of real effects can be inferred from the gross expression of apparent cause' (37).

Most critics have expressed the opinion that *Travesties* explores art's function in society. I am willing to believe that this might even have been Mr. Stoppard's psychological motive for writing the play. But I think it is much more forceful if read as a play about the nature or—if you wish—the reality of reality. This ties in with what he has done in his previous plays. *Travesties* combines various motives which have been touched upon earlier: the improbability of events, their openness to different and contradictory interpretations, the congruence of patterns on different levels of reality, especially of art and reality. And it is this congruence that Stoppard also draws upon to develop his technical construction in this play. As in *Rosencrantz and Guildenstern Are Dead* and *The Real Inspector Hound*, he uses a theatrical pattern for an overall structure. Only this time the extra-theatrical reality is not separately developed and set off against the play, but developed from within. Therefore it never loses its air of complete artificiality. But as such it provides a forceful metaphor for a life in Switzerland during a World War, for the artist's life today, for the madness of the war and the surrealist improbability of Lenin's revolution. It is therefore less of an exploration of the direct opacity and weight of reality than the earlier plays; instead it is a successful probing into the historical dimension of reality. But basically the problem remains the same.

As I see it, the fundamental question of what makes reality real is already implied in the unresolved issue between Kierkegaard and Hegel which Sartre still grapples with in his *Question de Méthode*: has the question of reality to be decided on the level of existential suffering of the individual or on the level of categorization.[33] Stoppard poses Kierkegaard's question several times: "Guil.: (fear, derision) Actors! The mechanics of cheap melodrama! That isn't death! (More quiet) You scream and choke and sink to your knees, but it doesn't bring death home to anyone—it doesn't catch them unawares and start the whisper in their skulls that says—'One day you are going to die' ... " (83). Or Carr talking to Tzara about the war: "Do you think your phrases are the true sum of each man's living of each day?—capitalism with the gloves off?—do you think that's the true experience of a wire-cutting party caught in a cross-fire in no man's land?" (40). On the other hand Stoppard's obsession with categorization and logical order seems to be an affirmation of Hegel and, for that matter, of modern sociology and interaction theory: the generation of the sense of reality has to do with a consensus in interpretation, with an intersubjective agreement on the logical levels of categorization and therefore with our ability to develop functioning systems of categories.

Categories are not only the instrument of analysis but—much more importantly—they also form a structure which is lived. Stoppard then goes on to show the very vulnerability of this structure and the concomitant sense of derealization. In doing this he subjects the audience to a theatrical mystification which dislocates their sense of reality. The philosophical point—as I see it—lies in the paradox with which he plays. The dichotomy between Hegel and Kierkegaard is also paradoxical; though the question of reality has to be decided on the level of categorization (consciousness, consensus, intersubjectivity, communication etc.), once the sense of reality is lost it cannot be regained within and through a system of categorization. This is a matter of trust, of faith, of an existential leap. One has to believe in one's own existence; once this belief is lost it cannot be regained by proofs. The very attempt to prove it is an indication that the conviction of really existing has been lost. To this extent the belief in reality corresponds to the theological problem of the existence of God: man has basically the same relation to both; for both have to be believed in and cannot be proved. This is the deeper significance of Professor Moore's futile exertions in *Jumpers*. As he says very aptly, "There is probably a calendar date—a moment—when the onus of proof passed from the atheist to the believer, when, quite suddenly, secretly, the noes had it" (25). And the attempt to silence the existential schizophrenic doubt in reality has to be as much of a leap as the Kierkegaardian leap into faith, if it is to transcend the categories in which modern man experiences himself. But transcended they must be, because they too are of a paradoxical nature. For, basically, modern man builds his life from two sets of categories: the one is provided by science (sociology, psychology, dialectical materialism), the other is provided by common sense. But both sets contain and relate to each other thereby violating the theory of types: historical, psychological, sociological categories explain the categories of common sense in which a life is lived; and the life lived produces the scientific theories which can be explained with reference to their origin. Within this self-relating cycle man can't find any hold and oscillates between categories which are too remote from his life to be psychologically relevant and others which are not true.

These glimpses at the underlying issue may demonstrate that it is a serious and fundamental one. The above description, however, touches only upon the ideological reflection of a general feeling of derealization for which various explanations have been put forward by the social sciences and cultural criticism. Thus it has been seen in the following contexts: of a collective identity crisis (Berger), of the personality-forming principle of other-directedness (Riesman), of a general mauvaise foie (Sartre), of the pervasive impression management and self-advertising (Goffman), of the disintegration of binding force of institutions (Gehlen), of the tendency towards automaton conformity (Fromm), or of a general self-alienation, one-dimensionality and role-playing compulsion (various Marxists and critical psychiatrists).[34] These hints seem to confirm that Stoppard's use of the theatrical metaphor is symptomatic. Not that it can be claimed that he is the first to use it in the manner described. Rather, he is openly following in the footsteps of Pirandello, Beckett and Genet. But compared to them Stoppard is much lighter. However, this light touch is also the mark of his originality, for with it he demonstrates that there is a tradition of modernity within which one can work and within which it is possible to combine philosophical and intellectual sophistication with entertaining high comedy.[35]

Nor is this the whole story as far as Stoppard's originality and his relation to tradition is concerned. With all his indebtedness to the theatre of the absurd with its various cross-currents and influences, Stoppard seems to be obsessed with techniques and concerns typically and genuinely surrealistic. This is the source of his interest in Dada, Tzara and Magritte. One theme which was developed first by Lautréamont[36] leads directly to the surrealists' and Stoppard's central problem: the improbable encounter of two unconnected objects (like Lautréamont's famous meeting of a sewing machine and an umbrella on an operation table). The arbitrariness of their relation (illustrated by the surrealist object trouvé) is profoundly significant because it characterizes also the relation between language and reality. For there is nothing virginal about the word virgin and — as William James once put it — the word dog does not bite. Technically this leads to the method of collage and pastiche, and intellectually to Wittgenstein's thought. We have seen that Stoppard combines all three aspects: wild coincidences in plot constructions, collage, and linguistic reflection. With the surrealists Stoppard shares the tendency to tease the audience out of their expectations; and like Stoppard the surrealists were fascinated by crime and crime detection, by the problems of contingency and probability, the relation of symbol and objects, code and representation, illusion and reality. And it is especially Magritte who uses the picture-within-the-picture technique in a way similar to Stoppard's use of the play-within-the-play, both developing problems strangely reminiscent of Wittgenstein's thought.[37] Thus Magritte paints ambiguous pictures confusing the difference between inside/outside, transparency/opacity, and representation and reality. He even once drew the picture of a piece of cheese, writing the following on it: 'This is a piece of cheese,' and put it under a cheese-cover; or he wrote on the picture of a pipe: 'This is not a pipe' (implying that it was a picture of a pipe instead). And, as if to illustrate Einstein's theory of relativity, he destroys the illusion of absolute space and time.[38]

It is true that Stoppard in his latest play *Night and Day* seems to be making a start in a new direction. For here he moves away from the multi-layered, technically intricate plots and logical paradoxes and gives a straightforward action which is set in a fictitious African country, a former British colony, whose dictator is threatened by a rebellion. This forms the background for a thorough treatment of British and, for that matter, Western journalism. Three British reporters turn up in the bungalow of a British mine-owner in Kambawe to cover the war and through their competition, cynicism and conflicts reveal the problematic character of the media in relation to third world realities. It is a play which, to my knowledge, presents one of the best comments on the contemporary debates on the role of the media started by the proposed declaration submitted to the twentieth General Conference of UNESCO in Paris by the Third World countries. But, though conventional in form, the play treats a subject which further analysis reveals to be less far removed from the typical Stoppard concerns than it would at first appear: the reality of a Third World civil war is in part created by the journalists who cover it while these same journalists are in their turn swallowed up by the war they describe. The play ends with the murder of one of them.[39] And in this play too Stoppard remains faithful to his typical characters, the heroes of language and interpretation: artists, theatre-critics, police inspectors, professors and journalists who not only change the world by interpreting it but who — Marx forgive me — help create it. This then is the final paradox: man is the creator of a reality of which he himself is a product.[40] It leads Stoppard to contribute to a general social theory of relativity which may be as unsettling as Einstein's.

NOTES

1. Cf. A. Righter, *Shakespeare and the Idea of the Play* (London: Chatto & Windus, 1962).

2. P. Furth, 'Nachträgliche Warnung vor dem Rollenbegriff.' *Das Argument* 13 (1971).

3. Confirmed by M. Karnick who let me see his thesis on the subject in manuscript (Freiburg 1978).

4. The quotation shows that this was already familiar to Shakespeare but the Surrealists gave it wider currency

5. R. J. Nelson, *Play within a Play* (New York: Da Capo Press, 1971); D. Mehl, 'Forms and Functions of the Play within a Play,' *Renaissance Drama* 7 (1965).

6. R. Dahrendorf, *Homo Sociologicus* (Düsseldorf: Westd. Verlag 1977); E. Goffman, *The Presentation of Self in Everyday Life* (Garden City, Doubleday, 1959). A. W. Gouldner, *The Coming Crisis of Western Sociology* (London, Heinemann, 1971); D. Schwanitz, *Die Wirklichkeit der Inszenierung und die Inszenierung der Wirklichkeit* (Meisenheim, Anton Hain, 1977).

7. Thus it has been even labelled as theater of criticism cf. N. Berlin, 'Rosencrantz and Guildenstern are Dead; Theater of Criticism,' *MD*, XVI (1973).

8. Perhaps the idea was suggested by Oscar Wilde who writes in *De Profundis*: 'I know nothing in all drama more incomparable from the point of view of art, nothing more suggestive in its subtlety and observation, than Shakespeare's drawing of Rosencrantz and Guildenstern . . . They are close to his (Hamlet's) very secret and know nothing of it . . . they are what modern life has contrivuted to the antique ideal of friendship' (London: Methuen, 1916, 33rd ed.), p. 140.

9. L. J. Gianakaris, 'Absurdism Altered: Rosencrantz and Guildenstern are Dead,' *DS*, VII (1968); R. Cohn, *Modern Shakespeare Offshoots* (Princeton, UP, 1976); W. Baumgart, "Stratt eines Epilogs: 'Hamlet's Excellent Good Friends,' Beobachtungen zu Shakespeare und Stoppard," in: R. Sühnel und D. Riesner (eds.), *Englische Dichter der Moderne* (Berlin: G. Schmidt, 1971); R. H. Lee, 'The Circle and its Tangent,' *Theoria* XXXIII; U. Broich, 'Montage und Collage in Shakespeare-Bearbeitungen der Gegenwart,' *Poetica* 4 (1971).

10. A. Callen, 'Stoppard's Godot,' *New Theatre Magazine* X (1969); R. Brustein, 'Waiting for Hamlet,' *The Third Theatre* (New York: Knopf, 1969); J. Levenson, 'Views from a Revolving Door: Tom Stoppard's Canon to Date,' *Queen's Quarterly* 58 (1971).

11. W. Babula, 'The Play-Life Metaphor in Shakespeare and Stoppard,' *MD* XV (1972); T. R. Whitaker, *Fields of Play in Modern Drama* (Princeton: U.P., 1977); C. W. E. Bigsby, *Tom Stoppard* (London: The British Council, Longmans, 1976).

12. There are two exceptions I know of: significantly enough one was written by the producer W. D. Asmus, 'Rosencrantz and Guildenstern Are Dead,' *Shakespeare-Jb.* 106 (1970); and H. Zimmermann, 'Tom Stoppards Publikumsverwirrung,' *Shakespeare-Jb.* (1978/79).

13. These and future references give the page number in the Faber editions of Stoppard's plays in brackets.

14. In this they are clearly meant to differ from Claudius who understands a play when he sees one just as well as he understands his own life.

15. E. Erikson, *Identity and the Life Cycle* (New York: International Universities Press, 1967).

16. R. Laing, *The Divided Self* (Harmondsworth: Pelican, 1965).

17. Cf. Andrew Kennedy, 'Old and New in London Now,' *MD* 4 (1969).

18. For the following account cf. Watzlawik, Beavin, Jackson, *Pragmatics of Human Communication. A Study of Interactional Pattern, Pathologies and Paradoxes* (London: Faber & Faber, 1968); Bateson, Jackson, Laing, Lidz et al., *Schizophrenie und Familie* (Ffm.: Suhrkamp, 1972); L. Wittgenstein, *Tractatus logico-philosophicus* (Ffm.: Suhrkamp, 1963).

19. This is the version in which the story was told to me by Gesine Hermes and I have tried to reproduce it from memory as best as I could. The motive is very old, a variation of it occurring in Homer's *Odyssey* when the hero plays on the meaning of his name (Udeis/Nobody) in telling Polyphemos that his name was Udeis. When Polyphemos cries for help and his relatives ask him who blinded him, Polyphemos answers: Nobody. Folk literature abounds with similar paradoxical situations.

20. For a survey cf. L. Bellak (ed.), *Schizophrenia. A Review of the Syndrome* (New York: Logos Press, 1958); Laing, op. cit.

21. This possibility of the drama to confuse intra- and extra-dramatic messages make its structure particularly interesting for interactionists. Cf. Bateson et al., p. 36.

22. The picture I have in mind is 'Les promenades d'Euclide' in the Minneapolis Institute of Art. He used the same method with 'La Condition Humaine I' (Spaark Collection), and on many other pictures he employs different though equally confusing techniques.

23. Social scientists have made the disconcerting discovery that an interpretation is accorded more credibility and prestige the more complicated it gets. This is an insight which literary criticism has still to take in. Cf. the experiments recorded in H. Garfinkel, *Studies in Ethnomethodology* (Englewood Cliffs, N.J.: Prentice Hall, 1967).

24. W. I. Thomas, *The Child in America* (New York: Knopf, 1927), p. 572.

25. Zeno's is certainly one of the most famous paradoxes: it consists in the proof that Achilles running ten times faster than a tortoise is nevertheless not able to overtake it provided the tortoise gets a handicap of 10 yards: when Achilles has covered the first ten yards, the tortoise is one yard ahead; when Achilles has covered that, the tortoise is still ahead by one tenth, then by one hundredth etc. ad infinitum: This is the problem of the infinitely regressing series, and Moore is concerned with it in connection with proving God as the First Cause.

26. There are several proofs of the existence of God which were devised and given currency by various scholastic philosophers. The most famous is the so-called ontological proof which is based on a logical fallacy showing the same paradoxical structure we are now familiar with: God is by definition the most perfect being. It belongs to the most perfect being that it exists, for if it would lack the quality of existence it would per definitionem cease to be most perfect. Ergo a most perfect being, which is only imagined, is an impossibility, ergo it must exist q.e.d. This proof was eventually demolished by Immanuel Kant, who argued that the qualification of existence cannot add or subtract anything from a concept, but was a comment about the whole of the concept on a higher level. This is an anticipation of the theory of types.

27. Here I completely agree with J. Bennett, 'Philosophy and Mr. Stoppard,' *The Journal of the Royal Institute of Philosophy*, 50 (1975).

28. Cf. Richard Ellmann, 'Travesties,' *Times Lit. Suppl.* (July 12, 1974).

29. Stoppard makes free with the temporal sequence of events: Tzara founded Dadaism in 1916, Lenin went to Russia in 1917 and Joyce produced Wilde's play in 1918.

30. In *Ulysses* Private Carr is quite an Orangeman and Jingoist, and Stoppard makes him voice equally patriotic sentiments in his play. Incidentally Joyce also uses the name of the consul in Zürich (Bennett) for the commanding officer of Private Carr.

31. Edmund Wilson, *To the Finland Station* is a very readable account of the development of socialism during the nineteenth century up to 1917. The question-and-answer chapter in *Ulysses* is the one preceding Molly's final soliloquy and lends itself very nicely to a comparison with Aunt Augusta's brazen way of questioning Jack Worthing. With the use of quotations from Shakespeare, Stoppard is also parodying Joyce's method.

32. Since the outbreak of the revolution in St. Petersburg Lenin wanted to return to Russia which, however, proved wellnigh impossible since Switzerland was surrounded at all sides by belligerent nations. Finally the German High Command let him travel through Germany in a sealed train because it wanted to back the Bolsheviks who were making propaganda for the end of the war.

33. Cf. J. P. Sartre, *Search for a Method (Question de Méthode)* (New York: Knopf, 1963). Sartre reformulates this question as the issue between existence and knowledge and tries to solve it by infusing Marxism with a shot of Existentialism. I think, however, that phenomenological sociology has taught us to regard the opposition between knowledge and existence as a fallacy. Instead I see it between different types of knowledge which are, in their turn, differently tied up with existence.

34. P. L. Berger, 'Towards a Sociological Understanding of Psychoanalysis,' *Social Research* 32 (1965); D. Riesman, *The Lonely Crowd* (New Haven: Yale U.P., 1950); J. P. Sartre, *L'être et le néant* (Paris: Gallimard, 1952); E. Goffman, op. cit.; A. Gehlen, *Die Seele im technischen Zeitalter. Sozialpsychologische Probleme in der industriellen Gesellschaft* (Hamburg: Rowohlt, 1959); E. Fromm, *The Sane Society* (New York: Rinehart & Co., 1955); H. Marcuse, *One-Dimensional Man* (Boston: Beacon Press, 1964). Cf. also R. Schacht, *Alienation* (London: Allen & Unwin, 1971) and G. Devereux, *Essais d'éthnopsychiatrie générale* (Paris: Gallimard, 1970).

35. In an interview published in the *Theatre Quarterly*, Vol. IV, No. 14, May–July, 1974, Stoppard expressly states his purpose 'to contrive the perfect marriage between the play of ideas and farce or even high comedy.'

36. Comte de Lautréamont (Isidore Ducasse), *Le Chants de Maldoror* (Paris: Corti, 1973).

37. Cf. Suzi Bablik, *Magritte* (London: Thames & Hudson, 1973), especially chapt. 8.

38. For collections of Magritte see the Editions of D. Larkin (London: Ballatine Books, 1972), R. Passeron (Paris 1970) and Suzi Gablik, op. cit.

39. One of the journalists is killed which may very well have a biographical background: One of Stoppard's idols was Noel Barber of the *Daily Mail* who got shot in the head in Budapest in 1956.

40. This paradox is the thesis of a book which has become rather influential: P. Berger and T. Luckmann, *The Social Construction of Reality* (Garden City, N.J.: Doubleday, 1966).

Harold Pinter:
The Metamorphosis of Memory

A. R. BRAUNMULLER

There's something beats the same in opposed hearts. (W. D. Snodgrass)

Audiences have long recognized Harold Pinter's interest in Kafka and Beckett. Recently, in a collection of poems and prose pieces, *Old Times,* a screen-play, and *No Man's Land,* two other figures have revealed themselves: Proust and Eliot. Their presence—"influence" is not quite the word—should come as no surprise. Pinter writes of *The Proust Screenplay,* "The subject was Time," and the same could be said for much of his own work from *Landscape* and *Silence* (both staged in 1969) forward.[1] Listening again to such earlier plays as *The Birthday Party* and *The Caretaker,* we can now also hear some of Eliot's rhythms, some of his verbal mannerisms, especially the jangling colloquialism and irreverent, "irrelevant" high diction.[2] *No Man's Land* goes further. Without shame or satire, it parodies lines from "Prufrock" ("I have known this before. The exit through the door by way of belly and floor") and alludes quite directly to the Fisher-King myth and romance matter of *The Waste Land* (Hirst has an obscure hurt and Spooner a chivalric persona, *sans peur et sans reproche).*

Proust, Eliot, and Pinter most truly converge, however, in the matter of time. Of course, this convergence does not exclude Kafka and Beckett: time and memory interest both writers, and Pinter can hardly have failed to read Beckett's *Proust,* more Beckett than Proust as it is. Examining some of memory's shapes in Pinter's plays, I do not mean to write literary history, an influential tale, because Pinter becomes and remains his own man. Rather, I wish only to suggest that these writers formulated modern artistic concerns in ways Pinter found congenial.

Given drama's necessary difficulty with any time but the present—as Thornton Wilder observed, "On the stage it is always now"—this interest surfaces most complexly in memory, specifically memory (mental traces of other times) as it constitutes identity, guides perception, and structures the characters' relation with their human and physical environments.[3] My image of memory as metamorphosis is double: memory re-shaped and memory re-shaping. Both changes occur throughout Pinter's plays. Yet, when Pinter transmutes time into memory, he has still not completely solved the preliminary technical problem: memory is only slightly more "dramatizable" than time itself. Pinter most frequently resorts to his great strength, language, and makes memory into memory-narratives or discourse about memory. Once moved to the verbal level, memory enters the plays full-bore. As the characters talk about their memories, for example, we can see them hypothesizing identities or relations; memory is sometimes a play-arena where new personalities may be shaped and tested. Elsewhere, as the elaborate memory-narratives unreel they become objects or icons. As Ionesco said of a very different technique, these objectified memories materialize the "unseen presence of our inner fears."[4] Before refining these suggestions, I should like to indicate how memory's various forms relate to earlier elements in Pinter's drama and to more conventional critical issues.

"Menace," word and idea, marks discussions and reviews of Pinter like some critical measle, and the symptoms (or dramatic effects) have been well catalogued.[5] The etiology has not, however, been clearly understood. Very simply, the proverbial "menace" of these plays arises from two other proverbial qualities—the suppression (or elision) of motive and the absence of self-explication. Pinter has always explained this quality on realistic grounds, and he has implicitly ridiculed the older, Ibsenite or Chekhovian methods. Deprived of personal statement, the audience must rely on the characters' interpretation of their environments. Since those characters are, among other things, almost uniformly aggressive and defensive, hostile and timid, they tend to find their static and dynamic environments very threatening. Whatever the different reactions, "the world *is* a pretty violent place."[6] These objectified, external threats characterize the stage-world *and* explicate the characters. They see around themselves those conditions and qualities which they fear within themselves and cannot, or do not, express. Thus Bert's few lines in *The Room* report how he drove his (invisible) truck:

I caned her along. She was good. . . . I kept on the straight. There was no mixing it. Not with her. She was good. She went with me. She don't mix it with me. I use my hand. Like that. I get hold of her. I go where I go. She took me there. She brought me back.[7]

The truck, carefully sexualized, becomes an object of Bert's hatred, a hatred transferred from its true object(s), and a threat of the punishment he could unleash. Any realistic reading of the play would regard the truck speech as otiose. Similarly, McCann's violently possessive tearing of a newspaper in *The Birthday Party* objectifies forces and tensions he cannot articulate; later, McCann's verbose partner, Goldberg, almost literally suffocates under his own fears.

Pinter's environments reach the audience partially interpreted and distorted by the characters' psychologies. Consequently, his celebrated emphasis on private space arises from their need to clear away uncontrollable or frightening mental states. The more controlled, ordered, and understood one of those famous "rooms" is, the more powerfully in mental control, the more stable, the characters feel. An obvious counter-example, the junk-strewn room of *The Caretaker*, demonstrates my larger point. This space belongs to Aston who associates order with death, an association Stanley's cleansed and corpsed appearance at the end of *Birthday Party* helps us accept. The play's untidy and defect-filled world assures Aston that he lives and invites him to make connections: plug to socket, gas stove to gas main, person to person. It is a landscape of the mind, and so are most of Pinter's sets, up to and into *The Homecoming*. Pinter's rooms may passively assure identity, but they can also threaten psychological incoherence.

Real or imagined objects and factual attributes of the environment achieve "menace" when they become instruments of aggression. The rather garish pistols of *The Dumbwaiter* give way to more terrifyingly ordinary objects—a vacuum cleaner and a statue *(The Caretaker)* or a glass of water and a cheese roll *(The Homecoming)*. Mick bombards Davies with epic recitals of London's bus routes and conquers the tramp's fumbling attempts at self-assertion ("You and me, we could get this place going") through a pitch-man's dream of a bourgeois paradise:

> I'd have teal-blue, copper and parchment linoleum squares. I'd have those colours re-echoed in the walls. I'd offset the kitchen units with charcoal-grey worktops. Plenty of room for cupboards for the crockery. ... You could put the dining-room across the landing, see? Yes.... You could have an off-white pile linen rug, a table in afromosia teak veneer, sideboard with matt black drawers, curved chairs with cushioned seats, armchairs in oatmeal tweed, a beech frame settee with a woven sea-grass seat, white-topped heat-resistant coffee table, white tile surround. (p. 60)

Such speeches (their relatives appear in almost every play) work in many ways, of course, but they principally reveal the extent to which the plays' realities have been mediated by the characters' needs, fears, and interpretations.

This quality of the plays—and, I shall argue, of memories in the plays—can produce some odd responses. Deprived of more conventional explanatory signals, audiences supply fictional structures to link the characters and organize the action. They regard the play's "world" as distorted but basically mimetic rather than as the characters' version of a world. Once this fiction-making begins, it moves all the data towards coherence and the convenient, traditional recognitions called "plot," "character," and "conflict." These fictions infest much writing about Pinter. We offer them because the plays deceptively invite us to compensate for their own ample but deliberate omissions. Supplying this fiction may engage us with the play, but it also leads to private and often rather dismissive versions of Pinter's "world view." Such a procedure arises, I repeat, partly from misunderstanding the plays' physical worlds. These worlds are in fact fragments of personality. Their reference is inward. They lie within the orbit of the characters' interpretation, and they are not separate from those personalities.

Popular "menace" or "menace-and-violence" interpretations tend to overlook the way these qualities originate within the characters. Curiously, such interpretation needs the realignment Pinter has given the "failure-to-communicate" school of criticism: he has gently pointed out that his characters do not fail to communicate, they fear and flee it. Silence and speech deliberately circumvent rather than hinder expression. So, too, while menace (or better, threat) is no doubt present, it is what the characters have made their world rather than the world *a priori*.

Pinter has moved away from violence, physical assault, and the ominous use of farcical stage devices. Of *The Caretaker,* he said, "I have developed ... I have no need to use cabaret turns and blackouts and screams in the dark to the extent that I enjoyed using them before."[8] Threat, fear, self-doubt, aggressive assertion and all the rest have certainly not diminished with the blackouts. Instead, memory has gradually subsumed many functions physical assault and other threats once fulfilled.[9] *The Homecoming* is a pivotal play in this development because it contains both physical violence and "memory-violence"; in it, we find the familiar issues of identity, relation, dominance and subservience moving into a wholly verbal realm. That realm is also a realm of memory. Eventually, the characters will acknowledge and discuss memory as the context of their private and public struggles.

The Birthday Party and *The Caretaker* have simpler versions of some later developments. In these plays, memory confirms and protects identity; loss of memory tilts the personality toward fragmentation. For example, when Stanley first encounters the more brutish of his tormentors-to-be, he finds his exit repeatedly blocked. Rather than challenge McCann, Stanley picks up a strip of the newspaper we have watched McCann methodically shred. This act disturbs McCann, and he commands, "Mind that" —

STANLEY: What is it?
McCANN: Mind it. Leave it.

Stanley now deploys a much more subtle attack:

STANLEY: I've got a feeling we've met before.
McCANN: No we haven't.
STANLEY: Ever been anywhere near Maidenhead?
McCANN: No.
STANLEY: There's a Fuller's teashop. I used to have my tea there.
McCANN: I don't know it.
STANLEY: And a Boots Library. I seem to connect you with the High Street.
McCANN: Yes?
STANLEY: A charming town, don't you think?
McCANN: I don't know it. (p. 42)

The assertion of previous acquaintance, like Mick's reaction to Davies— "You remind me of my uncle's brother" (*Caretaker,* p. 31)—offers the chance to mould an antecedent relation and an entirely new set of characters. Stanley can define his earlier relation with McCann as he wishes, but more important he can attribute whatever qualities he wants to both McCann and himself. Unlike the most sophisticated Proustian "involuntary" memory which comes unbidden and uncontrolled, this memory-form can modify the present through changing or creating a past. Proposing memory, "anteing" it up has dangers. Later, Goldberg will casually absorb Stanley's recollection: "A little Austin, tea in Fullers, a library book from Boots, and I'm satisfied" (p. 59). Stanley uses "remembered" detail to achieve conviction, but this sword has no handle, only a double blade. *Old Times* develops this kind of conflict very fully.[10]

During the birthday celebration itself, we hear a quartet of interwoven memories:

MEG (to McCANN): My father was going to take me to Ireland once. But then he went away by himself.

LULU (to GOLDBERG):	Do you think you knew me when I was a little girl?
GOLDBERG:	Were you a nice little girl?
LULU:	I was.
MEG:	I don't know if he went to Ireland.
GOLDBERG:	Maybe I played piggy-back with you.
LULU:	Maybe you did.
MEG:	He didn't take me.
GOLDBERG:	Or pop goes the weasel.
LULU:	Is that a game?
GOLDBERG:	Sure it's a game!

(pp. 62–63)

Here the remembering has its own energy, occasionally sustained through a flicker of shared detail (Ireland and game). The purpose—to create a world insulated from a thousand natural shocks—becomes clear in Meg's subsequent aria, "My little room was pink ... and I had musical boxes all over the room." The childish occasion (a birthday party), the childish game (blind man's bluff), and childish gift (the drum) all make this a plausible refuge, and other characters — especially the domineering Goldberg — offer glimpses of a safer, childish, past. This tactic shows the obverse of memory as domination: a malleable past may be brought forward to re-place a dangerous, uncontrollable present.

The faintly Stoppardian interrogation scene concentrates on Stanley's hypothetical past. Mention of sin leads to "Do you recognise an external force, responsible for you, suffering for you?" (p. 53), and that question produces an archetypally "random" number: "Is the number 846 possible or necessary?" The number only justifies the true topic, necessity and possibility. Rejecting both necessary and possible things, Stanley doggedly attempts to substitute a security of place for a secure self-conception. Since the interrogators aim to destroy Stanley's illusions about his right as well as his capacity to answer their questions, they eventually conclude that something ("846") may be necessary without being possible: "We admit possibility only after we grant necessity." The sensation that something is necessary without also being possible is of course foreign neither to the play nor to our experience of life. Memory escapes this practical inconvenience because the re-shaped memory admits all possibilities, indeed, it creates them to satisfy present necessities. Stanley lacks this metamorphic resilience, but *The Birthday Party* demonstrates its "possibility."

The Caretaker begins, appropriately enough, with a quest for origins. Aston gently quizzes his new acquaintance about his name, his jobs, and so on; this kind of inquiry doesn't really arise in *The Birthday Party* because

Stanley has already established a tenuous "present" in the boarding house. While Davies anxiously asserts his gentility—"I've eaten my dinner off the best of plates" (p. 9) and "I slept in plenty of beds" (p. 23)—his most famous attempt to establish himself involves the insurance cards and other papers long abandoned in Sidcup. Davies claims that bad weather and difficult travelling have prevented their retrieval; without the papers, he cannot resurrect "Davies" in place of "Jenkins." Aston soon asks an obvious question about the man and papers in Sidcup: "How long's he had them?" (p. 20). Davies' reply, "Oh, must be . . . it was in the war . . . must be . . . about near on fifteen year ago" reveals that he is drifting in time as much as in space. His identity—fictitious or fantasied or whatever—he chooses to locate in the past. Travelling to Sidcup is no answer and must be resisted, as his picayune complaints about Aston's gift of shoes demonstrate. This difficult journey towards a self means travelling in time, and Davies will repeatedly link a physical with a temporal disorientation.

His situation gives the word "where" a special status. Aston asks, "Where were you born then?"—

DAVIES (darkly):	What do you mean?
ASTON:	Where were you born?
DAVIES:	I was . . . uh . . . oh, it's a bit hard, like, to set your mind back . . . see what I mean . . . going back . . . a good way . . . lose a bit of track, like . . . you know. . . . (p. 25)

Davies treats his birth as a problem of memory. To know his birth(place), he tries to "set" his mind back to that moment and that place. Davies often uses "where" in a common, colloquial way: "I mean, with a bloke like you, you know where you are" (p. 61). Almost immediately, colloquial imprecision rises to a much more haunting cry: "I mean, if you can't tell what time you're at you don't know where you are" (p. 62). "Where"—location—hovers between sloppy speech and metaphor, just as Davies' substitution of himself for the absent clock shows him lost without time's fictitious external order. Davies needs a timekeeper and a settled location. Otherwise, his own emotional and mental coherence begins to collapse: "No, what I need is a clock in here, in this room, and then I stand a bit of a chance" (p. 62). His literal and figurative orientation depends on external forces and external objects. He defines himself in simple terms—not-Davies and like-Davies. Thus, he urgently needs to establish that others share his prejudices (against the "blacks" next door, for example); he must fix the value of the room's junk, and he must force those objects (like the disconnected gas stove) back into their familiar terrain.

Davies' need for circumstantial order is much more primitive than his host's. As Aston patiently fiddles with the plug and plans to build a shed (more important as plans for construction than as accomplishment), we recognize that he regards his own mental eccentricity rather equably. Aston's long, meditative memory-discourse ending the second Act may be largely a retrospective fiction, but it also represents his satisfying conception of his origins and his present state. Critics have recognized the play's basic construction—a series of triangular exclusions, a sequence of pairs against the odd man out.[11] This series ends with the two brothers at least temporarily reunited (re-connected like the plug and socket), though the process requires smashing the Buddha and expelling Davies.

Attacking Davies, the brothers make a separate peace. Since Davies' personal integrity requires an ordered physical and temporal environment, their attacks drive him either toward an extreme disorder (the junk room which Aston refuses to tidy) or toward an extreme but foreign order (Mick's *House and Garden* penthouse-fantasy which requires that Davies become an interior decorator). Davies must be denied any comforting connection with an environment he can order or arrange. These exchanges are intensely theatrical and employ concrete stage-images; they have evident relations with the way Pinter's stage manifests mental states. The two brothers also attack Davies' more intimate ways of maintaining his identity. Aston quietly forbids any unconscious repose by shaking Davies awake and complaining that he was "making noises":

DAVIES: Now, wait a minute. Wait a minute, what do you mean? What kind of noises?

ASTON: You were making groans. You were jabbering.
. . .

DAVIES: I don't jabber, man. Nobody ever told me that before. (p. 22)

This interrupted sleep and the accusation of dreaming become one of Davies' angriest complaints against Aston (pp. 62–63). In concert with his brother, Mick attacks Davies' memory:

MICK: Well, I could see before, when you took out that knife, that you wouldn't let anyone mess you about.

DAVIES: No one messes me about, man.

MICK: I mean, you've been in the services, haven't you?

DAVIES: The what?

MICK: You been in the services. You can tell by your stance.

DAVIES:	Oh ... yes. Spent half my life there, man. Over-seas ... like ... serving ... I was.
MICK:	In the colonies, weren't you?
DAVIES:	I was over there. I was one of the first over there. (pp. 50–51)

More elaborately than Goldberg, who absorbed Stanley's memory, Mick has begun to mould Davies' past. The tramp's anxiety forces him to accept a new past, and he cuts his precarious hold on the other memories he could conveniently arrange for himself. The brothers succeed, of course. In his last, stumbling monologue, Davies can no longer even articulate the memory of Sidcup and its feeble promise of personality:

> Listen ... if I ... got down ... if I was to ... get my papers ... would you ... would you let ... would you ... if I got down ... and got my. ... (p. 78)

First produced almost precisely five years after *The Caretaker*, *The Homecoming* combines earlier materials with important new departures. As before, violence threads through the characters' ambivalent relations and ambiguous identities, but Ruth and Teddy possess a new and more ambitious drive for control. They have returned (or arrived) "home" to displace Lenny and Max, themselves powerful descendants of earlier bullies like Goldberg and Mick. This displacement is clear enough in the play's individual struggles, in Ruth's annihilating decision to remain and Teddy's forceful escape, but another more subtle displacement accompanies these obvious ones. Physical threat and violence begin to fade before memory-violence. Even the crudely successful father and son seek to dominate through physical intimidation *and* through remembering their brutal or domineering pasts. At the very start, Max claims a superior knowledge of racing and race horses because "I was always able to tell a good filly by one particular trick. ... I'd stand in front of her and look her straight in the eye, it was a kind of hypnotism ... " (p. 10). Lenny soon tries his own "particular trick" and attempts to "hypnotize" Ruth with his memories of beating and kicking other women.

As earlier plays had hinted, violence expressed often returns upon the inventor's head. Near the end of Act I, Joey dismisses his father — "You're an old man. ... He's an old man" (p. 42) — and Max responds with a powerful blow which fells his boxer-son. Even as Joey falls, Max himself collapses, managing nonetheless to hit his brother Sam, who has moved to help him. Tension and suppressed violence provide energy, purpose, a reason for living; yet when they are released, they debilitate. Similarly, after the birthday calamities and a night teaching Lulu "things a girl shouldn't know before she's been married at least three times" *(Birthday Party,* p. 84), Goldberg collapses, gasping and making strange wheezing sounds. McCann revives him with reassurance and ritual resuscitation. Memory violence sometimes follows the same pattern. In *The Homecoming,* Sam has long treasured the secret knowledge (or fantasy) that Max's best friend MacGregor "had Jessie in the back seat of my cab as I drove them along" (p. 78). No sooner is this sustaining piece of meditated revenge spoken, than Sam himself collapses, near death.

Memory opens the way to a land where contradiction is futile and where dreams may be made retroactively true. Once rooted, memory confers power in the present. Shaping memory, however, and using it to shape the present are complicated, dangerous manipulations. Like violence expressed, they may reveal compensatory weaknesses. Ruth brilliantly uncovers such a memory-fissure when she dismisses the defeated Lenny, calling him "Leonard."

> *LENNY:* Don't call me that, please.
> *RUTH:* Why not?
> *LENNY:* That's the name my mother gave me. (p. 33)

Memory has traps as well as weapons; once put in play, the memory-terrain becomes another arena of struggle. This moment echoes at the play's end when Ruth calls her husband "Eddie." It is the name she gave him, and she has also become the family's "mother." These are, patently, small (though dramatically stunning) examples, but they recall memory's association with origins, beginnings, and still further back, with dear dead days beyond memory's metamorphic recall.

Lenny turns to just such a time-before-memory after Ruth rejects his proposition. Awakened by the shouting, Max comes downstairs to find out "who you got hiding here" (p. 36). Lenny responds to his earlier defeat and this present intimidation by asking "in a spirit of inquiry" about "the night you got me ... that night with Mum, what was it like?" (p. 36). Although Davies apparently ponders his birth, human beings cannot remember the moment of origin, of conception, "the true facts of that particular night — the night they were made in the image of those two people *at it.*" This almost incestuous violation, his son's ability to regard his parents as "two people *at it,*" horrifies Max and successfully stymies his attack, but Lenny's "spirit of inquiry" is more than off-hand familial torture. Between birth (or conception) and the moment one gains sufficient memories to be worth manipulating, there lies a period of emotional and mental helplessness, the period Max can fill with jolly moments of paternal care: "What fun we used to have in the bath, eh, boys?" (p. 46). This is also the period when Max claims he "commemorated" his father's name "in blood" — the blood of the butchershop and the blood of his own sons. Such periods, like those occasions when a potential attacker/victim is physically distant (Teddy in America, or Ruth before she met Teddy, for example), deny memory its ore and prevent that refining into effective fantasy which is both protection and attack.

Memory appears in many guises, and the examples I have mentioned so far point towards future developments, but they don't contribute very fully to *The Homecoming*'s own organization and effects. Yet, even in its fundamental dramatic subject—what R. F. Storch calls "the family's revenge against the mother"—the play introduces that hated figure, Jessie, through the survivors' memories of her.[12] They remember her everywhere, in Max's kitchen, in Sam's cab, in the very structure of the house (p. 21). The men, especially Max, seek to replace Jessie with Ruth and recompense their former humiliation and estrangement through exploiting her. The more Ruth seems to become a submissive version of Jessie, however, the more she becomes her avatar, and Max finally wonders whether Jessie has been too thoroughly re-created:

> You understand what I mean? Listen, I've got a funny idea she'll do the dirty on us, you want to bet? She'll use us, she'll make use of us, I can tell you! I can smell it! You want to bet? (p. 81)

Memory has done its job too well: it preserved hatred, it encouraged revenge, but it has also reproduced the past. Listening to the memories which distill years of experience into a series of pleated contrasts—"I left a woman at home with a will of iron, a heart of gold and a mind" (p. 46); "a slutbitch of a wife" (p. 47)—Ruth realizes she can cajole memory into serving up old vulnerabilities alongside ancient hatreds.

Ruth entices the men into making the first active move. That move leads not to success but to renewed enslavement. Appropriately enough, she employs a long memory-narrative of a time when she was "model for the body. A photographic model for the body" (p. 57). Memories often serve as dream-substitutes for Pinter's characters, and Ruth's memory of trips "to a place in the country" mingles random detail with vague narrative structure as a remembered dream often does:

> We used to pass a...a large white water tower. This place...this house...was very big...the trees...there was a lake, you see ...we used to change and walk down towards the lake...we went down a path...on stones...there were...on this path. (p. 57)

Unlike Lenny's violent memories, which achieve conviction at the price of giving Ruth detailed ammunition for her counter-attack, Ruth's own memory invites him to complete the story as he wishes.

Anxious to "take her up ... to Greek Street," Lenny accepts Ruth's apparent willingness to return to her former profession. Teddy's reaction when he overhears the conclusion of Ruth's memory is a telling hint of her success: "What have you been saying to her?" (p. 58). Even Ruth's husband believes Lenny has somehow elicited or extorted the memory, when the very reverse is true. Memories are the "unverifiable" medium *par excellence*: we do not know, we cannot know, and finally, we need not know, whether Ruth's memory is "truth," fiction, or some ingenious mixture. Memory's very pliability, its indifference to truth-tests, makes it both refuge and weapon, though (again) a skillful antagonist may make these advantages disadvantages.

More than any previous character, Ruth has recognized memory's metamorphic power. Through memory, she can shape and reshape her past; that power—its freedom from time-present—allows her to shape current relations. Ruth's (or Pinter's) discoveries blossom in *Old Times*. Characters gradually remember not just themselves but each other, conjuring venomous histories which cripple their subjects here and now. Remembering too facilely, too intricately, too viciously, however, rebounds upon the creator when he or she finally accepts an authoritative history which then proves vulnerable. In the end, Kate seizes memory's "high ground"—its link with origins—and conquers: "I remember you dead" (p. 71). From plays in which, revue-like, almost too much "happens," Pinter has advanced through *The Homecoming* to plays structured by remembered pasts. *Old Times*'s linear "plot" arranges a series of created and re-created past "plots," each one an element in the present conflict. *Old Times*'s most violent action is the pouring of coffee and brandy (stern enough, God knows): all the energy—the self-doubts and their poisonous interpretations of others—flows into creating the memories and using them to re-create the self and others. Max asked Ruth, "Who can afford to live in the past?" and thereby anticipated his own defeat. No mature Pinter character can afford not to live in the past, although the risks may prove costly. Indeed, a satisfactory manipulation of past living is all that permits present existence.

The lines of development, recession, and experiment which join *The Homecoming* with Pinter's subsequent plays are more complicated than I may adequately discuss here. If *Homecoming* is taken as a benchmark, however, one may say that *Landscape* and *Silence* are the most experimental and *No Man's Land* the superficially most conventional of the plays which followed. *Old Times* and *Betrayal* are more difficult to categorize, though types of memory do order their dramatic sequences. Memory's role in *No Man's Land* is in fact more complex than the play's apparent (Pinterian) conventionality first implies. It is also the play, I think, where one sees Pinter reacting most openly and characteristically to Proust's and Eliot's work. For these reasons as well as the fact that it has received less, and less complimentary, attention than *Old Times,* I include it here.

Near the beginning of *No Man's Land,* Spooner describes Hirst as "kindness itself ... now and in England and in Hampstead and for all eternity" (p. 17). The line appropriately echoes Eliot's *Four Quartets* because Spooner believes "The present is truly unscrupulous. I am a poet. I am interested in where I am eternally present and active" (p. 20).[13] Both men are "trying to run away from their own disenchantment"[14] with the unscrupulous, changing, betraying present, and each finds a characteristic solace — Spooner in elaborate memory-narratives, Hirst in a no less elaborate (and no more verifiable) photograph album.

Memory consequently becomes an explicit subject, rather than the tactic it was in *Old Times.* Spooner cross-examines his host about "the quaint little perversions of your life and times" (p. 30) and soon expresses dissatisfaction:

Is she here now, your wife? Cowering in a locked room, perhaps?
Pause.
Was she ever here? Was she ever there, in your cottage? It is my duty to tell you you have failed to convince. (p. 31)

Of course, Hirst's memories (and Spooner's, for that matter) do not seek "conviction"; rather, they create and protect a personality. Shards of the past do create a mosaic allowing an arid present existence. They also create an "historical" present, eternal and active, where Hirst retreats from Spooner's shoddy domineering strategies and where Spooner himself can escape Foster's and Briggs' spiteful mention of The Bull's Head and pintpot attendants (pp. 37–40 and 48–50, for example).

Like all very important subjects, memory can be made humorous. Sprucely sober, Hirst interrupts Spooner's champagne breakfast and recalls "Our last encounter — I remember it well. Pavilion at Lord's in '39, against the West Indies, Hutton and Compton batting superbly, Constantine bowling, war looming. Surely I'm right?" (p. 69). The two men pursue one another through an hilarious series of memory-fantasies, each accepting the other's insulting recollections and then topping them. Stella and Bunty Winstanley, Muriel Blackwood, Doreen Busby, Geoffrey Ramsden — a complete, extravagant Noel Coward cast — flicker in and out of equally extraordinary adventures — threatened horsewhippings, several sorts of seduction, betrayal, deceit, literary insult, and wartime heroics (or worse). Two superb memory-strategists struggle to learn if the means of defensive self-protection can subdue another person. They cannot, and the exchange ends with a return to whiskey, soda, and the photograph album.

Disappointed that Spooner isn't the man his memory would create, Hirst claims, "In my day nobody changed. A man was" (p. 78). Hirst's "true friends" reside in the photograph album. His youth and his friends don't change; only the light which fixes them forever changes: "It existed. It was solid, the people in it were solid, while...transformed by light, while being sensitive ... to all the changing light" (p. 45). These transformed images offer Hirst an eternal present like the one Spooner finds in his stories and his allusive literary fragments. The images objectify memory, they validate it, and they replace life. When Hirst finally considers showing Spooner the album, we grasp the images' power:

> They possess all that emotion ... trapped. Bow to it. It will assuredly never release them, but who knows...what relief...it may give to them ... who knows how they may quicken ... in their chains, in their glass jars.... And so I say to you, tender the dead, as you would yourself be tendered, now, in what you would describe as your life. (p. 79)

"The love of the good ghost" glancing sidelong from the album's pages halts the viewer; the images deaden him even as they quicken, so that "your life" becomes less lively than their imprisonment.

Briggs describes the images as "The blank dead" (p. 79), and Foster claims "Those faces are nameless, friend" (p. 84), but these qualities attract rather than repel Hirst. Blankness and anonymity welcome tenderness; Hirst may attribute every emotion, meaning, and relation to them. His photo-images recall Marcel's related images in *Remembrance of Things Past*: "a visual fragment that has lost all relation to reality except the capacity to suggest something lost, something infinitely worth seeking."[15] Associated with this album there is also what Eliot might call "death by water"—someone has drowned or is drowning in a lake or a dream or both. Memory holds the images and the watery death, and gradually we understand that the refuge has become a prison. Hirst cannot bear his grand life as man of letters any more than Spooner can stomach his much dirtier one, but memory releases them only into no man's land, "which never moves, which never changes, which never grows older, but which remains forever, icy and silent" (p. 95, echoing p. 34).

Like the characters of *No Man's Land*, Pinter has pursued memory into an icy, unchanging realm where the subject cannot be changed. Once only an occasional attack or defense, memory becomes a much more formidable bulwark, and then moves toward destructive self-immurement. Fragmentary pasts shored against ruin eventually form a constricting cell of "solitary shittery." His latest play, *Betrayal,* brilliantly reverses the locus of memory. As the play moves backward from present anguish and delusion to betrayal and then to original innocence and comic passion, the audience's memory becomes both subject and victim.[16] We are betrayed far more than the trivial usage the play first seems to have in mind. Pinter exploits a wonderful version of "dramatic irony" which makes our superior knowledge a liability rather than an illumination. Pursuing origins, baring "causes" whose "effects" we already know, *Betrayal* makes explanation and understanding harder and more equivocal rather than the reverse, as we anticipated. The less the characters know about their present and their future, the less reliable our experience of the play itself becomes. At the end, our memory's power to shape into coherence has been jeopardized. Pinter has maneuvered us from knowledge to ignorance. Understanding more about ourselves and our betrayals, we see how little we know.

NOTES

1. Harold Pinter, *The Proust Screenplay* (New York: Grove, 1977), p. x.

2. See Russell Davies' review of Pinter, *Poems and Prose, 1949–1977* (New York: Grove, 1978) and other works in *New York Review of Books,* 25 January 1979, pp. 22–24.

3. Thornton Wilder, "Some Thoughts on Playwriting" (1941), reprinted in S. Barnet *et al.,* comp., *Aspects of the Drama: A Handbook* (Boston: Little, Brown, 1962), p. 10.

4. Eugène Ionesco, *Notes and Counter-Notes,* trans. Donald Watson (New York: Grove, 1964), p. 29; cf. ibid., p. 104 and Karl-Heinz Stoll, *Harold Pinter: Ein Beitrag zur Typologie des neuen englischen Dramas* (Düsseldorf: Bagel, 1977), pp. 19–50 et passim.

5. Irving Wardle apparently first applied the phrase "comedies of menace" to Pinter's plays; see Steven H. Gale, *Butter's Going Up: A Critical Analysis of Harold Pinter's Work* (Durham, N.C.: Duke Univ. Press, 1977), p. 23.

6. Or so Pinter said to Lawrence Bensky in a 1968 *Paris Review* conversation reprinted in Arthur Ganz, ed., *Pinter, Twentieth-Century Views* (Englewood Cliffs, N.J.: Prentice-Hall, 1972), p. 29.

7. *The Birthday Party and The Room* (New York: Grove, 1961), p. 120. All quotations of Pinter's plays are from the same publisher's editions: *The Caretaker* (1961; rev. 1965); *The Homecoming* (1965); *Old Times* (1971); *No*

Man's Land (1975). Parenthetical page references are to these editions. American printings after the first and many British editions have minor verbal differences from the texts I quote. *Betrayal* has to date (March 1979) been published only in London (Methuen, 1978).

8. Quoted from Kenneth Tynan's BBC interview (28 October 1960) by Martin Esslin, *Theatre of the Absurd* (New York: Doubleday, 1961), p. 212.

9. Gale, pp. 174–75 et passim, disagrees.

10. "A World of Words in Pinter's *Old Times*," MLQ, 40(1979), 53–74 discusses this and other aspects of that important play.

11. See for example, Karl-Heinz Stoll, pp. 61–64 and Austin E. Quigley, *The Pinter Problem* (Princeton, N.J.: Princeton Univ. Press, 1975), pp. 114–15; both authors offer diagrams.

12. R. F. Storch, "Harold Pinter's Happy Families," reprinted in the Ganz collection (see note 6), p. 144.

13. Gale, p. 201, mentions *Four Quartets*; "Little Gidding," lines 36 ff. read, "There are other places / Which also are the world's end ... But this is the nearest, in place and time, / Now and in England."

14. Ionesco, p. 225; he is describing the characters of Roland Dubillard's *Naives Hirondelles*.

15. Roger Shattuck, *Proust's Binoculars* (New York: Random, 1963), p. 22; for Proust's extensive use of photographic imagery (including photo-albums as memory-images), see Beckett, *Proust* (1931; New York: Grove, 1957?), pp. 19–20 and Victor E. Graham, *The Imagery of Proust* (Oxford: Blackwell, 1966), pp. 103, 106, and 151.

16. Beckett's *Play,* in *Cascando and Other Short Dramatic Pieces* (New York: Grove, 1968), concerns another sexual triangle (two women, one man); rather than moving backward in time as *Betrayal* does, *Play* achieves similar effects through repetition. The final stage direction is *da capo*: "Repeat play" (p. 61).

Harold Pinter:
The Room as Symbol

HEDWIG BOCK

Harold Pinter was born in Hackney, London, in 1930. With Wesker, Osborne and Stoppard, he is chief among the dramatists who have made British drama world famous since John Osborne wrote *Look Back in Anger* in 1956. The first two dramatists of this group, Wesker and Osborne, intend social criticism, the other two do not, as they have often said, unless we accept that any presentation of events will reflect good as well as evil and therefore induce criticism. Although Pinter gives the impression that society is completely excluded from his plays—most of his characters are borderline cases who do not conform to any norm set by society—we nonetheless know that there is a society functioning outside Pinter's "rooms," and one of the main themes of Pinter's plays is the threat of the intruder from the outside, from society. The fact that in Pinter's plays there is neither analytical technique nor exposition, neither explicit nor implicit, to explain the past, gives the impression that there is no before and no outside either.

All of Pinter's plays have as their key symbol the "room," either as room, garden, house or van, which gives warmth and protection against a threatening world, but is a prison and a threat in itself.

Martin Esslin and others have interpreted this continuously threatening menace from the outside, the fear of being attacked and either annihilated by forces from the outside, or imprisoned, as having its roots in Pinter's Jewish descent. Although Pinter grew up in Britain during the Second World War with the constant threat of German invasion, the roots of this fear can be traced psychoanalytically to a much earlier stage of his being. The room in its various appearances is a symbolic remembrance of the womb, the symbiosis of mother and child, and the fear of being born, i.e. on the one hand of being exposed to a threatening world, on the other hand of not being born, and finally dying. Samuel Beckett once said that he "had retained a terrible memory of life in his mother's womb. He was constantly suffering from this, and had awful crisis, where he felt he was suffocating."[1] Harold Pinter seems to have been obsessed with both the fear of being driven out of the protective womb and not being able to leave it.

Although this symbol of the room is a female symbol and the key symbol in Pinter, the family structure in his plays is clearly patriarchal. The children in his plays are nearly all boys: in *A Night Out* (1958), *Tea Party* (1964), *The Homecoming* (1964); and in *The Birthday Party* (1957), Meg feels sorry for the woman who has given birth to a little girl. *The Dumb Waiter* (1957), *The Caretaker* (1960), *The Dwarfs* (1960), *No Man's Land* (1975), have no women characters, but exhibit the symbol of the room as womb. Women in Pinter's plays are either castrating mother figures or whores. Very often they are both, in real life, as Ruth in *The Homecoming*, or pretending, as Sarah in *The Lover* (1963), who seems to have children and to lead a dull middle-class housewife's life, but plays the whore in order to increase sexual satisfaction with her husband. It may be noted, that Pinter, who once said: "I just cannot write parts for intelligent women," has dedicated most of his earlier plays to his first wife, Vivien Merchant, and that she played the leading female roles in them. She has meanwhile divorced Harold Pinter; and his last play *Betrayal* (1978), dedicated to Simon Gray, offers completely new aspects. There are two families with sons as well as daughters, two "emancipated" wives with jobs, and the room as symbol of the womb has disappeared.

The following analysis will examine Pinter's plays and interpret them according to the aspects above: the meaning of the room, the woman in it, and the male-female relationship in several of Pinter's plays. It should be noted that these interpretations stress only one aspect in Pinter. A "total interpretation" exists as the sum total of all Pinter interpretations.

The Birthday Party[2] appeared on the stage in April 1958. It was Pinter's second play, written after *The Room* (1957). At the time, the press rejected *The Birthday Party,* now considered one of Pinter's major plays. It contains all the typical elements of Pinteresque style: dialogue with its silences and misunderstandings as non-communication, the theme of the intruder, the symbol of the room, its occupant and his problem of identity and autonomy.

The Birthday Party deals with Stanley Webber, a man in his late thirties, incapable of leading an independent life outside, who has taken refuge in a boarding house in a seaside resort. The owners are Meg and Petey Boles. Stanley, who is also afraid of sex—in this case Lulu—is finally and forcefully taken out of his refuge by two intruders from the outside, Goldberg and McCann.

Meg and Stanley are the central characters of the play. Meg certainly is the woman with the lowest intelligence of all Pinter's women. The comic effect of the play rests with her, her immense stupidity and inability to understand even her own reality. She takes no interest in anything, and considers her house a good house, simply because it is "on the list" (12). She is convinced that she is a good wife, since she keeps her house clean. Her activities consist of dusting the rooms in a rather ineffective way, going shopping to buy food and feeding whoever is near her. She is too lazy to read the newspaper, and asks Petey to choose "nice" passages to read to her. Her complete lack of self-esteem and her female inferiority complex come to the surface in an undeniable Freudian "penis-envy": she feels sorry for the woman who has just given birth to a little girl, since only the birth of a boy for her is a joyful event. When she tries to impress McCann, she boasts of her father, who, she says, was a "very big doctor" (60), but she does not mention her mother. As a typically Pinteresque woman she is identified with her room. She boasts of the room she had as a little girl, which was pink with lots of musical boxes all over the room. In other rooms of different colours lived lots of little brothers and sisters. She has never left the room. Even at her age, it is still her place. Stanley, as a man, who tries to cover his own inability and inferiority, boasts about his past as a great artist, also about places like Berlin and Vladivostok, where he says he will give concerts. Both, Meg and Stanley, in their boasting, adhere to the traditional role-models, deeply internalized into the female and male, or rather Pinter's, subconscious. The woman is immobile, emotional, with a fixation on anything male, in this case the father and Stanley. The man at least dreams about his own greatness, and of being the one who can move around the world.

Meg's relations with her husband Petey, after so many years of marriage, are based on an habitual arrangement, which works well for both of them. Petey is able to accept reality, is mobile, takes from Meg what he needs—the food in the mornings and evenings—but can go out. The room for him is neither prison nor protection, merely the place to which he returns after he has done his job outside. He is able to withdraw from Meg's mothering and feeding attacks. He is also able to go out during the birthday party that destroys Stanley. Goldberg and McCann can never be a threat to him. This leaves Meg with nobody to concentrate upon, to feed, and to satisfy her sexual interest. Since Petey withdraws from her misdirected mother instinct—as her husband he can be defined as the person who stays in the same house and sleeps in the same room with her—Meg has adopted Stanley as a substitute "son-cum-lover." Her sexual attraction to Stanley is mixed with aggressions: on the one hand, she goes into his room in the morning, tickles him violently, and says that she would like to go for a walk with him. On the other hand, she constantly castrates him. She fusses over him, expresses concern for his socks and even goes to the extent of inquiring, "Did you pay a visit this morning?" (23).

Stanley, for his part, was looking for what Meg can offer: the safety of the house as uterus, as protection against an outside world. Meg's and Stanley's weaknesses, her need to look after a son and his to find a mother, combine in neurotic arrangement. That Stanley also felt some attraction for his substitute mother is shown on a symbolic level. He wears glasses, which Goldberg and McCann break so that he cannot see, and blindness was the punishment for Oedipus for having sexual desires for his own mother.

Stanley's entrapment in this oedipal position, his inability to follow a father figure and leave, make him the helpless victim of Goldberg and McCann. Instead of going out when the intruders come in, he tries to defend what he calls "his" room, he tells them that the house is fully booked, that they cannot stay, that they must leave. Even Lulu cannot tempt him to go out, because outside is "nowhere" (26).

What we witness as Stanley's birthday party, therefore, is the ritual of his forceful and long overdue initiation into the world. The violence necessarily attached to the ritual brings his own violence to the surface. His only way to escape his symbiotic and incestuous relationship with his "mother"—Meg—is through murdering her, which he tries during the games played at the party. He can only experience sexual relations through aggression and through degrading women. He tries to rape Lulu who is a tart. His own "birth" takes place with violence and force. Whether we consider Goldberg and McCann as real or the product of Stanley's imagination, whether or not we consider them as agents of an evil society, they symbolize Stanley's fear and inability to grow up and take full responsibility for himself and others. The only alternative left for him, therefore, is "adjustment" and "integration." He will become a new "Mensch" (83–84). The glasses he gets back are broken, the umbilical cord and his oedipal connections with Meg are forcefully cut, but he cannot live without a mother, outside a mother. The van waiting for him is his coffin. What happened to him is exactly what Beckett describes in *Waiting for Godot*:

> Astride the grave and a difficult birth. Down in the hole, lingeringly, the gravedigger puts on the forceps. We have time to grow old. The air is full of our cries (...) But habit is a great deadener.[3]

In many ways Pinter's subsequent play *A Night Out*[4] may be considered as Stanley Webber's early case history. We observe a mother-son relationship as in *The Birthday Party,* but this time the son, 28 years of age, and therefore 10 years younger than Stanley Webber, tries to leave his mother's house to go to a farewell party for one of his colleagues. His mother, a widow, desperately tries to stop him from going out of the house, but the son goes, though with an extremely guilty conscience. His colleagues at the party make fun of his weaknesses, and he returns home to try and kill his mother who receives him with bitter reproaches for leaving her. His second effort to leave home takes him straight to a prostitute, whom he also threatens to kill. He does not have sex with her and returns home to his mother, his efforts having led to no results at all.

This time, dialogue and action are completely realistic. Albert's weaknesses and the threat which the world poses for him are a direct outcome of his relations with his mother. Again there is no father or other man with whom the son could identify to counter the overprotective mother and to teach him to be independent. The father obviously died a long time ago. We hear practically nothing of him. He is used as a weapon in Mrs. Stoke's battle for power over her son. She tells Albert that his father was always properly dressed, and brushes his clothes in order to keep him a couple of minutes longer in the house and to prove her motherly feelings for him. The son is reminded that the father had high hopes for him, and that it cost the parents a great deal of money to raise him. The natural outcome of all this nagging is Albert's guilt complex and consequent inability to leave his mother. The marriage of the parents was obviously not built on love; love is only mentioned when the mother asks Albert to confirm that he loves her. She never says that she loves him or anyone else. She merely needs him as an object of identification. She is a "non-person" except for her role as mother, which she should long since have given up. She therefore tries everything she can to keep Albert as her little son. Feeding him and cleaning the house is all that she is able to do. She has a great aversion towards sex, may have been frigid in her relations with her husband, since sex for her is dirt. She therefore tries to prevent Albert's relations with girls. His discovery of sex would mean his growing up and turning away from her. Therefore she does everything to strengthen their oedipal connections. "Matriarchy" seems to be the traditional family structure in the Stokes family: the father is dead and the dominating mother is the sole mistress of the house. A grandfather is never mentioned, but the grandmother and her room are ever-present. Though the grandmother died ten years ago, her room is still called "grandma's room," and the broken bulb he is expected to replace in it is used to prevent Albert from leaving the house.

Stanley, in *The Birthday Party,* seems to have escaped from his mother, returning to a substitute mother. His "regressus ad uterum" ends in the van as coffin and is therefore final. Albert in *The Night Out* has just reached the first stage of rebellion against his mother. He tries twice to leave the house, he returns twice, and the second time for him may be a final retreat unless he is born forcefully like Stanley. The battle between mother and son gives Albert only slight chance of victory. He does not leave his mother on his own accord, but makes use of an invitation to his boss's party. He does resist his mother's urging to put a new bulb into the grandmother's room. He also resists his mother's offer of his favourite dinner. He resists her questions about his sex life, and he finally gets the tie from her. But all this, together with her warning:

> You are all I've got, Albert. I want you to remember that. I haven't got anyone else. I want you...I want you to bear that in mind. (46)

is too much for him. She has created such a guilt complex in him that he does leave her, but even in the pub where he meets his colleagues he is not sure whether he should not return home at once. As Goldberg and McCann close in on Stanley in Meg's house, Albert meets his opponents and oppressors in the house of Mr. King. Like Goldberg and McCann they know about his weaknesses, his dependence on his mother and his consequent fear of sex. They know his inability to defend himself verbally against the accusation that he touched one of the girls, and physically against the attack by his colleague Gidney who has a grudge against him.

His return home to his mother as the only haven he has, at once confronts him with his reality: the nagging mother. His only way out is to attempt to kill her, but even this attempt will prove futile. He is the defenceless "little boy" for whom every encounter turns out to be defeating. The prostitute who picks him up offers him a chance to have sex, though in its most primitive form, but even here, without any personal consequences for him, he is unable to escape his own personality. Both the girl and he try to disguise the reality, that they are unable to change their situations in life. In her, Albert merely meets his castrating mother. Again he threatens to kill the woman as his only way to escape. The fact that he follows the prostitute shows that he can either have contact with women who prove to him that they are inferior and that sex is dirty—or be aggressive and try to kill them—or have no relations with younger women at all. He finally flips her money for a service he has not even taken.

However, he does not kill and cannot kill any woman. Symbolically he is unable to cut his oedipal relations. When he returns home, his mother is as alive as ever, castrates and infantilizes him as always, and pretends that nothing has happened:

> I'm going to forget it. You see? I'm going to forget it. We'll have our holiday together, in a fortnight. We can go away. (87)

Albert's "night out" after this is a mere farce, he will not leave the house except with his mother and will return with her.

Harold Pinter's *The Lover,*[5] first performed on television in 1963, is his only comedy. It is written with a very light hand and is quite entertaining. It introduces Richard and Sarah, a middle-aged couple, very well off, who live in a house in the country near London. Richard travels into London every morning. On leaving he casually enquires whether his wife's lover will come, which she confirms. The lover, Max, however, who visits the wife several afternoons a week, is Richard in different clothing. Sarah also wears clothes different from her morning attire when her "lover" arrives. An attempt of Richard/Max to break out of this role-playing proves to be a failure.

In *The Lover* we have the usual Pinter theme of the intruder, though on various levels of reality. There is the effort to break away from what seems to be a whore, to get out of fancy dress and into "respectable" clothes. For the first time in Pinter, we have what appears to be a respectable couple, very well off, since the husband can afford to leave his job in the afternoons as often as he pleases to do so. The couple lives in a house near London, "the furnishings are tasteful and comfortable" (49). Their marriage is success-ful, they several times assure each other of their love, an assurance we usually do not hear in Pinter's plays, as he does not go in for happiness. The couple has been married for about ten years, and their happiness is based on the invention of ritual games in which they both take roles and wear clothes they do not wear outside the games. What is "reality" and what is not, is difficult to decide. For Sarah both levels are at the point of combin-ing. Which shoes are most "comfortable" for her, she does not know herself. Sarah's game of being a respectable woman who is attacked in the park, of a whore who seduces a gentleman, and Richard's game of being the gardener, who attacks the respectable woman, are their way of heightening sexual satisfaction. A beautiful moonlit evening cannot stimulate them. The husband Richard, who kisses his wife on the check, is only the breadwinner, while Sarah is the wife, who stays in the house, gets the food ready, as all Pinter women do, and, madonna like, does not know about sex. For Richard, Sarah is an ornament he is proud to appear with in public. The house is his and if he wishes to do so, he could force her to leave. She is completely dependent on him. She is also more dependent on the games they play than Richard is. She is the one who begins to confuse her roles of madonna and whore, she is the one who wears the wrong dress and shoes at the wrong time, about whom we ask "Who is she, which one is her identity?" Sarah, however, knows perfectly well, that all is "our arrange-ment" (81). Richard, on the other hand, clearly separates both roles. There are his job in the City of London and his games at home. He is the one who breaks away, though we are not quite sure whether this is a new game he is inventing. After so many years of married life, this may be the stimulus he needs. Sarah, as Pinteresque woman the more dependent partner of the two, has internalized her role as sex object so well that she produces psychosomatic symptoms when Richard threatens her game: she gets a headache. At the same time, she knows Richard's weaknesses, is able to take revenge on him and force him to continue the games. She threatens not to feed Richard—in Pinter a dreadful thing for a woman to do—and when she finally gives in and gets Richard back to the games with the promise of boeuf bourgignon, she attacks him by telling him that she really is a whore and takes in lovers whenever her husband is not there. This is the final solution, they have again reached a balance—though rather delicate— Sarah is the respectable wife/madonna/feeding mother and also the whore, Richard's strength is her weakness, his weakness is her strength. And we may add, that they will live and love happily ever after, perhaps with similar interruptions of the games and new satisfaction for them when the old games become stale.

Most amusing and perhaps even very British are the symbols Pinter uses in this play: to drink tea means to have sex, to drink whisky the opposite. The "lover" wants to see the hollyhocks. Moonlight and a beautiful evening mean a good night's rest for both husband and wife, while shutting out the daylight by letting down the blinds, suggests the artificial nature of their games. That cigarettes are sex symbols is well known. In this play to ask for a light has this meaning. The couple light their own cigarettes when they do not play games. The bongo drum as instrument of ritual may also be mentioned.

If Pinter's *The Lover* is his one amusing play which represents a satisfactory, probably even happy relationship between husband and wife, *The Homecoming*[6] may be considered his most famous play. *The Homecoming* deals with a family of two brothers, Lenny and Joey, their father, Max, and his brother, Sam, who keep house together, and of Max's son, Teddy, who returns home for a visit from the United States with his wife, Ruth. In the end it is decided that Ruth shall not return with her husband to the States, but stay with the family and earn her keep as a prostitute.

Again Pinter presents us with his version of the female principle as possessive mother and whore, who seems to be at the root of all evil. Looking at the men first, they suffer from a massive oedipal syndrome, which explains the mother/whore woman as the sole type they are able to accept, and only then, if they debase her. Even so they can only establish some sort of highly aggressive contact with her. They are a group with obvious or hidden homosexual connections and have therefore been able to live without women until Ruth comes. Since the group's heterosexual desires are so weak, she will certainly be able to satisfy them all and also be part-time prostitute.

Out of this combination of oedipus complex and homosexuality, Pinter develops the group's attitude towards women in general as highly aggressive. Again, as in other Pinter plays, their constant wish to kill the mother/whore is their only way to overcome their oedipal desires. Lenny, one of the younger brothers, in his conversation with Ruth, tells her about a woman who, as he says, "started taking liberties" with him. He decides that she was "diseased":

> ...and so I clumped her one. It was on my mind at the time to do away with her, you know, to kill her, and the fact is, as killings go, it would have been a simple matter, nothing to it... But... in the end I thought... Aah, why go to all the bother... you know, getting rid of the corpse, and all that, getting yourself into a state of tension. So I just gave her another belt in the nose and a couple of turns of the boot and sort of left it at that. (32)

and about an old lady who asks him to help her with her iron mangle:

> I said to her, now look here, why don't you stuff this iron mangle up your arse? Anyway I said, they are out of date, you want to get a spin drier. I had a good mind to give her a work over there and then, but I was feeling jubilant with the snow clearing, I just gave her a short arm jab to the belly and jumped on a bus outside. (32)

The group's aggressive behaviour, their attitude towards women, was formed by the relationship between Max and the sons towards Jessie, Max's wife, who apparently died many years ago. Max has the most ambivalent attitude towards her, saying in one breath "she wasn't such a bad woman," and in the next "it made me sick to look at her rotten stinking face" (9).

Max himself was the one to look after the children, who bathed them and fed them, who played the mother's role and therefore stayed inside the house, while Jessie went outside and followed the same profession that Ruth takes up. Max's walking stick may be interpreted as a phallic symbol of old age and impotence. Lenny calls him "sexless" (72). But at the same time he brags about his ability to deal with horses, also a sex symbol, and puts the blame on family obligations for his not having had a career in horse racing. His lack of gender-identity is revealed in his birth envy: "I gave birth to three grown men" (40) is what he tells the family, and "...don't talk to me about the pain of childbirth—I suffered the pain, I've still got the pangs—when I cough my back collapses ... " (47). He seems to have been unable to satisfy his wife/whore's desires, for it is certain that she had connections with her husband's best friend, about which her husband may not even have known.

Ruth, Jessie's daughter-in-law, returns into the family as Jessie's reincarnation. Like all Pinter women, she exists as sex object. Therefore, the question of her becoming older is raised at one point, which would mean that she would then not be able to earn her money. The life she is going to lead in Max's family is the life she is accustomed to. She was a model of the body before she got married to Teddy, then had three sons and led a middle-class life as a professor's wife. Coming to her husband's family, for her, means "homecoming." When she sees the old life, she reverts to its patterns. She becomes what she has always been—a whore—and at the same time takes up Jessie's role as the all-possessive mother of the family. Unable to develop any personal attachment either to her own children and husband or the members of Max's family, she becomes their economic object. However, she is clever enough—more intelligent than Pinter's women so far—to make demands and get as much as possible out of the group of males before she signs a contract with them. Her three children seem to have slipped from her mind completely. The one question left at the end of the play is not, whether Sam is really dead and Max has had a stroke. It is the question of what will Ruth do when she is 50? The chances are that she will be a very efficient "madame."

The plays Pinter wrote after *The Homecoming*: *The Tea Party* (1964), *The Basement* (1967), *Landscape* (1968), *Silence* (1969), *Old Times* (1971), *No Man's Land* (1975), *Betrayal* (1978) have not reached the quality of his earlier plays. Nor have they been acted and analysed as often as the others. It may be argued that Pinter would have been considered a minor author, if he had only written what he wrote after *The Homecoming*. His plays have become variations on a theme, there is the male-female relationship as described above; the question of what is dream, nightmare or reality; and, in consequence, the question of identity of the characters concerned.

This is the case in Pinter's *Old Times*,[7] as Anna explains it:

> There are some things one remembers even though they may never have happened. There are things I remember which may never have happened, but as I recall them so they take place. (32)

This may be taken as the motto for nearly all of Pinter's plays. The meaning of *Old Times* is even less translucent than that of other plays.

The play deals with a middle-aged couple, Deeley and Kate, who live in a house outside London. In the beginning of the play the wife's friend Anna, who seems to be married and living on Sicily, comes to visit Kate, whom she has not seen for the last twenty years. There appears to be a strong rivalry between the intruder Anna and the husband Deeley, who knows about the friendship and its lesbian nature. The whole play may very well be Deeley's nightmare that Anna will do to him what he has once done to her: come in as the intruder and take Kate away. This does worry him not because he loves his wife—love is not mentioned in the play—but because this would mean his castration. Again we are presented with the Pinter principle of the woman as feeding mother/madonna/whore, this time split into two people. Kate, the parson's daughter, is the madonna with the "shy" smile, who folded herself from other people, that "they were no longer able to speak or go through with their touch" (64). Sex, as her forbidden fruit, is dirty, and when Kate tries to plaster Deeley's face with dirt, and thus acts against the role model Pinter ties her to, Deeley suggests a wedding instead. Anna, by contrast, is the whore whose face is dirty. She, like Deeley, has once taken the first steps in wooing the passive Kate. Anna has several times put on Kate's underwear, each time Deeley looked up Anna's legs, but she did not mind. In this new contest over Kate, she is the winner, and Deeley the "Odd Man Out." When he begins to feel uncomfortable, she tells him to go. In the end Anna and Kate are both on the divan, Deeley sits away from them in an armchair. The old connections between the two women are stronger than what he can offer.

Pinter's most recent play, *Betrayal*[8] was staged and published in the autumn of 1978. It is a play that may very well be compared to *Old Times,* since it also deals with old relationships. But events in *Betrayal* take place on a completely realistic level. The technique is more analytical than in any other of the Pinter plays. It is the story of two couples, Emma and Robert, Jerry and Judith. Judith does not appear on the stage. The couples each have two children, a boy and a girl. For the first time in Pinter we have a well balanced representation of women, men, girls, boys, and for the first time the wives as well as the husbands have jobs. The husbands are both connected with publishing, Emma runs an art gallery, Judith is a doctor, and the question may even be asked who are the more successful, wives or husbands.

The play deals mainly with the relationship of Emma and Jerry, who were lovers for seven years. At the beginning of the play their love affair has been dead for the last two years, and the marriage of Emma and Robert has come to an end the night before. It should be mentioned that all four children are legitimate. Also, though the wives have demanding jobs outside the house, Pinter again stresses their job as housewives. They cook or put the children to bed while the men have drinks.

The play as such may be considered not interesting, since it deals with rather unexciting every-day events. The dialogue tells us facts and is without depth. The play, however, becomes interesting when it is compared with other Pinter plays. The symbol of the womb as protection and prison no longer exists. Pinter himself has become conscious of the meaning of his key symbol, which Jerry and Robert discuss:

JERRY: Well, I suppose . . . boys are more anxious.
ROBERT: Boy babies?
JERRY: Yes.
ROBERT: What the hell are they anxious about . . . at their age? Do you think?
JERRY: Well . . . facing the world, I suppose, leaving the womb, all that.
ROBERT: But what about girl babies? They leave the womb too.
JERRY: That is true. It's also true that nobody talks about girl babies leaving the womb. Do they? (63)

In this play, Pinter seems to have overcome the fears which were urgent in his earlier plays. His women, who were never faced with the problem of leaving the womb, who were in fact the incarnation of the womb, who tried to hold the men in it, have also left the room. They are no longer interested in keeping one man, son or husband, tied to their apron strings. Accordingly the place of action changes with each new scene. Each one takes us back further into the past and explains the rather loose relationship between the two couples. But even though Pinter has now dissolved the old relationship between the men as sons and the women as feeding, overpossessive mothers and whores, he has not been able to develop a full and satisfactory—one is tempted to say emancipated— relationship between the sexes. The protagonists assure each other of their love from time to time, but they are not able to build up a close and warm relationship with one partner. Naturally, to see ideal relationships on the stage might be uninteresting, but, with the old problems, the old drive seems to have left Pinter. There is no intruder in the play, unless we take it for granted that everybody has intruded on everybody: Jerry on his friend Robert, when he started to make love to Robert's wife soon after their wedding. Robert when he found other women. Jerry's wife, when she had an affair with another doctor. The men are shocked when they hear about the unfaithfulness of their partners; the wives' feelings are not mentioned, but nobody tries to find a way back into a close relationship. The blame seems to be put on the wives' working, because they are often out when their men come in. Pinter feels that their marriages are therefore "Drying Out," as the title of the novel referred to in the play suggests. It is interesting to note that the violence, which is so prominent in Pinter's earlier plays, is still there. Although the characters in the play are all members of the middle or upper-middle class, Robert, at least, goes in for occasional wife-battering:

> It's true I've hit Emma once or twice. But that wasn't to defend
> a principle. I wasn't inspired to do it from any kind of moral
> standpoint. I just felt like giving her a good bashing. The old itch
> ... you understand. (41)

We do not hear what Emma thought about this treatment.

After reading and seeing *Betrayal* and looking back at the development of Pinter's plays, at the men being imprisoned in the womb, not wanting to leave it and finally leaving it, and at the women, who were — symbolically speaking—the womb and finally become human beings, with heads and brains, there remains the question of what Pinter will have to say in the future. Does *Betrayal* indicate, that Pinter's talents have come to an end, that he has finally left the "room" himself and has no more to say or does it indicate a new phase of creativity with new themes and new messages to give to his audiences? One is tempted to hope for the latter.

NOTES

1. Martin Esslin, *The Theatre of the Absurd*, rev. ed. (London: Eyre Methuen, 1974), p. 16.

2. Harold Pinter, *The Birthday Party* (London: Methuen & Co., 1960). All quotations from *The Birthday Party* are from this edition.

3. Samuel Beckett, *Waiting for Godot* (London: Faber and Faber, 1961), p. 90f.

4. Harold Pinter, *A Slight Ache and Other Plays* (London: Methuen & Co., 1961). All quotations from *A Night Out* are from this edition.

5. Harold Pinter, *The Collection and The Lover* (London: Methuen & Co., 1963). All quotations from *The Lover* are from this edition.

6. Harold Pinter, *The Homecoming* (London: Methuen & Co., 1965). All quotations from *The Homecoming* are from this edition.

7. Harold Pinter, *Old Times* (London: Eyre Methuen, 1971). All quotations from *Old Times* are from this edition.

8. Harold Pinter, *Betrayal* (London: Eyre Methuen, 1978). All quotations from *Betrayal* are from this edition.

The Fabulous Theater of Edward Bond

RUBY COHN

"If I had to name my theatre I would call it The Rational Theatre."[1] If I had to name Bond's theater, I would not call it rational but fabulous. Bond does not seem to me his most discerning critic, but then he has finer things to do—like write plays.[2] Although I shall not again quote Bond in order to disagree with him—and I shall quote only stingily from his essays—I realize that my view of his work diverges from his own. Bond's Fabulous Theater then, in the second and especially the third OED definitions:" 2. Spoken of or celebrated in fable or myth; 3. Of a narrative; Of the nature of a fable or myth." Bond's plays seek rational direction through theatricalization of fable. Roaming through time and place, his ten major dramas may be grouped for convenience: surface realism of *The Pope's Wedding, Saved, The Sea;* invented or embellished history of *Early Morning, Bingo, The Fool;* war fables of *The Narrow Road to the Deep North, The Bundle, Lear,* and *The Woman.*

Author not only of these ten plays, but also five minor plays, four stories, an opera libretto, a ballet, three translations, two adaptations, several film scripts, a volume of verse, and various essays. The last rubric bristles with exposition of ideas—"Millstones round the Playwright's Neck," "Censor in Mind," "The Murder of Children." In Bond's plays, however, he *dramatizes* ideas through lapidary phrases, theatrical scenes, vivid characters, and complex fables. Living with his family in a village near Cambridge, he is politically committed to the British New Left and artistically committed to all his work, major and minor.

The drama critic may skim over the minor works, written by request, but even they show him as an irrepressible fabulist. *Black Mass* (1970), *Passion* (1971), *Stone* (1976), *Grandma Faust* (1976), *The Swing* (1976). Blunt and funny agit-prop, they are not unrelated to Bond's opera libretto *We Come to the River* (1976). Written five years afer *Lear,* the libretto depicts a comparable education of the protagonist and stages the same dramatic metaphor of insight through blinding. When the General learns that he is about to lose his sight, revulsion wells up against his profession, against the caricature figures of his country, and against the soldiers he has ordered to commit atrocities. He sees himself tainted by the destruction of two families, and, refusing to serve any longer, he is committed to an insane asylum where the mad people kill him. The opera closes on two counter-pointed choruses—the war victims (including the dead) at the river and the madmen in the asylum. Played in three areas of a vast stage, each with its own orchestra, the opera is richly textured in sound, as well as socially sophisticated in theme.[3]

Agit-prop and libretto are not of course Bond's most resonant achievements, but they mark the areas of his commitment, the liveliness of his plotting, and the deadliness of his satiric instruments—mainly dialect and parody—that cut more sparingly in his major plays, which begin with *The Pope's Wedding* (1962). Before that he submitted to the Royal Court Theatre Writer's Group "two short plays ... one of which was rather Beckett-like, and the other rather Brecht-like in style."[4] Both masters are blended in *The Pope's Wedding,* but naturalized into Bond's theater idiom—pithy phrases, sixteen short scenes, individuals in tension with an established society. What Bond borrowed from Beckett (and perhaps from Raleigh Trevelyan's *A Hermit Disclosed*) is the hermit Alen, who fasci-nates the play's protagonist, Scopey. What Bond borrowed from Brecht (who learned it from Shakespeare) is the suggestion of a whole society in swift interchanges of incidental characters. What Bond borrowed from both playwrights is a nearly bare stage where the few props gain illumina-tion. *The Pope's Wedding* sets hermit and society in an invisible English countryside (Essex) that is bankrupt economically, culturally, morally.

Bond has explained his provocative title: "The Pope's Wedding is an impossible ceremony—Scopey's asking for an invitation for something that isn't going to happen, that *can't* happen."[5] What can't happen is, however, less simple and more shocking than a pope's wedding. Scopey not only asks for an invitation to an impossible event; he commits murder when the impossible can't happen, when he cannot enter another man's skin and soul.

Twenty-two year old Scopey, whose name relates only by sound to the titular pope, strains inarticulately against the limitations of his small farm-village world: he snatches a new handbag from eighteen-year old Pat, he excels in a local cricket match, he sneaks away from the victory celebration to enjoy Pat sexually, he marries her and offers to help her care for the old hermit Alen, the charge of Pat's dead mother. Gradually replacing his wife as the old man's caretaker, Scopey leaves his cricket team, and spends so much time with the hermit that he loses his job. All in the obsession to learn: "What yoo 'ere for?" By the play's last of fifteen scenes Scopey has strangled the hermit and *become* a hermit in Alen's hut, without penetrating the phenomenon of hermitage. The pope cannot wed.

What Bond has contrived in this naturalistic play is greater sympathy for the murderer than for anyone in his environment. Like Macbeth, Scopey commits no violence onstage. Like Macbeth, Scopey defies his social order, and like Macbeth, he is unfulfilled by mere worldly comforts. Unlike Macbeth, however, Scopey has no lexicon to express his frustration, and, true to the naturalist tradition that stems from Buechner's *Woyzeck,* he vents that frustration in violence. This seldom seen theater piece provides vivid scenic fragments—a distant cricket game, a postcoitus love scene, a terrified hermit in his hut. Empty community is juxtaposed with an empty hut; the former is filled with cheap consumer goods, and the latter with piles of newspapers, cans of food, and rudimentary furnishings. Through these voids rings Bond's stripped dialogue, pleading with the audience in Pat's final line: "'Elp!'"

The Pope's Wedding received a single initial performance at a Royal Court Sunday Evening, whereas *Saved* (1965) was a *succès de scandale* in the same theater. They are companion contrasts that barely hint at the variety to flow. The one is populated with rootless village youth, the other with rootless urban youth; most characters are in their early twenties. Sex sours into obsession for Scopey, and sex is displaced by concern for Len. The protagonist of *The Pope's Wedding* commits murder, and the protagonist of *Saved* watches while a baby is murdered. The protagonist of *The Pope's Wedding* chokes off his future in choking old Alen, but the protagonist of *Saved* may save or be saved by his adopted family. Bond claims: "Scopey is obviously Len in *Saved* ... "[6]

Scopey and Len alone probe their respective worlds with questions, however monosyllabic. Early scenes in both plays reveal their sexual joy in prowess, and both protagonists wish to sustain and domesticate such joy. Len rents a room from Pam's parents, who haven't spoken to one another in some twenty-five years. After Pam bears a child, she turns against Len and takes up with Fred. Len tends Pam and the baby, and he befriends Fred, who soon tires of Pam. Quarreling with Fred in the park one evening, Pam leaves the baby in its pram. Bored, the South London youths (including Fred but lacking Len) push the pram at one another, half plaything, half weapon. When that game palls, they dare one another to pull the baby's hair, pinch it, hit it, rub its face in a soiled diaper. Egging each other on, they throw stones at the target in the pram, but leave the park when the closing bell sounds. After "A long pause" Pam returns to claim her baby; she wheels the pram away, without looking inside—at her dead infant. It is this scene that grounded Bond's reputation as a playwright of violence, when he should have received acclaim as a scenewright of skill. With flawless rhythm, abrupt gestures punctuate the Cockney banter until, unheeded by anyone on stage, a baby lies battered to death.

When Fred is imprisoned for the death of the baby, Len brings him cigarettes. Confessing that he saw the stoning from a treetop, Len blames himself: "I didn't know what t'do. Well, I should a stopped yer." Again rejected by Pam, Len has a passing flirtation with Pam's mother, and finally decides to leave the "home," but Pam's father dissuades him: "I'd like yer t'stay. If yer can see yer way to." In the final scene of *Saved* each of the four "family" members is preoccupied with his own task, the father mailing a letter, the mother straightening the livingroom, Pam perusing the *Radio Times,* and Len fixing a chair. The single line of dialogue is Len's request to Pam: "Fetch me 'ammer." Nobody does, but Len fixes the chair anyway—the chair broken during a fight of the older couple—and the final silence is a harmonious lull in this household where words are blows. It is an open question who is saved in this drama where no one saves a helpless infant. Searching both individuals and their societies, these naturalistic plays do not yet show Bond the fabulist.[7]

With *Early Morning* Bond takes a giant step away from naturalism and into fable, although few critics recognized it at the time—1968. In that year of historic upheaval Bond contributed his own explosive version of history, one power bloodily displacing another on earth as in heaven. If *The Pope's Wedding* shocks by its title, and *Saved* by the scene of the baby stoned, *Early Morning* offends British shibboleths of history, religion, sexual ethics, and it does so through the length of a diabolically comic fable, which ends in heaven. Before the end, however, Bond has collapsed chronology to render ridiculous the prosperous reign of Queen Victoria, that bastion of English self-satisfaction. Far from her idyllic marriage to Prince Albert, Bond has the royal couple plot one another's assassinations. The Disraeli whom Victoria liked and the Gladstone whom she disliked (both Prime Minister after the real Albert's death) join conspiratorially with him. Queen Victoria's nine children are condensed into Siamese twins, Arthur and George (the former an actual name of one of her sons, the latter otherwise rich in royal resonance). The Florence Nightingale whom Victoria decorated and the John Brown who was her favorite manservant merge into a single character who is betrothed to the Prince of Wales, raped by Queen Victoria, named the first public hangwoman, compelled by her conscience to fornicate with dying soldiers, killed while catering to Disraeli and Gladstone simultaneously; in heaven she is the only one sensitive to the unregenerate humanity of Arthur.[8]

Outrageously, Bond claims: "The events of this play are true." Very loosely, they are. Victoria stood for victory of Capitalism over Chartism, respectability over morality, family cohesion over individual creativity, and repression over freedom throughout a widespread empire. It was during her reign that British "free" trade converted England into a consumer society. Brilliantly, Bond literalizes the metaphor: law, order, and uniformity are established when human beings consume one another's humanity—the stage cannibalism. But *Early Morning* is not Gothic melodrama, in which the great are debunked and the humble ennobled; the commoners—invented characters—are as cruel as the privileged, and the only one who shrinks from horrendous deeds (bordering on Grand Guignol) is the Arthur part of the Siamese twins, who—significantly—possesses their single heart. Immoral and moral aspects of the same character, George the Crown Prince accepts the Establishment on earth and cannibalism in heaven, but Arthur demurs in both realms. The heir of Len and Scopey, he probes the basis of behavior. "Why did you kill him—" he asks repetitively of the Len of *Early Morning,* a commoner whose violence and cannibalism on earth predict that of his betters in heaven. It is Arthur who designs a tug of war to annihilate opposing inhumane armies, and it is Arthur who refuses to accede to celestial cannibalism, even if George must waste away. It is Arthur who dominates the end of the play visually in Bond's revised version of *Early Morning.* In the original last scene (of twenty-one) Victoria nails Arthur (separated from George) into his coffin with her teeth. In the revised version Arthur rises from his coffin, unseen by the others who feast on his corpse. Only Florence abstains from food as she weeps for Arthur—early mourning—and pleads dirt in her eye. With Arthur visible on high, Victoria declares: "There's no dirt in heaven. There's only peace and happiness, law and order, consent and cooperation. My life's work has borne fruit. It's settled." But closing the play, and deflating Victoria's rhetoric is Len's request: "Pass us that leg."

Sympathetic as Arthur is on his second death and ascension to an invisible heaven, it is not he who endows the play with dramatic force, but rather the inventive shock of the whole fable. The first scene surprises Albert and Disraeli plotting Victoria's murder, the third reveals Arthur and George as Siamese twins, the fifth features a pastoral picnic with moments of shoe fetishism, Lesbianism between Victoria and Florence Nightingale, poisoning of Albert by Victoria, struggles for pistol and rifle, and wounding of George Prince of Wales. By Scene 12 George's body is decomposing, and Arthur marshalls a mammoth tug of war in which the losing army topples over a cliff, and the winners tumble to death when the cliff becomes an avalanche. Scene 16 finds the whole cast in a heaven which mirrors earth—its savagery, oppression, and pious rhetoric. Except for Arthur, all the inhabitants engage in candid cannibalism, and even he occasionally weakens into self-consumption. In the play's final scene Arthur's severed head makes love to Florence beneath her skirts, but George bites into the offending member. Arthur laughs loudly—his last sound in the play. As the whole cast picnic on Arthur's corpse, a celestial soldier pronounces his epitaph: "'E weren' a bad bloke. Juss couldn't keep 'is-self to 'is-self.'" This will be true of all Bond's fabulous heroes—acting in larger contexts than their mere selves.

Even today, when Bond's plays are beginning to command the attention they deserve, *Early Morning* has been less than popular. One of the few shocking plays to retain its shock power—*Look Back in Anger* is conservative; *The Blacks* is fast dating; *Godot* is already a classic—it is a Gothic farce that has tempted few directors—like Jarry's *Ubu* before recent appreciation. Arthur Arnold has acutely observed: "Shakespeare's early blunders with literal sons-in-the-pie cannibalism were never repeated, although the image is often repeated."[9] Bond does not even repeat the image, but human ferocity is often repeated—no later than his next play, the first to be set outside of England, but including English characters.

Narrow Road to the Deep North (1968), commissioned by the Canon of Coventry Cathedral for the International People and Cities Conference, was written in two and a half days, and it played to small houses in Coventry (English church plays have come a long way since T. S. Eliot produced *The Rock* for Canterbury Cathedral in 1934). Ostensibly treating the set theme of People and Cities, Bond creates Buddhists and Christians to theatricalize a plague on both their houses.

As in *Early Morning* Bond collapses chronology, but this goes unremarked in the unfamiliar history of Japan. The actual Bashio, a seventeenth-century poet and scholar, wrote a Japanese classic *The Narrow Road to the Deep North*, at once a travel account and what his translator calls "a monument he has set up against the flow of time." Bond plunges *his* Basho right back into time while mocking it. Bond takes only the title from the poet's bestknown work, and from another account an incident about an abandoned child. Subtitled "A comedy," Bond's play is set in "Japan about the seventeenth, eighteenth, or nineteenth centuries." This cavalier attitude toward time is one of the comic notes of the so-called comedy.

Bond's Basho becomes Prime Minister for a nineteenth-century British Commodore-imperialist. Before that, however, Bond's Basho behaves like the historical Basho on seeing an abandoned child: "Alas, it seems to me that this child's undeserved suffering has been caused by something far greater and more massive, what one might call the irresistible will of heaven. If it is so, child, you must raise your voice to heaven, and I must pass on, leaving you behind."[10] With few changes, Bond rhythms these words dramatically: "It hasn't done anything to *earn* this suffering—it's caused by something greater and more massive: you could call it the irresistible will of heaven. So it must cry to heaven. And I must go north." And north he goes, in search of enlightenment.

Fiction begins thirty years later, when Bond's Basho returns enlightened and again stands on his refusal—to serve as religious master to the young monk, Kiro. Basho's home city is in the grip of the warlord Shogo, who was once the child abandoned at the river. A Janus-figure, Shogo in a single scene saves Kiro from strangulation by breaking a holy pot, and a moment later condemns an innocent man to be thrown into the river. Having killed the Emperor in seizing power, he gives the infant-Emperor to Basho, to be brought up as a peasant.

Equally horrified by Shogo's sacrilege and cruelty, Basho travels north again, seeking not enlightenment but the power of an army led by an English Commodore and a Victorian Salvation Army sister Georgina. By Part II Georgina has replaced Shogo's atrocity with her efficient but even more oppressive piety. Fled on the narrow road to the deep north, Shogo and Kiro find not enlightenment but mutual interdependence, so that Kiro reluctantly follows Shogo south to conquer his city. Since the Commodore's conquest was waged in the name of the infant Emperor, Shogo kills five identically dressed children, one of whom is probably the Emperor, and Georgina goes mad. With Basho as Prime Minister, the Commodore has Shogo hacked to death. As Georgina blends a rape fantasy with a call on Jesus, Kiro disembowels himself by the very river where Basho first left the child. A man emerges from the river, scolding Kiro for not rescuing him. Kiro dies as the man dries himself. Barbarians control the city in this "comedy," but new life starts at the river and not on the narrow road to the deep north.

By 1978, a decade after *Narrow Road* was swiftly written, Bond revised it to *The Bundle*. Both plays begin and end at the river, but the adventurous mediating action diverges. The springboard is again Basho's refusal to stray from the narrow road to the deep north, to care for an abandoned child. Bond's new theater fable focuses more sharply on that child, soon grown to manhood. Like the abandoned prince in Brecht's *Caucasian Chalk Circle*, this child thrives on the sacrifices of his adoptive parents. Like the Water-Carrier in Brecht's *Good Woman of Setzchuan* this child is named Wang, and his society resembles China on the verge of the Communist Revolution. In Bond's stage world Wang is a prime mover of that revolution; the titular bundle is a child at the play's beginning and a cargo of rifles by the end.

With *The Bundle* Edward Bond claims that he has embarked on his third cycle of plays, which dramatize an analysis instead of a story, but story is rife in *The Bundle*. What Bond does dramatize is the diametric opposition of the ethics of Basho and Wang; Basho does not shelter the abandoned baby because he pursues self-indulgence on the road north. Wang does not shelter the abandoned baby because he pursues a single-minded goal of arming the peasants to withstand their oppressors. In the first *Narrow Road* as in *Early Morning,* one tyrannical power bloodily replaces another, and the only hope on the horizon is a naked nameless man at the very end of the play. In *The Bundle* hope rests firmly on peasants armed by Wang. At play's end two major characters address the audience directly. Basho, who has served the establishment in its oppression, is still seeking a metaphysical road, whereas the revolutionary Wang is frankly didactic: "To judge rightly what is good—to choose between good and evil—that is all that it is to be human." Before that unabashed declaration, however, the play vibrates with passionate characters—the poor Ferryman and his wife who adopt the infant that Basho spurns, the competitive peasants who cooperate as soon as their oppressors are overthrown, the bandits that Wang converts into a populist army, the soldiers and merchants in unregenerate self-interest.

More than in *Narrow Road* Basho weaves his delicate poems through *The Bundle,* but Wang is a poet too, and the play abounds in imagery of water, energy, vegetation. Basho has himself become a narrow road to a perennial north.

Although *Early Morning* and *Narrow Road* brim with fabulous material, it is in *Lear* (1971) that the fabulist achieves towering mythic dimension. Bond's own summary of his play juxtaposes myth unfavorably with reality: "Act One shows a world dominated by myth. Act Two shows the clash between myth and reality, between superstitious men and the autonomous world. Act Three shows a resolution of this, in the world we prove real by dying in it." The "we" extrapolates Bond's Lear whose death closes the play. It is with a sense of "we" that I write of Bond's Fabulous Theater—theater dramatizing dynamic events about a moral giant whose fate awakens not only pity and terror but complicity.

Bond is bold to risk a *Lear* that triggers comparison with Shakespeare's tragedy, but he thereby became England's major living dramatist. Most telling in both plays is the rechilding of the king, so that we experience the long painful fable of his education. Shakespeare's king moves from imperious rage to self-pity to contrition toward Cordelia, to compassion for the Fool, to "Poor naked wretches whereso'er you are," and, finally, to the utter humility of kneeling to Cordelia—before his variously interpreted death. Bond's Lear learns comparably: looking at the disfigured face of his daughters' victim, he confronts his own mortality. To protect his Fool-figure, the Gravedigger's Boy, he unhesitantly lies, and he later agrees to help the Ghost of the Gravedigger's Boy, to whom he did "a great wrong once, a very great wrong." After the death of Lear's daughters, he assumes responsibility for their atrocities. In the classical tradition, he sees morally after he is blinded; as Bond states it in his preface: "Lear is blind till they take his eyes away. ... Blindness is a dramatic metaphor for insight ... " Blind Lear offers asylum to deserters from Cordelia's wall, and he admits to her that there is no difference between his daughters and him. Finally, he learns that pastoral withdrawal is impossible within society. Failing to convince Cordelia to pull down the wall, he goes to the wall that he himself initiated, in order to undig it. In the revised end Bond has a junior officer shoot Lear, killing him instantly, but "The shovel stays upright in the earth." The wall workers are ordered to leave the scene. "The workers go quickly and orderly. One of them looks back." In that look back Bond punctuates the fabulous dimension; we should all look back on the education of his Lear; the autocrat is elevated to autodidact, wiping the slate of his mind with madness.

Bond has declared: "My plays are about the quest for freedom of one man" Lear's quest is strongly theatrical. He has to find his way through two walls—the first cruelly visible and the second a metaphor for well-wishers and sympathetic strangers. It is only when Lear can tear down the metaphoric wall that he acquires the resolution to assault the physical wall.

Of Bond's fabulous plays *Lear* has the hardest narrative drive through eighteen scenes (with fifteen scene changes). In *Lear* Bond also achieves increased complexity of character. Lear the royal villian learns to be a victim. Warrington-Gloucester is twice dehumanized; at play's start he is the king's principal and unprincipled adviser, telling him mechanically what he wants to hear; by the end of Act I he has been tortured into a terrified dangerous animal. Although Lear's daughters are caricature termagants, even they are momentarily appealing as the ghosts of the girls they once were. In contrast, the Gravedigger's Boy—an odd designation for a man—is immediately endearing in his simplicity and tenderness, but his ghostly guise slowly alienates us before his second violent death. Cordelia is ambiguous but completely unshakespearean; a priest's daughter with small charity, a pregnant wife with an adoring lover, an ungracious hostess who reacts to rape with a single gasp and a life of hatred—she selflessly leads a revolution and is just as selflessly deaf to Lear's plea that she learn by his errors.

In Bond's Preface to *Lear* he points out that seventy odd small roles may be viewed as "one role showing the character of a society," but there is diversity in that society. The king's soldiers are as practical and shrewdly humorous as the rebel forces. Farmers, prisoners, politicians—Bond distinguishes their diction and speech rhythms. So enmeshed is Bond's social fabric that the play's first director, William Gaskill, warned his actors: "If you relate too much you'll break up the scene."[12]

Scenewright Bond works in massive contours unlocalized as to time and place. Alternating between open air and prison scenes, the play begins and ends at the wall that is both. As the river will change from enemy to friend of man in *The Bundle,* so the wall changes from defensive measure to repressive symbol for Lear, and through Lear for us. It is hard to see a stage river, but a stage wall was massive set and prop at the Royal Court Theatre.

Less ceremoniously than Shakespeare, Bond plunges us *in medias res* in his opening scene; the division of *his* kingdom happens through civil war, when Lear's daughters marry invaders. War's confusions rage through Bond's violent play, its brutalities sometime skirting Grand Guignol. To some extent Bond builds the possibility for laughter into the very horror of such scenes as the businesslike torture of Warrington while one daughter knits and the other jumps excitedly, the wisecracks of the soldiers as the blood of the Gravedigger's Boy stains the freshly laundered sheets, the corrupt comments of the judge as mad Lear looks in the mirror, the autopsy of Lear's daughter — "Then let them anatomize Regan." — and the almost clerical crown-blinding of Lear. Director Gaskill rightly enjoined the Royal Court cast: "Never play the character, always play the situation."[13]

In Bond's *Lear,* as in Shakespeare's, images of vision and maiming abound, but most striking is Bond's domestication of Shakespeare's animal imagery. As king, Bond's Lear calls his people sheep and his enemies wolves. When mad, he sees himself as a dog and a mouse. The program for the Royal Court production pictures a monkey in a cage, but Lear's plea is wider, reaching out to horse and bird, and crying: "Let that animal out of the cage!" Lear's dead daughter is to him a blend of lion, lamb, and child. He compares the subservient farmer's family unfavorably to wolf, fox, and horse, and he accuses men of behaving like jackals and wolves. Sane and admired as a saint, Lear narrates a fable of a man's voice in a bird's body. His last fantasy wish is to be as cunning as the fox. These diverse images accumulate into a powerful illustration of Shakespeare's great line: "Unaccommodated man is no more but such a poor bare forked animal as thou art." Image and dialect, quip and anachronism, character and caricature, virtue and violence cohere theatrically in Bond's *Lear,* a fabulous drama.

Two years after this tumultous drama—in 1973—Bond completed two quieter plays, *The Sea* and *Bingo.* However, *The Sea* begins stormily, a man drowning while a paranoid coastguardsman ignores the desperate pleas of his friend who has managed to swim to shore. For the first time since *Saved* Bond returns to realism—of an East Coast English town in 1907. With the deftness acquired in sketching anachronistic societies, Bond swiftly—in eight scenes of which five take place by the sea—depicts an English village hierarchy, with Mrs. Rafi at the head, her social coterie just below her, tradesmen like the draper Hatch dependent upon her, and laborers like Hollarcut completely at her small mercy; she is a provincial Victoria—"The town is full of her cripples." Only Evens, a hermit and alcoholic, lives far from her in a beach-hut, so close to the sea that he alone ripples the realistic surface.

Although *The Sea* skirts the edge of fable, its story is more intricate than *The Pope's Wedding* or *Saved,* its society is more varied, and its characters do not precipitate into simple satire. In spite of Willy's frantic attempts at rescue, Colin drowns because Evens the wise hermit is too drunk to be helpful and Hatch the mad draper believes the coast is being invaded by extraterrestrials. Yet Evens is optimistically understanding of nature and society, and Hatch is more victim than villain. The dead man's fiancée Rose is devoted to him, and yet, on the advice of Mrs. Rafi, she joins Willy In leaving the town. Mrs. Rafi herself is at once self-pitying and self-critical.

Bond easily twists three plot-threads—the social hierarchy's daily doings, the conspiracy of the paranoid vigilantes, and the understated romance of the young lovers. Two—grotesque scenes—plays within the play—comment pointedly on the action. Mrs. Rafi is author, director, and actress in *Orpheus and Eurydice,* but she charms no one with her melodies (especially her rendition of "There's no place like home"), and, far from rescuing anyone from the underworld, she stifles everyone she touches with her well-gloved hand. She dominates the scene of Colin's funeral, theatrically set on a cliff overlooking the sea, with piano music and army guns sounding in the background, and a descant rivalry overriding any hint of grief. When Hatch interrupts the funeral with his fantasy, he seems no madder than the respectable townspeople at their service. In a harmonious final scene Evens the hermit enunciates a philosophy for the couple who will found a new society in this rightly named "Comedy": "Remember, I've told you these things so that you won't despair. But you must still change the world." The "things" Evens tells make the play resonate beyond specific realism. As loquacious a hermit as Alen of *The Pope's Wedding* was laconic, Evens comprehends the nature of the sea, and he enjoins Willy to comprehend human nature.

The protagonist of Bond's next play *Bingo* believes that he has failed to change the world, and he does despair. His name is also Willy—William Shakespeare of *Bingo: Scenes of Money and Death.* Bingo is a game played for money on numbered squares, and so is Bond's play. The "and" of the subtitle ties money, the goal of several characters including Shake-speare, to death, which grips several characters including Shakespeare.

Bingo belongs to the group of plays I designate as invented or embellished history, and Bond's Introduction to the published text enumerates his changes "for dramatic convenience."[14] Set in and around Shakespeare's still extant home at New Place, Stratford, in 1615–6, the play depicts a weak and bloodless bard, who is a virtual stranger in his own family and his own town, and who is confronted with the energies of nascent capitalism. Anxious about financial security, Shakespeare acquiesces to the land enclosures that starve out poor farmers and force them to migrate. The play's villian Combe—also named William—guarantees Shakespeare's holdings at the price of his silence in the protest against enclosure: "It pays to sit in a garden."

This public plot about Shakespeare, money, and death is balanced by a private plot — the whole in six scenes—about Shakespeare, money, and death, for Shakespeare's wife (never seen on stage) and daughter Judith are the money-hungry puppets he has made of them: "I loved you with money." Family love is dead, and Judith values her father's money above his life. In a parallel pattern that Bond learned from Shakespeare, he contrasts that family trio with a nameless family composed of his wise old servant, her mentally deficient husband, and their radical Puritan son. Mother loves husband and son, but son abhors the carnal appetites of his childlike father. Dispossessed by the enclosures, rebellious against such dispossession, the son accidentally shoots the father in a wintry confrontation of opposing forces.

Each half of the six-scene play pivots on an outsider's arrival in Stratford.[15] Part I presents a nameless, homeless Young Woman, soon sentenced to whipping "till the blood runs" and afterwards to hanging. She graphically binds the plot threads—given money by Shakespeare and blame by his daughter, fornicating with the feeble-minded Old Man, judged by landowner Combe in his office of magistrate. Her gibbeted body is visible throughout Scene 3. In Part II Ben Jonson is a slimmer binding thread. Stopping in Stratford on his walk to Scotland, vigorous with lived experience, Jonson confesses his long hatred of Shakespeare, shows the dispirited Bard the poison he has no courage to swallow, and is oblivious to the peasant-rebels at the next table of the inn.

Outsiders are gone after Scene 4, but Jonson's poison — acquisition unexplained—is in Shakespeare's possession in Scenes 5 and 6. Bedridden in the final scene, Shakespeare is beset by his hysterical wife, his importunate daughter, and the Puritan son rationalizing away his guilt at his father's death. The bard intones: "Was anything done? Was anything done?" When Combe enters his sickroom, Shakespeare swallows the poison as a medicine. He falls to the floor when Judith enters. Instead of tending him, she searches frenetically for his will, crying in disappointment: "Nothing." The "emptiness and silence" at play's start lead to the death and nothing at the end.

Shakespeare is Bond's second poet-villain, following Japanese Basho in serving capitalism and failing to support rebels. But Basho is virtually unknown to Western audiences, whereas Shakespeare is a culture hero. Compared to Bond's earlier shock effects, condemning Shakespeare is mild, especially since the play evokes sympathy for a man of exquisite conscience without self-pity. By unshakespearean soliloquies—pithy noun phrases, abrupt associations—Bond's stage bard is a rarity of conviction, but for few critics. Bond's portrait of old Shakespeare casts a shadow over the patina of comfort at New Place in Stratford, should one happen to visit it as I did—post-*Bingo*.

The most frequent scenic direction in *Bingo* is: "Shakespeare doesn't react," and uncannily, Patrick Stewart as Shakespeare rendered the passivity actively, silence projecting dismay at the ubiquity of suffering. In Scene 3 Puritans picnic near the gibbeted Young Woman, and they register no awareness of an abyss between such punishment and their prayers, but Shakespeare associates her fate with London bear-baiting at his theater. In Scene 4 Shakespeare hears the rebellious conspiracy counterpointed against Jonson's drunken confession of hatred. Scene 6 parades the Son and Combe, social antagonists, by Shakespeare's bed. What Director William Gaskill said of *Lear* seems just as true of *Bingo:* "I think the main moments are those when more than one thing is happening on stage at once."[16]

One might view *Bingo* (1973) and *The Fool* (1975) as Bond's classical and romantic play on the same subject—the writer's relationship with society (following facts only minimally about both the Bard and the Northamptonshire Peasant Poet). Although Bond does not obey the classical unities in *Bingo*, he approaches them, with setting in and around New Place, with time-span of a little over half a year. *Bingo* begins, like classical tragedy, close to its dénouement, driving the fable hard toward the dénouement—Shakespeare's willed death. *The Fool*, in contrast, moves back and forth geographically from Northumberland to London; the time-span is some forty years, and the plot rambles through several peripetias—John Clare seeking Mary and thus avoiding arrest, his refusal to expunge class criticism from his poems, his romanticizing of Mary while married to Patty, his commitment to an insane asylum, his brief escape from the asylum. Both Bond protagonist-poets avoid social action, but dramatic focus is more relentlessly on Shakespeare than on Clare.

The eight scenes of *The Fool* are only a slight increase over the six of

Bingo, but they are more liberally peopled—some forty speaking parts
against twelve. Digressions from the plot-line occur more often in *The
Fool*—a mummer's play within the play, a London prize-fight, between a
Black and an Irishman, alcoholic Charles Lamb and his mad sister Mary,
Irish vagabonds (which were eliminated in the Royal Court production).
These digressions are pregnant thematically, but they deflect apprehension
of the narrative line. However it is language that is of almost classical
limpidity in *Bingo* as compared with the variety of *The Fool*—the lugubri-
ous piety of the paraon, the gnetlemen's clichés, the pseudo-lyricism of
literary Mrs. Emmerson, the gambling slang of the boxer-backers, and
especially the rhythmic dialect of the villagers. Never mired in unnatural
diction, they express emotion through repetition of simple words, particularly " 'on't" which can mean don't, won't, can't, shouldn't, wouldn't, am
not. "On'y" and " 'on't" pulse through John Clare's mad self-awareness
before he is reduced to slavering consonants.

It would be wrong, however, to view *The Fool* as a romantic variant on
Bingo. Martin Esslin has succinctly summarized the central difference
between these two poets who have attracted Bond the playwright: "The
Shakespeare of *Bingo* is a highly successful artist who becomes enmeshed
in society's guilt precisely *because* he is a financial success and has to
invest his money, whereas *The Fool* shows the fate of an artist who cannot
support himself by his writing.... *The Fool* dramatizes the life story—and
the bewilderment—of an individual of great talent who lacks the self-
awareness which would enable him to master his personal destiny, just as
he also lacks the historical and political consciousness that would allow
him to make rational political decisions.... It is this lack of understanding
which makes Bond's Clare a *fool.*"[17]

John Clare, Peasant Poet, is Bond's Fool, but capitalism—far more
liberally represented than in *Bingo*—is guilty in robbing him of the Bread
and Love of the subtitle—Scenes of Bread and Love. Clare the Peasant
Poet undoubtedly attracts Bond by his precise participation in the natural
world, his pungent colloquial diction, his unabashed class-consciousness.
For that poet in that society Bond finds two main images—the prison (the
setting of Scene 4) and the madhouse (the final setting). Metaphorically,
they hem Clare in in all the scenes, and yet they are the only cooperative
communities in the play. Initiated by John Clare, insane laughter tears
through the prison. By the final scene mad John Clare is incomprehensible,
but mad Mary Lamb has no problem with his mumblings, and she imper-
turbably translates them into the words that magnetized him above bread
or love.

Bingo and *The Fool* are Bond's first plays to carry subtitles beginning
"Scenes of...." The phrase misleads one to expect a drama of high points

rather than the coherent structures, the theatrical fables they are. If *Bingo* coheres more deeply, *The Fool* ranges more widely. As scenes of money and death freeze *Bingo*, scenes of bread and love provide a dynamic of *The Fool*. Mary feeds Clare stolen bread; the prison warder gives bread to the prisoners; Mary Lamb has killed her mother with a breadknife. In a surrealistic scene of Clare's mad mind, Mary feeds bread to dead, blind Darkie, but he cannot swallow it. Even in his madness, Clare comes to understand the power of bread: "I am a poet an' I teach men how to eat." Durable love exists only between peasants who unite for bread—whether to present plays, steal goods, or comfort one another in prison—and their (invented) leader is pointedly named Darkie—a name that underlines Bond's scenic oppositions of light and dark. The first four scenes—Part I—are performed in darkness, and the last four—Part II—in increasingly bright light. Since no character in the play undergoes enlightenment, Bond may have intended light as a metaphor for the audience understanding. One can only hope, when the blindness of reviewers has receded into oblivion, that illumination will come.

We come finally not to a river but to a masterwork, *The Woman* (1978).[18] A play of unparallelled scale, *The Woman* is a dramatic analogue of *The Iliad* and—not *Odyssey* or *Aeneid* but *Ismeneid* or *Hecubaid*. Written before *The Bundle*, these "Scenes of War and Freedom" are viewed by Bond as the last in his second cycle of plays, whose aim is to de-mythologize the past, to reject the idea of "a golden age [in which] all the answers were known."[19] I view *The Woman* as the last to date of Bond's war fables, whose germ also lies in literature. In 1966 Bond told an interviewer that theatre could "go to the very roots of human nature. This is the sort of thing that happens in [Shakespeare's] *Lear* and *The Women of Troy*. ... I've been inspired, I suppose, by Euripides and Shakespeare ... and Chekhov."[20] We have seen in *Lear* and *Bingo* that Bond's inspiration is not uncritical. So too with Euripides.

The Greek playwright wrote two extant tragedies about Hecuba—*The Trojan Women* and *Hecuba*. In the one Hecuba is a national Niobe, mourning her city, and losing her only grandchild. In the other play Hecuba mourns her young son, slain by a treacherous friend. In both plays Hecuba is a raging vengeress, never seeking to comprehend her loss. Bond changes her vengeance. And if it seems academic to begin with Euripides, so did the mainly unappreciative London reviewers. More to the point, so did Bond.

Begun in 1975, Bond's early draft for *The Woman* set the first scene in Athens and the second on a nameless island. After a few months, Bond put the play aside for a year but thought about it: "I wanted to soak myself in the Mediterranean background and the place I went to a couple of years running was Malta, just to face the sun on the rocks, as it were, as simple as that. I reread all the extant Greek tragedies while I was there, and the comedies too. That was my preparation for *The Woman*."[21] Bond also admitted that he was probably influenced by what he had heard of the vast size of the Olivier stage, which opened in 1977 but has never used more than about one/third of its area; during rehearsals he wrote a poem on the Olivier, ending: "But this is a public stage/Where we speak of our times." To speak of our times Bond decided to direct his own play, insuring an epic sweep.

Structurally, *The Woman* is divided into two parts—fourteen scenes in Part I, nine in Part II. The cast is grouped as Greeks, Trojans (further divided into Bystanders, Soldiers, and Poor), Villagers, and, belonging to none of these, the Dark Man who has escaped from a silver mine. Greeks span both parts of the play, but only Hecuba of the Trojans survives to Part II, which belongs to the Villagers. In the program the scenes of Part I are indicated by their spatial setting, of Part II by their temporal setting.

Part I rewrites the *Iliad*. The Greeks attack Troy not for Helen but for a statue of the goddess of Good Fortune, and their forces are led not by Agamemnon but by Heros, who is married to Ismene. Familiar are the names (and roles) of Nestor and Ajax, but Thersites changes into a competent warrior and diplomat. In the Trojan camp Hecuba's one remaining son is simply called Son, but her daughter Cassandra, without prophetic gift, is the mother of the child Astyanax. The Villagers of Part II belong to Bond's fabulous invention. Neither Odysseus nor Aeneas wander toward the outlying island, but Heros and Nestor come seeking the statue of the goddess, which disappeared in the confusions of Greek victory. A blind Hecuba and amnesiac Ismene live among the islanders as mother and daughter.

Loosely joining these "Scenes of War and Freedom" (Part I being War, Part II Freedom) is the statue of the goddess, visible only once but verbally on many tongues. Four major characters play in both parts—the woman Hecuba, the Greek elder statesman Nestor, the handsome Greek hero Heros, and his humane wife Ismene. *The Woman* blends their stories within the societies of their ungolden age; more properly, it might be called a silver age since Athenian power rests on its farflung silver mines.

In the fifth year of Bond's Trojan War Priam dies of old age. A Greek delegation of Thersites and Ismene try to persuade Hecuba to surrender. When the two women meet in intimacy, they do not speak in Giralducian trivialities but in deep worry about loss of life. Hecuba convinces Ismene of what she has half-realized—that the Greeks will destroy Troy with or without the statue, and therefore Ismene refuses to return to a perfidious Greece. From the walls of Troy (across the vast red battle-field of the Olivier stage) she harangues Greek soldiers to go home (as American soldiers have been urged to go home from distant lands). Ismene fails in her self-imposed mission, and Troy falls not by invasion but by Trojan rebellion of the Poor against the military clique of Hecuba's Son. Trustingly, the poor Trojans deliver the statue to the Greeks, who nevertheless sack Troy, kill its men, and raze its buildings. The Greeks sentence Ismene to death by immurement, and she refuses her husband Heros' offer of poison to curtail her suffering. In the victory momentum, Heros orders the child Astyanax flung to death from the walls of Troy, Hecuba blinds herself with the gesture of Oedipus but without his guilt; and Part I closes on the return from Troy of drunken Nestor and his looting soldiers. (It is this last scene of Part I that most closely resembles Euripides' *Women of Troy*.)

Part II takes place twelve years later in a free world, a nameless island far from Athens; visually a gray tilted disc of uneven terrain. The island Villagers work hard at their fishing and play joyously at seasonal festivals. Even events, announced in the program by "a month later," seem to partake of each season's blight. First Nestor and his men are sent to invite Hecuba to Athens, to display their great city, and to find the statue of the goddess, which will bolster Athenian power. A month later a runaway crippled slave, the Dark Man, arrives at the hut of Hecuba and Ismene, fleeing the faroff silver mines. Another month and the Dark Man has made love to the Ismene he is the first to find beautiful, undisturbed by her amnesia; he promises Hecuba to care for her daughter. Still another month and Heros arrives personally to superintend the charting of the sea into rectangles through which the fishermen will search each day until they find the statue. To ingratiate himself with Hecuba, Heros spares the life of the runaway Dark Man. Still another month and Heros, unquenchable in quest as in war, tries to jolt Ismene's memory—about himself and about the statue. Three months later, a climax as winter approaches. Nestor returns from Athens to order Heros home. Hecuba, sensing danger, claims a prophetic dream whereby the statue will be awarded to the winner of a race around the island. Heros responds to this prophecy veiled in mystery, but Hecuba and the Dark Man methodically plot his death, which alone will free them all. After they succeed, Nestor has a momentary reflex for punishment, but Hecuba persuades him not to disturb the new *status quo*. The old warrior, ever flexible, leaves for his beloved Athens. Blind Hecuba is killed in the first storm of winter. Ismene and the Dark Man, both maimed but mutually supportive, face the new day and the new season.

This summary barely hints at the narrative richness of the drama, which is intensified by character complexity. Heros is brutal, but he is a man of immense civic pride. Nestor is wily, but he too loves his city. Even Hecuba, the compassionate woman, plays the old diplomatic game to gain her worthwhile ends. Ismene comes lying to the Trojans, and the Dark Man protects her in sexist fashion. By Part II each of the women—the title might mean Ismene or Hecuba, although Hecuba took the bows—is injured, but Hecuba blinds *herself;* Ismene refuses to poison herself, and she loses her memory when she is immured *by others.* Old Hecuba finally dies alone, but young Ismene couples in the traditional ending of comedy—to start a new society, however frail in the Silver Age. Part I of *The Woman* adheres to the spirit of Euripidean tragedy, but Part II limps toward New Comedy.

The Woman has a fabulous sweep, whose dramatic conflict pulls in fundamental oppositions. Not only Greece versus Troy, but warmongering men versus peace-plotting women. Scenically, this becomes white versus dark, with dark connoting peace. In the striking scene of Ismene's treason trial, the Greek men glisten in their white togas whereas Ismene wears midnight blue, but it is she who is morally innocent, forecasting the Dark Man of Part II, who will found a new humane civilization. Subtle and significant at the Olivier Theatre was Bond's (or his designer Griffin's) deployment of geometric forms to reenforce the morality. Essentially, war was rectangular and freedom circular. Although the colossal stage of the Olivier is roughly elliptical, it is backed by a fire-curtain in rectangular steel panels. Greek uniforms consisted of copper-colored rectangles from greave to jerkin. Greek generals sat on camp-stools with rectangular seats. In contrast, Hecuba, scheming for peace, wore a vast black circular cape that bore evidence of her past through the colored rectangles in its design; the other Trojan women echoed this costume. The Greeks were often blocked parallel to the rectangular wall panels, whereas the Trojans circled the stage—Hecuba herself, the Poor after they kill the Son, the captive women after the death of Astyanax. Ismene calling for Greek desertion crosses the stage-field in a wide arc.

The omnipresent circle of Part II is the raked disc of the island on which the Villagers dance in a smaller circle. Although blocking is freer in Part II, the now silver-clad Greeks still line up, and the whole cast circles around the Dark Man when he reveals his identity as a nameless miner. Hecuba's Part II rags are tie-dyed in circles, and her eyeband circles her head; she tests the eye she thought sighted with light from a small round lamp. When the Dark Man tease-tickles Ismene, she doubles up and turns around laughing. When the Dark Man tease-tickles Hecuba, she doubles up and rolls on the ground.

Which brings me to Bond the scenewright. Even unappreciative critics cited the power of certain scenes—the regal intimacy of the first Hecuba-Ismene meeting, Ismene's mission drowned out by Greek drums, the Trojan poor moving step up step to topple the Son and their joyous man-handling of the statue as they sing out: "To the Greeks," the rigidity of Ismene's trial disintegrating into a raucous game, Greek sentinels attacked by three veiled women with plague, the dance of the Villagers, the tickling scene, a terrifying storm with the most resonant thunder I ever felt in the theater.

Verbal imagery is more sparing than visual brilliance, but there are dazzling passages. Usually, the speech is formal by this master of the colloquial. Priests and diplomats take refuge in clichés; the soldiers, the poor, and the villagers in simple syntax. Not until Ismene's trial do images flow, with Troy compared to a wounded animal. Hecuba's words rise slowly to imagery. In Scene I of Part II she explains to Ismene their presence on the island in a long lovely passage, a fable rich in water and plant recollections. But to Nestor she affirms simply: "I've no wish for revenge." Perhaps the most moving speech of the play belongs to the Dark Man, ordered to identify himself as a contestant in the race. He starts: "I don't know," then exposes the underground life of the silver miner—a fable of enslavement.

With *The Woman* Bond reaches the pinnacle of his fabulous theater. Fortunately, his fecundity continues from play to fabulous play. Mid-career he may be known through his own poem about Shakespeare:

> He is not an academic
> His written words
> Are the echoes of speech
> His learning is prefaced
> By experience
> He does not come from school
> He goes to it.[22]

NOTES

1. Author's Program Note to *The Sea*.
2. Unlike Bond's reviewers, however, his critics have been discerning. I can recommend:
   Tony Coult, *The Plays of Edward Bond* (London: Eyre Methuen, 1978).
   Peter Iden, *Edward Bond* (Velber bei Hannover, Friedrich, 1973).
   Richard Scharine, *The Plays of Edward Bond* (Lewisburg: Bucknell University Press, 1976).
   Simon Trussler, *Edward Bond* (Harlow: Longman, 1976).
   Anticipated is Malcom Hay and Philip Roberts, *The Theatre of Edward Bond*.
3. I saw a German production in West Berlin, with superb blend of solos, choruses, orchestra.

4. William Gaskill quoted in Malcolm Hay and Philip Roberts, *Edward Bond, A Companion to the Plays* (London: *Theatre Quarterly Publications,* 1978), 8.

5. *Theatre Quarterly* editors, "Drama and the Dialectics of Violence," *Theatre Quarterly* 2, 5, Jan–Mar, 1972, 13.

6. *Ibid.,* 8.

7. Bond may have pondered a group of plays about Len, who, as the seventeen-year old brother of Bill, appears in *The Pope's Wedding,* and, at eighteen, in *Early Morning.* There is no cross-reference between the plays.

8. In production at the Royal Court, Bond changed some of these details. *Cf.* Hay and Roberts, 50–1.

9. Arthur Arnold, "Lines of Development in Bond's Plays," *Theatre Quarterly* 2, 5, Jan–Mar. 1972, 18.

10. Basho, tr. Nobuyuki Yuasa, *The Narrow Road to the Deep North* (Norwich: Penguin, 1966), 52.

11. Hay and Roberts, 14.

12. Gregory Dark, "Production Casebook of Edward Bond's *Lear* at the Royal Court," *Theatre Quarterly* 2, 5, Jan–March 1972, 27.

13. *Ibid.,* 31.

14. Samuel Schoenbaum discusses them in *Times Literary Supplement* (August 30, 1974).

15. This balance was reflected in Chris Dyer's panels at the 1977 Warehouse production.

16. Gregory Dark, 27.

17. Martin Esslin, "Nor yet a 'Fool' to Fame . . ." *Theatre Quarterly* 6, 21 (Spring, 1976) 44.

18. Although completed before *The Bundle, The Woman* was not published until May 1979. My analysis written prior to the publication of the text, is based on a typescript, for which I thank Cynthia Damoney of the National Theatre of Britain, and mainly on the Olivier production directed by Bond. For some helpful suggestions I thank Professor and Director Betty Osborn.

19. Hay and Roberts, 74.

20. Joseph F. McCrindle, ed. *Behind the Scenes* (New York: Holt, Rinehart and Winston, 1971), 135, 136.

21. Malcom Hay and Philip Roberts, "Edward Bond: Stages in a Life," *Observer Magazine* (August 6, 1978), 13.

22. Edward Bond, *Theatre Poems and Songs* (London: Eyre Methuen, 1978), 56.

Edward Bond

KATHARINE J. WORTH

On the morning of the day Bond's play, *The Woman,* had its first showing at the National Theatre in August, 1978, I interviewed him for the University of London Summer School, before a deeply interested audience of American and European graduates. He was charmed by their warmth and enthusiasm; but when I suggested that this might be a token of reactions to come from the general public, he pointed ironically to past experience which held a different augury. Certainly it is true that there has been much incomprehension and hostility in reviewers and so, alas, it proved to be again: review of *The Woman* with one or two exceptions, suggested a kind of mental collapse or panic before the size of the task before them. Good instant reviews of a play on such an epic scale are rather more than can reasonably be expected: a play of such stunning originality requires more time to assimilate than most theatrical fare; sadly, reviewers are not often prepared to convey to their readers that their judgments must be tentative on such occasions.

So, like many of Bond's plays, *The Woman* suffered from criticism well below the level on which the play operates. It was especially sad on this occasion, for it was a particularly important one. *The Woman* was the first play which had really used the great open space of the Olivier Theatre. It was the first play of Bond's to be performed in the National Theatre. By any standards it was a massive and deeply provocative play by the most original English playwright of his generation.

Yet the reviewers on the whole shrank from or collapsed under it. Was this because of defects in the play itself? One might have had reservations about this or that sequence or episode, but for anyone who experienced in the theatre the impact of scenes such as the fall of the citadel and the burning of Troy it should not have been possible to take the play on anything but the highest level and to judge it by the most exacting standards. Why is this so often found too difficult a task? Once it might have been said—and it is still true of many who read about him, perhaps without seeing the plays—that the violence in his plays is overwhelming and inhibits response to what else is there. That is hardly likely to be true nowadays, when scenes of much more explicit and gratuitous violence can be seen any night on the television screen. But in any case the violent episodes in Bond's play are part of a structure which lifts them out of the realm of the sadistic and intolerable. He shows characters fascinated by violence and using it, but their actions are part of an exploration of darkness which leads into equally memorable experiences of light and understanding, as I shall hope to show in this article.

More likely, reviewers and critics are staggered by the demands his plays make for a revolutionary new look at life. 'Revolutionary' is a key word for Bond's theatre, though it is not necessary, and indeed would be quite wrong, to take it in a narrowly political sense. Bond is setting out to do something beyond the circumscribed aim of shifting political allegiances. He offers us no less than a new mental landscape — which means of the past as well as the present, a new view of our whole cultural heritage. In *The Woman,* he takes a look, in his phrase, at our classical heritage; this means writing the story of the Trojan War with no Helen of Troy in it and with a strange blend of names and incidents from other classical legends, so that Hecuba is at times in familiar company with Astyanax or Nestor, at other times disconcertingly with characters who seem to have come from Sophocles rather than Homer. Purists may resent this, but was the Trojan War really as Homer told it? In what senses are the classical legends true? How is it that these people — Hecuba, Ismene, Nestor — seem so real to us that we resent their being given new episodes in their history as though they were people who had actually lived and even been known to us in the flesh? More than any living playwright except Beckett, Bond makes us vividly aware of how strange it is that we should all have this other world in the head. He exposes and tries to jolt and jostle deeply ingrained patterns of thought, forcing us to entertain new ideas about every sort of routine unquestioned assumptions, our notions of the Trojan war, Shakespeare, Queen Victoria.

This is the epic mode and of course Bond is often thought of as an epic playwright in the Brechtian sense of the word. There is the emphasis on reason, the social purposiveness and optimism; "The world is badly arranged and we must alter it." There is the irreverent and often extravagantly comical use of the past to indicate new patterns for the future; the abundance of articulate, witty characters with a strong tendency to preach; the enjoyment of making the audience uncomfortably aware of weak spots in their society. There is a similarly censorious view of romantic illusion — "All illusion is destructive" coupled with a strongly romantic faith in the infinite possibility of things. *The Sea* has for its close a lecture to a young man from a philosophical drop-out who gives him all the reasons to despair and then exhorts him to ignore them and go instead to change the world.

This is an ending the Shaw of *Man and Superman* or *Back to Methusaleh* would surely have approved. Bond too writes prefaces. If we were to judge by them and by his other polemical writings (including some of the poems) we would probably expect the plays to outdo Shaw in didacticism and to be rather short on comedy. Criticism of Bond's drama is in fact often unduly influenced by Bond's theorising. This is a pity because the plays follow the prefaces no more closely than, for instance, Shaw's *Heartbreak House* — that complex tragi-comedy — keeps within limits set by the topical, political speculations of its war-conscious preface.

What we find when we turn to the plays is comedy more droll and sympathetic than the prefaces would lead us to expect, also — and the two are inseparable — a much stronger sense of tragedy. Here Bond parts company both with Shaw who never allowed his comedy to move more than a pace or two into the pain and terror of tragedy, and with the Brechtian epic mode which shrinks from tragedy as a king of bourgeois, emotional self-indulgence. Bond is often thought of as being committed to the modern form of political epic which demands that good be judged in terms of public good and art be a conscious instrument to induce that good. He sometimes seems to place himself in that way, and of course politics are important in the action of his plays, as they are in life. But what makes his art so distinctive is his ability to hold his epic interests in tension with others, equally strong, in the inner life of individuals.

Tragedy is an essential perspective, for Bond as for his character, Evens, in *The Sea*, for whom a future without that dimension would be a nightmare: " ... without tragedy no one can laugh, there's only discipline and madness." Humour and tragedy are in a mysterious relation in Bond's plays: the public world continually fades into the deeply private, the world inside the head. Some of his most theatrically exciting and memorable scenes are those which give us glimpses of an interior inhabited by many kinds of strange ghosts. Right at the start of his career, in the seemingly naturalistic *Saved*, there is a curious ghost-like effect when the old man, Harry, joins Len for an intimate confessional scene, comically and suggestively dressed in long white combinations, pale socks and his head in "a skull cap of bandages." Later there are the hearty, cannibalistic ghosts of *Early Morning* who cannot be suppressed — they take over the whole action — and at the other extreme the wistful wraiths of *Lear* — the visionary figures of the bad daughters as they once were in childhood, and the deteriorating Gravedigger's Boy, with his "face like a sea shell" and eyes full of terror. And in *The Fool* the grotesque, filthy, ugly apparition of a once longed-for woman, an emanation from the depth's of a poet's mind.

In this region of his plays, where we go into the "deep of the mind," reason is no longer king, irrational elements surface and are given their place in the complex order of creativity. Contradictions can be admitted, paradoxes explored: the dark is shown to be the necessary complement of light. The mysterious relation between pain and true vision comes to the fore as we should hardly expect from a reading of the prefaces alone. Perhaps the effect is all the more powerful because there is something in Bond which resists the tragic view of life: the resistance is a source of tension in his drama; he creates an extraordinary sense of characters who are at some deep level wishing to be wrenched out of their habitual ways of viewing and thrust into perceptions they have hitherto avoided.

A characteristic pattern of classical tragedy in fact emerges. Characters are driven towards light and truth by their experience of the dark, an experience that is expressed often through traditional imagery of light and dark, sight and blindness. Bond changes the plot of Shakespeare's *King Lear* in his own version to put the blinding episode at the centre of the play making the victim not Gloucester but Lear himself. Ironically he is blinded by the 'good' Cordelia, who has been infected by the corruption of the very power she set out to destroy. When Lear and Cordelia confront one another at the end of the play, he at last understands where he went wrong, there is a Sophoclean irony in his cry to the woman who is about to repeat his mistakes: "How can I make you see?" Blindness, as Bond himself points out, is obviously being used here as a dramatic metaphor for insight. More subtly and strangely in *The Fool,* imagery of blindness is associated with a painful groping towards revelation. John Clare, running away from the asylum where he has been confined for years, wanders into a dream state where images, including the composite figure of the blind boxer and hanged man, emerge from the dark of night. The poet at least is recognising a truth about his life: "I wandered round an' round. Where to? Here. An' a blind man git here before me. The blind goo in a straight line."

The changes which occur in Lear and in Clare, as in all of Bond's central characters, are the climactic moments of his plays. And they are inner changes which do not always have the kind of reverberations in the public sphere that the Brechtian epic mode demands. Of course there is interaction of characters and there are effects on others of the mental and emotional changes of a Lear or a Clare. This is inevitable indeed, for Bond particularly deals with characters who wield influence over others with their exceptional gifts of expression as well as of mental grasp: it is no accident that two of his protagonists are poets, including the most famous of all, Shakespeare. Here again he is well in the tradition of classical tragedy, with its great men at the centre. For some of Bond's critics, the failure of his characters to achieve a Brechtian revolution, a public change on the grand scale, makes him seem a pessimist. In discussing *Lear* once with some German students I was surprised to find that they regarded the heroic ending of the play, when Lear is shot in the act of climbing the wall in an attempt to demolish it, to be deeply pessimistic. Nothing had changed by his death, they said; the wall was still there, his conversion had come too late. They did not seem aware that they were rejecting both the individual heroism and the possibility of tragic satisfaction which comes not from a 'happy ending' but from a movement of the spirit towards the truth. The movement which occurs in Lear's mind and is represented by his obviously doomed attempt to pull down the wall is nevertheless a triumph and it took all the suffering in the action to bring it about, for at the start of the play when we saw him giving his pitiless orders to execute workers who were impeding the building operation, we could never have imagined that by the end this same man would be seeing the dread wall as an instrument not of defence but of self-imprisonment and self-destruction.

Such victories are the only victories in which tragedy is interested. But of course one can understand the students' reaction, not just because of the special significance the wall symbolism must have for Germans, but because in the play itself there is a strong didactic pressure: towards the end Lear is seen as a kind of guru, moralising in parables to a community which we are invited to think of as learning from his experience and being changed by it. The possibility of change on an epic scale is indeed something Bond must believe in, for, as I began by saying, he sets out in his plays to make us see the whole of history in a new light, re-order our mental landscape, unfix some of its most familiar features, from the Trojan War to Victoria and Albert.

But after all, this landscape exists nowhere but in the mind and deep changes in that region can only be brought about in life by a rather slow and complex process and can only be made convincing in the theatre by a technique of great subtlety such as Yeats described: 'A deep of the mind can only be approached through all that is most human and most delicate'.

So now we come to a central paradox of Bond's drama. He can give us both worlds. This master of epic, this iconoclast and melodramatist, also commands a style which is 'most human and most delicate,' a technique of Chekhovian exactness and humorous sympathy which allows him to test the great sweeps of his action through the minute particulars of individual lives. Without such testing (as he said to me in another of our interviews) what would the great events be worth? It is his ability to turn from the public to the private, to go into the hidden regions of the mind where nothing is simple, where public and private are inextricably mixed, that gives one confidence in his epic actions.

I want now to consider how the method works in a few plays, concentrating especially on two most important elements. One of these is humour. Bond has in abundance a humour we tend to think of as peculiarly modern, the style of Beckett in *Endgame* which shows at its best when cir-cumstances are most dark. Bond's too is a droll, dry humour; sometimes wittily fantastic and grotesque, as in the absurd chasing after Arthur's head in the cannibal picnic of *Early Morning,* sometimes mundane and reassur-ingly homely. It is this humour which helps to make his approach to the mind's interior 'most human.'

Secondly, imagery. As one could not fail to observe, just from reading his stage directions, Bond is a master of stage imagery. The look of his stage—its customary bareness, its few symbolic objects—is an important means for him of moving easily between public and private worlds and of heightening and focusing our attention, to bring us further into the mental landscape inhabited by the characters. Here Bond is in a modern European tradition which first became naturalized in the English theatre by Beckett. Lighting, groupings, spatial arrangements, function in Bond's plays as in Beckett's, with great poetic economy, for a subtle variety of dramatic purposes. Like Beckett too, Bond is deeply responsive to visual art and often has specific paintings in mind in planning his scenic arrangements; Rembrandt, for instance, is in the background of the autopsy in *Lear.* Objects—sparse, starkly visible in empty spaces—acquire enormous sig-nificance. They are used to indicate place, both external and internal; they tell us where we are in the public world and they suggest prevailing moods, passions, obsessions of the characters. I will draw my illustrations from the later plays because they have as yet received relatively little critical discus-sion, but I need first to mention *The Pope's Wedding* (1971) to show how at the very start of his career Bond had evolved his highly distinctive tech-nique. Though to its first critics it seemed, like *Saved,* a naturalistic play (and largely is that), the stage direction at the beginning gives us a hint that we are also going to be in a more private and inner world: "The objects are very real, but there must be no attempt to create the illusion of a 'real scene.' In the later scenes the stage may be lighter and Scene Fifteen may be played in bright light."

What would be the function of the bright light, if the scene were to be played in this way? Scene Fifteen represents the temporary return to the mundane world of housekeeping, pub crawls, 'normal' relationships with wife and friend of the increasingly withdrawn Scopey. For a moment only he comes into the bright, public arena before going back to the room of the hermit, Alen, which he has made his own by murdering the old man and strangely entering into his place. In the final episode, back in the hermit's room, Scopey is seen sitting surrounded by piles of largely unopened tins of food with nearby the dead body of the hermit, the man who accumulated food that he could not eat. Later plays, especially *The Fool,* show us that this has become a favorite metaphor of Bond's for certain modes of human behaviour. The riddling element is strong in that last scene: the hermit was a riddle to Scopey and Bond wishes to draw us into Scopey's position where we are acutely conscious of the limitations on our 'knowing' the inner life of other people. So before we come into the dim region of mental impasse represented in the final scene through the delphic symbolism of the tins, we must first be given some light of a more normal kind. And so Scene Fifteen closes with a piece of dumb show in which light has a crucial part; Scopey alone on the brightly lit stage, going through a series of commonplace actions, cutting a slice of bread, unbuttoning his cuffs, drinking tea and then, for a long moment doing nothing at all, just staring at the cup and saucer. Light and silence are being used with a kind of sad irony to draw attention to how little we can see: we are in a position close to Scopey's own in relation to the hermit. He could not penetrate the mystery of that self-willed isolation, nor can we learn from him—who is so inarticulate—the full explanation of the state of mind which has driven him to his strange act. Like him, we can only grope towards understanding; what can be shown has been shown.

In the plays that follow *The Pope's Wedding*, however harsh or fantastic their events or vast their sweep, Bond always finds room for scenes that illuminate difficult inner experience through stage imagery of great delicacy and precision and with a dry humour which keeps the human perspective. I want now to look at some instances of this technique for exploring the deep of the mind in the later plays, beginning with *The Sea*

In *The Sea* humour has an especially vital and subtle role. It first builds up and then undermines the imagery of funereal melancholy, which it is the business of the play to destroy. We see the process beginning in the rehearsal for the play of Orpheus and Eurydice which Mrs. Rafi's ladies are performing in aid of the coastguards' fund. There is obviously a relation, though at first it may seem only one of caricature, between this absurd piece and the tragic event with which the play opens, the drowning of the young man, Colin, fiancé of Mrs. Rafi's niece, Rose. They play will show Rose surmounting her grief and rediscovering love with another young man, Colin's closest friend, Willy. He too has to surmount a potentially crippling sense of grief and horror at the death of his friend. The play opens with a scene which conveys his emotional shock; wind and sea storm, the friend drowning, Willy himself rushing along the beach desperately calling for help and meeting only the drunken indifference of the coastguard and the obsessive hostility of the deranged draper, Hatch. Bond wants to show the necessity for moving away from grief, especially in the phase of youth, when emotion becomes exaggerated and unbalanced. The comical rehearsal scene serves as a warning against histrionic exaggerations.

We could not miss the false notes in the expressions of grief in the play within the play. Bond exploits them ruthlessly for comic effect. Mrs. Rafi, playing Orpheus, grandiloquently describes her own actions: "Wearily I sit down on a rock and survey the dismal scene, I take out my lute and sing 'There is no place like home.'" When Mrs. Tilehouse, her bullied companion, timidly suggests that this might not be the most appropriate song for Orpheus to sing, Mrs. Rafi, as usual, is contemptuously dismissive; her performance, she says, will be one of the highlights of the evening. Her mind is not on the scene, still less on the inner experience it was meant to express, but on herself being carried away by her own performance: 'Moved by the atmosphere I have created, I cry—together with a large part of the audience, if things go as usual.'

This narcissistic luxuriation in grief is a long way from the natural and touching sorrow of the young girl who has just lost her lover. So far as character is concerned, the Orpheus episode might be thought of as expressing Mrs. Rafi rather than Rose. It does so, but it has implications for Rose and indeed for all the characters, if they were able to perceive them. It offers a warning, serious under the fooling, against over-intensity and false prolongation of feeling. Rose too is inclined to fall into exaggeration, for instance in a later scene on the beach with Willy when she says, "Now I have nothing to live for. There's nothing to look forward to. I don't know what I shall do. I can't think of anything to make one day pass." In her, of course, the exaggeration is excusable: still, it is touched with adolescent fantasy: she must grow up.

The rehearsal is certainly farcical, with Mrs. Tilehouse ludicrously called upon by Mrs. Rafi to crawl under the stage and splash water to represent the sea, while Mafanwy has to represent the dog, Cerberus, by making movements behind a sheet held by ladies in bathing attire. 'Why must I be a dog?,' complains Mafanwy, 'Last year I was the monkey. If we did a pantomime, you'd make me the cat. I want to be one of the floral maids-of-honour who greet Orpheus with rose petals and song when he comes out of hell.' 'You'll be a dog,' says Mrs. Rafi—and there is no more argument. This is all good comic stuff, but through it come warnings and messages which have to be taken seriously. Mrs. Rafi, acting the crossing of the Styx, sees 'a white thing shining down in the darkness' and is told by Rachel, an absurd Charon, with a punting pole and a straw boater, that it is the reflection of Narcissus condemned to haunt these waters for ever. Mrs. Rafi's reaction, 'Ah horror! Ah horror!,' is in her usual vein, exaggerated and unfeeling, but there is a hint in this imagery of real horror, the narcissism which afflicts not only her victims but also Mrs. Rafi herself. The self-love which distorts her gifts and abilities and makes her so brutal in her handling of weaker people like Mrs. Tilehouse and poor Hatch, also makes a lonely and unloved figure. She becomes almost a tragic one towards the close of the play when she reveals her awareness of what she is preparing for herself, drawing a terrifyingly accurate picture of her old age, when she will be bullied by her revengeful companion:

> Take me down to the beach. I want to see the sea. You don't want to see the sea. You saw the sea yesterday. The wind's bad for your head. If you misbehave and catch a cold we'll shut you up in bed. You'll stay there for good this time.

Intimations of that sombre knowledge come through the seemingly insignificant comedy of the Orpheus episode. Even the vicar's ludicrous rendering of his lines as Pluto turns serious when he warns Mrs. Rafi, playing Orpheus, to abandon the pursuit of Eurydice: 'Oh man, a god pleads with you. You may not put your hand into the iron sea to pluck out the glittering thing.' But it is all blatantly play-acting. Then the rehearsal is brought to an abrupt end by the routine firing of the coastal battery guns, the curtains are drawn back and the sea is restored to view, bringing back the memory of Colin's drowning and fearful reality. The sea took away, but we have since learned that it also restores:

> Everything is washed up. Our coast is known for it. You throw a handkerchief into the sea one day and pick it up the next.

And the sea does return the body of the young man. The madness of Hatch is allowed to work itself out on a corpse, not on a living creature: under Willy's eye he stabs at the dead, committing an 'innocent murder.' So when the Orpheus episode ends, and the sea comes back to view, returning Rose and Willy to real life, they have been given a warning through the farce not to linger too long in the genteel room where the curtains are drawn to shut out awesome reality and where histrionics and fantasies obscure and stunt true feeling. And in opening themselves to reality, they rediscover joy. The play ends when they resolve to plunge again, swimming together in that sea which drowned one young man but which, as we have seen, really does return everything in the end.

In the play which followed *The Sea* there is a particularly interesting relationship between comedy and visual imagery. *Bingo* has nothing like the buoyant comic atmosphere of *The Sea*: the ageing, dying Shakespeare who appears on Bond's stage has long since parted company with the young man who wrote *As You Like It*. His plays indeed are not mentioned, except in one scene, which is also the only scene that could possibly be described as comic. Shakespeare and Ben Jonson meet in The Golden Cross and talk—or rather Ben Jonson drags remarks out of a reticent Shakespeare and holds forth to him. There is much fun in this conversation, though always a dark background remains: later in the scene the room is

KATHARINE J. WORTH

used for a conspiratorial meeting by a group who are resisting the threatened enclosure of common land. And tragedy is never far off even in Jonson's talk; under its comic surface a confession of inner suffering builds up, a hatred for the barbarism of the age. He carries poison with him to end it all if life becomes too grim.

But Jonson is also jovial, combative, curious and above all professional. He brings firmly into the play a reminder that Shakespeare is Shakespeare: whatever his failings as a citizen—he is tacitly supporting the enclosures which threaten the livelihood of the poor—or as husband and father—he is shown to be estranged from both wife and daughter—still, he has written those plays. Bond gives us an amusingly unexpected perspective on them. 'Your recent stuff's been pretty peculiar,' says Jonson, probing into Shakespeare's current activities, 'What was *The Winter's Tale* about? I ask to be polite.' Shakespeare neatly sidesteps this by an equally polite 'What are you writing?'

This is an antidote to solemnity, but nevertheless the comedy has a serious function, bringing before us not just a general idea of Shakespeare's plays but in particular those late plays which keep so fine and precarious a balance between comedy and tragedy, light and dark, spring and winter. This play too is a Winter's Tale. It might seem totally to lack spring notes: Bond's Perdita is a truly lost girl, the Beggar for whom there is no happy ending but instead a miserable death by gibbetting. Shakespeare can do nothing to help her (though he tries), any more then he can help other victims of the social order. Bond's point is, of course, that he is inhibited by his own commitment to that order as a rentier: the internal divisions caused by the failures in public and private life lead in the end to his taking the poison which Jonson gave him. In his death scene he lies on the floor in agony asking repeatedly, 'Was anything done?' while his daughter, Judith, unfeelingly searches the room for his will, muttering 'Nothing' as she fails to find it in one place after another. It might seem that her 'Nothing' is being presented to us as the appropriate answer to Shakespeare's question, that in fact his life is to be seen as a failure.

But of course this would be nonsense as who should know better than Bond. He has told us that his first experience of Shakespeare, seeing *Macbeth* as a boy, transformed his life:

> It was the first thing that made sense of my life for me; the first time I'd found something beautiful and exciting and alive. For the first time in my life I became real. (M. Hay and T. Roberts, p. 7)

Bond the socialist may disapprove of Shakespeare's bourgeois leanings, Bond the playwright may—legitimately—speculate on the possibly demoralizing effect of social pressures on Shakespeare's moral life. But when Shakespeare asks 'Was anything done?' Bond knows that we all, like him, must answer 'Yes.' For anyone who knows the plays at all must have had their lives thereby enriched as his was. That recognition is written into the play, although we might perhaps overlook it in the novelty of seeing Shakespeare presented as a man, with the usual difficulties, and inner doubts rather than as a god (Bond's irritation with that view of course colours his own). Still he reminds us of Shakespeare the artist, and it is a measure of his craftsman's economy and sense of dramatic decorum that he touches in these reminders with such swift, fine brush strokes. He knows we can be relied on to complete the picture for ourselves; any more overt references would risk tipping the balance towards Shakespeare the god.

Bond's humour is always a saving grace. Characteristically, then, it is in the comic interchanges with Jonson, that we are given the first reminder of Shakespeare's creative life, in that droll reference to the *Winters Tale*. Then an image develops: Jonson gives a description of the act of writing: 'Fat white fingers excreting dirty black ink.' It conveys the bitterness in his character, his resentment of his bondage. In the scene which follows the striking and repellent image is given a visual projection and its quality is transformed. Shakespeare, drunk from his convivial meeting, makes his way to his house across a snowy field, a black figure against the whiteness and emptiness. The unbroken whiteness is emphasised in the stage direction and in Shakespeare's soliloquy. It is an open space, 'Flat, white, crisp, empty' and Shakespeare observing it, muses: 'How clean and empty the snow is. A sea without life. An empty glass .... ' Insidiously the scene suggests to us the idea of a pen moving over a blank white page, filling it with words, words with magical reverberations like *The Winter's Tale*. For the first time Shakespeare is alone and talking, revealing his mind; we can see that behind the taciturn, reserved style he has preserved throughout, there is an imagination constantly at work, observing, registering, creating images, giving shape and colour to the emptiness. As earlier on he had responded to and celebrated the beauty of the Young Woman, as no-one else could, seeing her, even in her squalid death as 'Still beautiful,' so now he makes a poem out of the icy desolation. The dark figure moving on the virgin snow like the pen moving over the virgin page subtly reminds us that there is a positive answer to that question 'Was anything done?'

My next illustration is the episode from *The Fool* which I have already mentioned in speaking of Bond's stage settings. I want now to look more closely at the subtle and economical working of the stage imagery in this haunting scene. The opening stage direction gives us clues to the nature of the experience which is to be expressed; it is one of public and private life.

Clare, ragged and exhausted, wanders on stage, seeking his home and coming into an 'open space' where all that can be seen by the night light, is the figure of the Boxer sitting on a boundary post 'Hunched forward in the pose of The Thinker.' The detail of the boundary post recalls to us the social conditions which have played a sad part in Clare's breakdown: the land which seems so free and open has in fact been claimed and marked out as his own by Lord Milton: the enclosure of hitherto common land was the source of the disasters earlier in the play when Clare's friend, a brother of his wife, Patty, was among those hanged for their share in riots of protest. Clare and the Irish itinerant workers who come into the scene later are eventually warned off the land by the Keeper as trespassers.

But the boundary post should also have suggested to us by the end of the scene a limit of a different sort, the limit upon the extent of self-exploration the mind of the poet, Clare, is able to achieve. For *The Fool* is not concerned simply with the inequities of nineteenth-century society and their destructive effects on a rural poet. We are to see into the poet's mind where personal desires and dreams play as crucial a role as public pressures: the two cannot of course be separated from one another. The open space is the region where Clare for the first time in the play is seen looking into his own life in private and is confronted with a truth which it may be beyond his power at this stage to recognise fully. There is a paradox, so the scene suggests, which cannot be resolved by any change in social conditions. Clare's poetic imagination which fills his mind with tunes and gives him words to render the true experience of his place and time as no one else can, also creates images and false illusions which prevent him from tasting the true joy of his own life. In his wife, Patty, he has all the love he should need—this is the view Bond himself has suggested to me—but it has not been enough. He cannot get out of his head the vision of the girl, Mary, to whom he once made love, at the start of the play, and has not seen in the flesh since. Of course there is something dubious and puritanical in the idea that he *should* need no more than Patty can give him: whether this is how we must see the situation is open to question, but there can be no question that his dream of Mary has been debilitating.

It has indeed become a tired reflex by the time of the final episode, so the stage direction suggests; Clare enters the scene calling on Mary 'routinely.' Then he sees the Boxer and at once identifies him as 'The Paddy,' whom he had watched years before, in the brief period of his fashionable success, in a boxing match in Hyde Park, against a much superior negro. A complex network of associations is touched off by the sight of that bowed figure, for us the audience as well as for him. We recall the Hyde Park scene, which hinted at Clare's final fall from social favour by drawing a visual parallel between one stage audience—Clare and his

patrons — and the other, cruder group who urge on their respective pro-
tegés, the super-confident negro and the battered Irishman to ever more
sadistic display and have no feeling for them outside their function as
money-winning boxers. Clare on that occasion identified himself with the
defeated Irishman and was especially fascinated by his ability to take
punishment: 'Wow! Seen knockin' at fairs but I on't see a man git to his feet
after that! On't knew a man could stand so much!' The image has never left
him, in fact the habit of thinking and speaking of himself as a boxer is one of
the reasons for his wife, Lord Milton and the rest thinking of him as mad.

The stage imagery has first conveyed to us then the sense of defeat and
the uneasy concern with punishment which Clare has experienced after his
transient celebrity as a writer. This might be described as his public life.
Now we go into his private woe. Another figure enters, this time one which
could just be taken as real (though not for long). It is Mary, older now like
Clare himself, battered and, in the words of the stage direction 'grotesque,
filthy, ugly.' Her appearance can easily enough be accounted for by the
hard life with the gipsies on which she had just embarked when Clare last
saw her. Bond later thought, so he told me, that he might have made her
appearance still more grotesque, to leave the audience in no doubt of the
symbolism; here was an illusion which had always been totally destructive.
'Ghosts are always corrupt,' he says in the preface to *Lear* and Mary is a
ghost of something that has never really been, for there was no sign in her
two brief meetings with Clare that she understood, let alone shared, his
desire for an idyllic love. Her acceptance of him as a lover was casual,
fleeting; a world away from the tenacious love of Patty or the capacity for
ardent passion in Clare himself. It is made painfully clear in the laconic
interchanges he has with this wreck of a woman how his passion has been
wasted. 'Come lookin' for you,' he says, explaining his wandering, 'I
thought a you all the time. On't you think a me?' 'Can't say I hev,' she says,
then goes on to mock the idea of him as he is now as a lover: 'Want summat
a sight more appetizin' fore I put myself out this time a night.' Clare is
galvanised into an agonised appraisal of what this romantic dream has done
to him: 'An' all those years my life was waste. You on't there. Ony in my
head. That drove me mad. I'd a stood the rest with you.'

There is a suggestion of weakness in his words, a hint that his dream
has reduced and undermined his true strength. Wildly he tries to reject the
thought (which his mind is forcing on him), protesting that he is not
defeated, turning to the Boxer, challenging him to fight, to put on a display
for the lady, punching him on the arm. And then he sees the face. It is not
the Boxer of memory but the friend who was hanged in the riots, Darky,
with a burn mark on his neck. And he is blind, so he says, because of the
punishment he has received: 'Punch punch or summat — knock all the sight

out of my head.' Memory and imagination have created a composite image in which ideas of defeat and punishment are associated with an idea of failed vision. In this encounter we are at the heart of the play and in the deepest layer of Clare's mind. Terribly, the Boxer gropes his way towards Clare, to return the punch he was given. Clare is struck, staggers, passes out. Then we are shown that the figure of Mary is only a figment, for she and the Boxer have a strange interchange, in which he tells her of his terrible hunger and she tries to feed him with bread which he cannot swallow for the pain in his throat.

Even at this ghostly climax, Bond carefully maintains a link with the public world, for we are always to be kept aware of its pressure on the private lives. The apparitions leave the stage, not mysteriously, but on a quite realistic note, as the Irish itinerants are heard approaching. 'Hide till thass safe,' says Mary and they leave, as on come the three Irishmen looking for a place to spend the night and bringing with them the sense of flesh and blood and a coarse, jovial humour which helps to keep the whole episode rooted in reality.

It also points up, however, the intense privacy of the episode their arrival has interrupted and also the power of Clare's inner vision to impose itself on external reality. For he continues to speak of the apparitions as if they were really there, so convincingly indeed that one of the Irishmen, believing there is a real woman hidden in the background, offers to give Clare bread in exchange for his handing her over. Clare, pitifully sunk in his dream, can only say that it depends on her, drawing from the Irishman the comment, 'If the lady says yes to you she'll say grace when she sees me.' There is pathos in this encounter between the earthy, practical Irishmen and the poet who has gone so far into a world of his own. Yet the scene ends with something unexpected, an upsurge of power in Clare, not in worldly terms, for he as well as the Irishmen are driven off by the keeper, told to keep on the path and get off the land, and Clare knows that when he gets home there will be nothing to do but wait till 'they' come for him. But in terms of the poet's vision there is a sense of power and a new recognition. He interprets the episode we saw enacted by the apparitions:

> I dreamt I saw bread spat on the ground, and her say:
> Waste, I risk my life!
> 'No,' he says, 'Bread on't waste. Thass on'y seed you
> threw on the ground.'

He begins to think about bread, or seed, in a metaphorical sense going from one to another, tasting of other mouths. The blindness of the Boxer becomes the metaphor for insight: 'An' a blind man git here before me. The blind goo in a straight line.' Yet still he seems to be thinking of Mary as someone he should have lived his life with. Then he, the poet, would have been able to save her from rags, the Boxer from blindness—and himself from madness. It is only at the end of this deeply touching soliloquy that there comes a blinding moment of truth: he admits for the first time that Mary had no real existence: 'No one there. Never was. On'y the songs I make up on them.'

The last scene of the play is set in the asylum, in a pleasant, comfortable room, we might note (a setting which should frustrate any attempt to interpret the play as a diatribe against nineteenth-century social conditions, especially its clinical treatment of madness). It is one of Bond's most moving scenes. Patty comes, reluctantly, timidly but determinedly to visit Clare, now far sunk in illness and unable to formulate his words properly. He has to be interpreted by Mary Lamb, one mad person speaking for another, as we are in a way invited to see it. Clare has lost sense of time and events; he cannot accept or remember the death of their two sons. And so we will never know whether the flash of true understanding at the close of the previous scene still lights his way; whether he knows now that the dream of Mary was a mirage and that faithful Patty was his true love. All we can be sure of is her faith—and that there was the moment of revelation.

My final illustration is from *The Woman,* a play which provides an especially strong demonstration of Bond's skill in drawing profound and complex effects from a bare stage and a few arresting objects. This is a play of public life. Almost everything happens in the open, outside the walls of Troy or on the island where Hecuba and Ismene find refuge. There is realism in this—a Mediterranean quality of open air living—and there is the feeling of epic. Of all Bond's plays it most needed a massive space for performance such as it received in its first performance by the National Theatre company. The great open stage of the Olivier Theatre, which directors normally fill in with stage scenery and buildings, became Bond's characteristic 'open space,' a space given significance by the dominating, bleak and beautiful metallic wall which circumscribed it. When Greeks held the stage, this wall shut them out of Troy: when Trojans, the same wall shut them in. In the final triumph of the Greeks a section of the great wall was raised to show an equally vast looking space behind, lit up with red flames; no anticlimax here, as a modern stage representation might easily have been, but a shattering visual image of the fall of Troy, entirely equal to the size of the imaginary event.

The scene I am discussing occurs towards the end of the first part after the taking of the city. The characters are gathered by the gap in the wall; it is 'half filled with rubble' and there is a noise of hammering. The Trojan women sit there with their 'refugee bundles' and nervous children who are too frightened to sleep, looking like any sad group in a television news programme such as we can see almost any day of the week. These women, however, ally themselves with the women of antiquity by answering to names such as Cassandra and Hecuba. In one section of the wall soldiers are completing the walling up of Ismene, bringing in terrible echoes from yet other ages. Bond makes the gap in the wall the site for a desolate grouping which seems to express the woe of women in every era.

Through this same gap comes another kind of woman, the Woman over whom Greeks and Trojans have been contending, the professed cause of the long siege. This is not a living woman, the Helen of Troy of tradition. Bond takes the story away from the personal and adds layers of irony to his drama by making Homer's Helen of Troy into what shw has always been really, an image in the minds of men. She becomes for him a stage image, a statue, representing the Goddess of Fortune and essentially a property—to be set up on an altar, carried in procession by Trojans and by Greeks and now, in the scene I am discussing, flaunted before the defeated Trojan women on its way to the Greek ships. Bond envisaged the statue as 'a plain, gray, schematized female shape, of worn, but not smooth stone, about three-quarters life-size, exaggerated in length not thickness.' The blend of modern and primitive in that account is finely in keeping with the fusion of old and new achieved throughout the play. In the National Theatre production the statue had an appropriately archaic, remote appearance, though perhaps not quite the degree of abstraction Bond had first imagined. However, it was sufficient to give visual emphasis to the ironic point made by the contrasting treatment of the statue and the live women in the play.

The statue is an abstraction, an idea of woman which has no effect whatever on the way the men, led by the glamorous and brutal Heros, treat the actual women in their lives. Their worship of the Woman is bound up with the lust for power; according to the chance of war they adore or revile her as when the Trojans eject her from their temple calling 'Bitch! Bitch! No more bitch! Out!' Worship of the Woman even seems to involve a hardening in the men against feminine attributes like compassion and distaste for war. Heros condemns his wife to an especially terrible death and is quite cold when Hecuba pleads with him to spare the life of her grandson, Astyanax.

At this climactic moment Bond finds a stage image equal to the mighty status of his story. The Trojan wall, this glittering, dominating visual image takes on a fearful life. It has already become for Hecuba a fearful thing, the cruel height from which the little boy is to be hurled to his death. But she does not know that Ismene is imprisoned in it. So for her it is as if the wall itself speaks when the voice of Ismene is heard, begging Heros to spare the child, pathetically suggesting that Heros might adopt him. 'Listen,' Hecuba calls, 'the ground spoke! Yes—speak—speak!' When she is told the truth she recoils from Heros, calling him a monster, and he behaves like one reiterating the death sentence on Astyanax, sparing her nothing: 'He'll die and you'll see his body.' The child is dragged out and Hecuba goes through the gap in the wall, as Heros thinks, to kill herself in despair. He relishes the thought of her death, brutally calling after her 'Find a beam and hang yourself.'

What happens instead confounds him and is a great turning point in the play. Hecuba does not die. She returns through the dread gap, afflicted, seemingly broken, having blinded herself. But she has survived, and in her new helplessness she has gained a strange new power. She has defeated Heros; for she will never as he has commanded, see Astyanax dead. Instead she calls on the killer to be brought to look at her, speaking with mysterious authority as if she had take on the attributes of the goddess, though a mother goddess rather than a casual dispenser of fortune: 'Let that man see my face!,' she calls, 'Fetch that manchild to my feet and make him see my face.' Heros responds with a cry of 'bitch' a word that is taken up and repeated by Ajax and Thersites in a ritualistic chant, which recalls the Trojan chorus, of imprecations against the goddess: the echo reinforces the growing suggestion that Hecuba has acquired in her agony new insight which gives her numinous power. All these hints and suggestions are taken up in the second part of the play, when Bond moves further away from the traditional story and allows his optimism freer rein by showing the triumph of Hecuba over Heros, the womanly attributes of common sense and devotion to life over masculine vainglory. The Woman is lost in the sea—recurring symbol of creativity in Bond's drama—and Hecuba too is drowned there, but not before she had ended the tyranny of Heros and made possible a new life for Ismene and the cripple who becomes her lover. The scene which I have been discussing, however, ends on a note which tests the audience's response in a characteristically uncomfortable way. The women have left the scene and the aged Nestor appears with a band of soldiers, exulting in the carnage, looting and rape which has restored to him a sense of his youth. The parental feeling just experienced in so poignant a form in the laments for Astyanax, is horribly travestied in his affectionate address of the soldier as 'Son' and 'My boy.' And yet in the theatre there is also an almost unavoidable sense of relief at the joviality and good humour of the episode after the unremitting bleakness of what has gone before. It is a temptation for the audience to enjoy the contrast and the jollity— certainly this was so in the National Theatre production when Nestor was played by Andrew Cruikshank with rich humour. Yet it is a scene of the utmost beastliness; a reminder that we cannot afford to think ourselves too far above or separate from actions such as Nestor and his cronies exult in.

Through two state objects, a wall and a statue, Bond encompasses that great event, the fall of Troy, and the other, inward event which is bound up with it, the putting on of new power by the women. He has evolved a technique of formidable flexibility. We can only speculate whether, perhaps, like Ibsen (or dare we say, Shakespeare?), he is going through a phase of 'history plays' and may move out of it into some other which we cannot as yet imagine. The possibility of his giving us surprises on so grand a scale is real—and one of the many reasons why Bond must be thought of as a major playwright of our time.

BOOK LIST

Coult, T.   *The plays of Edward Bond* (London: Eyre Methuen, 1977)

Hay, M. and P. Roberts   *Edward Bond: A Companion to the Plays* (London: TQ Publications)

Taylor, J. R.   *The Second Wave: British Drama for the Seventies* (London: Methuen, 1971)

Worth, K.   'Edward Bond' in *Revolutions in Modern English Drama,* (London: Bell + Sons, 1973)

See also interviews with Bond in Gambit No. 17 and *Theatre Quarterly* 2, 1972 (also in this issue, Production Casebook no. 5: Lear).

Simon Gray

RÜDIGER IMHOF

> I once informed the Master of a Cambridge College, whom I did
> not recognise, that the lady with whom I had just conversed was
> a ghastly old woman. He courteously identified her for me as his
> wife. Five minutes later I told this as an amusing anecdote to a
> new man who revealed himself as their son.[1]

This brick sounds as if it has been dropped by Simon Hench, in *Otherwise
Engaged*, or, more appropriate still, by Peter, in *Dog Days*, who with
unrivalled impudence manages to affront almost everyone at a publishing
party, including "the Horatio Bottomley of Women's Lib" (53)[2], with a rich
variety of deliberate bricks; in point of fact, however, Simon Gray himself
was the agent.

Despite the phenomenal West End success of both *Butley* and *Otherwise Engaged*, Simon Gray has received only scant attention from critics
who have assessed British drama of the seventies. There seem to be three
explanations, at least, for this neglect. Firstly, Mr. Gray's dramatic output
may be considered not worth the critics's ink, consisting, at best, of
material suitable to guarantee full houses for West End impresarios, but
lacking the intrinsic literary value to qualify as 'serious' drama. Thus
Bernard Levin, in his offhand way, asserts that "the plays . . . are no more
than entertainment bonbons dressed above their station as philosophical
statements about mankind's condition."[3] Admittedly, the *œuvre* is mixed
in quality. The early plays are fairly lightweight, relying, as they do, on a few
clever theatrical contrivances; and the last venture, *Molly*, is of mediocre
calibre only, if not one of Mr. Gray's least successful pieces. However, the
plays of the middle period, from *Butley* to *Dog Days*, notwithstanding their
minor deficiencies, present a well-matched marriage of features of the
drawing-room comedy with those of the problem play. They do not claim to
be concerned with philosophical statements about the *conditio humana*;
they are much more modest in their pretensions. At his most prolific, Mr.
Gray is a playwright who has devoted his creative abilities to fathoming
phenomena of human interaction. Pronouncing on his artistic goal, he has
said that he wants "to give people a new perception of life, different from

their own. I certainly don't set out to shock them; indeed I'm surprised when they are shocked."[4] A more pertinent reason for the critical neglect seems to be that critics have never really bothered to look behind the façade of easy entertainment that the plays undoubtedly possess. If they had, they would have been able to discover serious and valid thematic concerns, which have no parallel in what is commonly known as West End comedies. Lastly, critics may have been prevented from giving Mr. Gray his due as an important dramatist of the 'second wave' by the very fact that his successes were scored in the West End. Critical quarters, rightly or wrongly, hold the West End in pretty low esteem with regard to the 'literary' quality of its productions. The West End is thought to cater, above all, for audiences, recruited from innumerable tourists who during the summer swarm the length and breadth of London in search of easy entertainment, such as "Whodunnits," US-imported musical extravaganzas, nude shows à la *Oh! Calcutta!,* revivals of classics, and the occasional original production of 'serious' drama, if an impresario is willing to run the risk of a financial disaster. According to this view of the West End, plays which are staged there cannot—exceptions proving the rule—be worthwhile. Hence it may be that, if Mr. Gray gets a mention at all in a study on contemporary British drama, he is perfunctorily treated, in one breath with Alan Ayckbourn and David Creegan[5], simply as a farceur. Oleg Kerensky's attempt at discussing the plays[6] fails to do justice to them, because the author confines his remarks largely to plot synopses, which are seldom enough spiked with feeble-minded forays into literary criticism. Reviews apart, there is, at the time of writing, only one serious article on Simon Gray,[7] which focusses on one specific aspect of one play. No effort has been made to provide a study of Mr. Gray's dramatic *œuvre,* and it would appear only fair to refrain from pronouncing judgment on the playwright, either overtly or covertly, until such an evaluation has been undertaken. Nor has Mr. Gray felt it part of his duty to gain greater prominence for his plays by commenting on them in interviews and explaining what he is striving to express. Only with reluctance has he consented to be publicly questioned about his work.[8] In fact, he has lately come to believe, as Arnold Wesker has informed the present writer: "I've given up talking to critics and academics about things I've written. No good ever comes of it in my experience."[9] This view is not without some back-firing irony, as Mr. Gray is an academic himself.

He was born on Hayling Island, Hampshire, 28 October 1936[10], the second son of a physician of Canadian extraction. During World War II, he was evacuated to Canada. Aged 14, having returned with his brother to England, he became mixed up in the Great Tube Ticket Machine Swindle, whereby he inserted a Georgian penny, purchasable for twopence, instead of a florin, and thereby acquired a ticket and three sixpences change. He worked his racket until he and the rest of the gang were caught red-handed on Victoria station by three policemen. He went to Westminster School in London and continued his education at Dalhousie University, Halifax, Nova Scotia, from 1954–57, where he received a B.A. honours degree in English. From 1958–61, he went to Trinity College, Cambridge, chiefly because he wanted to study under F. R. Leavis, whom he regards as the greatest critic of the century and the best teacher he has ever met.[11] At Trinity College, he got another B.A. honours degree in English. After his time as Harper-Wood student at St. John's College, Cambridge (1961–62), and subsequently as Research Student at Trinity College (1962–63), he worked as Lecturer in English at the University of British Columbia, in Vancouver, from 1963–64. Before he took up his present post as Lecturer in English at Queen Mary College, London, in 1968, he was Supervisor in English at Trinity College.

Simon Gray made his debut as a stage-dramatist in October 1967 with *Wise Child*. Previously, he had published three novels: *Colmain* (1963), *Simple People* (1965), *Little Portia* (1967) and had succeeded in making a name for himself as a moderately reputable television playwright with *The Caramel Crisis* (1966), *Death of Teddy Bear* (1967), *A Way with the Ladies* (1967) and *Sleeping Dog* (1967). In 1969 he was to bring out his fourth novel: *A Comeback for Stark*, under the pen-name of Hamish Reade. The dramatic writings may be classified into three groups. There are the early plays, which critics have chosen to label as Ortonesque farces; Simon Gray maintains that he had not read or seen any of Orton's plays when he wrote *Wise Child*[12]; in his view, the play owes more to Dickens, for whom he has a penchant, than to Orton. These were followed, from *Spoiled* onwards, by plays which on account of related themes and compositional affinities form a second category. The last and most recent group unites quasi-documentaries or, in other words, works founded upon historical events, and, in the case of *The Rear Column*, introduce a new element into his writing for the stage by tackling abstract moral values, whereas hitherto he was mainly concerned with specific and concrete problems of interhuman relationships, especially so in his middle period.

Throughout his as yet brief career, Simon Gray appears to have been fascinated by people endeavouring to dominate and possess each other. The battle for positions in interactional constellations is one of the salient dramatic motifs in his plays. The theme of homosexuality, which permeates many of his pieces, is not so much a sensational feature added to attract the attention of his audience, as an integral concern in his investigation into human social behaviour; it is more, as Rober Barker has argued[13], an illustrative image than a realistic matter, forming one significant aspect of the issue of dominance and subservience. Connected with this theme is that of friendship between two men, which is shown to be more profound and far-reaching than marital bonds. Another of his primary interests is the personal difficulties arising for the characters out of their unrelinquished sexual desires; in a number of instances these entail a break-up in marital relationships. Many of the characters are human failures, or, in Wundale jargon "plops," small-scale crooks, spoiled children, unsuccessful public school teachers, disillusioned literary critics and editors, paranoiac military officers, and sexually frustrated women, who try to compensate for their acute sense of inadequacy by dreams of sexual prowess, by destructive behaviour toward others, or by a deliberate retreat into solipsism. Compositionally, Mr. Gray often adheres to the traditional formula of the well-made play; he is a careful craftsman, who is much concerned with getting the shape of his plays right; his technical skill is particularly evident in *Butley, Otherwise Engaged,* and *The Rear Column,* which are embellished with a convincingly worked out dramatic texture. Almost in the form of a structural pattern, there is a tendency to concentrate on a dominant figure who is presented in a series of encounters with, preferably, one of the supporting cast. This practice was abandoned in *The Rear Column,* which is one reason to suppose that this play marks a new phase in his writing. With a consistency suggestive of a deliberate compositional policy, a large number of his pieces are open-ended, as if the author were shying away from offering easy solutions to the problems dealt with. Quite a number of the characters are obsessed with idiosyncratic linguistic phrases. For instance, Godboy, in *Dutch Uncle,* has a pathological preference for the word 'merely,' and Joey, in *Butley,* employs the phrase "in point of fact" to a degree that Ben Butley sees fit to comment: "Matters of fact and points of fact have been cluttering your syntax since you started going steady with that butcher's boy" (49). Others, such as Butley or Simon Hench, indulge in taking someone's loose grammatical use of words quite literally, by which ploy Mr. Gray manages to endow his plays with comic effects. Unlike Orton, who is often at the tip of the tongue of people who talk about the early Gray and who, at his most convincing, relies heavily on knockabout farcical turns, Simon Gray's humour is largely linguistic in kind.

The present study will concentrate on Mr. Gray's work for the stage. The decision to neglect the TV pieces, of which only *Man in a Side-Car* (1971), *Two Sundays* (1975) and *Plaintiffs and Defendants* (1975) are in print, was taken because the TV plays are, by and large, muddled and mediocre dramatic exercises; on account of their compositional weaknesses, they will add little to Mr. Gray's reputation as a playwright; further, they exploit themes that were treated far more satisfactorily in the stage-plays of the middle period. As the greater number of them have not been published, it was felt more serviceable to the reader to disregard those which have been printed so that more space would be available to discuss particularly *Butley, Otherwise Engaged,* and *The Rear Column* in greater depth.

Wise Child, staged at Wyndham's Theatre, London, on 10 October 1967, with John Dexter as director, is a not altogether successful first play that vacillates between farce and problem play. Its lukewarm impact on an audience derives mainly from two causes. Firstly, from the tired theatrical device of having a male character wear women's clothing for most of the time; the audience is left guessing whether whiskey-addicted Mrs. Artminster is in fact a lady. Sir Alec Guinness, who in the original production played Mrs. Artminster, called the play an updated version of Brandon Thomas's *Charley's Aunt* (1892). Secondly, from the compositional contrivance of correlative sexual advances made by two characters in adjacent rooms at the same time: while Booker, the hotel manager, is attempting to seduce Jerry, Mrs. Artminster has persuaded the hotel maid, Janice, to strip for him on the fraudulent pretence of seeking to verify whether her attractive "bubbles" are indeed real and not just foam or stuffing. The play's shortcomings, however, outweigh these redeeming qualities by far. They concern, first and foremost, the relationship between two small-time criminals. Jerry has picked up Jock, when he found him hiding from the police after Jock had committed his last crime. It was Jerry's idea that Jock wear women's clothes and that they book themselves in at a sleazy provincial hotel as mother and son. Jerry has forced Jock (Mrs. Artminster) into submission, threatening to give him away to the police unless he accepts his terms. "You treat me to threats and police to make me beg" (18), Mrs. Artminster remonstrates. Jerry provides money by applying for all sorts of jobs, making himself unsuitable during the interview and claiming lavish expenses for attendance. Jock counteracts Jerry's efforts to keep him in the subservient position by repeatedly comparing him to his former partner, Derek, who was everything that Jerry is not. It comes as a more than slightly unconvincing turn in the plot, when Mrs. Artminster, or Jock, near the end of the play, outspokenly rebels against Jerry's dominance, claiming that he can no longer bear to be deprived of all he yearns for, including women, because he is confined to staying in his hotel-room. He wants to be free again (68), for which purpose he tries to put an end to the sadomasochistic relationship with Jerry, regardless of running the high risk of being tracked down by the police. As if in a last desperate attempt to prevent Jock from leaving him, possibly because he learns that his partner has tried to sell him off to Booker for £200, Jerry kills Booker, puts on Janice's clothes, and it appears that the two will go on leading their questionable mutual existence, but with the rôles reversed.

Jerry has an immature, insecure, fragile, repressed, childish nature, and may have been drawn to Jock out of a recondite, juvenile admiration for criminals. His problems are, in the main, presented credibly; they may be out of, say, one of those plays that John Elsom has labelled "plays of middle-class decline," a play by Peter Shaffer or John Mortimer. But these psychological handicaps together with the sado-masochistic relationship in which the two crooks stand to each other seems slightly out of place in the overall farcical context of the play. The ambiguity and unspecific nature of the central human conflict seem to indicate the difficulty on Mr. Gray's part of deciding whether he wanted to write a full-blooded farce or a problem play. *Wise Child* lacks the verbal charm of Mr. Gray's other pieces; in fact, it is obtrusively verbose for most of the time. The longish speeches of the characters give the play a static effect which runs counter to its farcical, knock-about intentions. It is a play that invites comparison with Orton's *What the Butler Saw*, or, even more strikingly, with Alan Bennett's *Habeas Corpus*. When measured against Orton's mastery in contriving hilarious farcical situations or Bennett's specimens of witty repartee, the weakness of *Wise Child* becomes only too apparent. It is, one should not forget, Mr. Gray's first stage-play, in which he may have been exploiting new territory. As *Dutch Uncle* evidences, he was quick to establish himself as an expert of more than moderate status in this field.

The plot of *Dutch Uncle*, first produced in March 1969 by the Royal Shakespeare Company under the direction of Peter Hall, deals with Perkins Godboy's attempts to gas his wife, May, in an enormous cupboard, so that he can have an affair with Doris, the wife of the upstairs neighbour, before he gasses her too. Godboy is motivated by his Raskolnikov-like infatuation with murder, in particular, by his admiration of one James Ryan O'Higgs, who, in cold blood, "polished off his wife and tenant in a week, and ... kept the police at bay by clever lies" (12). There is also his over-riding desire to attract the attention of Inspector 'Mannerly' Hawkins, against whose fastidious methods of investigation he wishes to test his own ingenuity as a murderer. Too many unexpected and unprovided-for events, alas, run counter to poor Godboy's plans. Every time he presumes his wife to be in the cupboard and turns on the gas, she has, in full view of the audience, but unnoticed by him, come out of it; all he eventually achieves is to gas his guppies. Similarly, when attempting to kill Doris, first he is interrupted by a number of people who intrude at the wrong moment, and then he falls victim to his own inability, for he simply anaesthetises himself, and Doris can escape. As to his allegedly unprecedented game of cat-and-mouse with the police, Godboy misreads Hawkins's presence in his house as evidence for the Inspector's investigation into the presumed

disappearance of May Godboy; whereas, in fact, Hawkins is on the trail of
the Merrit-Street rapist, who turns out to be Doris's husband. The play
ends with May Godboy accidentally shutting her husband in the cupboard,
and Mr. Gray leaves it open whether Perkins Godboy will ever emerge.

What the characters have in common is that their behaviour is determined by unfulfilled wishes, and, especially in the case of Perkins Godboy,
by an acute sense of failure. Like George Riley, in Tom Stoppard's *Enter a
Free Man,* or Simon Hench's brother Stephen, in *Otherwise Engaged,*
Godboy, more or less overtly, knows that he is a 'greyish' character in
terms of socio-conventional standards, unable to make a lasting impression
on his fellow men. Desperately, he clings to his memories of his allegedly
important operations in his capacity as Special Constable during the war,
but these are thrown into a comical light by his admission that he was only
one of the most insignificant of subalterns, "checking padlocks in the
evening" (43). His sense of futility is presently enforced by his wife, who
keeps him under her thumb and nags him about his inability to satisfy her
sexually. By way of a remedy for his meaningless existence, he has con-
cocted a plan, which is intended to prove him to be a match for Inspector
Hawkins, in whom he sees all the authority and efficiency he himself is
lacking. By imitating "gasser O'Higgs'" criminal actions, he dreams of
engaging Hawkins in a "real battle of wits" that will undeniably establish
him as superior to the authoritative, ingenious Hawkins. The trouble is that
the Inspector is not at all interested in Godboy, and that Godboy's plans
come to a farcical end.

May Godboy hankers after the sexual satisfaction her former husband
was able to give her. She still regards herself as a "warm woman," with "a
lot of life" in her, but one whose emotional fire is turned into embers by
Godboy. Eric's problems are comparable to May's. He is frustrated in his
desire for sex and love by his wife and driven to raping other women in
Merrit Street. Doris is a timid, repressed girl, and, in a way similar to
Godboy, unable or unwilling to satisfy her husband's longings, or so May
sees it: "if you made your Eric welcome, he'd be up there, inside, and you
know who I mean, who a man ought to be inside of. You don't give him what
he needs, Doris Hoyden, and he'll do what I'm doing to him, who doesn't
give me the same" (35). Even Inspector Hawkins is conditioned by an
unfulfilled wish. Godboy regards him as a true-born policeman, without
blemish; the others know or, as in Doris's case, have experienced that he is
a womanizer. He is the Dutch uncle of the title, who seizes upon every
opportunity for a flirt or an affair. Having arrested Eric, after passionately
kissing his wife, he promises to be like a Dutch uncle to Doris in the same
ambivalent manner in which he persuaded female Constable Hedderly to

join the police force. Hawkins's dream is to remain "boy eternal" (90), and his amorous escapades are a means to prove that to himself and avoid growing old.

Roger Barker has argued[14] that Godboy's inability to satisfy his wife sexually is really a rebellion on his part against the rôles he is forced to play by society and by his wife. Godboy's sexual failure, however, so convincingly ties in with his other weaknesses, which make him a 'plop,' that Barker's assertion appears to overstate the case. Besides, Godboy is too dotty to be convincing as a rebel, however small-scale.

Spoiled, presented on 24th February 1971, in the Haymarket Theatre, directed by Stephen Hollis, marks a new departure for Simon Gray, after the Ortonesque farces of the first period. Mr. Gray may be said to have now turned to exploring in greater depth problems of interhuman relationships in terms of the interactional principle of dominance and subservience. *Spoiled* is based on the often-used ménage-à-trois motif, but Mr. Gray is unable to bring out the conflicts inherent in the situation that arises from Richard Howarth's inviting an over-mothered pupil, Donald, who is trying to prepare for his O-Level examination in French by some concentrated cramming, to stay with him and his pregnant, slightly hysterical wife, Joanna. Too many problems are touched upon without being fully accounted for, so that the ultimate outcome is disappointing. We may applaud Howarth's well-intentioned tirade against the dangers of overweening parents and his presumably equally well-meant warnings to Donald against the problems of a homosexual relationship, and also the way in which he is built by Gray into an understanding, sympathetic teacher. Mr. Gray strains our credulity when, out of the teacher-pupil situation, he contrives the seemingly most important event in the play that unites teacher and pupil in a homosexual encounter. After this incident, Howarth meets his wife outside the bedroom. She simply stares at him "and goes away" (75).

The play suffers at least from three defects. It fails to convince us that Joanna is right in calling her biscuit-devouring husband's tutorial efforts an act of "self-indulgence," for up to the point where Howarth misuses his power over Donald—which power, Mr. Gray appears to be hinting, is inherent in every pupil-teacher relationship—to satisfy his latent homosexual bent, he seems sincerely concerned about Donald's welfare. Moreover, why do the interactional manœuves taking place between Howarth and Donald find their climax in this homosexual union? Is it because Howarth, like Stephen in *Otherwise Engaged,* may be a "latent pederast," who upon learning that his pupil has a homosexual friend thinks he must not let the opportunity slip? There is reason to believe that Howarth has some kind of sexual axe to grind with Donald, for otherwise there is little to justify his deliberate talking to the boy about various sexual matters. On the other hand, that may again only be a well-meant attempt at liberating the overmothered Donald, as he tells Joanna. But then, by so doing, he embarrasses the boy out of all proportion, which, of course, could be interpreted as an intentional strategy on Howarth's part to force Donald into submission. Lastly, the marital conflict, which the audience is made to think is brought into light by Howarth's interest in his pupil, is not only disappointingly unspecific—if it does not simply involve the effect that Joanna's pregnancy has on the husband-wife relationship, as Howarth is inclined to think: "One of the facts of marriage," he enlightens Donald, "is that ladies, when in an advanced state of pregnancy, tend to be a trifle, um, dramatic, poor dears" (69)—but is even downright confusing. Joanna complains about Howarth's late-night marking of exercise-books, nags him about his penchant for biscuits, reprimands him for not having loved her since she became pregnant, yet, on top of all these accusations, does not omit to caress (40) him, calling him "a liar, self-indulgent, lovable, sexy and exhibitionist" (40), which comes as another surpise in the play, as Howarth has in no way betrayed any tendency to being an exhibitionist. The play, then, is as muddled as Joanna's verdict on Howarth.

With *Butley*, we approach that part of Simon Gray's *œuvre* to date on which his claim to fame rests. The play was first presented in London, on 14 July 1971, at the Criterion Theatre, directed by Harold Pinter and with Alan Bates starring in the title rôle. It is the first in a group of three that focus on one principal character who is supported by a varying number of secondary characters. Structurally, these plays consist of a series of encounters, involving, almost as a rule, the protagonist and one of the supporting cast, with each constellation or partner functioning in such a way that one specific character trait of the protagonist is brought to the fore. The chain of constellations may appear random, at first sight, but is, in fact, carefully calculated.

Butley opens and closes with a student coming into Ben Butley's office for a tutorial. In between these framing events, the audience bears witness to how Ben's seedy world collapses. Act I falls into seven different constellations; it has Butley and Joey together on stage for most of the time; their communicational jockeying for positions is interrupted five times by other characters and ends temporarily when Butley's wife, Anne, arrives and, after Joey has left, reveals that she is going to marry another man. This revelation constitutes a minor climax; it is minor inasmuch as it does not lead the play's true dramatic conflict to its peak, but is rather a secondary strand in the plot. Act II has again seven different constellations; the corresponding climactic event to that at the end of Act I and also the major climax in the play is reached when Butley competes against Joey's latest friend, Reg, for the possession of Joey. If one regards Butley's battle for dominance as the main dramatic event, the plot-structure may, at least to a certain degree, be likened to the traditional pattern, as formulated by Gustav Freytag: exposition, inciting force, the building up of the conflict, the moment of final suspense, and catastrophe. The exposition does not make up a unit on its own, but is integrated into the building up of the climax; it is handled in an analytic manner, as it were. The inciting force may be seen in the fact that Joey has spent a weekend with his new companion, which arouses Butley's jealousy and gives rise to the battle for dominance, built up gradually until it is brought to its climax in the last section of the play. There is a moment of final suspense, when, after his unsuccessful contest with Reg, Butley asks Joey to stop his bleeding wound, and there is a flicker of hope that Butley has at least managed to degrade Joey in the eyes of Reg, with the possible consequence that Reg will not have him after all. The catastrophe is reached when Butley eventually has to acknowledge that he has lost on all socres and is too old to begin anew, as he tells Gardner, who could have been Joey's possible successor.

The play's main dramatic spring is Butley's battle for the possession of Joey. The two men have lived together before and after Ben's brief marital interlude, and without having to take recourse to assessing the relationship in homosexual terms—for Mr. Gray has convincingly argued that Ben is not the man to indulge in a homosexual relationship[15]—one may assert that Joey means a lot to Ben; possibly besides the nursery rhymes, his relationship with Joey is about the only thing that still has meaning in Ben's pessimistic world. Butley's fight is against Joey for keeping him in submission, but also, of course, against his actual rival, Reg. Mr. Gray colours it by bringing in Ben's marriage problems as well as his disparaging attitude towards his students and his colleagues, represented by Edna, "the human contraceptive."

In his competition, Butley employs a series of strategic moves. Because Joey has spent the weekend with Reg, Ben is jealous and feels vindictive toward him. When, for instance, Joey betrays his genuine interest in whether he will get his lectureship, Butley keeps him on tenterhooks about what has happened in the meantime, arguing that "a member of the department has his knife out" (15). There are three main targets of attack. Firstly, Ben aims at degrading Joey; he criticises him for associating himself with a butcher's boy from the north of England, or tells him bluntly that his wife thinks little of him, mainly because he is a homosexual. Secondly, he seeks to disparage Reg by harping on Reg's homosexual inclinations and speaking disdainfully about Reg's family. Thirdly, he teases Joey about the lectureship. What he hopes to achieve through his tactical efforts is—as Joey well knows—to embarrass him and make him feel guilty. Butley is quick to change his strategy when a new situation has been created by Joey's refusal to come with him to Bianchi's, because of his appointment with Reg. Here, it appears, Ben is made to realise for the first time that his harangues, which, we can safely assume, have frequently been part of their daily routine, may not have had their desired effect. Now Butley strives to counteract Joey's plan by repetitive threats to ring Reg and invite himself to join them. Joey is, by nature, no match for Butley; he is too weak to make more than feeble attempts at fighting back, as, for example, when he reciprocates Ben's revelation that Anne does not trust him by telling Ben that Reg hates him and echoing Ben's bitchiness:

> BEN.   You never told me this before.
> JOEY.   You never asked me before (25, cf. 21)

Joey has always been in the subservient position. He does not even have the strength to tell Ben what he knows about Tom and Anne. The real battle takes place between Butley and Reg. Only after Reg has cleared the way does Joey make a true effort to sever his connections with Ben. By means of, more or less, subtle innuendoes and verbal gauntlets, Butley desperately fights for Joey, laying the major emphasis of his attack on Reg's homosexuality and bossing him around by deliberately calling him back a number of times when Reg is making for the door. When all the hurly-burly is done, Butley has lost and Reg has won. Reg has Joey firmly under his thumb; he has already usurped Ben's place, and, before knocking Ben down, he tells him unequivocally that Joey will leave him. Reg, then, does not, as Ben had hoped, cook Ben's kidneys (70), but 'cooks his goose.'

As the title implies, the play's predominant thematic concern is a character portrait of Ben Butley, or, to be more precise, the portrait which can be drawn by presenting him in the last lap of his race against loneliness. Ben is a relatively complex figure, almost—in E. M. Forster's terminology—a 'round' character. He is a highly intelligent, messy, seedy, vindictive, indiscriminately destructive, spiteful man, who, behind a façade of sardonic wit, hides his vulnerability and essential solitude. He may have been a good teacher once, but he has developed into a student-hater. It is possible that Ben has undergone a process of disillusionment about the merits of teaching when overshadowed by administrative and academic excesses; this is a reason, to be sure, which Mr. Gray chooses to leave for the audience to infer. More likely, Ben's development may stem from the difficulties appertaining to his person, his life, and attitude towards those around him. The messy, seedy condition of his part of the office mirrors the disorderly state of his existence. Butley's main weakness is that he is unable to organise his life properly and strike up viable relationships with other people, possibly because he has too possessive a nature. At the root of his vindictive, destructive behaviour lies the conscious or semi-conscious acknowledgement of personal failure: his marriage broke up after only a short time, and his relationship with Joey is about to approach a disastrous end. By way of compensation, Butley projects his own inadequacies onto those he is concerned with; his retaliatory actions spring from the egotistical conviction that everyone is trying to get at him; no-one is excepted from his cynical wrath.

The vindictive actions are, of course, not taken by Butley merely for the sake of fun. They are stratagems to cover his frustration at seeing his cake turned into dough by those he thought he possessed; his destructive behaviour is really a means to camouflage his vulnerability and the ineluctable loneliness of his situation. Despite the witty, self-assured airs he gives himself, he is deeply wounded by both the two devastating revelations. After Anne has informed him that she will divorce him, "he breaks off, trembling" (42). And at the end of his excruciatingly merciless battle for Joey, when with Joey's moving office all hope is lost, he openly admits that he is too old to begin again. So Ben is not only bleeding from the cut caused by a dull razor-blade, but bleeding profusely from the wounds inflicted upon him by the events which the play presents. Probably the only time that a statement of Ben's approximates his real feelings is when he answers Joey's question about why he engaged himself in the Gardner intrigue: "Perhaps I had a sense of vacancies opening up in my life" (55). At bottom, Butley is a lonely man, afraid of being left to himself, like Jeff, in *Otherwise Engaged*, "he has got nowhere to bloody go and he does not want to go there yet" (59). He has a special predilection for Eliot. In a way, he is like Prufrock, with the notable difference that he does have the strength to force the moment to its crisis.

One critic has argued that "it is difficult to account for the great success of [the play]."[16] Many may not have been impressed by the character of Butley, and it must be admitted that he lacks the universal validity and metaphorical transferability to make the play into a profound contemporary dramatic statement. But then, Mr. Gray was most certainly not striving to make such a statement. His dramatic output offers ample proof that he is not at all aiming at, say, moral messages, as for instance Tom Stoppard is; he appears to see his duty as a playwright, first and foremost, in entertaining his audience, which is as legitimate a goal as using the stage as a substitute for the soap-box. It is probably unfair to suggest that he has nothing of particular value to tell his audience, apart from some verbal jokes he strings together in music-hall fashion. The middle plays of his *œuvre* to date establish him as a very subtle craftsman, who, almost in a Shavian manner, has learned that the only way to put across his ideas is to present them in a beribboned box of assorted laughs for the audience.

There is no denying that most critics were intrigued by Mr. Gray's verbal wizardry. The funny instances of repartee, *e.g.*

JOEY.   ... What's the matter with your chin?
BEN.   I'm trying to cultivate cotton wool on it ... (9)

the comic effects resulting from taking a character's loose grammatical use of words literally:

MISS HEASMAN.   Yes. She said she didn't get to see you
                                   often owing to administrative tangles.
BEN.   Mrs. Grainger got into administrative
                                   tangles? (14)

or the combination of verbal and situational jokes, as when Butley, trying to get up after Reg has knocked him down, explains to puzzled Edna: "Living theatre. Next time round in Polish" (71), all of which he was to cultivate to near perfection in *Otherwise Engaged* —these features are apt to guarantee a theatrical success, when employed in as skillful a manner as Mr. Gray's. And if one digs deeper into the subtext of the plays, one can find how cleverly the serious thematic targets are woven into what may appear on the surface to be a loose series of insignificant, easy-going events. This is, incidentally, also Harold Pinter's dramatic method[17]. If one takes into account the dominant dramatic motif in Mr. Gray's middle plays, the battle for positions, which again is the dominant motif in Pinter[18], as well as dialogue passages such as:

JOEY.   ... I left it with Reg.
BEN.   Reg? Who's Reg? (...)
JOEY.   Reg is his name.
BEN.   Whose name?
JOEY.   Ted's.
BEN.   Reg is Ted's name?
JOEY.   The one you call Ted is the one I call Reg. He calls
                himself Reg too.
BEN.   How sweet.
JOEY.   In fact, everybody calls him Reg except you. You
                call him Ted.
BEN.   Why do I do that, I wonder. (10)

which could be straight out of a Pinter Play[19], it is obvious why Harold Pinter was eager to direct *Butley* and *Otherwise Engaged*.

Otherwise Engaged is Simon Gray's most fascinating work for the stage. It was first presented on 30 July 1975, at the Queen's Theatre in London's Shaftesbury Avenue, and won its author the Evening Standard

Award for 1975. Again as in *Butley,* Alan Bates acted in the leading rôle, and Harold Pinter was the director. At the centre is the character of Simon Hench. In a manner comparable to the formal procession of Tempters and Deadly Sins in a morality play, he is brought into contact with assorted bores, boors, and creeps. Dave appears four times, Stephen three times, Jeff twice, Wood, Davina, and Beth just once. A possible logic behind this pattern of 'diminutive returns' may be this: the less important the problems connected with an intruder is, the more often he reappears, as if the author wanted to lay an additional stress on the whimsicality as well as impudence of the visitors. The play is structured by means of a carefully designed texture of internal rhymes and incremental repetitions. Thus, at the beginning and, approximately, half way through Act I, Simon puts on a record from his newly-acquired *Parsifal* box; each time Dave interrupts. The second attempt functions as a kind of caesura, dividing the lesser from the more serious problems with which Simon is faced. The next time Simon tries to play the recording—and this time successfully so—is at the end of the play, with the second repetition bringing the dramatic action back to its beginning, as it were; in other words, similar to the structure of *Butley,* the events in *Otherwise Engaged* are framed. With the exception of Dave, each visitor is either introduced or drawn into an often unpleasant brief verbal exchange with his predecessor. Wood makes his entrance after five prior intrusions on Simon's privacy by other characters, and he reappears, albeit only via the answering machine, in Act II, again after five preceding visits by other figures. Davina's invented suicide in Act I is echoed with incremental force by Wood's seemingly real suicide near the end of the play. Jeff's violent act of throwing his drink in Davina's face has its counterpart in Simon's throwing his drink in Jeff's face. The motivation for Stephen's appearance in Act I is disappointment and despair; in Act II it is the opposite. Act I ends with Simon's allegedly true admission of having been unfaithful to his wife; near the end of Act II, we have Beth's revelation about her affair with Ned.

Otherwide Engaged is about egotism, inconsiderateness, and the indifference of people to the concerns of those around them; it is also about a lack of sensibility in human beings. In more concrete terms, the play deals with a handful of characters who are so deeply immersed in their personal problems that they consider themselves to be the focal point of everyone else's interest. It has become something of a convention among reviewers to define Simon Hench as a cold-hearted, cynical, uncaring brute. The none-too-perceptive German critic of *Die Zeit* argued that the play was "a comedy about the total indifference of an intellectual."[20] It is, however, by no means indisputable that *Otherwise Engaged* is a comedy at all. J. R. Taylor writes:

> Toward the beginning of the play [Simon] appears to be a very
> decent sort of chap amiably putting up with a succession of
> bores and boors and creeps when all he wants to do is listen to
> his recording of *Parsifal;* by the end of the play our image of him
> has changed considerably ... , as we gradually incline to the
> belief, expressed most explicitly by his wife, that he can put up
> with all this just because he hardly notices and what he does
> notice he does not care about. He is indifferent ... ; he is im-
> pregnable ... ; he may seem to be otherwise engaged, but
> in all probability he is merely switched off.[21]

Notwithstanding other arguable assertions in Mr. Taylor's comment, if
Simon is regarded as being totally unfeeling toward the difficulties of his
wife, friends and acquaintances, it is only fair to add that those bores, boors
and creeps Mr. Taylor speaks of are equally insensitive to Simon's interests. Furthermore, there are a number of good reasons to suppose that the
characters who barge into Simon's living room are to a greater extent
'otherwise engaged' than Simon himself. To give but one of these reasons
before we enter into a more penetrating discussion: not to any of those who
do their best to heap their worries onto Simon's shoulders does it ever
occur, before unleashing their torrent of self-pitying language, whether she
or he is imposing upon Simon. In fact, Stephen comes to see his brother in
spite of the telephone call in which Simon told him that he had better not
come as he was expecting Jeff Golding.

Even those who favour a negative interpretation of the central character in *Otherwise Engaged* will agree that not all the problems with which he
is confronted are equally weighty. Some are simply rooted in material
interests, others are of more complicated origin. On the superficial level,
one would have to place Dave and Davina. Both of them seek to *use* Simon
for certain petty material wishes. Dave is the insufferable lad from upstairs
who wears the non-conformist uniform of—what has come to be called—
the progressive student. He shows no sense of civilised behaviour or
decency, at least, that is, from the old-fashioned bourgeois standpoint. His
mental activities are largely confined to provoking bourgeois Simon by
spreading himself about in the Hench household and to sponging fishfingers
or Nescafe as an aid to seduction. Simon treats him according to his
deserts. Davina tries 'to put the make' on Simon to obtain a contract for her
as yet unpublished book on "Major Bloody Barttelot." She gets wittily
turned down, although she manages to interest Simon in her book.

The verbal exchanges resulting from Stephen's appearance are
symptomatic of most of the other encounters, and a more detailed analysis
of them may serve to illuminate the pattern of Simon's reaction. Stephen
comes in in a state of utter depression. Taking up Simon's description of

Ned as "a bit of a failure" (12), he wonders whether people regard him as a failure, too: "A middle-aged public school teacher with five children to boot" (13). At any rate, he has come to *use* Simon as some kind of sounding board to get the feeling of failure off his chest. Simon, despite his annoyance at Stephen's intrusion, betrays, or simply pretends, interest by asking such questions as are necessary for Stephen to be able to communicate the sad events that happend to him in the course of his interview for the Assistant Headmastership. He enquires: "Why, what's the matter?" (13), and, furthermore, he tries to stop Stephen in his self-pitying analysis of why he failed by offering words of consolation which are at first nothing but pertinent and reasonable. But then he loses interest when, after his third attempt at cheering up Stephen, he realises that there is no stopping him in his self-abuse, and he asks one of those funny irrelevant questions. In a disarmingly witty manner, he meets the most preposterous of all of Stephen's explanations, namely that he did something which he had not done since he was twelve—he farted, by asking: "You haven't farted since you were twelve?" (15), and taking exceptional interest in what the fart sounded like, or, later on, what herbs the Headmaster uses for his herbal coffee. By the very irrelevancy of the question, he tries implicitly to hinder Stephen in going on as well as to make him realise the banality of his arguments and the waning curiosity on his part to continue the conversation, a waning curiosity which, because of the triviality of Stephen's agonizing, is fully understandable. It should be noted, however, that, notwithstanding these irrelevant enquiries, Simon goes on to console Stephen, as when he argues: " ... even if they suspected that your single fart heralds chronic incontinence, they'll have to appoint you ... " (16). And, interestingly, Stephen acknowledges his brother's efforts: "Actually it would be better, if you don't mind, not jollying me along with reasons and reassurances. I shall have to face the disappointment sooner or later ... " (16); he says this even though one of the reasons why he came to see Simon was, after all, to be jollied along.

When Stephen returns in Act II, he is again possessed by a paramount desire: this time he wants to unbosom his happiness at having gotten the job. But Simon frustrates him in his zeal to communicate in interminable detail by asking irrelevant questions about pansy wine and nut cutlets. The feeling of being frustrated breeds aggression in Stephen, and consequently he lets off steam by accusing Simon of despising his person, his job, his wife and family, in short — of being indifferent, "absolutely indifferent" (48). His diatribe culminates in the revelation that Simon's wife is having an affair. As he is frank to admit afterwards, this revelation was an act of revenge on Simon: " ... I suppose I meant to hurt" (50). Similarly, Dave, when he meets with Simon's determined refusal to lend him the coffee machine, which is coupled with an unequivocal pronouncement of what Simon really thinks of Dave, tries to turn the tables on Simon by asserting that through keeping him as a "special deserving case," Simon is seeking to salve his conscience (46). Even Wood's suicide at the end of the play may be nothing but a comparable act of revenge. For it remains entirely undecided, since Simon switches the machine off before we are able to tell whether Wood does in fact pull the trigger.

Jeff is an old-fashioned sentimentalist, who hankers after the bygone days of the muffin-man. From the outset, he leaves no doubt as to the purpose of his visit. He wants to cry on Simon's shoulder about what presents itself to his mind as a totally unjust and grim vicissitude of fate: he has fallen in love with his ex-wife in the middle of Oxford Street. The pathetic snag in Jeff's affair is that his ex-wife is now married to a Cambridge don. Jeff, like Dave, Davina and Stephen, wants to *use* Simon. He endeavours to vent his despair; but he is more outspoken about his intentions. Before embarking on his narrative, he lays down the guidelines for Simon's response: "What I want from you is an attentive face and a cocked ear, the good old-fashioned sympathy and concern for which you're celebrated" (21). So he, too, is in search of an ear into which he can pour his sad story, and he is in search of sympathy for his situation, which, objectively speaking, is too pathetic to warrant true compassion. Admittedly, Simon is not in the least interested in Jeff's story, but why should he be, there having been so many similarly preposterous Jeff sagas, and why, indeed, should he suffer himself to be told yet another, this time involving "bitch Davina?"

The dialogue between Simon and Wood is a brilliant dramatic achievement, a balancing act between farce and tragedy. Wood has come to satisfy his somewhat depraved, self-tormenting curiosity about whether Simon has had sexual intercourse with Wood's fiancée. He shows a surprising degree of prurient interest in the deed. Understandably, Simon finds Wood's obsession "frankly Mediterranean, and the enquiry into method depressing." Wood behaves rather provocatively, at first, bombarding Simon with remarks about his homosexual experiences at Wundale; he nosily pries into Simon's motives for not having children, and then bluntly asks him about the sex with Joanna. With justification, Simon replies: "Look, Wood, whatever your anxiety about your daughter, I really don't think, old chap, that you should insinuate yourself into people's homes and put a question like that to them. I mean, good God, you can't possibly expect me to dignify it with an answer, can you?" (37). Yet, he answers Wood's question, and this answer is interesting. For it remains open whether he did have sexual intercourse with Joanna. If we take Simon's words about fidelity meaning more "than a suck and a fuck" with the likes of Davina as being true, the answer is, in all probability, a lie, designed to lead Wood on. Simon, it appears, invents the whole story so that he can get back at Wood for Wood's abnormal insinuations by offering him an opportunity for revelling in his self-torture. Shortly afterwards, Wood obliges with a complete recital of his ploppy past, which has led him "from masturbation to matrimony to monogamy" (39). So once more, it is the "good old-fashioned sympathy" that the intruder is after, for a problem Dantesque in the purity of its hopelessness. It should be clear that Wood does not really want to ascertain whether Simon did have sex with Joanna, for, as he admits, Joanna habitually sleeps around with a lot of boys (41).

Beth is given the climactic position in the play. The problems attached to her appear to be the most serious, if only in that they concern Simon directly. Given the stage at which they are presented, they take on the significance of a final test, as it were, to verify whether Simon is able to keep his calm at all costs and whether he will treat Beth and her difficulties in the same flippant way as all the others. He behaves, however, in his usual irreverent manner and does not want to get involved in a discussion of Beth's affair. Mouthing Ned's judgment on Simon, Beth asserts:

> You're one of those men who only give permission to little bits of life to get through to you. He says that while we may envy your serenity, we should be revolted by the rot from which it stems. Your sanity is of the kind that causes people to go quietly mad around you. (56)

But Simon has his own and, on close inspection, very weighty reasons for not entering into a discussion and instead confining himself to "the other words" (53). He knows that such a discussion would be hurtful, and he does not want to hurt Beth. Besides, he holds that "the worst thing you can do to an important problem is discuss it" (52), since people understand as much as they need without having to be told. Thirdly, unlike Beth, he is well aware that a discussion would only be reasonable if it brought about a change in the state of events, be it either that Beth leaves Simon for Ned or that she breaks with Ned. In such an outcome, Simon does not believe. At the end of the verbal contest, therefore, he asks:

> Excuse me, but what precisely has all this been about? You complain of my reticence over the last ten months, but what good has all this exposition served, what's it been for, Beth? Ned's not going to leave his wife, I don't want you to leave me, you don't even think you're going to leave me—we have a perfectly sensible arrangement, we are happy enough together you and I, insultingly so if you like but still happy. (57)

Beth, on the other hand, insists on a discussion, finding him, who has known about the affair and because of his knowledge has taken her to bed with even greater satisfaction, a freak. Simon's reaction may be considered freaky, but then from a different, equally valid, point of view it is only rational. Simon is a rationalist, and to accuse him is to accuse this type of character altogether. Beth's behaviour is an act of "infantile agonising," and it stems partly from vanity and hurt pride. Her accusations are, ultimately, conditioned by the same motives as those of Stephen, Dave, Jeff, and Wood. Whereas Wood tries to revenge himself by threatening to kill himself, Beth springs the surprise on Simon that she is pregnant and does not know whether Ned or Simon is the father. After that, Simon "sits in a state of shock." He is deeply irritated and agitated by the news. Only once in the course of the events does he lose his self-control, and this is when, after Beth's revelation and Dave's and Wood's retaliatory moves, Jeff accuses him of having tipped the police off, he throws his drink in Jeff's face.

Simon, then, is confronted with a number of people whose sense of delicacy and feeling for other people's right to privacy has been dulled by "triumph or disaster ... like a drug" (50). They have no qualms about bothering Simon with their more or less trivial worries but are disgusted when they are compelled to acknowledge that their problems have failed to win Simon's sympathy. In a way, Simon is like Parsifal. He too—though in contrast to Parsifal he does it deliberately—fails to ask the right questions so that his visitors may tell their quaint little stories full of human catastrophe. They can, as Simon diagnoses their symptoms, take his "courteous metaphors literally, but ... can't take [his] literals literally" (52). If it is true, as John Donne states in *Devotions,* that "No man is an island, entire of itself; every man is a piece of the continent," this continent can only exist if each is willing to put his share of compassion, sensibility and tolerance into the bargain. Perhaps this is the message *Otherwise Engaged* may be conveying to its audience, if the audience is looking for one.

How perfectly 'normal,' or 'British' Simon's way of dealing with the intruders is may be discerned when it is compared with the manner in which Laurence Olivier reacted to Tom Stoppard's private reading of his play *Jumpers*. As Ken Tynan reports, he had invited Stoppard to his Kensington flat so that Stoppard should read *Jumpers* to Olivier, John Dexter and Tynan. Stoppard arrived with the script and a number of cards that bore the names of the individual characters. Reading the parts, Stoppard would hold up the cards so that his audience knew who was speaking. Stoppard's recital developed into a disaster; after two hours he had not got further than the end of Act I, and he was frantically shuffling the pages of his script and brandishing cards. Within an hour, Olivier had fallen asleep. When he awoke, he stared at the ceiling where some spotlights were dimly gleaming. Stoppard looked expectantly in Olivier's direction. Clearly Olivier was choosing his words with care. At length, he said: "Ken, where did you buy these lights?"[22]

As the "Author's Note" to *Dog Days* tells us, the play was begun before the final draft of *Butley* was in production. Mr. Gray kept working on it, besides a number of other pieces, for the next two years "in an increasing state of muddle." "Characters from one play would slip into another, change name, age, occupation and even sex, before either slipping into yet another play or back into the first." The plays referred to are *Otherwise Engaged, Two Sundays,* and *Plaintiffs and Defendants,* all of which were completed and produced before *Dog Days.* Even though the four works relate to each other because of themes, motifs and structural characteristics they have in common, and even though *Dog Days* may be called — as the jacket-note states — "a companion piece to *Otherwise Engaged,*" exploring in greater depth Simon's/Peter's relationship to his brother Stephen/Charles as well as his marital difficulties, there is reason to suppose that *Dog Days* forms part of a trilogy of sorts with *Two Sundays* and *Plaintiffs* ... , rather than that the play is part of a tetralogy. In *Plaintiffs* ... , *Two Sundays,* and *Dog Days,* there are the same *personae* and the same thematic issues. *Dog Days* begins like *Plaintiffs* ... with Peter and Joanna about to enter upon their affair. As anticipated in *Otherwise Engaged,* the two have been brought together by Joanna's wish to show some of her cover-designs to Peter. But Peter is very different from Simon Hench, despite his witticisms and relish for deliberately misunderstanding people. Niddy repeats her "big jobs" for Charlie from *Two Sundays;* Alison is again pregnant; Charlies has applied for the Assistant Headmastership at Amplesides; the Headmaster is a vegetarian and is extremely fond of home-made retzina; Joanna has had a similarly disastrous affair with Josh, as in *Plaintiffs;* and lastly, to name only the most prominent parallels between *Dog Days* and the two TV plays, in each of the pieces the statement recurs "old friends are like old habits. It doesn't matter whether you like them, they are what you've got." (40)

As to the composition of *Dog Days,* Mr. Gray has resorted to the formula which is familiar from *Butley.* The events are again framed — at the end, there is an almost verbatim repetition of the scene with which the play begins — and, minor modifications apart, they are organised according to the structural pattern of the well-made play. Thematically, *Dog Days* is basically about the process of disillusionment and, consequently, of facing up to one's own shortcomings, in this case those to which Peter is subjected. In the first half, he is clearly akin to Butley, vindictive, deadly with his tongue, disenchanted with almost everything, given to heavy drinking bouts, a bit, too, like Osborne's Jimmy Porter, wholly indiscriminate in his attacks on all around him. Peter claims he acts out of boredom, possible from the sterile sex-routine in his marriage (36f.). Later on, he explains that his behaviour is grounded in frustration (83) and discontent. It may also stem from a deep-seated dissatisfaction with the moral standards of contemporary society; he argues with Charlie:

> One isn't *allowed* to commit [adultery] these days, it's stopped qualifying as a sin. Why, for lots of blokes in publishing it's become such a habit that half of them don't even enjoy it ... That's all that's meant by a permissive society now ... (47)

Most importantly, Peter's pose is a rearguard attempt to struggle against his suppressed realization that he is really like Charles. They have based their lives and relationship on a lie. Peter has told Charles about affairs he never actually had, for the only reason that Charles wanted Peter to live out his own fantasies. They are both all relationships and no self (77). The peak of Peter's self-revelation is reached when he confesses: "All these years I've sneered at you for practising what I was ashamed to realise in myself" (79).

After the 'trilogy,' Mr. Gray must have noticed that he was slipping into a formula and that he had exhausted the thematic potentials inherent in either *Butley* or *Otherwise Engaged*. Consequently, he applied his energy to a different venture. As if following Davina, he wrote a play on "Major Bloody Barttlelot." But to suggest that he did so after realising he was falling prey to his own thematic mannerisms is not quite correct, as he began work on the play in 1971, when *Butley* was being produced and the plays of the middle period were occupying his mind. The "Author's Note" informs us that Tony Gould supplied the idea. Having planted in Simon Gray's mind something that promised to be potential matter for a play, Tony Gould left him to struggle, on and off, for seven years with what finally was presented at the Globe Theatre, on 22 February 1978, as *The Rear Column* under the direction of, again, Harold Pinter.[23]

The jacket-note declares that *The Rear Column* and *Molly* "mark a new departure for Simon Gray as a playwright." As with the previous assertion about Mr. Gray turning his hands to other matters after the middle period, this contention is true, and at the same time it is open to contradiction. *The Rear Column* is different from the plays which we have dealt with so far in that it is based on an historical event and as a semi-documentary seeks to express concerns which have no parallels in the other pieces. If pressed to single out the major conflict in *The Rear Column* in abstract terms, one could argue that the play is about blind compliance with military orders *versus* the necessity to disregard these orders on humanitarian grounds; or: the conflict of two kinds of responsibilities — the responsibility to military instructions *versus* the responsibility to common sense; military honour *versus* humaneness. Like *The Caine Mutiny, The*

Rear Column deals with the obligation to humanity of a handful of officers to take a stand against their paranoid superior. What makes the claim that the play is a new departure objectionable is that very early in his career as a playwright, Mr. Gray wrote a piece which was likewise based on an historical event. This quasi-documentary was *Death of a Teddy Bear*, screened as one of B.B.C.'s Wednesday Plays in 1967 and later adapted for the stage as *Molly*. Thus, in a sense, all subsequent works are more of a new departure than *The Rear Column*.

Whereas, to some extent at least, the play is novel in thematic respects, the compositional method is fairly reminiscent of the middle pieces, although there are occasionally more characters involved in a scene than hitherto and the scope of the relational interplay is wider than in either *Butley* or *Otherwise Engaged*. *The Rear Column* weaves its story around the historical incident concerning the rear column Stanley left behind at Yambuya base with orders to hold the fort until some recondite Arab slaver, called Tippu-Tib, would supply 600 porters so that, with the help of the 300 still at camp, 900 loads could be transported. It covers a time-span of more than one year and brings the story of Major Barttelot and his men to life in such a way that the various conflicts resulting from the interplay of the characters call forth in the viewer a discussion of moral standards. The compositional pattern is again indebted to the Freytagian scheme: Scene i serves, above all, an expository function, introducing in turn the major characters and laying down the basic dramatic situation. In addition, the scene contains the inciting event, which consists of the quarrel of Ward, Bonny, and Troup with Barttelot over the jungle provisions. Further, by way of arranging certain character constellations, *e.g.* Ward and Jameson, Bonny and Barttelot, it points at possible alliances among the men. The whole play is circular in its progression. At the beginning, Jameson refers to one of his "trips out after Stanley's departure" (1), on which occasion he traded a woman for two turtles. In III, i, he comes back from another of these forays and again he has traded a woman; this time in order that a cannibal feast could be staged. The quarrel over the correct interpretation of Stanley's instructions—in I, i—is taken up at the very end of the play, where Stanley comments on Barttelot's ludicrous assumption as to the meaning hidden in his orders. There are, worth noticing, further circular compositional patterns. Act II, scene i resembles I, i in that it too presents Troup's rebellion against Barttelot's directives. II, ii like I, ii ends in apparent reconcilement; after a joint Christmas dinner, drinking brandy and smoking cigars, the men appear to be at peace with one another. Act III, scene i refers back to the first scene of the previous acts; the conflict between Troup and Barttelot is here brought to its climax, with Barttelot refusing Troup the quinine he needs against the fever. Before the conflict is resolved, Jameson intervenes; he gives Troup his ration of quinine, and, in the way of a last minute hope, brings the news about the possible delivery of the 600 porters within the next month. III, ii offers the 'catastrophe.' Through Jameson's cannibal feast, which in a macabre fashion is analogous to the reconciliatory dinner in the second scene of Act I and II, the main conflict, which results from the antagonism between Troup and Barttelot, is resolved. By tying the end of the play to the beginning so that the initial situation out of which all conflicts arose is thrown into a dubious light, Mr. Gray provides a semantically telling frame for a series of nightmarish acts of lunacy and inhumaneness, which are counterbalanced by Troup's endeavours to appeal to the common sense of his fellow-sufferers in order to put an end to their futile wait. The triple circuitry of the play's progression is an adequate formal expression of the futility of the whole enterprise at Yambuya.

Probably the major conflict in the play is generated by Barttelot's determination to carry out Stanley's instructions to the last letter, which means staying at Yambuya in spite of more than considerable doubts that Tippu-Tib will ever come, and the intention of Troup, in particular, not to have his life ruined by "some private misunderstanding between Mr. Stanley" (10) and the major. The issue raised by this antagonism is whether honour and obedience to military instructions is to be rated higher than the need to ignore the orders when it is only too obvious that the person responsible for enforcing the instructions is out of his wits. The play appears to come down on the side of Troup and to pronounce, albeit implicitly, judgment on the others, who fail him in his efforts to initiate the necessary steps against Barttelot. Ward, for instance, echoes the Major's conviction about honour being the only valid cause for waiting, even though he is aware, on the strength of a number of instances where Barttelot's abnormal reasoning is refuted, that Barttelot is insane; even more importantly, it is Ward's sincerest belief that "there are no noble causes in the Congo" (16). Troup and the attitude he embodies is defeated, then, by the cowardice of the others, who cover their weakness to come to a decision by empty verbalising about honour and patriotism.

The other thematic issues are in different ways also related to moral standards, be it the question of whether flogging is a justifiable way to enforce obedience among the natives, or whether Jameson, who sacrifices his life for Troup, is to be condemned because he was responsible for arranging a cannibal feast in order to make sketches of how a thirteen year old girl was eaten by a native chief. The otherwise morally sacrosanct Jameson maintains that he did nothing particularly terrible: "Good Heavens, we've flogged them to death, we've watched them die by the score, what does it matter, one nigger girl" (71). One of the questions here is whether the extraordinary situation in which the men find themselves in Yambuya has dulled their moral judgement and sense of humaneness, which is certainly the case, and turned them into brutes whose "conduct is unbecoming." It would be interesting to discuss *The Rear Column* jointly with Barry England's *Conduct Unbecoming,* if only because both pieces deal with correlative moral issues.

As most moral arguments that the play proposes are connected with certain *dramatis personae,* a brief discussion of them might not be out of place here. Bonny is an opportunist, quick at gauging the personal advantages inherent in a given situation. He respects Barttelot as his Commanding Officer because he realises that by allying himself with the Major he will gain favour. For the same motives, he readily associates himself with Stanley at the end. He is the only one to steal from Stanley's provisions (62), but does not admit the theft. Ironically, Stanley calls him "the only survivor, in the moral sense" (73). Jameson is a very interesting case. He is "a gentleman of leisure," immensely forthright, ingratiating and helpful. Bonny sizes him up correctly as the peacemaker at Yambuya (13). In almost Solomonian fashion, he suggests to Barttelot that he give the men half the provisions they demand: "That way, you'll be recognising their claim, while representing Stanley's ultimate authority" (22). Jameson abhors the flogging and votes against it; he simply cannot abide seeing someone being tortured. In a metaphorical sense, he kills the 'snake' at Yambuya, which is Troup, who, at least from Barttelot's point of view, sows the seeds of discord among the men. But Jameson appears to have two faces: he is capable of giving away his ration of quinine to save Troup, thus bringing about his own death, and at the same time, he helps to arrange a monstrous cannibal feast. The staging of the feast may be an intentional operation, an heroic move. Knowing full well that Tippu-Tib would never come with the 600 porters, Jameson can have been motivated to draw the sketches and give some of them to Tippu-Tib, who would show them to Stanley, in order to put an end to Barttelot's lunacy and the misery of their existence. His deed virtually destroys the Major, and, for all we know, causes Stanley's return to Yambuya, which in turn completes the absurd wait of the rear column. Perhaps Stanley rightly assumed that Jameson would keep a check on Barttelot (74), who asked especially for Jameson to be left with him at Yambuya, thinking he would have things his own way with the gentleman of leisure and not realising that all the while he was under his control (68).

Barttelot is strikingly reminiscent of Captain Queeg, in *The Caine Mutiny,* suffering, as does his counterpart, from paranoia. One of his *idées fixes* is that Stanley is plotting to ruin his career, "his reputation at home," through orders "some of them impossible to perform" (10). There is no gainsaying this suspicion, as Jameson corroborates the view. Barttelot refuses to give the men their provisions, because, so he asserts, Stanley did not mention provisions in his instructions. To make his stance even more preposterous, he racks his brain not only about what Stanley actually stated in his orders, but, more so, about "what he's left out!" (12). Barttelot embodies a curious mixture of an eccentric sense of military duty and of personal honour. The flaw in the Major's pose is that he is the first who wants to leave the 'sinking ship.' He plans to have himself invalided home by means of a letter written by Bonny, whom he mistakes for a doctor. At heart, Barttelot is a weakling. But Mr. Gray does not portray him in starkly negative terms. For he makes him confess his conversation with Bonny to Jameson; Barttelot argues it could have meant a solution: "I'd be out of the trap honourably and the rest of you'd be out of this trap, too, d'you see?" (23), while in one breath he contends that in reality he would never have done it (23), Bonny's letter being just something "to confirm I'd made a choice—a choice not to go back even though I'd be left off" (23). The entire plan is merely a means to prove to himself that he is not the coward he actually is.

Ward is a cynic; to Troup's remark that he thought cannibalism had been "wiped out in these parts, by Stanley himself... There was a long report in the *Times*" (7), he replies: "The local chiefs probably haven't received their copies yet" (7). From the start, he knows the exact nature of the ordeal of the rear column. It is he who characterises Tippu-Tib for what he is; he describes the hopeless situation at Yambuya as "constant sickness punctuated by floggings" (4), remarks on Stanley's actions as being motivated by egotism" (16), refutes most of Barttelot's arguments (40) and is aware of the possibility that, what with the severe conditions in which the Major and Jameson had to live, they may be "a trifle mad" (15). In spite of these insights, he falls victim to the madness bred by Barttelot, when he exceeds the flogging he has to supervise, and betrays himself to be too undecided, perhaps even too weak, to contravene the military orders and take sides with Troup. He calls himself "a patriotic Englishman" (16). With cynical undertones, he explains that he felt it was his duty to sign up with a Welsh adoptive American to rescue an eccentric German employed by the Egyptians to maintain their interests in South Equatorial Africa (16). To some extent, he is like Osborne's Jimmy Porter; he too cannot find any true causes for his energy. "There are no noble causes," he tells Jameson, "and never have been. In the Congo there are only cannibals and other natives, Arab slavers, European interests and magnificent opportunists" (16). His anger at what the world and the old good causes have come to has been transformed into impotent cynicism. But as Jameson knows, Ward is, behind the façade of his witty irreverence, a serious man, "who's not yet discovered what it is he came here to find." (17). It is he who sees to the honourable burial of Jameson, when all the others condemn Jameson for his part in the cannibal feast. In the end, overwrought by the human bestiality he experienced at Yambuya, Ward vanishes without trace.

Even though Stanley appears in person but for a brief period in the play, most of it being some kind of 'waiting for Stanley,' the treatment he receives at the hands of Mr. Gray is none too flattering. Maybe he was as recondite and despicable a character as the abominable Tippu-Tib, and a callous ego-maniac to boot. The character of Stanley is a case in point to exemplify in what way Mr. Gray has developed as a dramatist. In the previous plays, there was generally one character who, because he possessed disparate traits, could loosely be called complex, while the rest consisted of flat embodiments of particular attitudes. Now in *The Rear Column*, Simon Gray has succeeded in endowing his *dramatis personae*, down to the insignificant Stanley, with conflicting features. This method of getting away from the hitherto practised clash of stereotypes adds a new dimension to his work. To be true, in the middle period there was always the tendency of presenting the case with Ardenesque detachment, as it were, leaving it up to the spectator to draw his own conclusion. In a much more intense and unsettling manner, *The Rear Column* confronts its audience with a number of conflicting arguments, whose spokesmen are far from arousing either sympathy and understanding *or* rejection and condemnation. What has been intensified in Mr. Gray's dramatic method is the active participation and creative involvement of the perceiver. Naturally, every work of art is constituted in the communicative process which, brought about by the artist's product, takes place between the object and the perceiver. The brilliance and quality of a given work of art is in direct relation to the degree in which it engages the viewer in this communicative act. Simon Gray's work has undeniably gained in eminence, as far as this aspect is concerned. *The Rear Column* appears quite a far cry from the easy-going farces of the first period. Add to this the greater richness of subject-matter and theme of the later plays as well as the more far-reaching, universal significance of the themes, and it should be easy to subscribe to the view that Simon Gray has undergone an important change: from a farceur to a playwright who, in almost Shavian fashion, has managed to put his serious concerns across to a West End audience in a chocolate-coated guise of sheer entertainment.

It is a pity that after the high hopes which may have been aroused by *The Rear Column*, *Molly* is a disappointment. The play was originally presented at Charleston to open the New Spoleto Festival in May 1977 and was first seen in Britain at the Watford Palace Theatre in November of the same year. *Molly* is loosely based on the Alma Rattenbury case (1935), which was brought to Mr. Gray's notice, when on a train journey to Cambridge he happened upon a paperback edition of *Ten Famous Trials*. When Kenneth Trodd asked him if he would like to try his hand at a full-length television play, he did not bother to reconstruct the exact happenings, but instead took as his point of departure the effect that the dozen or so pages in the book had had on him. *Death of a Teddy Bear*, as the original piece was called, was therefore "not *about* Mrs. Rattenbury and the murder in which she was involved," so Mr. Gray informs us in the "Author's Note." Subsequently, in a number of drafts he tried to adapt the television version for the stage; the first of these attempts was made in 1972, or about then. The last variant, which was the one presented at Watford and since published in the Methuen edition, is among Mr. Gray's least satisfactory dramatic exercises.

The story of Mrs. Rattenbury seems to have remarkable dramatic potential, as the numerous dramatizations by diverse hands, including Terence Rattigan with *Cause Célèbre* (1977), show; however, Mr. Gray has not managed to put them to effective use. After a disastrous marriage, in which she suffered a miscarriage, Molly emigrated to Canada. There she was lucky to infatuate a successful businessman, a sexagenarian, called Teddy Treadley. Teddy was still dynamic at that time, though unable to satisfy Molly's sexual longings. As she "needed [her] sex" (114), she took to having affairs with other men on the sly. When the play starts, the Treadleys have just returned to England. The Teddy we come to know has been reduced to a deaf, dotty old man, who knocks back whiskey galore and keeps rabitting on about a song his wife composed in protest against seal hunting. Molly employs the seventeen-year old Oliver, as chauffeur, gardener and handyman. Seducing him, when her husband has gone for a walk, she begins another affair to satisfy her sexual appetites. For the shy, awkward, unawakened boy, who has never known "anything about any of that" (104), it is a dazzling and shocking sensation; he has fallen deeply in love with Molly, who considers him a mere functionary in her zest for sex. When Teddy, having been warned by the companion-housekeeper, Eve, about the goings-on, fires Oliver, the boy in a fit of outrage, fostered by jealousy, stabs Teddy to death. Molly takes the deed upon herself and thus shields her lover; she is put on trial, sent to jail, but eventually set free after Eve has disclosed the whole truth and Oliver is convicted and hanged.

The play clearly strives to investigate the psychological motives for Molly's behaviour as well as to deal with the effect that her endeavours to meet her sexual needs have on the true victim of her doings: Oliver. And this is precisely where Mr. Gray's attempt goes wrong. The character of Molly is a disaster. Her desperation, which is the first of her character traits we are presented with—"She . . . stares around her with an air of desperation" (81)—is never fully explained. The only reason offered to the viewer's rationale is that she is in desperate need of a lover. Her aversion to killing, which led to the anti-seal hunting song and which finds expression in her remark: "You see, I hate anything being killed by people ... " (105) is another of the loose ends Mr. Gray is unable to tie up into an acceptable character study. Her entreaty that Oliver should forthwith refrain from shooting rabbits is plain silly and, on top of that, wholly unserviceable to the play's thematic interest. For it is difficult to see how the anti-killing attitude winds up with the killing of Teddy and her shielding of Oliver. Surely she does not take the deed upon herself because she cannot stand a killing. Probably the greatest mystery involves the theme of childishness that we are made to believe permeates the play, when, in fact, it does not. We may be inclined to interpret Molly's excessive strategy of offences and apologies, which she practises with great success on Eve, as a trifle childish, but then we are left without any clear evidence as to why she is childish. Her disastrous marriage cannot be a reason; perhaps it is an intrinsic character blemish, or Molly has never grown up. One factor that contradicts the childishness motif is that she accepts full responsibility for the murder by covering up for Oliver. Molly is a highly strung creature and again her maxim: "Because if we didn't lie to people we love and live with, we wouldn't be able to love and live with them. See." (103), reads childish, at least idiosyncratic, but it is too eccentric to ring true. Her attempt to explain the events in her household by asserting: "We're all children in this house, all of us. That's what caused it, you see" (132) fails to convince. Teddy is surely not childish; he may be deaf, impotent and senile, but not necessarily childish. Eve is all but childish, she is a mother-figure, who has grown severe because no-one ever asked her to marry him so that she could have children of her own; thus she looks upon the Treadleys as her child-substitutes. Molly's ineffably sad story of her failed marriage (115) is ill-equipped to account for her sexual longings; it simply does not, in any sense, justify her outcry: "I need my sex" (114). Of course, the dramatic substance is of a high explosive character, especially the effect of her sexual ravishing of Oliver. If Mr. Gray had wanted to exploit this effect more fully and focus his attention on it, he would have had to write quite a different play; in the present form, we are moved but slightly by Oliver's desperation.

Desperation also seems, at times, to have been one of the determining factors behind Mr. Gray's creative activities, the desperation caused by the fact that a playwright is constantly in need of ideas potent enough for new plays. Most of the middle plays bear witness to Mr. Gray's predicament, and so does *Molly*. If Mr. Gray were not earning his living as a professional teacher, many of his dramatic pieces, notably those he wrote for television, would tempt one to categorise them as pot-boilers. Whether he is able to offer us a theatrical experience which can compare with *Otherwise Engaged* or even surpass the thematic originality as well as the compositional mastery of this play, is a question which, of course, the future will have to decide. *The Rear Column* may be seen as an effort in this direction; the issues it raises are not without interest, but the play does not cause profound reverberations in our minds. At present, it can only be hoped that *Molly* was not Simon Gray's swan song.

NOTES

1. R. Morley (ed.), *Robert Morley's Book of Bricks*, (London: Weidenfeld and Nicolson, 1978), p. 121.

2. The numbers in brackets refer to the following editions of Simon Gray's plays: *Wise Child* (London: Faber, 1967); *Dutch Uncle* (London: Faber, 1969); *Spoiled* (London: Methuen, 1971); *Butley* (London: Methuen, 1971); *Otherwise Engaged* (London: Methuen, 1975); *Dog Days* (London: Methuen, 1976); *The Rear Column and other Plays* (incl. *Molly*) (London: Methuen, 1978). Mr. Gray's most recent piece, *Close of Play* (London: Methuen, 1979), to be staged at the National Theatre under Harold Pinter, was published after the present article was completed.

3. B. Levin, "A Powerful Dose of Guilty Passions," *The Times* (29 October 1978), p. 39.

4. O. Kerensky, *The New British Drama. Fourteen Playwrights Since Osborne* (London: Hamilton, 1977), p. 143.

5. Cf. J. R. Taylor, *The Second Wave* (London: Methuen, 1971).

6. O. Kerensky, *op. cit.* pp. 132–144.

7. S. N. Blaydes, "Literary Allusions as Satire in Simon Gray's *Butley*," *Midwest Quarterly*, XVIII (July 1977), pp. 374–391.

8. "Interview with Ian Hamilton," *The New Review*, III (January–February 1977), pp. 39–46; "Simon Gray, Author of *Butley*, Talks to *Plays & Players*," *Plays & Players*, XIX, p. 2, (August 1972), p. 33; "Complex Simon," *The Observer* (7 September 1975), p. 7.

9. Letter from Arnold Wesker (10 August 1978).

10. Not in 1935 as the anonymous writer of "Complex Simon" stated in his *Observer*-article.

11. Cf. "Complex Simon."

12. "Simon Gray, Author of *Butley*, Talks to *Plays & Players*."

13. R. Barker, "Simon Gray," in: J. Vinson (ed.), *Contemporary Dramatists* (London, New York: Macmillan and Co., 1977), p. 316.

14. R. Barker, *op. cit.*, p. 316.
15. "Simon Gray, Author of *Butley,* Talks to *Plays & Players.*"
16. O. Kerensky, *op. cit.*, p. 137.
17. Cf. R. Imhof, *Harold Pinters Drametechnik* (Bonn: Bouvier, 1976), *passim.*
18. Cf. R. Imhof, *op. cit.*, pp. 89–125.
19. Cf. R. Imhof, *op. cit.*, pp. 137–194.
20. B. Henrichs, "Ein Erfolgsstück. Warum"?, *Die Zeit* (4 February 1977), p. 30; my translation.
21. J. R. Taylor, *"Otherwise Engaged," Plays & Players,* XXIII, 1 (October 1975), p. 22.
22. K. Tynan, "Withdrawing with Style from the Chaos," *The New Yorker* (19 December 1977), p. 82.
23. Tony Gould has recently published his own version of Stanley's rear column: *In Limbo, The Story of Stanley's Rear Column* (London: Hamish Hamilton, 1979).

Division and Unity in David Storey

PHYLLIS R. RANDALL

David Storey is one of those rarities, a novelist and a playwright. Moreover, he has been successful as both, as attested by five awards for his six novels and seven awards for the eleven plays that have been produced. Despite this generic division, however, all of his writings are of a piece. It is instructive to examine both this unity and this division in Storey for the light that can be shed on Storey as a playwright.

Many have noted that David Storey's novels and plays frequently deal with the same themes, backgrounds, and activities, sometimes even with the same characters and incidents. The accompanying chart of Storey's works that have been released for publication shows some but by no means all of the connections between his works.[1] Some connections are close enough in theme and background or details of characters and incidents to justify labeling certain works as pairs—for example, *This Sporting Life* and *Flight into Camden*, or *Saville* and *In Celebration*. Some are not exactly pairs but have close connections, nevertheless. *Radcliffe* and *The Contractor*, for instance, are connected because of the appearance of Ewbank, a peripheral character in the novel, as a central character in the play. Other connections are more tenuous. *This Sporting Life* and *The Changing Room*, for example, share a naturalistic look at professional rugby, but are otherwise very different.

The chart shows also that Storey's works fall fairly readily into two main groups. The first, which includes the novels *This Sporting Life*, *Flight into Camden*, *Radcliffe*, and *Saville*, and the plays *The Changing Room*, *The Contractor*, *In Celebration*, and *The Farm*, are all concerned with— among other themes which vary from work to work—the disintegration of the family. In the first two published novels, where the theme is less central, the protagonists, who have broken away from the stifling atmosphere of their puritanical, working-class parental home, find it impossible to establish their own family unit. *Radcliffe* and *Saville*, both longer, more ambitious works, do centrally reveal the disintegration of a family, the Radcliffes to madness and obliteration of ancestral home (accompanied by rapes, murders, and suicides), and the Savilles, more quietly, to physical removal of son Colin, the central pin of the family (accompanied by arguments, lying, and defiance of standards of parental morality). The family of the plays may be a literal one, as the Ewbanks of *The Contractor* and the Slatterys of *The Farm,* or an artificial "family" created by society, as the rugby team of *The Changing Room* and the tent crew of *The Contractor.* In all these works, however, though there may be some moments of unity (the disparate individuals of the rugby team unite to play and win a game, those of the tent crew to raise a tent, the emphasis or the concluding point of view is on the disintegration, the breaking apart of the family.

The second major group, allied to the first in a number of ways, is united by a focus on the theme of the disintegration of the individual personality, often to madness.[2] Since that theme was latent in the first two novels and explicit in *Radcliffe,* the novels themselves are connected; J. R. Taylor has noted, for example, that *Flight into Camden* and *Pasmore* are virtually the same story told from different perspectives.[3] While the first concentrates on Margaret Thorpe's attempts to build a family, the latter concentrates on a person like her partner, whose disintegrated personality makes family building impossible. Both *Pasmore* and *A Temporary Life* were parts of a projected long novel, so they might even be considered a pair, although it should be noted that Storey has stated that *A Temporary Life* is a "transposed" section while *Pasmore* was lifted whole.[4] *A Temporary Life* is paired with *Life Class* in setting (an art school), in a repeated character (the headmaster, called Wilcox in the novel, Foley in the play), in the repetition of a key incident (the exchange of urine specimens for objets d'art in the office of the headmaster), and in the nature of the central characters (disenchanted art teachers who live in a limbo of inaction). Neither Colin Freestone *(A Temporary Life)* nor Allott *(Life Class)* offers much resistance to life's buffeting. Nor do the inmates presented in *Home* (Freestone's wife is also in a mental institution), who have had encounters with life which were meager and fruitless and who have found security at last in insanity. *The Restoration of Arnold Middleton* belongs in this grouping, sharing with *Pasmore* and *A Temporary Life* a teacher protagonist, who, like Pasmore, is on the verge of insanity. It does have one important difference from the rest of the works, however; Arnold Middleton does at last fight back and at the end of the play gives evidence that his refuge will not be insanity but a coping with the world. It is interesting to note that this is Storey's first play and an early work.

On the entire chart, only *Cromwell,* Storey's one attempt at a drama with a political statement, is unconnected to the other works. Perhaps not incidentally, Storey now finds that play a "disaster."[5] Though puritanism is pervasive in Storey, *Cromwell* is outside the themes, activities, and background material that connect the other works.[6]

One other way in which Storey's works are connected is that they are, while not precisely autobiographical, heavily reliant on the circumstances and activities of Storey's own life. Hence many of his writings include a Yorkshire and/or coal-mining background (all of the novels plus *In Celebration, The Contractor, The Changing Room,* and *The Farm*). In particular, they present working-class parents ambitious for their children, especially through education, and, consequently, guilt-ridden children trying to please but feeling more and more alienated *(Flight into Camden, Pasmore, A Temporary Life, Saville, In Celebration, The Contractor,* and *The Farm)*. Moreover, characters tend to occupy the kinds of jobs in Storey's own background—teacher *(Flight into Camden, Pasmore, A Temporary Life, Saville, In Celebration, The Restoration of Arnold Middleton, The Farm, Life Class)*; rugby player *(This Sporting Life, The Changing Room)*; tent raiser *(Radcliffe, The Contractor)*; and farm laborer *(Saville)*.

The major underlying source of all this evidence of oneness in his writing is, paradoxically, the division Storey has felt in himself. He has referred to this division many times in interviews, mentioning that his life "has always been contrary,"[7] and that he "lives Left and thinks Right."[8] In his Introduction to the 1968 edition of *This Sporting Life*,[9] he traced the origins of this awareness of division to his growing-up years when he lived at the edge of a coal-mining town with one view toward the colliery and the other toward the Pennines, making him aware of the split between the intentions of nature and the intentions of man. Even that early, however, he was aware of a similar split in himself. He liked to be with people but was happiest when alone painting pictures or writing poems. When guilt at trying to withdraw from his coal-miner father's values made him sign on as a rugby player, there was a still more dramatic split between his life as an art student during the week and a professional rugby player during the weekend. This division, the crucial one in his life, he has explained fully in "Journey Through a Tunnel," published some eighteen years ago in *The Listener* (1 August 1963, pp. 159–61). After turning down a chance to enter Reading University in order to enroll in the Wakefield Art School, he won a scholarship to the Slade School of Art at the University of London. At the time he was still under contract as a rugby player for Leeds. This meant that every Friday, after a week of art classes, he had to catch a train for Leeds in order to make the game that weekend. During his regular four-hour trip he thought

> of the life I was leaving behind me, that of an art student in
> London, at the Slade, enjoying a freedom that had exceeded my
> greatest dreams; and...of the life to which I was now returning,

the north of England, the West Riding, the very place from which, only a few months before, I had escaped with a relief that was beyond any measuring. ... I seemed, through these two activities, to be trying to resolve two sides of my temperament which were irreconcilable—the courtship of a self-absorbed, intuitive kind of creature with a hard, physical, extroverted character: the one the very antithesis of the other. (p. 160)

This split, Storey saw, was made all the more intolerable because the part associated with the hated northern end of the journey, the football end, was reinforced by the mores of Yorkshire, specifically West Riding, an "intensely and even obsessively puritan region" (p. 160), which distrusted the lone and solitary man, preferring the man in the marketplace or on the rugby team, the man in a social unit. The work ethic of the North is strong and simple: work is good and indolence is evil. But in his own particular working-class area, the coal-mining region, Storey observes that the ethic is amended to "physical work is good, and mental work is evil" (p. 160), with mental work being anything that is done from a sitting position. The artist, then, is viewed not just with suspicion "but with condemnation" (p. 160).

In order to "accommodate the two extremes of this northern, physical world and its southern, spiritual counterpart" (p. 160), Storey began to takes notes, to keep a journal of his thoughts as he made the London-Leeds trip. Those notations eventually led to his first two novels, one in which he tried to isolate the northern, physical temperament, what he came to think of as the masculine temperament, in the character of rugby-player Arthur Machin in *This Sporting Life*, and the other in which he isolated the southern, spiritual temperament, the feminine one, in the character of secretary Margaret Thorpe in *Flight into Camden*. He had found a way to survive the journey through the tunnel. As he put it, "those four hours during which I inhabited no place, no time, and in which there was no meaning, could in fact be given a structure and a purpose—that of the novels themselves" (p. 161). To Storey, then, the novels are "like acts of despair. A drowning man cries out and begins to swim: I find that, metaphorically in the same darkness and distress, I began to write novels" (p. 161).

It would be impossible to overestimate this central division in Storey's life. It gave him not only the impetus to switch from painting to writing as his creative outlet, but also the major theme which unites all of his work— the struggle to make life work on both the external and the internal levels. Hence the two major divisions of his works shown on the chart, one group concentrating on the dissolution of the interior self and the other on the dissolution of the social unit of which the self is a part. It is the integration of these contrarieties that is the goal of Storey's long-planned definitive novel, of which *Pasmore* and *A Temporary Life* were excerpts and the first three novels preliminary skirmishes. Indeed, J. R. Taylor speculates that "the battle" between inner and outer lives is the essential of Storey's creativity.[10]

The point to be made here, however, is that this acknowledged division has had two noteworthy mutations that bear on Storey as a writer of plays. The central division between the exterior and the interior self was bridged originally when Storey turned to novel-writing, an action which he found a more "social" activity than painting pictures. So he gave up painting as a profession, turning to it now only in moments of despair.[11] But play-writing involves even more "social" activity than novel-writing, and the first mutation can be seen in the fact that Storey writes in both genres. Just as the dichotomy once was seen as a division between northern and southern, between "hard, physical, extroverted" and "self-absorbed, intuitive," now there is a split between novelist and playwright. The former is the isolated, solitary figure who broods above the page; the latter is the one who enjoys rehearsals and works closely with the director, who says that "at least the plays ... take me out of that writing cubicle."[12] But the ramifications of this familiar division between the solitary and the social halves now differ from those of the original dichotomy. This time it is the novel-writing which seems to be associated with the northern terminus. Storey has said that when he first began to write he consciously adopted his father's mining hours as his own working hours.[13] Still today, he says, "I sit down to eight hours of slog a day and do a shift of prose."[14] If the novel-writing is the work of solid, day-by-day hard labor, it is the playwriting which is the fun, the "holiday" as he has called it.[15] Now the dichotomy lines up the work ethic of the northern temperament with the novel-writing, and the play-writing, which has aspects of a social activity also deemed desirable by the same northern ethic, comes without effort, seems indeed intuitive, a characteristic of the southern terminus. For the plays are written quickly, usually in no more than five days. Furthermore, Storey claims that he is not in control of the impulse for creating plays. That impulse (he calls it a "magical process"[16]) strikes suddenly. As he explains it, "The plays just pop out of their own accord."[17] When he sits down consciously to write a play, as sometimes he has tried to do, the results are, to use his own words, "an absolute mess."[18] This is not to suggest that Storey fails to rewrite or alter his original texts. He has spoken of the cuts made in *The Contractor* in rehearsals, for example. Nevertheless, the original version came quickly and as a whole. In the case of *The Contractor*, most of the cuts were restored by opening night.[19]

So the first mutation of the original division produced not only a

PHYLLIS R. RANDALL

playwright but also a new division between the conscious writer in day-by-day control of his material and the unconscious, intuitive writer from whom material seems to flow unexplained and unbidden. The former produces novels, the latter plays. It is tempting to speculate that one of the reasons Storey considers himself a novelist who happens to write plays and not the other way around, despite the fact that he feels there is more potential in plays than in novels,[20] is his own deep-rooted distrust of "easy" work compared to "hard," a legacy of his puritan background.

Considering such a central split, virtually a personal and artistic schizophrenia, it is surely not a coincidence that a number of Storey's novels and plays come in pairs. Already noted in the conscious pairing of the first two novels, but it is the pairing of novels with plays which not only gives evidence of a second mutation but also reveals a reason for the strong irony of the plays.

What Storey is doing often in these pairings is looking at the same themes from different points of view, from different ends of the tunnel, as it were. "I like to work the same thing over from different angles...it's a bit like Cézanne or someone painting the same thing over and over again in different versions."[21]

It is not just that he uses the same themes, however. His 1976 novel, *Saville*, is paired with his play of nine years earlier, *In Celebration*, but these works share a great deal more than theme. In both there are three sons of a coal miner and his wife. In both, a son with artistic aspirations who is alienated from his environment is the central focus. His name is Colin in the novel and Andrew in the play, but even the names reappear. In the novel Colin's older brother is named Andrew, while his two younger brothers are Stephen and Richard. In the play, Andrew's younger brothers are named Stephen and Colin. In the play the Shaws are the family examined; in the novel a family called Shaw are the neighbors of the central family, the Savilles. In each family a first-born son dies (or has died) unexpectedly of a pneumonia-like disease, and the mother has attempted suicide early in the marriage. In each work the central figure is jealous of the attention given to another son and is bitter about both parents pushing him via education into a world he finds uncongenial, a world which his parents themselves do not admire. Colin Saville attacks his father by saying, "The job I end up with you say you despise" (p. 402),[22] while Stephen Shaw agrees with his brother Andrew that their father has "raised us to better things which, in his heart—my dad—he despises..." (p. 86).[23] Both lines are very close to Storey's own words in an interview with Mel Gussow: "When I was 17 or 18, I began to realize that my father was educating us for a society that he himself despised."[24]

258

All of these "borrowings" (and there are others, including a bomb shelter incident, a teacher's visit to the home, and home lessons from a father who has to learn the material to teach it, whether Latin conjugations or decimals) are not so strange as they might seem at first glance when we recognize Storey's working habits. As a day-by-day laborer at novel-writing, one who had intermittent bursts of playwriting (which often come when the novel in progress bogs down), Storey is usually several books and plays ahead of his publishers and producers. According to an interview published in 1977, he had "at least another half dozen" novels in hand and only about half of his twenty plays had been produced.[25] In the *Saville–In Celebration* pairing it was the novel *Saville* that he began first in 1965, but after getting to the father/son sledding scene, it bogged down and he abandoned it. Two years later he wrote *In Celebration*—in three days— then picked up *Saville* again, wrote one hundred or so pages, and then again abandoned it. Finally, in what for Storey is a burst of speed in novel-writing, akin to his pace and inspiration in playwriting, he picked it up yet again in 1974 and finished it a year later.[26]

The difference in Storey's handling of such similar incidents, charac- ters, and themes is revealing. One notable difference is that there is dif- fused focus on the alienation theme in the genre in which we might expect it to be sharp, that is, in the play. It is Andrew, literate and aggressive, who expresses anger and bitterness; his declared aim in returning for his par- ents' anniversary party is revenge against them. And it is the silent Steven, the crying brother, who exemplifies despair. The third brother, a labor relations negotiator, has bought the dream of materialistic success and remains oblivious to any problems in adjusting to middle-class professional life. In the novel, however, our focus is solely on Colin Saville, who is bitter, angry, and despairing. Neither of his younger brothers has similar feelings. Quite the contrary, for the next younger is very much an Arthur Machin type, a born rugby player, all body and no spirit, full of action, not introspection. So it is the more recently completed work, the novel, which more overtly concerns the split talked about in the 1963 "tunnel" article than does the play.

Another difference needs to be pointed out. Colin Saville lashes out verbally at both parents, lashes out physically at his hated younger brother, and, at the end of the novel, leaves his home and its limiting environment. The play is strikingly different. The despairing, crying Steven, who has lost what Andrew calls his "re-vitalizing spirit," makes no accusations, while the vital, accusing Andrew directs most of his venom to his brothers, some as well to his uncomprehending father, and none at all to his mother, whom he considers the source of the family's problems. At the end of the play, each brother will go back to what he was doing before it began. The threatened confrontation with the mother will never take place, and she can go on, like Meg at the end of Pinter's *The Birthday Party,* believing that she was "the belle of the ball."

It is the novel, then, which has action and open conflicts, and the play which has no action to speak of (three sons come home to take their parents out to an anniversary dinner party) and which *avoids* conflict. This reversal of what we might expect in the handling of the same material and themes in the two genres is not unusual in Storey, but typical. The novels tend to contain dramatic confrontations of a man (or woman in *Flight into Camden*) seeking accommodation—within himself (*This Sporting Life, Pasmore*), with another (*Radcliffe, Flight into Camden*), or sometimes even with society at large (*A Temporary Life, Saville*). The sought-for change is almost always a psychic necessity. The plays, on the other hand, tend to reveal the acceptability of stasis—not the desirability, but the acceptability—even by the characters who are echoes of the ones in novels. As the now spiritless Steven says, "The world's as real as anything else; you don't compromise yourself by taking part in it." Since the "real world" is more often lived around an event than during the event itself, "taking part" means accommodation to mundane, day-to-day living: life before and after a wedding, not during the wedding itself; before and after a family celebration, or a game, or the homecoming of a prodigal son with his fiancée, not the celebration, the game, or the homecoming itself. In terms of the themes of *In Celebration,* this acceptability of the real world means that since revenge will not change parents, they might just as well be tolerated the way they are. Once educated for life in the professional middle class, one finds the values of the working class no longer obtain, so one might just as well live with whatever values he can and forget the rest. Despair is better than nothing, for despair at least may lead to art.

The second mutation of Storey's art, then, is that the conscious work is still dominated by the desire to bridge the original split, to integrate the contraries, while the "unconscious" work is a reflection of the acceptance of life on life's own unhappy terms, of the impossibility of integration. The plays contain a subconscious, an intuitive, feeling that the world goes on despite the collapse of an integrated personality or of a family, despite the collapse of standards of education or of art, or even despite the collapse of empires—all ideas that have been suggested in various Storey plays.

Therefore, uniting to play a game of rugby is a statement of faith in a life that amounts to the dust the janitor sweeps under the rug at the end of *The Changing Room,* just as uniting to set up a tent is, even though the tent will be ruined (*The Contractor*). And attempting to reach out and touch each other's lives, even if the attempts fail, is worthwhile for the inmates of

Home. For all their night-school courses and plans and radical ideas, those in the Slattery family of *The Farm* do not improve or even change, and yet the bickering and barren family is held together by threads as ephemeral as the steam from the porridge that brings them together at the end. And Allot of *Life Class* can keep what little integrity he has left despite being buffeted by whatever life dishes out—his wife leaving him, the rape of the model in his class, his firing. In each case, so long as there is a moment of unity in the disintegration-of-the-family plays or a modicum of self respect and integrity in the disintegration-of-the personality plays, then life is acceptable on whatever terms life sets. With that acceptance, there is no longer any need to turn oneself into an ape (like Arthur in *This Sporting Life*), or return to the stifling womb (like Margaret in *Flight into Camden*), or murder and go mad (like Leonard in *Radcliffe*), or become a collector of refuse (like Colin in *A Temporary Life*). There is not even a need to run away to the promise of the South (like Colin in *Saville*).

This is not to suggest that Storey has never consciously thought about life's impassiveness in the face of an individual's problems in coping. Indeed, he has incorporated his own ability to outlive his felt disintegration in the rewriting of *The Restoration of Arnold Middleton,* his first play, which went through many re-writings and therefore does not qualify to fit into the category "intuitive."[27] In the original version produced in Edinburgh, Arnold Middleton commits suicide; in the final London production, Storey changed the ending to have him recover. As a reflection of Storey's outliving his own despair the London ending is the truthful one, though Storey now claims that the original ending was "more logical and honest."[28]

There is also one novel which, like *In Celebration,* lacks dramatic confrontations. *Pasmore* ends with the protagonist back with his family, back at his university job, but unsure whether his life is better or worse. "Yet something had changed. It was hard to describe. He had been on a journey. At times it seemed scarcely credible that he had survived. He still dreamed of the pit and the blackness. It existed all around him, an intensity, like a presentiment of love, or violence; he found it hard to tell."[29]

The difference, however, is that both Arnold Middleton and Pasmore engage in a struggle with their interior demons, a struggle which Storey feels is virtuous. "There is no choice, for all of us there is, I believe, the obligation to try to bring the pieces together, at least in touching distance."[30] That, of course, is the goal of his long-planned novel. It is as well the attitude which separates him from R. D. Laing, the psychiatrist author of *The Divided Self,* with whom he otherwise shares many ideas.[31] In reviewing Laing's *The Politics of Experience* and *The Bird of Paradise,* Storey finds Laing's descriptions of man and the world mutually destroying each other true but the treatise incomplete. What Laing should do, Storey declares, is show how to come back and live in the world in spite of the mutual destruction.[32]

Whether or not Storey as playwright is consciously aware of the incongruity of himself as the despairing artist of the "tunnel" article writing plays about acceptability, certainly it is true that the prevailing tone in his plays, as William Free has noted, is ironic.[33] Though the deeply felt schism is still the source of his more recently published novel, what seems to have happened is that some of those attributes of the once hated northern end of the journey, deeply rooted in Storey's psyche, are so much a part of him that when he writes from inspiration—that is, when he writes plays—the attributes are seen as acceptable, some, for example work, even desirable. Though there is irony in *In Celebration*—the clear-sighted Steven is too much blinded by his own tears to finish his book on the ills of modern society; and Andrew, who rails about the "revitalizing spirit," paints pictures only of geometric figures, "not a sign of human life in them," he declares (p. 26)—the irony of the despairing artist writing plays of acceptability is perhaps strongest of all in *The Contractor*. Despite all the sources of real and potential conflict in that play—lazy workmen, a wary father/son relationship—work is accomplished. The lazy, quarrelling English and Irish workmen, full-witted and half-witted, unite long enough to put up a tent. And the Ewbank family, separated by education, geography, age, and goals, do unite and decorate the tent. Those moments of unity through work are dramatic both visually (the erecting and decorating of the tent) and emotionally (the family's dancing to the music which only they can hear, the workmen's peace over cake and whiskey). But to what avail? The "art" that each group has structured and worked for, the tent and the decorations, are in ruins before our eyes in the last act. The workmen go back to bickering. The members of the family separate and go their own ways. Even the Storey surrogate, potential-artist Paul, far from being an artist-savior figure, is less forceful and dynamic than his crude, drunken, materialistic father. And though the tent contractor Ewbank is unhappy with his university-graduate son's joblessness and constant wandering, it is this same crude, materialistic Yorkshireman who does not begrudge his son either the money that supports his travels or the freedom to turn down the lucrative family business.

So the division between physical north and spiritual south found in most of the novels, including the most recent, is dimmed in the plays by irony. In the genre which seems to come from "inspiration," his plays, Storey has undercut the value of the spirit—London, freedom, art school, intuition—and built up the value of the physical—Leeds, puritanism, rugby, work. It is as if, having lived within the tunnel so long, Storey has come to recognize not only some of the values inherent in the once-hated Northern end of the tunnel but also some of the limitations of the Southern. Where once one end held promises, now a tenuous balance between the two seems all that is possible. It is a balance that obtains as well between novels and plays, a division with its own kind of unity.

NOTES

1. Two plays have been produced but, as of this writing, not published; *Sisters*, which opened for a three-week run at the Manchester Royal Exchange Theatre September 12, 1978; and *Early Days*, which opened April 11, 1980, at the National Theatre. Also not included on the chart is *Mother's Day*, which opened September 22, 1976, at the Royal Court in London. It was published with *Home* and *The Changing Room* by Penguin Books in 1978, after the chart was compiled.

2. Albert Kalson investigates the madness theme in "Insanity and the Rational Man in the Plays of David Storey," *Modern Drama*, 19 (1976), pp. 111–28.

3. *David Storey* (London: Longman Group, 1974), p. 11. Taylor points out as well the interconnections between these two novels and *The Restoration of Arnold Middleton, In Celebration,* and *The Farm.*

4. John Higgins, "David Storey: Night and Day," *Times*, 16 Sept. 1976, p. 13, col. 4.

5. Frances Gibb, "Why David Storey Has Got It in for Academics, the Critics and 'Literary Whizz-Kids,'" *Times Higher Education Supplement*, 4 Feb. 1977, p. 9, col. 4.

6. See John J. Stinson, "Dualism and Paradox in the 'Puritan' Plays of David Storey," *Modern Drama*, 20 (1977), pp. 131–43, for many insights into puritanism in Storey's plays.

7. Philip Norman, "World Without End," Sunday *Times*, 26 Sept. 1976, p. 32, col. 4.

8. Michael Billington, "Making Life Work on Two Levels," *Times*, 4 April 1970, p. 21, col. 3.

9. (London: Longmans, Green & Co.), pp. vii–x.

10. Taylor, p. 6.

11. Norman, p. 32, col. 5.

12. Higgins, p. 13, col. 5.

13. Ibid.

14. Mel Gussow, "Talk with David Storey, Playwright and Novelist," *New York Times Book Review*, 28 Aug. 1977, p. 11, col. 3.

15. Mel Gussow, "To David Storey, a Play Is a Holiday," *New York Times*, 20 April 1973, p. 14, col. 4.

16. Gussow, "Talk with David Storey," p. 11, col. 3.

17. Gibb, p. 9, col. 5.

18. Gussow, "Talk with David Storey," p. 11, col. 3.

19. Ronald Hayman, "Conversation with David Storey," *Drama*, No. 99 (Winter 1970), p. 48.

20. Gibb, p. 9, col. 4.

21. Victor Sage [Interview], *The New Review, 3*, No. 31 (1976), p. 64.

22. All references to *Saville* are from the 1976 edition published in London by Jonathan Cape.

23. All references to *In Celebration* are from the 1969 Grove Press edition.

24. "Talk with David Storey," p. 29, col. 2.

25. Gibb, p. 9, col. 4.

26. Details of the writing of *Saville* from personal communication, 2 Dec. 1977.

27. Frank Cox, "Writing for the Stage," *Plays and Players* (Sept. 1967), pp. 40–42ff., relates the history of how the play was brought to production.

28. Taylor, p. 15.

29. (Avon Books, 1972), p. 190.

30. "Introduction," *This Sporting Life* (London: Longmans, Green & Co., 1968), p. x.

31. Anita Guiton notes that the homecoming-from-the mental hospital-scene in *A Temporary Life* reads like a passage from Laing's *Sanity, Madness, and the Family* in "Comments on David Storey's *Pasmore* and *A Temporary Life*," *Delta*, 53 (1975), p. 20.

32. "Passionate Polemics," *New Society*, (26 January 1969), pp. 137–38.

33. "The Ironic Anger of David Story," *Modern Drama*, 16 (Dec. 1973), 307–16.

Relationships among Storey's Works

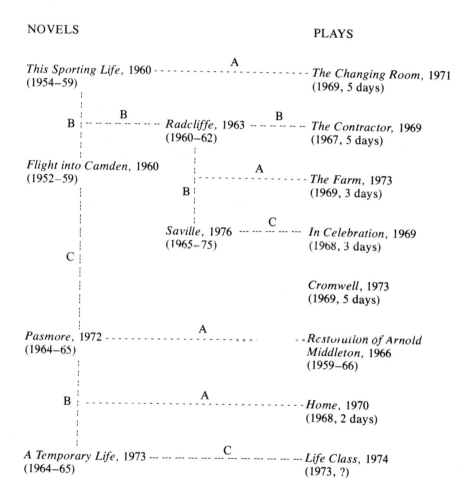

NOVELS   PLAYS

This Sporting Life, 1960 — A — *The Changing Room*, 1971
(1954–59)   (1969, 5 days)

B — B — *Radcliffe*, 1963 — B — *The Contractor*, 1969
(1960–62)   (1967, 5 days)

Flight into Camden, 1960
(1952–59)   A — *The Farm*, 1973
                B   (1969, 3 days)

Saville, 1976 — C — *In Celebration*, 1969
(1965–75)   (1968, 3 days)

C

Cromwell, 1973
(1969, 5 days)

Pasmore, 1972 — A — ·· *Restoration of Arnold*
(1964–65)   *Middleton*, 1966
                                      (1959–66)

B — A — *Home*, 1970
(1968, 2 days)

A Temporary Life, 1973 — C — *Life Class*, 1974
(1964–65)   (1973, ?)

Year after title, publication or first production date
Year(s) under title, writing dates

A line - - - - - - - some relationship
B line -- -- -- -- -- strong relationship
C line --- --- --- --- --- "paired" relationship
(All dates verified by Storey, December 1977.)

Trevor Griffiths:
Playwriting and Politics

ALBERT WERTHEIM

Trevor Griffiths is one of those rare politically committed playwrights who is able to move audiences without harranguing them, who is capable of political suasion without the self-conscious dramaturgy of Brecht, the agonizing and accusatory prefaces of Edward Bond, or the overt prog-agandizing of John Arden and Margaretta D'Arcy. As a leftist writer, Griffiths always addresses the struggle of the proletariat—frequently localized in the working class of his native Midlands—against the forces of capitalism, government and the bourgeoisie. Although some of his plays, including perhaps his two finest, *The Party*, and *Comedians*, have been written for the theatre, he frequently writes plays for television as well. Griffiths' interest in television is a realistic and pointed one, for as an exponent of the working class, he recognizes that the working class is not likely to be influenced by the drama presented for affluent playgoers in the West End or even by that presented at the Royal Court. A wide spectrum of classes, including workers, are, however, likely to see and be influenced by what they watch on the telly. In a *Plays and Players* interview, Griffiths remarked, "It's in television that I think, as a political writer, I want to be, because very large numbers of people, who are not accessible any other way, *are* accessible in television."[1] Griffiths has been writing dramatic pieces for radio, television and the stage since the late 1960s, and has begun to build an impressive body of work. As in the case of other relatively young playwrights (Griffiths was born April 1935 in Manchester), the early pieces of Griffiths may be viewed as finger exercises and it is in his more recent plays—especially *The Party* (1973), *Comedians* (1975), and *Through the Night* (1975)—that one feels the presence of a playwright of tremendous power able to use drama to convey a political message force-fully and feelingly.

Three of Griffiths' early works deal with the drama of political struggle among management, union and workers in a strike or threatened strike situation. The radio play *The Big House* (first broadcast on 10 December, 1969, BBC Radio 4), directed by Alan Ayckbourn, is an unusually effective play, for it presents a labor struggle within a Midlands factory and presents as well the interplay of a new, enlightened managerial class with an older often comically anachronistic yet still powerful class of petty industrial tyrants, who see their relationship to the men who work under them like that of commanding officers to those of lowest military rank or of slavemasters to slaves. More historical in character are the stage play *Occupations* (first produced 28 October, 1970) and *Such Impossibilities,* a television play written in 1971 but never aired. *Occupations,* called by Peter Ansorge the most successful political play of the 1968–1973 period,[2] examines the actions of Kabak, an operative of the revolutionary government in Soviet Russia, and Gramsci, a founder of the Communist Party in Italy, during the proposed occupation of the Fiat automobile factories in Turin during 1920. *Such Impossibilities* charts the involvement of Tom Mann, Secretary and agitator for the Transport Workers Federation, during the 1911 strike of the Liverpool Seamen's Union. All three dramas lucidly etch the struggle of the exploited workers in the face of big business and government.

Such Impossibilities is the most simplistic and polemical of the three plays, for it depicts an unequivocally heroic Mann, exploitive ship owners and a dastardly police force which, contrary to its agreement with the union, acts as a tool of a capitalist, management-government alliance literally bludgeoning the workers to the ground. *Occupations,* by contrast, is a far more complex play in which the title refers to the occupation of the Fiat plant by workers locked out by the owners, but refers as well to the occupations of the principal characters, their vocations and what commands their allegiance. In a moving confrontation between Kabak, the Russian agent, and Gramsci, the leader of the Italian workers, Griffiths forces his audience to consider two opposing revolutionary views. For Kabak, the workers in Turin are part of a pragmatic scheme to effect a Communist revolution in Italy. Gramsci, however, argues that his love for the workers and concern for their personal welfare precede his commitment to revolution:

> You would be wrong to see this ... love ... as the product of petit-bourgeois idealism. It is the correct, the only true dialectical relationship between leaders and led, vanguard and masses, that can ensure the political health of the new order the revolution seeks to create. Treat masses as expendable, as fodder, *during* the revolution, you will always treat them thus. (Pause) I'll tell you this, Comrade Kabak, if you see masses that way, there can be no revolution worth the blood it spills.[3]

Perhaps because of Gramsci's priorities, his workers do not finally effect a revolution but accept a settlement; and their failure, the play's closing moment suggests, helps bring about the rise of Mussolini fascism in Italy. When Gramsci's workers capitulate, Kabak reveals that his occupation is less that of advisor to an incipient Italian revolution than that of negotiator in Italy to effect a loan for Russia from Fiat in return for trade rights. What makes *Occupations* a truly political play is that Griffiths does not compel his audience to take sides but rather to see the complexities inherent in political situations. The power of industry, the precedence of immediate needs over revolutionary idealism among the workers, the humanity of Gramsci, the role of corruptible government officials, the pragmatism of Kabak and the several aspects of his mission in Italy are dramatically orchestrated by the playwright to provide a sophisticated lesson in situational politics.

With its Midlands setting and with its freedom from the limitations imposed by recreating an historical event, Griffiths' radio play *The Big House* is at once the most simplistic but the most immediately effective of his early published pieces.[4] The accents and the grievances of the factory workers in the face of exploitive industry, a factory manager with the model of a naval command for his relationship to his men, and a union leader who is the spineless tool of management create a dramatic situation more immediately recognizable than the political situation in 1920 Turin or 1911 Liverpool. One might classify *The Big House* as an agitprop radio play, for it is more polemical than political. All sympathy is with the workers and with the particular worker whose dismissal leads to unrest in the factory and whose plight is presented with a good deal of sentimentalism. The title of the play obviously refers to the factory, but "the big house" is also a cant term for a prison; and it is from this double meaning that the play is forged. What is important in *The Big House* for charting Griffiths' development is his attention to the specifics of working conditions in England, and more importantly, to life among the working classes. It is between this interest in the contemporary exploited British proletariat and an interest in historical politics that Griffiths' later plays seem to move.

Of his more recent plays, Griffiths' *Absolute Beginners,* a television play (broadcast 19 April 1974 by BBC TV), has most in common with the historical dramas, *Occupations* and *Such Impossibilities,* for it is a portrait of the shrewd but unfeeling pragmatism of Lenin. It is a portrait far different from the fanciful one offered by Tom Stoppard in *Travesties,* in which Lenin seems a dotty revolutionary whose schemes for returning to Russia show more imagination than sense. Griffiths' Lenin seems devoid of pity and of any concern for the personal lives and feelings of his fellow revolutionaries. Successfully effecting the revolution is Lenin's sole concern, but, the playwright tacitly implies, it was after all this unlovable, purely pragmatic politician who was the one finally able to turn ideas into reality, to direct the most significant social and political revolution of our century.

Those like Lenin, loveless but unwavering in their loyalty to revolution, are few. Those with good intentions, but who compromise, are many. Politics is more often than not fraught with compromise, and thus it is the compromisers as well as—and sometime more than—the idealists whom Griffiths examines. In seeing the dramatization of compromise the audience becomes aware of political ideals, the subversion of those ideals by the personal motivations of those in the political arena, and the inevitable confrontation of political ideals with the politically possible. Griffiths is concerned with both those who compromise and those who sell out. The idea of compromise and betrayal is present in *Occupations* but emerges with more clarity in *Sam, Sam,* a play written during 1968–1969 but not produced until February 1972. Here Griffiths describes political compromise not in an historical setting but in contemporary England. A schematic play, *Sam, Sam* juxtaposes two brothers, Sam 1 and Sam 2. The one an example of working class life with its frustrations, shabbiness but also fellowship; the other a teacher who has escaped from his working class background, who espouses leftist political ideals, but who, like Osborne's Jimmy Porter, also harbors a sadomasochistic desire for domination by his wife and, more significantly, by the monied class and bourgeois values she represents. Sam 1's description of his life is presented in the style of a stand-up comic, a foreshadowing of *Comedians*. The picture of Sam 2 in his vacillation between his working class loyalties and his bourgeois life suggests that *Sam, Sam* is an initial draft for Griffiths' first major play *The Party,* which was performed by the National Theatre (20 December 1973) and starred Laurence Olivier as an aging Trotskyite idealist and Ronald Pickup as Joe Shawcross, a dramatic portrait developed from the cartoon of Sam 2.

The Party is Chekhovian in its overall conception,[5] for it brings together a variety of tragicomic characters, all affiliated with leftist politics and the Communist Party, for a social and political gathering, a party, at the London SW 7 well-appointed home of television producer Joe Shawcross, who like Sam 2 has become affluent and largely shed his working class origins. Like Sam 2, Shawcross has a working class brother and a bourgeois wife. The play as a whole satirizes a spectrum of fashionable leftist stances among Shawcross and his intellectual friends on the night of May 10–11, 1968, the night the leftist students in Paris are mounting the barricades. *The Party* is a play about people for whom leftist party politics is simply the excuse for, ironically, an all night party in rooms hung with Hockneys and filled with expensive furniture, records, and an ample supply of drinks. Griffiths sets the tone for his bitter view of middle-class leftists, who make a travesty of party ideals, through a prologue in which an actor portraying Groucho Marx uses the text of Karl Marx as a basis for his comedy routine. The use of a comedy routine delivered by a professional comedian to evoke political consciousness harks back to the stand-up comic manner of Sam 1 and looks ahead to the subject matter of *Comedians*.

Griffiths' comment on fashionable leftism in contemporary Britain is an acid one. The radical-chic partygoers in *The Party* congregate in a room filled with material possessions and the symbols of material wealth, a bitterly ironic setting for those presumably devoted to an anti-materialist ideology. Into that room comes an alien figure, a true believer whose lifelong devotion to Marxist ideals italicizes the mere posing of Shawcross and his friends. The sixty-year old John Tagg, a disciple of Trotsky, still hoping to effect social revolution in England is a moving, tragic figure. Like Lenin in *Absolute Beginners* and like Tom Mann in *Such Impossibilities*, Tagg has sacrificed his life, his energies, his chance for family life and personal happiness for the revolutionary cause. He is not, however, tragic because he has terminal cancer and will die without seeing his dream fulfilled, but because he has misspent his time among the intellectual poseurs rather than among those people more likely to effect revolution. Among the shallow middle and upper-class leftists at Shawcross' home, Tagg has a moment of insight in which he realizes that even the leftist students, the new intellectuals, demonstrating that night in Paris will one day make their own compromise with bourgeois society. The close of Tagg's long speech in Act I is filled with both political and tragic recognition:

> The party means discipline. It means self-scrutiny, criticism, responsibility, it means a great many things that run counter to the traditions and values of Western bourgeois intellectuals ... But above all, it means deliberately severing yourself from the prior claims on your time and moral commitment of personal relationships, career, advancement reputation and prestige. And from my limited acquaintance with the intellectual stratum in Britain, I'd say that was the gravest hurdle of all to cross. ... The intellectual's problem is not vision, it's commitment. You enjoy biting the hand that feeds you, but you'll never bite it off. So those brave and foolish youths in Paris now will hold their heads out for the baton and shout their crazy slogans for the night. But it won't stop them from graduating and taking up their positions in the centres of ruling class power and privilege later on.[6]

Pointedly, Griffiths has this climactic and moving speech received not with thunderous applause or a sense of renewed commitment among the assembled group but with the tinkle of coffee cups wheeled in on a trolley by an *au paire* from Communist Czechoslovakia. The revolution in England when it comes, Griffiths implies, will not begin in London SW 7 or among the intellectuals but among the exploited working class, in their factories and in their shabby towns.

Once again Griffiths dwells on the working class leftist who sells out for bourgeois security, career and advancement in *All Good Men,* a television play produced a month (31 January 1974, BBC TV) after the opening of *The Party.* Again Ronald Pickup played a television producer this time one filming a documentary about an aged Labour politician from Manchester who has spent the better part of his life seemingly striving to better conditions among the working class. As the drama develops, it becomes clear that his life has been one of bourgeois compromises. A far more interesting television play is *Through the Night* (broadcast 2 December 1975, BBC TV), written at the same time as *Comedians* though produced afterward. In *Through the Night* as in *Comedians,* Griffiths shifts his gaze from an overtly political arena and sets his play among the working class. *Through the Night* deserves a good deal more attention than it has received and than it will receive here. Its subject matter, a working class woman's mastectomy in a national health hospital, is an unusual one particularly, so it would at first seem, for a playwright like Griffiths. On one level, it is a far more upsetting play than Peter Nichols' *The National Health* which likewise shows the dehumanization of patients by hospital staff bureaucracy. It is an indictment of a system that treats the disease without treating the patient, a form of health care that reflects no care at all for those it purports to help. On quite another level, however, the playwright's treatment of Christine Potts, whose breast is removed without her being told it will be or why it will be, and who is given no post-operative counseling, goes beyond the parameters of bio-ethics. It becomes just one aspect of the overall debilitation families like those of Christine Potts experience at the hands of the ruling class in Britain. The scene on which the play closes, a covert party held among patients in defiance of the hospital staff is, then, more than an affirmation of a human community in which individuals minister to one another; it is the first rudimentary act of social cohesion among the hospital inmates who are kept ignorant and whose organs are violated by the medical establishment. It is likewise a first rudimentary act of social cohesion among a working class depersonalized and exploited by an educated ruling class.

By far Griffiths' most significant play to date is *Comedians,* which was first performed at the Nottingham Playhouse on February 20, 1975. It marks a quantum jump from Griffiths' previous work, for it moves away from the drama of politicians and political history yet very much remains a political drama. The characters of *Comedians* are all stand-up comics, the funny men whose mission seems to be to take our minds off our worries through the escape valve of laughter. The important lesson *Comedians* teaches us, however, is that all human relationships, even those of comedian and audience, are fraught with implicit and significant political attitudes. In *Comedians* Griffiths so brilliantly probes the political nature of comedy that no member of his audience will again be able to hear a comedian or see a comedy without the acute realization that the comedy or humor heard or seen is by its very nature making a political statement as well as a concommitant statement about a comedian's implied regard for his audience.

Comedians announces its subject from the moment the play begins, for it opens with one of the most primitive of all comic gestures, scribbled graffiti, which a school caretaker is judiciously and angrily removing from a schoolroom blackboard, From the very start, then, Griffiths suggests that comic gesture, even in its primitive form, is a medium for expressing a response to the world. The play itself concerns six diverse students in a night school class for aspiring stand-up comics and their teacher, Eddie Waters. The school situation by its very nature suggests that comedy involves more than the ability to tell a joke, that there is indeed a discipline, an art, and a meaning to comedy, that there is something to teach about the nature, shape and content of a comedy routine. The night of the play is, moreover, a kind of graduation exercise, for the students will perform at a local Manchester club, where they will be seen and judged by a London talent scout. Griffiths thus sets up a series of interrelated polemics, for there are two very different examiners for the class, the teacher and the talent scout; there is the theory of the classroom and the praxis before an audience; and there is the question of truth to the comic self versus shaping truth to please the talent scout and thereby receiving the economic opportunities he can offer. Comedy and morality become, in short, conflated and inseparable issues.

The political coloration of the polemics in *Comedians* is focused in the political differences between Eddie Waters and Bert Challenor, the agent sent up from London to scout Waters' students. Challenor represents in the world of comic entertainers a political tyranny to which Eddie Waters asserts that he has failed to submit:

I never joined his ... Comedy Artists and Managers Federation, for a kick-off. They took it bad, for some reason. I didn't like what they stood for. I've been a union man all my life, it wasn't that. ... They wanted the market. ... They wanted to control entry into the game. I told 'em no comedian *(odd, particular emphasis)* worth his salt could ever 'federate' with a manager. *(Pause, sniff.)* And as far as I'm concerned no comedian ever did. (13–14)[7]

For Waters, the comedian to be a comedian must remain a free agent, free to express himself, free to transmit his comic vision of society, and free to diagnose and perhaps suggest a cure for the ills of society. Challenor's Comedy Artists and Managers Federation (CAMF) is a cartel that seeks to monopolize comedy, control it, and by extension control the comedians' comic visions. Those who have sold out, federated with a manager and subjugated themselves to CAMF, have surrendered their independence to become tools of a comedic dictatorship that keeps its subjects, the audience, in line by annihilating comedy as a heuristic medium and replacing it with comedy as a means for feeding already existing human prejudices and for promoting dull complacence with the social and political status quo. The political confrontation is, moreover, not merely hypothetical, for the aspiring comedians are members of the British working class in the Midlands. They are dock workers, delivery men and van drivers. For them success means a way out of their economic and social class. Though not all of them cognize it concretely, the comedians are given, Griffiths implies, the choice of using their talent to break through class barriers without questioning those barriers or of using their talent to examine the injustices of the class system and suggesting thereby the need for the destruction of class barriers altogether. How each comedian presents his act becomes, then, a significant political gesture.

Comedians is neatly divided into three parts: the classroom preparation, the performances, and the aftermath. The first act introduces the six students, the range of whose minds is suggested by the jokes they tell during the classroom warm-up exercises. When one of them recites a particularly obscene original limerick, Eddie Waters, in his role as teacher, takes the opportunity to hold forth on the implications of the limerick and on the proper use of comedy. The obscene but seemingly frivolous contents of the limerick contain, as the students and the audience become aware, an attitude toward humanity and, by extension, a definable political point of view. When the limerick has been recited, Waters replies with a political image: "The traitor hates the truth. The traitor distrusts the truth" (18) and "The traitor destroys the truth" (19). He proceeds to show that the humor of the limerick is engendered by misogynistic impulses as well as by deep-seated negative attitudes toward sexuality. "It's a joke," Waters explains, "that hates women *and* sex" (22). He goes on to place the limerick in the same class as jokes that stimulate laughter by merely invoking class, national and racial prejudice. Using the anti-Jewish joke as one case in point, Waters shows clearly that this sort of humor stems from precisely the identical source that brought Hitler his success and enabled him successfully to practice mass genocide. Through Waters, Griffiths thus forcefully identifies the congruence between the origins of politics and the origins of humor.

The lesson of Act One, perhaps the major lesson of the play as a whole, is one of the oldest lessons about the nature of comedy. It is that used properly comedy, like tragedy, can be a teaching device and a means for initiating change. For Griffiths and for Waters comedy that garners laughs without teaching is no comedy at all but something inherently insidious and potentially dangerous. The point at issue is the difference between comedy and entertainment, and this is what Waters attempts to teach the young men who have come to him for instructions:

> We work through laughter, not *for* it. If all you're about is raising a laugh, OK, get on with it, good luck to you, but don't waste my time ... It's not the jokes. It's what lies behind 'em. It's the attitude. A real comedian—that's a daring man. He *dares* to see what his listeners shy away from, fear to express. And what he sees is a sort of truth, about people, about their situation, about what hurts or terrifies them, about what's hard, above all, about what they *want*. ... a true joke, a comedian's joke, has to do more than with release of tension, it has to *liberate* the will and the desire, it has to change the *situation*. . . But when a joke bases itself upon a distortion—a 'stereotype' perhaps—and gives the lie to the truth so as to win a laugh and stay in favour, we've moved away from a comic art and into the world of 'entertainment' and slick success.

The italics, which are Griffiths', serve again to couple the idiom of comedy with that of politics. The point is refined as one of the students asks whether the limerick does not indeed use comedy to liberate fears, the fears of sex and of women. In replying that while the limerick liberates fear, it does not do anything to eliminate or alter that fear, Waters thus brings the notion of comedy around to the idea of comical satire as Ben Jonson, John Marston and others defined it.[8]

A good, brief working definition of comical satire can be found in Jonson's Prologue to his comedy *The Alchemist,* where he writes:

> Though this pen
> Did never aim to grieve, but better men,
> Howe'er the age he lives in doth endure
> The vices that she breeds, above their cure.
> But, when the wholesome remedies are sweet,

And in their working gain and profit meet,
He hopes to find no spirit so much diseased,
But will with such fair correctives be pleased.[9]

For Jonson and his contemporaries, as Alvin Kernan has so well explained elsewhere, the comic art and the healing art are closely allied.[10] And it is precisely that view of satire as a sanative art that informs Eddie Waters' definition of comedy as well:

We've got to make people laugh till they cry. Cry. Till they find their pain and their beauty. Comedy is medicine. Not coloured sweeties to rot their teeth with. (23)

The action of Act One makes it clear that Waters' classroom message, his definition of comedy, has its effect upon two of his students, Ged Murray and Gethin Price, both of whom proceed to tell darkly humorous anecdotes that stem respectively from the fear of fathering a mentally defective child and from the violent resentment of class prejudice among educators. Their anecdotes are Griffiths' excellent examples of the sort of comedy that leads to tears rather than to guffaws, but the sort of comedy that, at the same time, allows the teller and the audience to see objectively, and perhaps purge, shared fears and outrages. Waters' definition of comedy is, however, only one of two in *Comedians;* and the other view also has its coverts. Waters' valedictory address on comedy is countered well by Challenor's contrary salutatory words of advice to the graduating night school comedy class:

A couple of ... hints. Don't try to be deep. Keep it simple. I'm not looking for philosophers, I'm looking for comics. I'm looking for someone who sees what the people want and knows how to give it them. It's the people pay the bills, remember, yours, mine ... Mr. Waters's. We're servants, that's all. They demand, we supply. Any good comedian can lead an audience by the nose. But only in the direction they're going. And that direction is, quite simply ... escape. We're not missionaries, we're suppliers of laughter. (33)

For Griffiths the two disparate views have clearly defined moral and political biases. Waters' is sanative and seeks change; Challenor's corrupts the audience by aggravating rather than changing their vices. The one is revolutionary and liberating, the other fascist and enslaving.

Act Two of *Comedians* is Trevor Griffiths' brilliant *tour de force,* in which the theories of Act One are put into practice, and each of the students plays his act in front of an unseen audience at a Manchester social club and, of course, in front of the actual theatre audience of *Comedians*. By arranging the theatre audience to be the unseen audience at the Manchester club, Griffiths skillfully enforces a new consciousness in each playgoer. The politics of comedy are made clear in the first act and thus in the second act each time the enlightened spectators laugh at the jokes of those comedians who feed already established prejudices, those who follow Challenor's dicta, the spectators should become acutely aware that their laughs for the jokes of a "traitor" are a vote of confidence for those who would enslave us and leave us to our own sicknesses. In Act Two, then, not only the comedy of the comedian but the response of the audience becomes a political act.

In their several acts, the students of Eddie Waters take their disparate comic and political stands. Two of them, Sammy Samuels the Jewish comedian and George McBrain the Ulsterman, alter their acts to please Challenor. Both are funny but theirs is a destructive humor, for both feed on obscenity for its own sake and feed, more importantly, on the audience's knee-jerk responses to a host of prejudices. Their jokes are made at the expense of blacks, Jews, the Irish, Pakistanis, people with physical defects, women's liberation, and wives. Their humor feeds xenophobia and fears of marital incompatibility. It is they, of course, who are singled out afterwards by Challenor and offered an entree into the successful CAMF organization. The act of Mick Connor the Irishman and the brother act of Phil and Ged Murray are undone by their inability to make a clear comedic and political commitment. Connor begins with an incisive satire on racial and national prejudice in England but in an attempt to please Challenor, Connor's act deteriorates into a series of discrete jokes made at the expense of Irish and Catholics. Since Mick himself is Irish and Catholic, the jokes are clearly self-destructive or masochistic as well a means for supporting the very prejudices against which the opening of his act had taken so moving a comic stand. More obviously disjunctive is the act of the Murray brothers, an act with Swiftian comic potential. The comic routine of the Murrays involves the smaller brother, Phil, holding the large and rather simple looking Ged upon his knee as a ventriloquist's dummy. Dressed in the garb of a Manchester City football supporter, complete with rosette and rattle, Ged can direct the comedy and prove to be no dummy. With the contrast inherent in ventriloquy routines, in which a would-be sophisticated ventriloquist is outsmarted by his dummy, with the clever device of a Brobdingnagian dummy and a Lilliputian ventriloquist, and with the contrast between the white collar Phil and the blue collar Ged, the Murrays have the markings of what might be a powerfully satiric act. Their routine, however, flies asunder when Phil suddenly and awkwardly decides in midcareer to ditch the rehearsed routine and pander to Challenor by telling an irrelevant and very negative anti-Pakistani joke. Ged refuses to go along, refuses to sell out to Challenor's definition of comedy. The result is civil war and a comedy act devastated by the political and moral separation of the two brothers.

The high point of the second act and of *Comedians* as a whole is the performance of Gethin Price, who is all along marked as someone apart from the others, as Waters' favorite student, and as the one member of the class with true comedic talent. Price's act is a stunning display of black comedy, a chillingly comic *danse macabre,* a controlled venture into the area in which comical satire borders on tragical satire and in which the strong medicines of the satirist very nearly become the corrosives of the sadist. Like the Murrays' routine, Price's also depends on dummies. In this case two mannequins representing an upper class couple in evening dress and with *"a faint, unselfconscious arrogance in their carriage"* (50). They are accosted in lower class Midlands rhetoric by Price, who has presumably just been to the Manchester City football match. The mannequins as members of the upper class are literal as well as metaphorical 'stuffed shirts.' Their failure to respond to Price strikingly communicates the upper class' practiced response to the working class. They neither see nor hear their social and economic inferiors. What Griffiths achieves here is precisely what O'Neill wished to achieve in *The Hairy Ape* when he confronted Yank with the puppet-like Fifth Avenue churchgoers. As Price works to communicate with the aristocratic mannequins, he conveys the frustration of his class:

> Been to the match, have we? Were you at t'top end wi' lads? Good, wannit? D'you see Macari? Eh? Eh? *(Silence.)* P'raps I'm not here. Don't you like me? You hardly know me. Let's go and have a pint, get to know each other. . . . You do *speak,* do you? I'm trying to *talk* to you. Say some'at. Tell us what kind of day you've had. Are you on the buses? (51)

As the mannequins persist in their silence, the silence that increasingly becomes the indifference of the upper classes to the lives of those beneath them, Price becomes increasingly rude and violent. His garrulous friendship finds its true name:

> You can laugh, you know. I don't mind you laughing. I'm *talking* to you. . . . There's people'd call this *envy,* you know, it's not, its hate. (52)

Reminiscent of Vendici in Cyril Tourneur's *The Revenger's Tragedy,* Price makes the scourge of satire draw blood. Pinning a marigold between the female dummy's breasts, Price steps back as the audience begins to notice that *"a dark red stain, rapidly widening, begins to form behind the flower."*

Price's satire demonstrates the cruelties of British class distinctions while it conveys the message that unless action is taken, class warfare and bloodshed is imminent.

Price's muse is indeed a cankered one. His satire not only invokes the social ills created by class barriers but suggests the destructive means for remedying those ills. In the last moments of his act, however, Price is able to retreat from his murderous fantasy translating it into a call for political rather than homicidal anti-social action:

> Who needs *them?* Hunh. Who needs them? We manage. United. Uni-ted. Docherty, Docherty. You won't keep us down with the tiddlers, don't worry. We're coming up *there* where we can gerrat yer. ... I shoulda smashed him. They allus mek you feel sorry for 'em, out in the open. (53)

He then ends his act by picking up a tiny violin and playing "The Red Flag." In short, Price's black comedy, his sharp satire, is a brilliantly comic but unfunny means for laying bare Britain's social divisiveness and for suggesting the political cure that could bring sanative social change. Challenor of course cannot understand Price's comedy and is disgusted by it. He tells Price afterwards, "Personally, I found the content of your act. ... how shall I put it? ... repulsive" (60). But what Griffiths shows in Price is what Northrop Frye has called the "genius" that "seems to have led practically every great satirist to become what the world calls obscene."[11]

Gethin Price's chilling performance ends Act Two but not *Comedians*, for there is an important third act to follow. In it, Challenor reviews or misreviews each comic's performance in perfect accord with his preference for comedy as entertainment over comedy as education. The confrontation between this teacher and the students goes as expected. More significant, however, is the confrontation that follows between the teacher Eddie Waters and his star pupil Gethin Price, for in that confrontation Griffith distinguishes between Waters' hatred of a system he is prepared to tolerate and Price's hatred of a system he is prepared to destroy. Having shown in the first acts the difference between fascist comedy and the comedy that opposes it, Griffiths proceeds to differentiate among the opposers between arm-chair liberals and true revolutionaries. Waters understands the beauty of Price's satire, but says, nonetheless, "It was ugly. It was drowning in hate. You can't change today into tomorrow on that basis" (65). The difference between the two men is that, as Gethin says to his mentor, "Maybe you lost your hate, Mr. Waters" (65). As for most great satirists from Juvenal and Persius to the present, what informs Price's satire is a hatred not of men but of the vices and outrages that men create. In a discursive speech, largely and perhaps wisely cut by Mike Nichols in the New York production of *Comedians* he directed, the audience learns that Waters had come face to face with the greatest of vices and outrages ever created by men, the concentration camp at Buchenwald, and that he was frightened by the recognition that something inside of him loved as well as deplored Buchenwald. And it is that recognition that has brought him to avoid rather than attack what he hates, and thereby to give a tacit tolerance to those things he would as a young man have sought to excoriate from society. As Griffiths sees it, this stance of avoidance or grudging acceptance is one necessarily inimical to comedy as satire, and inimical as well to political activism.

In the final moments of *Comedians,* Price and Waters part ways with Price countering Waters' acceptance with "I stand in no line. I refuse my consent" (68). Unwilling to surrender his truth, the truth of class oppression, the truth that insists on the need to resist the fascist impulse in society, Price leaves Eddie Waters' classroom to sharpen his scalpel of satire, to promote a vision of revolution and to "wait for it to happen" (68). That *it* presumably being the revolution itself. Griffiths has Waters continuing to serve in his role of teacher of comedy and *Comedians* ends amusingly with Waters' finding a new student. For Griffiths, Waters is important as a teacher, for like all good teachers he is a means to an end. It is he who provides the initial insight that separates Challenor's destructive vision of comedy as feeding already existing prejudices from the idea of comedy as a means for change. It is the student, however, who must put the classroom theory into praxis. Likewise, it is Waters' liberalism or democracy that becomes a necessary prior stage for the revolutionary Marxist.

After the action of *Comedians* concludes, there is still one more teacher, one more comedian, one more comic routine to appraise. And that is the teaching and comedy produced by Trevor Griffiths himself in his own comedy, *Comedians*. In a sense, then, Trevor Griffiths creates in *Comedians* the very yardstick by which he himself must be measured. *Comedians* is itself a witty, pointed comedy, entertaining and full of laughs. But it is not entertainment and laughter that is an end in itself, for true to the old Horatian *utile dulce* formula, *Comedians* educates as it entertains. It teaches the audience first the difference between a fascist comedy that brings out the worst in people, providing a comic fix to aggravate already vicious habits, and a comedy that appeals to our better selves and seeks to liberate us—sometimes painfully—from our addictions. It is difficult to see or read *Comedians* without recognizing for the rest of one's life the implicit political stance of any comic one hears. It is clearly Griffiths' hope that likewise no member of the audience will get to the close of the play without being radicalized. *Comedians* is as powerful and moving as it is because

Griffiths recognizes that a comedian's comedy act is also a political act and that the power of comedy properly directed can effect social and political change. Similarly, Griffiths implies, the playwright can also, through his drama, effect social and political change. It is with some interest, then, that one can look forward to the political drama Griffiths is likely to produce in the future.

NOTES

1. *Plays and Players,* April 1972, pp. 82–83. Griffiths expands on this point more fully in his preface to the edition of *Through the Night* and *Such Impossibilities* (London: Faber and Faber, 1977).
2. *Disrupting the Spectacle* (London: Pitman, 1975), p. 64.
3. Trevor Griffiths, *Occupations* and *The Big House* (London: Calder and Boyars, 1972), p. 50.
4. This essay is concerned only with Griffiths' published works. For a description of all his works, published and unpublished, see Malcolm Hay, "Theatre Checklist No. 9: Trevor Griffiths," *Theatrefacts* 3 (1976), pp. 2–8.
5. Griffiths has recently prepared a new English version of *The Cherry Orchard* (London: Pluto Press, 1978) that emphasizes Chekhov as a herald of the Russian Revolution.
6. Trevor Griffiths. *The Party* (London: Faber and Faber, 1974), pp. 52–53.
7. Trevor Griffiths, *Comedians* (New York: Grove Press, 1976). All quotations are from this edition. Parentheses following quotations indicate page numbers in this edition.
8. This idea is explored by Patricia Meyer Spacks in her essay "Some Reflections on Satire," *Genre* 1 (1968), pp. 13–30. In it she writes that the satirist "usually seems to believe—at least to hope—that change is possible. Personal change, in his view, leads to social change; he insists that bad men make bad societies. He shows us ourselves and our world; he demands that we improve both. And he creates a kind of emotion which moves us toward the desire to change" (13).
9. Ben Jonson, *The Alchemist,* ed. Alvin Kernan (New Haven: Yale University Press, 1974), p. 25.
10. *The Cankered Muse* (New Haven: Yale University Press, 1959), pp. 25–30.
11. *Anatomy of Criticism* (Princeton: Princeton University Press, 1957), p. 235

BIBLIOGRAPHY
KIMBALL KING

The following bibliography has been provided as a convenience to scholars who wish to read more about the playwrights discussed in this volume. A list of books and articles which survey the new English drama from a broader perspective is also included. In most cases only plays written for the stage have been listed. Radio and Television plays and screenplays by the authors included are listed in *Twenty Modern British Playwrights* (New York: Garland, 1977) and *Contemporary Dramatists* (London: St. Martin's, 1973). Also the B.B.C. has extensive microcard listings of radio and television plays.

GENERAL

Armstrong, W. A. *Experimental Drama*. London, G. Bell and Sons, 1963.
    This well-edited collection of essays contains an analysis of John Arden and N. F. Simpson by Katharine Worth along with her essay on Osborne, Martin Esslin's on Pinter, and Laurence Kitchin's on Wesker, among others.
Brown, John Russell, ed. *Modern British Dramatics: A Collection of Critical Essays*. Englewood Cliffs, Prentice-Hall, 1968. 9–10, 47–57, 117–21.
    This is one of the 20th Century Views series and provides a collection of essays on the New Drama. Brustein and Marowitz are among the contributing authors. Strongest emphasis is on Osborne though other authors are discussed.
————. *Theatre Language: A Study of Arden, Osborne, Pinter and Wesker*. London, Allen Lane, 1972.
    Brown chooses to study Pinter, Osborne, Arden and Wesker because of the wide attention they have all attracted, the scope of their experimentation, and their similar backgrounds as English dramatists of the same age. Rather than describing their careers and the content of their plays, Brown explores how each has "controlled theatrical reality in words, actions, and time, so that the plays say what the authors want to say now, to present audiences and in present theatrical conditions."
Brustein, Robert. "The English Stage." *Tulane Drama Review* 10 (1966), 127–33.
    Brustein provides glancing mention of Pinter, who "excludes statement from his work altogether," and emphasizes the role of Osborne and Wesker in the New Drama.
————. *Season of Discontent*. New York, Simon and Schuster, 1965.
————. *The Theatre of Revolt*. Boston, Little, Brown, 1964.
Cohn, Ruby. *Currents in Contemporary Drama*. Bloomington, Indiana University Press, 1969.
    This is a sophisticated study of trends in recent theatre. Cohn pays particular attention to certain stage views of the hero on the modern stage. Osborne, Shaffer, Pinter, and Bolt are among the British writers discussed.

Esslin, Martin. "Brecht and the English Stage." *Tulane Drama Review* 11 (Winter 1966), 63–70.
This is an analysis of Brecht's influence on Osborne, Arden, and other English dramatists.

_____. *Relections: Essays on Modern Theatre*. Garden City, Doubleday, 1969.
Esslin discusses Osborne, Pinter, and other English dramatists of this period.

Hall, John. "British Drama in the Sixties—A Note from London." *Texas Quarterly* 10 (Summer 1967), 15–19.
A flamboyant essay discusses, briefly, Pinter, Fry, Bolt, Arden, Osborne, Wesker, Peter Shaffer, and Charles Wood. Hall feels that Pinter is the most important of these.

Hall, Stuart. "Beyond Naturalism Pure." *Encore* (November-December 1961), 12–19. Reprinted in *The Encore Reader*.
The treatment by Wesker, Arden, and Osborne of the anti-hero of contemporary culture is seen to be an extension of the naturalist mode of presentation. Osborne is particularly successful in combining naturalism with a subtle symbolism, thereby making protagonists like Jimmy or Archie part of a metaphoric design.

Hahnloser-Ingold, Margret. *Das Englische Theater und Bert Brecht*. Bern, Francke Verlag, 1970.
Hahnloser-Ingold gives a detailed analysis of Brechtian elements in the plays of Auden, Osborne and Arden. The discussions of Osborne's *Entertainer, The World of Paul Slickey* and *Luther* are particularly interesting.

Hammerschmidt, Hildegard. *Das historische Drama in England (1956–1971): Erscheinungsformen und Entwicklungstendenzen*. Frankfurt, Humanitas Verlag, 1972.
Hammerschmidt explores the fascination of English dramatists since John Osborne with historical figures. Bolt, Osborne, Whiting, Saunders, Pinter, and Arden are some major playwrights who have written "modern" history plays.

King, Kimball. *Twenty Modern British Playwrights: 1956 to 1976*. New York and London, Garland, 1977.
This is a comprehensive annotative bibliography of twenty major English dramatists, from John Arden to Charles Wood alphabetically.

Kitchin, Laurence. *Mid-Century Drama*. 2d ed. London, Faber and Faber, 1962. 119–22.
Kitchin admires Pinter's ability to compress action, to intensify feelings and emotions. He compares him to Chekhov. In general he admires the staging techniques, use of dialect and other verbal innovations of the realists such as Osborne and Arden.

Klotz, Günther. *Individuum und Gesellschaft in englischen Drama der Gegenwart*. Berlin, Akademie-Verlag, 1972.
Osborne and Wesker are discussed as products of the English class system and their alternative approaches to social issues and individual responsibility are compared.

Lumley, Frederick. *New Trends in Twentieth Century Drama: A Survey Since Ibsen and Shaw*. New York, Oxford University Press, 1972.

Lumley surveys dramatists in many nations and eras but devotes a full chapter to recent British playwrights, Arden, Pinter, Wesker, Shaffer, and Osborne among others.

"Playwriting for the Seventies: Old Theatres, New Audiences, and the Politics of Revolution." *Theatre Quarterly* 6 (Winter, 1976–1977), 35–78.

Theatre Quarterly has devoted a major part of this issue to an assessment of recent British Theatre. Comments by Arden, Wesker and others provide insights into current trends.

Taylor, John Russell. *Anger and After: A Guide to the New British Drama.* London, Eyre Methuen, 1962.

This is a classic study of Osborne, Wesker and the dramatists of the Royal Court Theatre after 1956.

_____. *The Second Wave: British Drama for the Seventies.* New York, Hill and Wang, 1971.

This book is an indispensable reference guide for the new drama. It includes essays on more than twenty English playwrights.

Vinson, James. *Contemporary Dramatists.* London, St. Martin's, 1973.

This general reference work includes entries for nearly all living major playwrights. For each author a biography is given, a full list of his plays and other literary contributions and a brief analysis of his major themes and techniques.

Wellworth, George. *The Theater of Protest and Paradox: Developments in the Avant-Garde Drama.* New York, New York University Press, 1964.

Wellwarth discusses French, German, English and American dramatists who are challenging traditional political or social values or those whose staging techniques are innovative. Of the British dramatists, Pinter, N. F. Simpson, Osborne, Wesker, and Arden are featured.

Weise, Wolf-Dietrich *Die Neuen englischen Dramatiker in ihrem Verhältnis zu Brecht.* Hamburg, Verlag Gehlen, 1969.

The influence of Brecht on Wesker, Osborne and Arden is analyzed in detail. Weise also devotes a chapter to John Whiting, Robert Bolt and Peter Shaffer, younger playwrights who similarly draw on Brechtian themes and techniques.

Worth, Katharine J. *Revolutions in Modern English Drama.* London, G. Bell, 1972.

Worth discusses the changing shape of drama in the seventies. She notes new varieties of realism in plays by Wesker, Storey and Mercer and new forms of melodrama and epic theatre in works by Arden, Alan Plater and Charles Wood. Finally she discusses the departure from tradition in works by Orton, Barnes, Williams and Bond.

JOHN ARDEN

All Fall Down. 1955.

Armstrong's Last Goodnight: An Exercise in Diplomacy. 1965.

Ars Longa, Vita Brevis. 1964.

The Bagman; or, the Impromptu of Muswell Hill. 1972.

The Ballygomkeen Bequest. 1972.

The Business of Good Government: A Christmas Play. 1963.

Fidelio. 1965.

Friday's Hiding. 1966.

The Happy Heaven. 1964.

Harold Muggins Is a Martyr. 1968.

The Hero Rises Up: A Romantic Melodrama. 1969.

Ironhand. 1965.

The Island of Mighty. 1971.

Left-Handed Liberty: A Play about Magna Carta. 1965.

Live Like Pigs. 1961.

The Non-Stop Connolly Show. 1975.

Play Without Words. 1965.

The Royal Pardon; or The Soldier Who Became an Actor. 1966.

Serjeant Musgrave's Dance: An Unhistorical Parable. 1960.

Soldier, Soldier. 1966.

The Soldier's Tale. 1968.

The True History of Squire Jonathan and His Unfortunate Treasure. 1968.

The Waters of Babylon. 1964.

Wet Fish. 1968.

When Is a Door Not a Door? 1968.

The Workhouse Donkey. 1963.

Wozzeck. 1964.

Adler, Thomas P. "Religious Ritual in John Arden's *Serjeant Musgrave's Dance*." *Modern Drama* 16 (1973), 163–66.

    In response to Mary B. O'Connell's suggestion that *Serjeant Musgrave's Dance* is a folk ritual based on the medieval mummers' play, Adler posits that the first dance in the play contains more specifically religious elements and that Musgrave's hoisting of the skeleton and his dance around it is a grotesque parody of the crucifixion. Musgrave's failure, Adler argues, is that his plan for vengeance is antithetical to the meaning of the cross. But the ultimate deaths of Altercliffe and Musgrave in the play may, in fact, be an expiation for their violence and "one step closer to inaugurating God's dance of love and peace on earth."

Blindheim, Joan T. "John Arden's Use of the Stage." *Modern Drama* 11 (1968), 306–16.

    Because Arden has attributed his concern with practical matters, such as set decoration and the logistics of manipulating a large cast, to his architectural training, Blindheim examines the "architecture" of Arden's plays and shows how their structure ranges from traditional realism to anti-illusionism to experimental "vital theatre." Sources from theatre history, particularly medieval and eighteenth-century plays, are cited, but Blindheim stresses the originality of Arden's highly structured stage technique.

Bonford, François. "Falstaffian Characters in Two Plays by John Arden." *Revue des Langues Vivantes* (Bruxelles), 38 (1972), 164–74.

Bonford sees Arden's plays as presentations of moral conflict embodied in antagonistic characters rather than Brechtian political dramas. *Armstrong's Last Goodnight,* and to some extent *The Workhouse Donkey,* are compared to Shakespeare's *Henry IV.* Bonford compares the thematic conflicts in the plays in an attempt to clarify Arden's "message."

Day, P. W. "Individual and Society in the Early Plays of John Arden." *Modern Drama* 18 (1975), 239–49.

John Russell Taylor and J. D. Hainsworth are among the very few critics who, according to Day, have attempted to analyze Arden's work. Day examines their interpretations before proposing his own—that the structure of Arden's first plays is based upon the conventional music-hall format, overlaid with conventional plot-lines, such as comedy intrigue, soap opera, and thriller. Arden's strong portrayal of social structure, according to Day, polarizes his characters into "acceptors" and "non-acceptors." From this conflict arise dramatic paradoxes, self-interest and social concern

Hahnloser-Ingold, Margrit. *Das englische Theater und Bert Brecht: Die Dramen von W. H. Auden, John Osborne, John Arden in ihrer Beziehung zum epischen Theater von Bert Brecht und gemeinsamen elisabethanischen Quellen* Bern, Francke, 1970.

This book is divided into four parts. The first offers a survey of the new British dramatists, including Arden, and the second is an analysis of Brecht's career and techniques; parts three and four demonstrate thematic and structural similarities between the German and the English playwrights.

Hunt, Albert. *Arden: A Study of His Plays.* London, Eyre Methuen, 1974.

Hunt states the thesis of his book: "that the revolutionary content of Arden's plays make stylistic demands that are outside the normal range of the established theatre." The author provides an analysis of Arden's major works, and traces the playwright's increasing political commitment.

Klotz, Günther. "Ein irisches Vermächtnis: *The Ballygombeen Bequest* von John Arden und Margaretta D'Arcy." *Zeitschrift für Anglistik und Amerikanistik,* Leipzig, 22 (1974), 419–24.

Klotz discusses the play which John Arden and his wife Margaretta D'Arcy have written together as an exploration of Anglo-Irish tensions. Klotz surveys the new drama briefly, summarizes Arden's career, and praises the play.

Marowitz, Charles, and Simon Trussler. "Who's for a Revolution: Two Interviews with John Arden." *Tulane Drama Review* 11, ii (1966), 41–53.

In the first interview by Walter Wager, Arden discusses the reasons for his playwriting, his education, where he writes and at what pace, his tastes in European and American drama, and his relationships with other playwrights, with his neighbors, and with television. The interview by Trussler concerns the themes and characters of several Arden plays, including *Left-Handed Liberty, Armstrong,* and *Ars Longa.*

Trussler, Simon. "Arden—An Introduction." *Encore* 12, v (1965), 4–8. [This issue of *Encore* is devoted to Arden.]

Arden's "relative failure to win a mass audience" is here attributed to his flight from the metropolitan setting, his sophisticated and frequently obscure language, and his stylization and modification of Brechtian devices. Trussler maintains that Arden is not an amoral dramatist, as J. R. Taylor has suggested, but rather a dramatist who rejects dogma in favor of practical and thus malleable honesty. Trussler chronicles Arden's professional career calling him "the most consistently impressive of our contemporary dramatists."

Worth, Katharine J. "Avant Garde at the Royal Court Theatre: John Arden and N. F. Simpson." In *Experimental Drama*. William A. Armstrong, ed., London, G. Bell, 1963. 206–14.

Worth compares the works of Arden and Simpson. She finds both playwrights concerned with language and claims of Arden that he "evolves a rough, highly coloured, figurative language, based on a curious amalgam of northern dialects." She contrasts Arden's world of real life situations and major issues and his use of poetry and prose to Simpson's fantasy world and use of common speech.

PETER BARNES

The Bewitched. 1974.

The Devil Is an Ass. 1973.

Frontiers of Farce. 1976.

Leonardo's Last Supper. 1969.

Lulu. 1970.

Noonday Demons. 1969.

Pawns; the Plight of the Citizen-Soldier. 1971.

Red Noses, Black Death. 1979.

The Ruling Class. 1968.

Sclerosis. 1965.

The Time of the Barracudas. 1963.

Esslin, Martin. *Jenseits des Absurden*. Wien, Europa Verlag, 1973.

Hennessy, Brendan. "Peter Barnes." *Transatlantic Review,* nos. 37–38 (Autumn–Winter 1970–71), 118–24.

In this interview Barnes says the inequities of the class system still prevail in the home counties, if not in London. He looks for verbal techniques and expressions "like the Elizabethan's or Jacobean's." Hennessey feels in this area he is like the young Shaw, seeking "medieval rhythms" in the dialogue of his historical plays. Barnes states that *Noonday Demons* is the "purest expression up to now of my interest in [religious] belief," and he specifically refers to the alienation effect of his plays, although Brecht is not mentioned.

Richmond, Theo. "The Visible Worm." *Guardian*, 6 January 1970, p. 6.

Taylor, John Russell. *The Second Wave: British Drama for the Seventies*. New York, Hill and Wang, 1971. 206–208.

Taylor surveys Barnes's career as a playwright and screenwriter briefly but concentrates on *The Ruling Class,* which he calls "a glittering satirical charade."

EDWARD BOND

A-A-America! 1976.

Bingo: Scenes of Money and Death. 1974.

Black Mass. 1970.

The Bundle. 1978.

Early Morning. 1968.

The Fool. 1975.

Lear. 1971.

Narrow Road to the Deep North. 1968.

Passion. 1971.

The Pope's Wedding. 1969.

Saved. 1965.

The Sea. 1973.

Stone. 1976.

The Woman. 1978.

The Worlds. 1980.

Barth, Adolf. "The Aggressive 'Theatrum Mundi' of Edward Bond: *Narrow Road to the Deep North." Modern Drama* 18 (June 1975), 189–200.
    Barth argues that *Narrow Road* ... is a "secularized theatrum mundi [that] in one way or another still maintains the archetypal hope for a 'heavenly Jerusalem' which should supplant Shogo's type of city as well as Georgiana's. ... " The solution, however, is neither personal nor spiritual, but is rather to be sought in the social realm. The play is inconclusive as to whether Basho will realize this hope.

Coult, Tony. *The Plays of Edward Bond.* London, Eyre Methuen, 1977.
    In 83 tight pages Coult discusses Bond's attitudes toward religion and superstition, nature and politics, and the family and the individual. The chapter on "backgrounds" provides a remarkably concentrated and useful survey of both the playwright's achievements and his problems with censorship.

Duncan, Joseph E. "The Child and the Old Man in the plays of Edward Bond." *Modern Drama* 19 (March 1976), 1–10.
    Duncan discusses the symbolic use of age in Bond's plays. The process of man's learning to accept, not reject, reality and to facilitate change are related to this symbolism.

Esslin, Martin. "Bond Unbound." *Plays and Players,* 16 (April 1969), 32–34.
    Esslin sees *Saved* and *Narrow Road to the Deep North* as both sharing "the disastrous influence of a morality based on an intellectually bankrupt religion" and "the *horror* of violence which expresses itself in *images* of violence." He reviews the current performances, finding fault with the "superficially effective clichés" of *Saved.*

Gross, Konrad. "Darstellungsprinzipien im Drama Edward Bonds." *Die Neuren Sprachen,* 22 (1973), 313–24.

Gross studies Bond's major works and systematically analyzes them in terms
of dialogue, scene structure, symbolism, time, space, and moral meaning.

Hay, Malcolm and Philip Roberts. *Edward Bond: A Companion of the Plays.*
London, TQ Publications, 1978.

Hay and Roberts provide a chronology of major events in Bond's life, a
bibliography of primary and secondary works, comments by Bond on his plays
and description of the plays in production.

Hobson, Harold, and others. "A Discussion with Edward Bond." *Gambit* 5 (1971),
5–38.

The discussion focuses on *Saved, Early Morning,* and *Narrow Road to the
Deep North.* Bond makes several remarks of critical interest: "The villain of this
piece is Basho," "I had this central character who runs all the way through my
plays: he turns up as Scopey in the first one *(Pope's Wedding)* ... he's Len in
Saved... Arthur in *Early Morning.*" Several comments seem designed to arouse:
"I mean we would be much saner if we were cannibals." He talks about *Lear,* in
progress, while Jane Howell, actress in and producer of several Bond plays,
offers her criticism of Bond's art. Bond mentions Chekhov and Wood as
dramatists he admires.

Klotz, Günther. "Erbezitat und zeitlose Gewalt." *Weimarer Beiträge,* 19, x (1973),
54–65.

Although he mentions *The Pope's Wedding* Klotz focuses on Bond's *Lear* and
its many parallels with and departures from Shakespeare's *King Lear.* The issues
of power and authority which are apparent in the Shakespearean classic have
been adapted, rather drastically, to comment on the contemporary world scene.

Mehlin, Urs. "Die Behandlung von Liebe and Aggression in Shakespaeres *Romeo
and Juliet* und in Edward Bonds *Saved.*" *Shakespeare-Jahrbuch* (Heidelberg),
(1970), 132–59.

Mehlin finds fascinating and convincing similarities between Shakespeare's
Romeo and Juliet and Bond's *Saved.* In particular, they are both set in an
oppressive society, which thwarts expressions of love and tenderness, and are
marked by the unexpected eruption of violence and the death of innocents.

Oppel, Horst and S. Christenson. Edward Bonds *Lear* und Shakespeares *King
Lear.* Mainz, Academie der Wissenschaft und Literatur, 1974.

Peter, John. "Violence and Poetry." *Drama* 117 (Autumn 1975), 28–32.

Peter argues that *Bingo* and *Narrow Road* share the same object: "the utter
inadequacy, indeed the harmfulness, of the artist as a social animal...." "Like
most of Bond's plays, *Bingo* is a play of conscience." "...But a moral view of life
means seeing it in terms of this and their consequences. Morality demands the
responsibility of logic," something Bond fails to provide in *Saved, Early Morning,* and *Lear.* Peter likes *The Sea* because it "presents not unmotivated puppets
but people." *Bingo* fails because it is improbable and overwritten.

Scharine, Richard. *The Plays of Edward Bond.* Cranbury, N.J., Associated University Presses, 1976.

Scharine provides the most thorough study in English to date of Bond's plays,
from *The Pope's Wedding* to *The Sea.* In his final chapter he provides a useful
summary of Bond's themes and techniques, emphasizing Bond's despair over
man's self-destructiveness, which is only partially mitigated by his seldom
realized potential to change course.

Wendt, Ernst. "König Lear und der Seiltänzer." In *Moderne Dramaturgie*. Frankfurt, Suhrkamp Verlag, 1973, 13–37.

Wendt compares Bond with Jean Genet, pointing out their shared revolutionary spirit and harsh assessment of society.

Wiszniowska, Marta. "Elizabethans on Modern Stage: Shakespeare and Marlowe versus Marowitz and Bond." *Studia Anglica Posnaniensia,* no. 8 (1976), 157–66.

Wiszniowska discusses recent adaptations of Shakespeare on the English stage, often by playwrights making a revolutionary statement. She provides a sustained analysis of Bond's use of Shakespeare's *King Lear* in his own play, *Lear.*

Wolfensperger, Peter. *Edward Bond: Dialektik des Weltbildes und dramatische Gestaltung.* Bern, Francke Verlag, 1976.

Wolfensperger devotes a full chapter each to *The Pope's Wedding, Saved, Early Morning, Narrow Road to the Deep North,* and *Lear.* He explores Bond's controversial themes and clarifies the intentions behind his innovative techniques.

SIMON GRAY

Butley. 1971.

Dog Days. 1976.

Dutch Uncle. 1969.

The Idiot. 1970.

Molly. 1977.

Otherwise Engaged. 1975.

Plaintiffs and Defendants. 1975.

Rear Column. 1978.

Spoiled. 1968.

Sleeping Dog. 1967.

Stage Struck. 1979.

Two Sundays. 1975.

Wise Child. 1967.

Blaydes, Sophia B. "Literary Allusion as Satire in Simon Gray's *Butley.*" *Midwest Quarterly* 18 (July 1977), 374–91.

Gray's allusions to T. S. Eliot, Yeats and the middle-class nursery poets provide an ironic backdrop for Gray's views of the English class system and for the changes he perceives in the values of educated people in our time.

Hamilton, Ian. "Simon Gray." *The New Review* 3 (January/February 1977), 39 46.

This interview provides the most thorough biography of Simon Gray available. It discusses his childhood in France and Canada, his education at Westminster and Cambridge and various graduate fellowships he pursued after Cambridge. Gray admires Henry James, Dickens, and George Eliot, but believes no great novels are presently being written. The adaptation of a short story on television brought him in contact with Ken Trodd and other television writers and eventually his work found its way to the legitimate stage. Gray and Hamilton discuss the relative merits of the protagonists in *Otherwise Engaged* and *Two Sundays* and the playwright stresses his present commitment to theatre and quality television.

Taylor, John Russell. "Three Farceurs." In *The Second Wave*. New York, Hill & Wang, 1971. 156–71.
  Taylor sees Gray as primarily a farceur without a wide-ranging appeal. The article was written prior to *Butley* and *Otherwise Engaged* and hence describes only the early plays and their resemblance to Joe Orton's work.

TREVOR GRIFFITHS

All Good Men. 1974.

Apricots. 1971.

The Big House. 1969.

Comedians. 1975.

Jake's Brigade. 1971.

Lay By. 1971.

Occupations. 1970.

The Party. 1973.

Sam, Sam. 1972.

Such Impossibilities (television)

Thermidor. 1971.

Tip's Lot. 1972.

The Wages of Thin. 1969.

Through the Night. 1975.

Barnes, Clive. *"Comedians."* New York Times Theater Review, 29 November 1976, 34:1.
  Comedians: "One of the funniest, and almost certainly the dirtiest comedy in seasons." —a comedy with an esthetic, moral, and above all, political purpose. Griffiths makes us believe in the stand-up comedians who wander on in a striking semblance of reality. Part of the reason is play's shape, which is perfect for discussing the wieghty matter of comedy, its function, purpose and reward. In the final revelation through Gethin Price, Griffiths apparently suggests to world Socialists something less compromising or smug than social democracy.

Hay, Malcolm. "Trevor Griffiths Checklist." *Theatrefacts* 3 (1976), 2–8.

Harold Hobson. "It's a Battlefield." *Sunday Times* (London), 8 May 1975, 33c.
  Hobson claims Griffiths' *All Good Men* illustrates the differences between political drama in the 1970's and its counterpart in the early days of the *Royal Court Theatre*. Osborne, Wesker and others in the 1950's were passionately committed to their causes whereas Griffiths and Donald Caute remain "intellectually detached." They leave commitment "to their characters." The play deals

with an elderly labor minister and his left-wing professor son. The former espouses gradual change; the latter favors Marxist-style confrontation. In the final act the son betrays the father—not maliciously we are told, but out of a sense of objective political commitment.

J. W. Lambert. "Joking Apart." *Sunday Times* (London), 23 February 1975, 37a.
   Comedians, Lambert feels, shows the influence of David Storey. The character Gethin is the "most interesting" anti-hero since Jimmy Porter. The play itself is built around a double conflict—a negative and positive attitude toward the comic in the theatre; and a division within the author between his "natural humanity and the iron corset of an *idée fixe* (Marxism)."

Marowitz, Charles. "New Playwrights Stir British Stage." *New York Times,* 20 June 1976, II: 7, 15.
   Marowitz comments on the new playwrights connected with the Portable Theatre, such as David Hare and Griffiths. The latter's early plays are briefly discussed.

Wardle, Irving. "Basement Theatre." *The Times,* 15 December 1970, 7c.
   Wardle calls Griffiths "a discovery of Manchester's stables theatre whence I hear excellent things of his full-length piece, *Occupations.*" However, Wardle, scorns the *Wages of Thin,* which he calls "yesterday's graffiti" carved "on a cherrystone." The play derives from Pinter's the *Birthday Party* and Orton's *Loot,* but is basically "an empty joke poorly told."

JOE ORTON

Entertaining Mr. Sloane. 1964.

Loot. 1967.

"Until She Screams." 1969.

What the Butler Saw. 1969.

Fraser, Keath. "Joe Orton: His Brief Career." *Modern Drama* 14 (1971), 413–19.
   This is a critical discussion of Orton's major works. Fraser concludes that *Entertaining Mr. Sloane* and *Loot* will be "among comedies still performed in fifty years."

Gordon, Giles. "Joe Orton." *Transatlantic Review* 24 (Spring 1967), 93–100. Reprinted in *Behind the Scenes.* Ed. Joseph F. McCrindle. New York: Holt, Rinehart and Winston, 1971.
   Orton discusses *Entertaining Mr. Sloane* and *Loot,* his views of himself as a playwright, his term in prison, his morality and taste, and his writing history.

Lahr, John. "Artist of the Outrageous." *Evergreen Review* 14 (February 1970), 30–34, 83–84.
   Lahr combines selections from Giles Gordon's interview with critical comment on Orton's work. Lahr feels that Orton reveals "social insanity" and his use of farce extends "to an audience the possibility of humility and care."

———. *Prick up Your Ears: The Biography of Joe Orton.* New York, Knopf, 1978.
   This is the first full-length study of Orton's meteoric rise as a dramatist, his troubled personal life, and his violent death.

Smith, Leslie. "Democratic Lunacy: The Comedies of Joe Orton." *Adam International Review* 40, nos. 394–96 (1976), 73–92.

Smith indicates that Orton is no mere farceur or absurdist but that his plays are sharply satirical, reflecting his distrust of modern institutions and the need for reform.

Taylor, John Russell. "British Dramatists—The New Arrivals—No. 7, The Late and Lamented Joe Orton." *Plays and Players* (October 1970), 14–17.

This is an overview of Orton's works. Those plays produced during his lifetime, Taylor feels, are evidence of his "genuine and extraordinary" talent. Those produced posthumously seem, "at best, rough drafts."

_____. *The Second Wave: New British Drama for the Seventies.* New York, Hill and Wang, 1971. 125–40.

This is a reprint with slight revision of the article appearing in *Plays and Players* cited above.

JOHN OSBORNE

A Bond Honoured. 1956.

The Devil Inside. 1949.

The End of Me Old Cigar. 1975.

The Entertainer. 1957.

The Entertainer. 1957.

Epitaph for George Dillon. 1958.

Hedda Gabler. 1972.

Inadmissible Evidence. 1965.

Look Back in Anger. 1957.

Luther. 1961.

A Patriot for Me. 1966.

Personal Enemy. 1953.

The Picture of Dorian Gray: A Moral Entertainment. 1973.

A Place Calling Itself Rome. 1973.

A Sense of Detachment. 1973.

Time Present and The Hotel in Amsterdam. 1968.

Very Like a Whale. 1971.

Watch It Come Down. 1975.

West of Suez. 1971.

The World of Paul Slickey. 1958

Banham, Martin. *Osborne.* Edinburgh, Oliver and Boyd, 1969.

Banham's emphasis is on Osborne's impact as a leader in a new theatre movement rather than on the playwright's social or political appraisals of English life. The individual plays are studied in terms of their expert craftsmanship and the new life they bring to the English stage.

Bieshaus, E. G. "No World of Its Own: *Look Back in Anger* Twenty Years Later." *Modern Drama* 19 (March 1976), 47–55.

On May 8, 1956 John Osborne's *Look Back in Anger* changed the direction of drama written in English, but now we only respond to it as an event and not a play that takes us into its world and compels us to accept that world on its own terms. Although the play engages our emotions, it fails to engage our minds. The reasons for this intellectual failure are the play's transparent structure, its arbitrary motivations, and its bogus characterizations. It is only because Jimmy's anger is so open that audiences and readers respond in spite of themselves.

Cagerne, Walter, ed. *The Playwrights Speak.* New York, Walter Wager, 1967. 127–28.

A BBC "Face to Face" interview—the general achievements, themes, goals of Osborne's career are discussed. Osborne appears to be a thoroughgoing theatre professional. He is defensive about charges that his later plays lack the social bite of *Look Back in Anger.* As an artist he wants the freedom to explore many ideas and techniques in the theatre.

Carter, Alan. *John Osborne.* Edinburgh, Oliver and Boyd, 1969.

A full length study of Osborne as a social protest playwright. All of the author's plays through *Hotel in Amsterdam* are discussed. Carter's knowledge of English social issues and Osborne's response to these is valuable, especially to readers a decade later.

Farrar, Harold. *John Osborne.* New York and London, Columbia University Press, 1973.

All of Osborne's plays are flawed and at least five are "bad." He is not a playwright of ideas, yet he is an exciting dramatist because "he has articulated as fully as any writer the central experience of his age."

Gersh, Gabriel. "The Theatre of John Osborne." *Modern Drama* 10 (September 1967), 137–43.

This article offers a biographical interpretation of the first decade of Osborne's career as playwright. The ups and downs of Osborne's fame and prosperity are related to his plays and the characters are seen to manifest the playwright's own slightly paranoid vision of life. Gersh offers some good insights but his conclusions are highly speculative.

Hahnloser-Ingold, Margrit. *Das englische Theater und Bert Brecht: Die Dramen von W. H. Auden, John Osborne, John Arden in ihrer Beziehung zum epischen Theater von Bert Brecht und den gemeinsamen elisabethanischen Quellen.* Bern, Francke, 1970.

The Brechtian influence on Osborne is given its fullest treatment here. The author's study of Arden is equally thorough. Brecht's techniques are defined and compared to copious selections from the English writers.

Hayman, Ronald. *John Osborne.* (World Dramatists). New York, Ungar, 1972.

Hayman suggests that Osborne is preoccupied with his heroes' quest for a kind of existential self-definition and suggests that his plays therefore lack thematic and stylistic variety. Though it is debatable whether Osborne's dominating protagonists are the weakness or the strength of his plays, Hayman's insightful analysis in separate chapters of Osborne's works from *Look Back in Anger* to *West of Suez* is well-organized and informative.

Huizinga, J. H. "'Look Back' Looked Back On." *New Review* no. 29 (1976), 59–62.

Huizinga remembers *Look Back in Anger*'s critical reception and examines the angry young man that engulfed literary London throughout 1956. Jimmy Porter as the first of the angry young men cashed in on what Anthony Crosland has called "the obsessive terror amongst English intellectuals of seeming priggish," as well as of their compulsive identification with working-class heroes. Huizinga presents a farcical cross-examination of Jimmy Porter in order to get to know this representative young man who supposedly typified young England. He discovers an imposter who fooled the literary England that hailed him as "archetypal" and his creator as a writer of profound insight. From this he determines that the future is not quite so dark as believed because the young men are far too busy abusing their long suffering relatives to have any time or energy left for revolutionary action outside the home. He then presents another cross-examination, this time with Osborne, who tells him that young England's as busy as ever indulging in paralyzing despair at its own unexplained plight and rendering it socially significant by nationalizing it.

John Osborne: A Symposium. London, Royal Court Theatre, 1966.

Ten years after *Look Back in Anger* opened at the Royal Court, dramatists connected with the theatre, such as John Arden and other literary personalities, evaluate Osborne's achievement.

Karrfalt, David H. "The Social Theme in Osborne's Plays." *Modern Drama* 13 (May 1970), 78–82.

Modern man's sense of isolation from his community and its institutions is seen to be a source of despair in Osborne's plays. The playwright's sympathy lies with protagonists who confront a meaningless world with an existential awareness.

Murphy, Brian. "Jimmy Porter's Past: The Logic of Rage in *Look Back in Anger*." *Midwest Quarterly* 18 (July 1977), 361–73.

The roots of English discomfort with the class system are explored by Murphy who re-evaluates the phenomenon of Osborne's early success in *Look Back in Anger*.

Northouse, C., and T. P. Walsh. *John Osborne*. Boston, G. K. Hall, 1974.

One of the most recent and most thorough bibliographies of Osborne's works. The annotations are perceptive and detailed. Foreign citations, however, are somewhat scanty. The secondary bibliography is arranged alphabetically under the year it was published. Critics of popular culture will appreciate this approach since one can see the impact of each Osborne play on audiences and watch the growing popularity of the playwright. But it is time-consuming to survey the writings of a single critic since his articles may be listed in many different sections.

Oppel, Horst. "John Osborne: *Look Back in Anger*." In *Das moderne englische Drama: Interpretationen*. (Ed. Horst Oppel) Berlin, Erich Schmidt, 1963. 316–30.

Oppel begins by citing the enormous impact *Look Back in Anger* has had on English theatre. He explores the social issues in the play and analyzes the imagery from a psychoanalytic viewpoint—for example, the sexual imagery of the bears and squirrels game. He concludes that, although the play is excellent,

Osborne, like most modern dramatists, has not found a dramatic form that fully suits his talents. He is caught instead between naturalistic and psychological drama.

Peinert, Dietrich. "'Bear' and 'Squirrel' in John Osborne's *Look Back in Anger.*" *Literatur in Wissenschaft und Unterricht* 1 (1968), 117–22.
Peinert does an extensive imagery study of *Look Back in Anger,* which he uses as the clue to understanding the play's psychological undercurrents.

Taylor, John Russell, ed. *John Osborne: Look Back in Anger, A Casebook.* London, Macmillan, 1968.
This casebook is a testament to the legendary impact of *Look Back in Anger.* Many English and foreign reviews of performances are given. Essays by Osborne which elucidate his social ideas are included. Evaluations of the play are provided by George Wellwarth, Katharine Worth, Lindsay Anderson, and other distinguished theatre critics. Taylor's introduction provides a balanced overview.

Trussler, Simon. *The Plays of John Osborne: An Assessment.* London, Victor Gollancz, 1969.
Trussler's full-length study of Osborne contains plot-summaries and critical interpretations of all the author's plays to date. The study is rather impressionistic. Trussler does not impose a set thematic structure or overemphasize biographical details, but his admiration for the playwright is consistent.

Tynan, Kenneth. "John Osborne Talks to Kenneth Tynan—Candidly." *Atlas* 16 (September 1968), 53–57.
The playwright discusses his own career and contributions in the context of the modern theatre. He discusses his theme of anger, the new school of drama that has grown up around him, his new play *Time Present,* and his explorations of other media, such as TV and film. Osborne gives an overview of the major social issues facing England in 1968—problems of drug abuse, student rebellion, changing values and traditions.

Worth, Katharine J. "The Angry Young Man: John Osborne." In *Experimental Drama.* Ed. William A. Armstrong. London, G. Bell, 1963. 147–68. Reprinted in *John Osborne: Look Back in Anger, A Casebook.*
In this largely affirmative evaluation of Osborne's career, Worth asserts that the playwright applied social criticism in the mode of Shaw and Galsworthy to the contemporary English scene with great success. She sees progress in his continued craftsmanship and conceptualizing.

HAROLD PINTER

"Applicant." 1961.
The Basement. 1967.
Betrayal. 1978.
The Birthday Party. 1959.
"The Black and White." 1960.
The Caretaker. 1960.

Bibliography

The Collection. 1962.

"Dialogue for Three." 1963.

The Dumb Waiter. 1960.

The Dwarfs. 1964.

The Homecoming. 1965.

The Hothouse. 1980.

"Interview." 1965.

Landscape. 1968.

"Lost to Go." 1961.

The Lover. 1965.

Monologue. 1973.

Night. 1970.

A Night Out. 1961.

Night School. 1967.

No Man's Land. 1975.

Old Times. 1971.

"Request Stop." 1964.

The Room. 1960.

Silence. Landscape and Silence. 1969.

A Slight Ache and Other Plays. 1968.

Tea Party. 1965.

Baker, William, and Stephen Ely Tabachnick. *Harold Pinter.* Edinburgh, Oliver and Boyd, 1973.
   Baker and Tabachnick explore Pinter's Jewish background and pay close attention to ethnic details in his plays.

Benstock, Shari. "Harold Pinter: Where the Road Ends." *Modern British Literature*, 2 (Fall, 1977), 160–68.
   No Man's Land, Pinter's strongest statement yet on the theme of the power struggle, portrays an intellectual duel whose spoil is survival itself. Language becomes the ultimate weapon, Hirst's Beckettian silences matching Spooner's prolixity. Benstock sees a great deal of T. S. Eliot in the drama with *No Man's Land* as Eliot's wasteland, a vast barren expanse occupied by those who are neither "living nor dead." The major theme of this play is the conflict between present and past, and Pinter—in a very Eliot-like mode—shows the present and future combining to become, paradoxically, both a summation of the past and its refutation. Pinter's characters seem motivated by a most basic tendency of human behavior—the unspoken, and perhaps unconscious, desire for supremacy over other persons, whether by intellectual, psychological, or physical force.

Bensky, Lawrence. "Harold Pinter: An Interview." *Paris Review,* 10 (Fall 1966), 13–37. Also in *Writers at Work: The Paris Review Interviews.* 3rd series. New York, Viking, 1967. 347–68.

Pinter discusses, among other topics, his career as a playwright, his writing methods, the reception and writing of *The Room, The Birthday Party, The Caretaker,* and *The Dwarfs,* the difficulties of directing his own plays, the violence and humor in his plays, the relative lack of autobiography in his works, and his traditional outlook on writing plays. Pinter also devotes time to explain how his characters develop, come alive, for him.

Brustein, Robert. "Thoughts from Abroad." In his *The Third Theatre.* New York, Alfred Knopf, 1969. 117–22.

Brustein is concerned by "Pinter's reluctance to invent in his works anything more than atmosphere." Although he finds the first act of *The Homecoming* promising, he concludes that the denouement is "mere exploitation of the bizarre."

Burkman, Katherine H. *The Dramatic World of Harold Pinter: Its Basis in Ritual.* Columbus, Ohio State University Press, 1971.

This excellent book reveals the archetypal patterns behind Pinter's dramatic situations. She argues for the very deep humanity of his plays.

Cohn, Ruby. "The World of Harold Pinter." *Tulane Drama Review* 6 (1962), 55–68.

This valuable early essay on Pinter views the playwright as a "spiritual sin" of Bechett and the "angry young man." Cohn believes Pinter's anger is directed at dehumanizing forces in society and that he attempts to reveal human values by presenting bitter dramas which make us loathe the forces of dehumanization.

_____. "Latter Day Pinter." *Drama Survey* (Minneapolis), 3 (1964), 367–77.

Pinter like most contemporary playwrights explores the themes of illusion versus reality. Plays such as *The Birthday Party* are enigmatic because they depict the very subjective nature of our experience.

Dukore, Bernard F. "The Pinter Collection." *Educational Theatre Journal,* 7 (1974), 81–85.

Form is content in Pinter's work. *The Collection* concerns a group of potential adulterers. There are unsuccessful attempts to establish their innocence or guilt. Desire for power is seen as the key in sexual relationships.

_____. "The Theatre of Harold Pinter." *Tulane Drama Review,* 6, iii (1962), 43–54.

This is an examination of Pinter's major plays. Pinter presents "an unreal reality or a realistic unreality," which is "a horrifying picture of contemporary life."

_____. *Where Laughter Stops.* Columbia, Missouri, University of Missouri Press, 1976. Dukore discusses the tragicomic aspects of Pinter's plays through *No Man's Land.*

_____. "A Woman's Place." *Quarterly Journal of Speech,* 52 (1966), 237–41.

Dukore sees four pairs of characters between the generations in *The Homecoming.* Each parallels the other in character and actions among "a cluster of interwoven images; battles for power among human animals, mating rites, and a dominant wife-mother in a den of sexually maladjusted males."

Esslin, Martin. *Harold Pinter.* Hannover, Friedrich Verlag, 1967.

This is the German version of Esslin's book-length studies of Pinter, though it only covers the early plays.

_____. Pinter, *A Study of His Plays,* 3rd ed. London, Eyre Methuen, 1976.
This book is an expansion of Esslin's earlier work on Pinter, *Harold Pinter: The Peopled Wound.* It includes analyses of *No Man's Land* and other recent works by the author. Esslin emphasizes the absurdist beginnings and the Beckett influence, and discusses Pinter's characters in existential terms. He blends Sartrean philosophy with Freudian psychology in a curious and interesting way.

Fischer, Peter. "Versuch über das scheinbar absurde Theater." *Merkur,* 19, ii (1965), 151–63.
Pinter makes a fine example of an Englishman who employs the non-sequiturs, ellipses and other stylistic devices of the continental absurd tradition.

Fricker, Robert. *Das moderne englische Drama.* Göttingen, Vandenhoeck, 1964. 166–70.
Fricker ends the book with Pinter, whom he considers basically an absurdist.

Gale, Steven H. *Butter's Going Up: A Critical Analysis of Harold Pinter's Work.* Durham, Duke Press, 1977.
This is a brilliant thematic analysis of Pinter's plays through *Old Times.* It contains a valuable chronology.

Ganz, Arthur. "A Clue to the Pinter Puzzle: The Triple Self in *The Homecoming."* *Educational Theatre Journal* 21 (1969), 180–87.
Ganz disagrees with Lahr and Schechner who find Pinter is deliberately obtuse; he then analyzes *The Homecoming* to demonstrate Pinter's clarity.

_____, ed. *Pinter: A Collection of Critical Essays.* Englewood Cliffs, N.J., Prentice-Hall, 1972.
This is a useful "Twentieth-Century Views" collection of essays on Pinter, most of which have been printed elsewhere.

Goetsch, Paul. "Das englische Drama seit Shaw." In *Das englische Drama.* Ed. J. Nünning. Darmstedt, Wissenschaftliche Buchgesellschaft, 1973, 403–507.
Since Shaw, Goetsch finds a much greater concern in English drama for confronting social issues. Pinter's complaints about society are not specific but he portrays an alarming, threatened world.

Gussow, Mel. "A Conversation [Pause] with Harold Pinter." *New York Times Magazine,* 5 December 1971, 42–43, 126–36.
In this long informative interview Gussow focuses attention on *Old Times* and Pinter's relationship with Beckett. In addition, Pinter discusses playwriting, screenwriting, his interest in poetry, his political views, and the reactions of critics to his plays. Also the topic of pauses and silences in his plays and their "meaning" is discussed.

Guthke, Karl S. "Die metaphysische Farce im Theater der Gegenwart." *Deutsche Shakespeare-Gesellschaft West. Jahrbuch, 1970,* 46–76.
Along with Stoppard and Beckett, Pinter is a dramatist who sees the perverse humor in man's control by an arbitrary fate. The bitter comedy of Shakespeare's *King Lear* is in this tradition.

Habicht, Werner. "Der Dialog und das Schweigen im 'Theater des Absurden.'" *Die Neueren Sprachen,* N.S. 16, ii (1967), 53–66.
Habicht compares Ionesco, Beckett, and Pinter in their approach to absurdism. Ionesco shows us the horrors of conformity and Beckett is concerned with the paradoxes of existence. Pinter illustrates man's basic separation from this community.

————. "Theater der Sprache: Bemerkungen zu einigen englischen Dramen der Gegenwart." *Die Neueren Sprachen* 7 (July 1963), 302–13.

Habicht provides some background on English "nonsense-literature," alluding to Edward Lear and Lewis Carroll. He shows that N. F. Simpson derives materials from this tradition and Pinter also, to a lesser extent.

Hinchliffe, Arnold P. *The Absurd.* Critical Idiom Series. London, Methuen, 1969. 82–85.

This is a general study of the genre including an overview of Pinter's work through *Landscape*.

————. *Harold Pinter.* (TEAS 51.) New York, Twayne, 1967.

This Twayne series biography provides useful biographical data, extensive plot summaries and a useful survey of criticism. Hinchliffe's interpretations of the plays and his discussions of language are sophisticated and thorough.

————. *Harold Pinter.* New York, St. Martin's, 1975.

This is an elaboration of the biography with more emphasis on interpretation and the inclusion of more recent plays.

Hollis, James R. *Harold Pinter: The Poetics of Silence.* Carbondale, Southern Illinois University Press; London, Feffer & Simons, 1970.

This is a survey and critical discussion of Pinter's major plays, focusing particularly on the "playwright's relationship to and utilization of language." Hollis includes an introductory section on modern drama in general.

Imhof, Rüdiger. *Harold Pinter's Dramentechnik.* Bonn, Bouvier, 1976.

Imhof provides one of the most comprehensive studies of Pinter's dramaturgy, exploring systematically all of the methods, effects and symbols that have given Pinter his reputation as a master craftsman of the stage.

————. "Pinter's Silence: The Impossibility of Communication." *Modern Drama* 17 (1974), 449–60.

This is an interpretive examination of the characters in *Silence*. Imhof sees Pinter as portraying "the essential qualities of the characters" as well as their interrelationship. Each of them is attempting to communicate, "to establish a true relationship," but they can only communicate their own problems and concerns and cannot hear the other characters.

Lumley, Frederick. *New Trends in Twentieth-Century Drama.* New York, Oxford University Press, 1967. 266–73.

Lumley's book provides an overview of Pinter's work, through *The Homecoming*. Lumley feels that Pinter "has no axe to grind, no significance is to be attached to his themes, nor do they mask any abstract idea."

Mengel, Ewald. *Harold Pinter's Dramen im Spiegel der soziologischen Rollentheorie.* Frankfurt, Peter Lang, 1978.

This is a fascinating study of the role-playing of various Pinter characters and of the sociological pressures which motivate their seemingly peculiar behavior.

Messenger, Ann P. "Blindness and the Problem of Identity in Pinter's Plays." *Die Neueren Sprachen* 21 (1972), 481–90.

In many of Pinter's plays blindness, light and dark imagery, and problems of vision are associated with physical or spiritual death. In addition, "The ideas of sight and blindness, along with light and darkness, are traditional metaphors for knowledge and ignorance, which Pinter uses, again traditionally, to image forth the problems of identity."

Milberg, Ruth. "1 + 1 = 1: Dialogue and Character Splitting in Harold Pinter." *Die Neueren Sprachen* 23 (1974), 225–33.

A discussion of the "basic dialogue form" of Pinter's best known plays as well as the themes of lack of communication, the influence of the past, illusion vs. reality, sexual games, and the fragmentation of the male characters.

Müller-Zannoth, Ingrid. *Der Dialog in Harold Pinters Dramen*. Frankfurt, Peter Lang, 1977.

Müller-Zannoth examines the dynamics of Communication in 12 of Pinter's plays, ranging in time from *The Room* to *Old Times*.

Powlick, Leonard. "Temporality in Pinter's *The Dwarfs*." Modern Drama 20 (March 1977), 67–75.

Powlick investigates the themes of time and memory in *The Dwarfs*, which Pinter wrote both as a novel and a play.

Quigley, Austin. *The Pinter Problem*. Princeton, N.J., Princeton University Press, 1975.

Quigley, using the linguistic theories of Wittgenstein and others, brilliantly demonstrates that language is a weapon to Pinter's characters who are engaged in a life-and-death struggle.

Schlegelmilch, Wolfgang. "Der Raum des Humanen: Zu Harold Pinters *The Caretaker*." *Die Neueren Sprachen* 13 (July 1964), 328–33.

This is an examination of the room as symbol in *The Caretaker*. It symbolizes the derelict state of Aston's inner life, Mick's loss of inner life, and Davies' lost identity.

Stoll, Karl Heinz. *Harold Pinter*. Düsseldorf, August Bagel, 1977.

Stoll devotes a chapter each to a close reading of the text and subtext of *The Room; The Birthday Party* and the *Dumb Waiter; A Slight Ache* and *The Caretaker; The Homecoming;* and *Old Times*. In the last part of the book Stoll discusses Pinter's drama against the backdrop of Bond's, Osborne's, Arden's and Wesker's plays.

Tetzeli von Rosador, Kurt. "Pinter: *The Homecoming*." In *Das englische Drama*. Ed. Dieter Mehl. Düsseldorf, August Bagel, 1970. 319–33.

Tetzeli describes the happenings in *The Homecoming* and discusses critical appraisal of the work. He then discusses the Freudian and existential elements in the play that make it such a challenging enigma.

Trussler, Simon. *The Plays of Harold Pinter: An Assessment*. London, Gollancz, 1973.

Trussler examines each of Pinter's works, major and minor, through *Old Times*. This is an extremely thorough study which includes a chronology and cast lists. He feels that Pinter is "a consummately skillful craftsman who has very little sense of his own art."

Worth, Katharine J. "Harold Pinter." In *Revolutions in Modern English Drama*. London, G. Bell, 1972. 86–100.

Worth writes that "Pinter is the conjuror who comes into the realist tradition, takes over the well-worn material ... and works a dazzling transformation act with it." While indebted to Beckett, Pinter, with his interest in "the revelation of character," is even more Chekhovian, indebted as well to Coward. "Quietness" and "secrecy" are key elements in his plays; hence the appropriateness of the "closed" situation. "Pinter's drama might be called all sub-text ... the action poised between inner and outer reality," best demonstrated in his use of ritual, akin to Eliot's.

TOM STOPPARD

After Magritte. 1971.

Dirty Linen and New-Found-Land. 1975.

Enter a Free Man. 1968.

Every Good Boy Deserves a Favor. 1968.

The Gamblers. 1965.

The House of Bernarda Alba. 1973.

Jumpers. 1972.

Night and Day. 1979.

Professional Foul. 1978.

The Real Inspector Hound. 1968.

Rosencrantz and Guildenstern Are Dead. 1967.

Tango. 1968.

Travesties. 1975.

"Ambushes for the Audience: Toward a High Comedy of Ideas." *Theatre Quarterly* 4 (May–July 1974), 3–17.

   Stoppard is asked some penetrating questions by the journal's editors and answers openly and articulately. He discusses his early background, his education, and his first play, *A Walker on the Water.* The philosophy behind *Rosencrantz and Guildenstern Are Dead* is explored as well as Stoppard's approach to problems of stage craftsmanship. His strong aversion to totalitarian governments, especially fascism and Marxist-Leninism, his career as theatre critic, and his preferences in the modern theatre are covered in detail.

Asmus, Walter D. *"Rosencrantz and Guildenstern Are Dead." Shakespeare-Jahrbuch* (Heidelberg), 106 (1970), 118–31.

   Asmus ponders the question of the seriousness of *Rosencrantz and Guildenstern Are Dead.* Unlike Bond, who called the play "a crass little metaphysical exercise," Asmus feels Stoppard may be on the verge of making a significant philosophical statement. The article contains elaborate parallels between *Hamlet* and Stoppard's play, especially passages dealing with theatrical metaphors.

Bennett, Jonathan. "Philosophy and Mr. Stoppard." *Philosophy* 50 (January 1975), 5–18.

   This intriguing essay examines the philosophical content of *Jumpers* and *Rosencrantz and Guildenstern.* Bennett finds the philosophical content of the former "academic"; it has no relation to structure, and Stoppard simply plays with the concepts: "he has nothing to say about [them]." *Rosencrantz and Guildenstern* seriously treats such concepts: "the central one is the concept of *reality,* and grouped around it are *identity, memory, activity,* and *death."* The play's strength derives from the importance of the concepts and "from the sheer pertinacity and complexity and depth of the conceptual exploration."

Grossley, Brian M. "An Investigation of Stoppard's 'Hound' and 'Foot.'" *Modern Drama* 20 (March 1977), 77–86.

It is the parodic and satirically self-referential quality of Tom Stoppard's plays that sets him apart from the playwrights of the fifties. He remains the theatrical critic and aims his derision at the mores of drama, and especially at the age-old detective figure of Sophocles's Oedipus. In *The Real Inspector Hound* Stoppard leads us all up the garden path in order to show us that the detective play has come in every sense, to the end of the road. ("Hounded" to death:) Satirically, the play within the play exposes and undermines both critics (Birdboot and Moon) as they become an integral part of the action. The division between Moon's failure and Birdboot's success as critic, between players and audience, between mystery and solution, furthers a kind of Platonic dualism and the concept of question and answer. Like Rosencrantz and Guildenstern, Moon and Birdboot are dead because the play calls for this death. Both the detective play and its commentators have confounded each other at last, and generically, Stoppard has brought about a mercy killing. *After Magritte* is a comic sequel to *Hound;* however, Stoppard's concern and formal approach remain unchanged. Foot is wildly exaggerated for comic effect and assumes a variety of meanings. The play parodies itself and the structural metaphors germane to the activity of the detective plays which Stoppard reinforces by flagrant theatricality. The final scene yields a circularity of design and *After Magritte* is denied an ending. These plays are "mock celebrations of a detective, of those who believe in him, and of the concept of drama which concerns itself with solving riddles."

Gabbard, Lucian P. "Stoppard's *Jumpers:* A Mystery Play." *Modern Drama* 20 (March 1977), 87–95.

Gabbard discusses the various levels of "mystery" in Stoppard's *Jumpers,* seeing it as a sophisticated combination of a detective and philosophy lesson and a religious statement.

Gitzen, Julian. "Tom Stoppard: Chaos in Perspective." *Southern Humanities Review* 10 (Spring 1976), 143–52.

Stoppard's success stems from his brilliant use of predominantly harmless techniques of farce. Nevertheless his comedy derives from the serious promise that our society is in imminent danger of going out of control. The failure of control is seen by Stoppard to be spiritual or moral as well as physical. He resembles Eliot here and shares the latter's belief in the importance of order. In *Jumpers, Rosencrantz and Guildenstern Are Dead* and *Enter a Free Man* the rapid scene-changes, frequency of character movements, and overall symmetry of plot typical of his plays are further evidence of the playwright's artistic control which defies the very chaos it portrays.

Hayman, Ronald. *Tom Stoppard.* London, Heinemann Educational, 1977. 143 pp.

Hayman's study provides a very useful chronology of Stoppard's life and a bibliography of his writings. The book contains a series of interviews with Hayman and a brief analysis of all of Stoppard's major plays, including in some cases, reviewers' reactions. Problems of interpretation are mainly left to the reader.

Keyssar-Franke, Helene. "The Strategy of *Rosencrantz and Guildenstern Are Dead.*" *Educational Theatre Journal* 27 (March 1975), 85–97.

Keyssar-Franke discusses *Rosencrantz and Guildenstern* in terms of Stoppard's "dramatic strategy," the effect of the play on an audience. The audience is to be forced to a recognition that they can no more alter their fate than Rosencrantz and Guildenstern could alter theirs. She examines the play minutely to determine the effect of each element in terms of Stoppard's strategy.

Levenson, Jill. "Views from a Revolving Door: Tom Stoppard's Canon to Date." *Queen's Quarterly* 78 (Autumn 1971), 431–42.

Here Stoppard is analyzed as a playwright of the Theatre of the Absurd, emphasizing similarities between him and Beckett in theme, form, and characterization. Levenson explores the plays (both radio and stage) through *Real Inspector Hound* and includes Stoppard's novel in an effective comprehensive study.

Robinson, Gabriele S. "Plays Without Plot: The Theatre of Tom Stoppard." *Educational Theatre Journal* 29 (March 1977), 37–48.

Stoppard writes of the anxiety and confusion of life, of the helplessness of the individual caught up in forces impervious to reason. His characters are the victims of accidental calamities. He adds such farce to his philosophy that the result is more funny than painful. Robinson surveys first the subject of the major plays and then their form in order to reach some understanding of Stoppard's achievement, of both the success and the failure of his plays without plot. He is at his best in parody and at his weakest when he wants his characters to express a meaning or feeling of their own.

Taylor, John Russell. "British Dramatists—The New Arrivals: No. 4, Tom Stoppard." *Plays and Players* 17 (July 1970), 16–18, 78.

This is a brief overview of Stoppard's work through *After Magritte* (1970). Taylor sees pattern or structure as one of Stoppard's primary concerns, coupled with completeness of effect. Stoppard recognizes the necessity for "intelligence and conscious art in the shaping of his material."

————. *The Second Wave: New British Drama for the Seventies,* New York, Hill and Wang, 1971.

Reprint, with minor revision, of the article above.

Whitaker, Thomas R. "Playing the Player: *Rosencrantz and Guildenstern Are Dead.*" In *Field of Play in Modern Drama.* Princeton, N.J., Princeton University Press, 1977. 9–17.

Whitaker briefly discusses *Rosencrantz and Guildenstern* from a philosophical viewpoint. Does man only exist when he is acting out a role in a play? He admires Stoppard's first major success for aesthetic reasons but views it as a kind of exercise in futility.

DAVID STOREY

The Changing Room. 1971.

The Contractor. 1969.

Cromwell. 1973.

Edward. 1973.

The Farm. 1973.

Home. 1970.

In Celebration. 1969.

Life Class. 1975.

Mother's Day. 1978.

The Restoration of Arnold Middleton. 1967.

Sisters. 1978.

Clark, Susan Mauk, Ph.D. "David Storey: The Emerging Artist." *Dissertation Abstracts* 37: 647A.
   Despite good reviews and impressive literary awards, Storey has received little scholarly attention. One reason is that he is a young writer who has only begun his literary career, so many critics prefer to sit back and watch. He also defies bourgeois values with his non-characteristic mining town background. He also resists categorization. Clark uses a general format in tracing his progress from the novel, *This Sporting Life* to the drama, *Life Class* and sees Storey's works as dealing with his attempts to reconcile the physical and spiritual life, while structurally searching for the ideal medium. She also discusses Storey's innovations in staging traditional literary plays, his poetic naturalism, the successes and failures of his style which she predicts, in time, will be known as "Storyean."

Free, William J. "The Ironic Anger of David Storey." *Modern Drama* 16 (December 1973), 307–16.
   According to Free, Storey is most like Pinter and Osborne, but differs from the former in his use of dramatic space — in which tension is released rather than built up — and from the latter in his ability to dramatize the meaning of his characters' lives instead of having characters rage about their lack of it. The article includes sensitive and detailed readings of *In Celebration* and *The Contractor.*

Kalson, Albert, "Insanity and the Rational Man in the Plays of David Storey." *Modern Drama* 19 (June 1976), 111–28.
   Kalson investigates the tormented protagonists of David Storey's plays. Man seems doomed to isolation and defeat, but the rational man attempts to make a contribution, however meager, to his world rather than to resort to passivity or violence.

Shrapnel, Susan. "No Goodness or No Kings." *Cambridge Quarterly* 5 (Autumn 1970), 181–87.
   Shrapnel traces the changes in dramatic language in Storey's plays from a language commensurate to the exposure of domestic relations on a naturalistic level in *Arnold Middleton* and *In Celebration,* to a language which is purposefully incommensurate to the tragedy of human experience in *The Contractor* and *Home. The Contractor* succeeds because of its refusal to buttonhole its message, and *Home* because of its near perfect imitation of the texture of an everyday speech which is both mundane and in a way comforting to those who use it.

ARNOLD WESKER

Chicken Soup with Barley. 1958.

Chips with Everything. 1962.

The Four Seasons. 1965.

The Friends. 1970.

I'm Talking About Jerusalem. 1960.

The Journalists. 1974.

The Kitchen. 1960.

Love Letters on Blue Paper. 1977.

Menace. 1963.

The Merchant. 1976.

The Nottingham Captain: A Moral for Narrator, Voices and Orchestra. 1971.

The Old Ones. 1972.

The Old Ones by Arnold Wesker. 1974.

Roots. 1969.

Their Very Own and Golden City. 1966.

The Wedding Feast. 1974.

Anderson, Michael. "Arnold Wesker: The Last Humanist." *New Theatre Magazine* (Bristol), 8, iii (1968), 10–27.
  Wesker's sympathetic portrayal of man's aspirations and failures, his "combination of the visionary and the realist," and his tragic perspective which reveals his belief in the dignity of man, classes him as a humanist playwright. This article discusses both the intimate connection between political thought and the rhythms of human life, and the need to combat failure and disappointment "with the warmth and passion of argument" in Wesker's trilogy, *Chips with Everything,* and *Their Very Own and Golden City.*

Habicht, Werner. "Theater der Sprache. Bemerkungen zu einigen englischen Dramen der Gegenwart." *Die Neueren Sprachen,* 7 (July 1963), 302–13.
  Habicht contrasts Wesker's use of language with N. F. Simpson's. He finds Wesker's more realistic dialogue less effective than Simpson's absurdist-influenced language. The latter conveys man's loss of values and disintegrating humanity more appropriately.

Hayman, Ronald. *Arnold Wesker.* Contemporary Playwrights Series. London, Heinemann Educational, 1970.
  Besides two interviews and a selected bibliography, this book provides play descriptions and summaries of critical reactions to *The Kitchen,* the trilogy, *Chips with Everything, Their Very Own and Golden City,* and *The Four Seasons.* In the first interview, Wesker talks about his life and the autobiographical strain in his writings, while in the second, he and Hayman discuss particular snatches of dialogue in his plays.

Klotz, Günther. "Individuum und Gesellschaft im englischen Drama der Gegenwart. Arnold Wesker und Harold Pinter." *Weimarer Beiträge,* 19, x (1973), 187–91.

Although the 1950s opened up English drama to polemical onslaughts by angry writers, progressive drama is doomed, Klotz feels, in an imperialistic society where theatres are run for profit. Pinter and Wesker are both caught up in this conflict. Wesker defends the dignity of man but Pinter denies the social function of art and dooms his characters to submit to fate.

Leeming, Glenda, and Simon Trussler. *The Plays of Wesker: An Assessment.* London, Gollancz, 1971.

In this thorough work, Leeming and Trussler closely examine the themes, characterization, structure and language of Wesker's plays from *The Kitchen* through *The Friends*. They also discuss *Fears of Fragmentation,* a collection of Wesker's lectures and essays, and provide a chronology of Wesker's career as a playwright, a complete set of cast-lists of London productions and rivivals of his plays, and a bibliography of work by and about the dramatist.

Oppel, Horst. "Arnold Wesker: *The Chicken Soup Trilogy.*" In *Das moderne englische Drama: Interpretationen.* Ed. Horst Oppel. Berlin, Erich Schmidt, 1963. 345–71.

Oppel notes the theme of the Wandering Jew running throughout Wesker's work along with a preoccupation re the working class world. Taken together these themes provide a kind of unity for the dense and far-ranging materials of the trilogy. Oppel points out characterizations which are not fully developed and plot contrivances, but he concludes that Wesker's dramaturgy is rich in human experience. He also mentions Wesker's fondness for the poets, D. H. Lawrence and Dylan Thomas, and for the playwright, John Osborne.

Ribalow, Harold U. *Arnold Wesker.* (TEAS, 28). New York, Twayne, 1966.

In this thorough study of Wesker's works and life, Ribalow attempts to "clarify Wesker's plays within the patterns of recent British social, cultural, and literary trends." He analyzes characters and themes in Wesker's plays from *The Kitchen* through *The Four Seasons,* discusses *Pools,* a short story, and *Menace,* a little-known play, explores the effects of Wesker's Jewishness on his life and writings, and provides a history of Centre 42, a summary of critical articles on Wesker, and a selected annotated bibliography of criticism.

Rothberg, A. "Waiting for Wesker." *Antioch Review,* 24 (Winter 1964–65), 492–505.

This is a personal glimpse of the optimistic, lively and yet "melancholy driving, ambitious" playwright in his Centre 42 office. Wesker briefly explains his trilogy of plays, *Chicken Soup with Barley, Roots,* and *I'm Talking About Jerusalem,* which deal with socialism in politics, love, and art. The article also provides a short history of Centre 42, the "cultural revolution" geared to involve the individual and community in the arts, with a list of its activities which include photo exhibits, folk festivals, theatre activities, and poetry readings.

Seehase, Georg. "Abbild des Klassenkampfes." *Zeitschrift für Anglistik und Amerikanistik,* 16, iv, (1969), 392–405.

Seehase claims that in both the nineteenth and twentieth centuries elements of working-class culture can be seen in bourgeois literature and "proletarian literature proper." He calls Wesker a twentieth-century bourgeois writer who has great sympathy for the working class.

CONTRIBUTORS

ENOCH BRATER is Associate Professor of English Language and Literature at the University of Michigan. He has written widely on modern and contemporary drama, and recently edited the special number of *The Journal of Modern Literature* devoted to Samuel Beckett.

ALBERT R. BRAUNMULLER has divided his energies between English Renaissance and contemporary drama, and has published several essays in both fields. He is Associate Professor of English at the University of California, Los Angeles.

HEDWIG BOCK is Lecturer in the English Department at the Universität Hamburg, where she teaches modern English and American literature, mainly twentieth-century drama. She has published on Arthur Miller and Edward Albee.

JOHN BULL is Lecturer in English and Drama at Sheffield University. His main areas of interest are eighteenth-century English literature and modern drama. He is editor of the *Penguin Book of Pastoral Verse*, and is currently working on post-1968 drama in England.

RUBY COHN is the author of a vast number of distinguished books, articles and reviews primarily on Samuel Beckett and on modern drama. Among her most noted books are *Samuel Beckett: The Comic Gamut* (1962), *Currents in Contemporary Drama* (1969), *Dialogue in American Drama* (1971), *Back to Beckett* (1973), and *Modern Shakespeare Offshoots* (1976). She is Professor of Comparative Drama at the University of California, Davis.

BERNARD F. DUKORE is Professor of Drama and Theatre at the University of Hawaii. He has edited several volumes of dramatic criticism and theory, and he has edited a number of anthologies of drama. His publications in the field of modern drama are vast and include *Bernard Shaw, Director* (1971), *Bernard Shaw, Playwright* (1973), and *Where Laughter Stops: Pinter's Tragicomedy* (1976).

STEVEN H GALE is the author of *Butter's Going Up: A Critical Analysis of Harold Pinter's Work* (1977) and *Harold Pinter: An Annotated Bibliography* (1978) as well as a number of essays and reviews largely on Harold Pinter and other modern dramatists. He is Chairman of the Department of English at Missouri Southern State in Joplin, Missouri.

FRANCES GRAY worked for a year in BBC Radio. She has taught in schools and colleges, and is currently lecturing in English and Drama at Sheffield University. She is at present completing a book on radio drama.

RÜDIGER IMHOF teaches at the Gesamthochschule in Wuppertal and is a specialist in contemporary British drama. His several publications include a recent book, *Harold Pinters Dramentechnik* (1976).

KIMBALL KING is Associate Professor of English at the University of North Carolina. His special interest is modern drama and he is the author of a significant reference work, *Twenty Modern British Playwrights* (1977).

MARGERY M. MORGAN is Reader in English at the University of Lancaster. Among her several publications in the area of modern British drama are two particularly well known studies: *A Drama of Political Man: A Study in the Plays of Harley Granville Barker* (1961) and *The Shavian Playground* (1972).

PHYLLIS R. RANDALL is a specialist in contemporary drama. She teaches at North Carolina Central University, where she is an Associate Professor of English.

HENRY SCHVEY is Assistant Professor of English at Leiden University in The Netherlands. He has written a recent study on the plays of Austrian painter Oskar Kokoschka and has published a number of articles on modern literature including essays on Eugene O'Neill, Dylan Thomas, Edward Albee and Sylvia Plath.

DIETRICH SCHWANITZ is Professor of English Literature and Philology at the Universität Hamburg. His publications include monographs on the theory and history of drama. He is the author of *George Bernard Shaw, Künstlerische Konstruktion u. Unordentliche Welt* (1971) as well as other works on Sterne, Jane Austen, Robert Musil, Huxley and Shakespeare. His main interest lies in the field of theory and sociology of literature.

ALBERT WERTHEIM teaches at Indiana University, where he is Professor of English. His special interest is English and American dramatic literature, and he has published widely on Shakespeare, Renaissance and Restoration drama, and on modern drama. He is completing a book on the Elizabethan playwright James Shirley.

KATHARINE J. WORTH is Head of the Department of Drama and Theatre Studies at Royal Holloway College, University of London. Her publications include *The Irish Drama of Europe* (1978) and *Revolutions in English Drama* (1973). She edited *Beckett the Shape Changer* (1975) and has published articles on modern drama in various journals and symposia.